Private Property and Public Power

Private Property and Public Power

Eminent Domain in Philadelphia

Debbie Becher

Oxford University Press is a department of the University of Oxford.
It furthers the University's objective of excellence in research, scholarship,
and education by publishing worldwide.

Oxford New York
Auckland Cape Town Dar es Salaam Hong Kong Karachi
Kuala Lumpur Madrid Melbourne Mexico City Nairobi
New Delhi Shanghai Taipei Toronto

With offices in
Argentina Austria Brazil Chile Czech Republic France Greece
Guatemala Hungary Italy Japan Poland Portugal Singapore
South Korea Switzerland Thailand Turkey Ukraine Vietnam

Published in the United States of America by
Oxford University Press
198 Madison Avenue, New York, NY 10016

Library of Congress Cataloging-in-Publication Data

Becher, Debbie 1970–
Private property and public power : eminent domain in Philadelphia / Debbie Becher.
pages cm
Includes bibliographical references and index.
ISBN 978-0-19-932254-1 (hardcover : alk. paper) — ISBN 978-0-19-932255-8 (pbk. : alk. paper) 1. Urban renewal—Pennsylvania—Philadelphia—Case studies. 2. Eminent domain—Pennsylvania—Philadelphia—Case studies. 3. Homeowners—Pennsylvania—Philadelphia—Case studies. 4. Real estate investment—Pennsylvania—Philadelphia—Case studies. 5. City planning—Moral and ethical aspects—Pennsylvania—Philadelphia—Case studies. 6. Land use, Urban—Government policy—Pennsylvania—Philadelphia—Case studies. I. Title.
HT177.P47B43 2014
307.3'4160974811—dc 3
2014001399

9 8 7 6 5 4 3 2 1
Printed in the United States of America
on acid-free paper

CONTENTS

LIST OF FIGURES AND TABLES

FIGURES

TABLES

ACKNOWLEDGMENTS

I don't believe that there is any such thing as true sole authorship. Many of the ideas I express in this book emerged from conversations with others. And my extensive research would have been impossible without others' incredible and repeated generosity.

This book started as a dissertation to complete my Ph.D. in Sociology at Princeton University, where I received more intellectual support than I had imagined possible. During my time at Princeton, Paul DiMaggio brilliantly and repeatedly eased my way forward. I am exceedingly grateful for his consistent generosity of mind and spirit; his excitement about, interest in, and insights into my work; and his many careful readings of my drafts. Kim Scheppele was my primary guide to smart and creative methodology and to legal sociology. She patiently discussed my findings during every stage of the research, often warning me not to simplify the lessons too early and directing me down promising new paths. Kim managed to push and support me in so many ways that I respect and admire. Miguel Centeno graciously guided and motivated me well before my dissertation and continues to do so well beyond it. He offered an attentive ear and amazingly astute advice about countless decisions and about my writing in ways that only someone with such a vast wealth of knowledge and enormous respect for people and history could. Viviana Zelizer charitably shared her intense curiosity and uncommon vision about economic transactions with me. She helped me communicate clearly without violating the complexity of my subject. Hendrik (Dirk) Hartog's fascination with American law has infected and inspired me, and I am extremely grateful to him. He showed excitement about my work that helped me to believe in it, and he always posed the questions I wanted to answer but had not yet learned how to ask. Beyond Princeton, the University of Pennsylvania Law School's Wendell Pritchett, author of the best article on eminent domain and economic development in existence, helped to launch my research by lending his expertise on that very subject—as well as on local governance and Philadelphia.

Colleagues and friends in the academy contributed immensely to the writing and ideas in the dissertation and its extensive revisions for this book. Without a doubt, the most crucial contributions came from my intellectually and emotionally brilliant writing partner, Emily Zackin. Emily read practically every draft of every section of this book, and she made remarkably thoughtful, clear, and creative suggestions for improvement every time. The book would have been dramatically different—and, I'm sure, much worse—if not for Emily's generous dedication to it and to me.

Several colleagues, mostly in law and sociology departments, have provided astute feedback on the book's prospectus and chapters; they include Robert Beauregard, Nicholas Blomley, Herbert Gans, Arthur Kirsch, David Madden, Michael Mcquarrie, Eduardo Peñalver, Jonathan Rieder, Gregory Smithsimon, and Josh Whitford. Others have lent their ears and minds to in-depth conversations that led me to important insights: Richard Briffault, Richard Brooks, Keith Brown, Wendy Cadge, Nitsan Chorev, Robert Ellickson, Howard Erlanger, Joshua Guetzkow, Leslie Hinkson, Alexandra Kalev, Alexandra Klass, Karyn Lacy, Gregoire Mallard, Isaac Martin, Christopher Niedt, Intisar Rabb, Lynn Sagalyn, Hana Shepherd, Jodi Short, Sara Shostak, Richard Shragger, Laura Stark, Richard Swedberg, Henry Walker, Laura Weinrib, and Cristobal Young. In addition, many Princeton professors gave sage advice and engaged me in important discussions about this research while I was in graduate school. I thank Elizabeth Armstrong, Sara Curran, Mitchell Duneier, Patricia Fernandez-Kelly, Marion Fourcade-Gourinchas, Eddie Glaude, Stanley Katz, Doug Massey, Katherine Newman, Devah Pager, Nell Painter, Alejandro Portes, Mario Small, Valerie Smith, Paul Starr, Cornel West, Bruce Western, and Robert Wuthnow.

The American Academy of Arts and Sciences (AAAS) and the Brookings Institution challenged me to bring this research to interdisciplinary audiences. I received unbelievable intellectual support while on one-year fellowships at each institution. At AAAS, the program's chair, Patricia Meyer Spacks, and my fellow Visiting Scholars with similar interests, Andrew Jewett, Jason Petrulis, Angus Bergin, and Daniel Amsterdam, were particularly helpful. From the Brookings Institution's Metropolitan Policy Program, Alan Berube, Jennifer Bradley, Bruce Katz, Alice Rivlin, Martha Ross, Audrey Singer, and Margaret Weir (visiting from University of California–Berkeley) all deserve special thanks.

Barnard College at Columbia University, where I came after completing those fellowships, has provided just the right kind of support for me to finish the book and launch my career as a professor. In addition to the people mentioned above who have read and commented on the writing, others who have ushered me through this work include Elizabeth Bernstein, Susan

Campbell, Flora Davidson, Kimberley Johnson, Christel Kesler, Jennifer Lena, Peter Levin, Debra Minkoff, and Jacquelyn Olvera.

My deepest gratitude goes to over a hundred people, mostly in Philadelphia, who offered up their personal experiences so that we all could learn. They shared their lives and work with me in informal discussions and formal interviews. They responded to numerous questions, some of which may have seemed ignorant or rude, with grace and generosity. My heartfelt appreciation extends to those of you who go unnamed in this book—whether because you asked to remain anonymous or because I did not quote you directly or relay your specific stories—and the many of you whose names do appear herein. The book will likely disappoint those of you who had particular hopes about what I would write or just hoped that I would be able to tell your story the way you told it to me. I am personally disappointed that space limitations forced me to leave out so many of the beautiful and important insights you gave me. Still, I hope that your talking, my listening, or my writing has brought you some satisfaction.

One of the things that makes this project so unique is the window I opened into Philadelphia government. That window would have been closed without significant efforts by key people to create access for an independent researcher. I am enormously grateful to Lew Rosman, of the City of Philadelphia Law Department, and John Kromer, at the University of Pennsylvania Fels Institute of Government and formerly of the Office of Housing and Community Development, for helping me make crucial connections. Michael Koonce and Hope Yusem generously gave me access to the City of Philadelphia Redevelopment Authority's offices, files, and people. Eva Gladstein did the same at the Philadelphia Mayor's Office of the Neighborhood Transformation Initiative and Empowerment Zone, and Ira Goldstein invited me into The Reinvestment Fund, a nonprofit that consulted for the city on blight policy. These gracious people even provided me with my own offices, from which I could easily review files, talk to employees, and simply make a nuisance of myself.

Several other organizations inside and outside Philadelphia allowed me to observe professionals in action and/or use their files: the Appraisal Institute, the Bureau of Revision of Taxes of the City of Philadelphia, the City of Philadelphia Mayor's Office of Information Services, the Institute for Justice, the Jefferson Square Community Development Corporation, Lorman Seminars, the Office of the Prothonotary of the Court of Common Pleas of Philadelphia, the Office of the Clerk of the Council of the City of Philadelphia, the Pennsylvania Bar Association, the Pennsylvania Association of Redevelopment and Housing Authorities, and the Philadelphia City Commissioners Voter Registration Office. I also thank

Temple University Urban Archives, University of Pennsylvania Law School, and the University of Pennsylvania Library for making their resources available.

Fellowships and grants for my research were plentiful and necessary. In addition to many Princeton programs, I thank the American Association of University Women, the AAAS, the Brookings Institution, the Hauser Center for Nonprofit Organizations, the Horowitz Foundation for Social Policy, the Mellon Foundation, the National Science Foundation (Grant Number SES-0648083), the US Department of Housing and Urban Development (Grant Number H-21536SG), and the Yale Law/Princeton University Arthur Liman Fellowship Program. Princeton University, in particular, provided stellar institutional support, through the Department of Sociology and through these interdisciplinary programs: the African American Studies Program, the American Studies Program, the Center for Human Values, the Department of Sociology, the Fellowship of Woodrow Wilson Scholars, the Global Network on Inequality, the Graduate School, the Policy Research Institute on the Region, and the Program in Law and Public Affairs.

I was also lucky to have terrific research assistants and consultants who completed large chunks of work with enthusiasm. Jack Baney performed magic with his remarkable, skillful copyediting of the final manuscript. Al Parker produced expert maps and went out of his way to track down various kinds of information for me. David Gehosky took perfect photographs. In addition, the book is a product of Tessa Landreau-Grasmuck's English-Spanish translation, Michelle Lappen's fact-checking, Ben Mearns's spatial analysis, Bongani Moyo's data entry, Jon Stover's literature searches and census summaries, Alissa Weiss's archival collection and organization, and Amanda Wagner's mapping.

Despite the significant support listed above and all of the support I have omitted, any opinions, findings, and conclusions or recommendations expressed in this book are mine and do not necessarily reflect the views of any of the supporting agencies or individuals.

My stamina—and I needed a lot of it—came largely from friends and family. My friends Jennifer Allen, Josh Asch, Pat DeVito, Heather Green, Karen Greene, Matthew Kirsch, Diego Matamoros, Josh Schachter, Darby Shaw, Alex Walker, and many of those mentioned above as colleagues, showed sustained interest in my progress and well-being, and they encouraged me to keep going. I have also been blessed by the love of my mom and dad, Bernice Weinstein and Jacob Becher; my sister and brother, Elise and David Becher; my brother's mom, Larisa Sosunova; my honorary parents Edie Patterson and the Imbraguglios; my in-laws Cheryl, Mike, Eric, and Leah Carpenter and Mark Mendelsohn; my extended families the Halcoussises, Pages, and Preises, and my beautiful nieces and nephews, Ava, Max, Renee, and Trevor. All of you made me laugh, smile, and turn upside down, and you created much more room in my heart. Thank you, dear people, for putting up with me throughout this project.

In the very final stages of my work, I was exceptionally fortunate to enlist the help of James Cook, my dedicated editor at Oxford University Press, and his dynamite assistant Peter Worger. James's excitement about the manuscript, his honest and careful suggestions, and his expedience have made the last steps of this process exceedingly more delightful and rewarding than they might have been.

My loving partner, Caryn Carpenter, was also a fantastic editor of the most crucial kind. Countless times and well before James saw the manuscript, Caryn talked me through convoluted early drafts and helped me figure out what I wanted to say. Indeed, every step of the way, Caryn shed her own beautiful and brilliant light on my ideas, fears, and excitement. I am forever grateful.

I am deeply indebted to all of the people and institutions listed above and to literally hundreds more whose names do not appear here. Perhaps one of my greatest talents is getting other people to help or join me in my endeavors.

LIST OF ACRONYMS

ASCTB	American Street Community Trust Board
BRT	Bureau of Revision of Taxes of the City of Philadelphia
CDC	Community Development Corporation (generic name)
CLI	Community Leadership Institute
EZ	Empowerment Zone—the national Empowerment Zone program, all of Philadelphia's three Empowerment Zone projects, or the American Street Empowerment Zone
HACE	Hispanic Association of Contractors and Entrepreneurs
IJ	Institute for Justice
JSCDC	Jefferson Square Community Development Corporation
L&I	City of Philadelphia Department of Licenses and Inspections
NLDC	New London Development Corporation
NSNP	Norris Square Neighborhood Project
NTI	Office of the Mayor's Neighborhood Transformation Initiative
OHCD	Office of Housing and Community Development of the City of Philadelphia
PCPC	Philadelphia City Planning Commission
PHA	Philadelphia Housing Authority
PIDC	Philadelphia Industrial Development Corporation
RDA	Redevelopment Authority of the City of Philadelphia
TRF	The Reinvestment Fund
UNAD	United Neighbors Against Drugs
URA	Urban Renewal Area

Private Property and Public Power

CHAPTER 1
Investment and Government Legitimacy

EXPERIENCES WITH EMINENT DOMAIN

When JoAnn King stepped outside her South Philadelphia house one Saturday morning in January 1998, she noticed a bright orange sign on her front door.

"Danger, keep out," the sign read. "This house is condemned by order of the Philadelphia Department of Licenses and Inspections."

Unbeknownst to JoAnn, politicians had decided to demolish all the houses on Leithgow Street—nicknamed King Street because she, her mother, and three of her siblings lived there in separate homes—and replace them with a parking lot for Mount Sinai Hospital.[1] They could do it legally. City officials were authorized to take private property via eminent domain to remove blight and promote redevelopment. If JoAnn and her family members didn't leave on their own, the city government would pay them what it deemed to be just compensation and force them to leave. JoAnn was shocked and incensed at such a blatant abuse of government's eminent domain powers.

Before those signs appeared, none of the Kings had intended to move. In 1965, JoAnn's parents, Dorothy and Richard King, Jr., had left the house they were renting to buy one just a bit farther south, on Leithgow Street in South Philadelphia.[2] They had been the first African Americans on their little block, and their street had been packed with Italian and Irish families.

These families had slowly left, however, as their jobs along the Delaware River began to dry up in the 1970s and 1980s. Some new, mostly African-American families had moved in, but many of the houses that had been abandoned by older residents simply lay vacant for years. Many were later demolished, leaving the once straight line of two-story brick row houses pockmarked with vacant lots. The buildings that remained had deteriorated, and eventually "drugs were rampant throughout the community."[3]

And yet, Dorothy and her husband had spread their roots. The neighbors with whom they had been friendly had offered them the opportunity to purchase many of the houses they left behind, and the Kings had done so. Between 1976 and 1984, they had bought houses within spitting distance of four of their five adult children—JoAnn, Shirley, Mary, and Richard, III.[4] They had made the place theirs, calling it King Street and closing it down annually to celebrate Independence Day and Dorothy's birthday. By the late 1990s, the Kings' houses were not in great condition, but they were comfortable. The Kings did not think they could sell the houses for more than $20,000 or $30,000, even if they wanted to. Nevertheless, they were counting on what Dorothy's husband, Richard, Jr., who died in the 1980s, had always said: "One day, this land right here will be very, very valuable."[5] They all remembered how he had beseeched them to never leave the community because they were "sitting on a gold mine."[6]

Initially, the Kings and other residents were confused about the origins of the condemnation signs on front doors, but they soon learned that some formidable powers wanted their houses condemned. The Councilman for the First District, Frank DiCicco, had already renamed the area Jefferson Square, after the park to the north. Mount Sinai Hospital had been asking for government-supported redevelopment before DiCicco even took office in 1995, and DiCicco had paid architects to draw a redesign that replaced Leithgow Street with an expanded hospital parking lot. This replacement was part of a larger plan to get rid of dangerous, unsafe housing and to build houses that attracted people from the city's outskirts and suburbs. The rainmaker Vince Fumo, a Pennsylvania state senator since 1978, supported DiCicco and the project, as did some of the community's veteran African-American leaders, including Reverend Fitchett of Mount Moriah Temple Baptist Church. Center City Philadelphia was gentrifying, and development pressures were pushing south.

The Kings, however, had no intention of accepting DiCicco's plan. They and their allies organized tirelessly, with Dorothy knocking on her neighbors' doors to ask for their support in opposing the city's plan. Many neighbors turned her away because they wanted to move, did not want to fight, or were not interested in getting involved. However, Dorothy received help from some sympathizers, including the preacher of Saint John's Episcopal Church, a professional community organizer from a nearby settlement house, and a Community Legal Services of Philadelphia attorney. Peggy

King Brookins, the one King daughter who had moved away to Germantown in North Philadelphia, came back to help. Neighbors who were not targeted for condemnation nevertheless saw the injustice and felt compelled to get involved. At a packed public meeting, Mary Black called out to Reverend Fitchett, "Judas! . . . You are Judas! You are trying to deceive us!," causing family members and friends to howl.[7]

These efforts eventually forced DiCicco to revise his plans for the neighborhood dramatically. Just as originally envisioned, their homes would be torn down, and Leithgow Street would be erased. But instead of a parking lot, new housing would stand in its place. Just as originally planned, outsiders would be sold some of that new housing. But older homeowners would not be pushed out of the neighborhood with only meager compensation and a need to find new housing on their own. Instead, homeowners would have the choice to stay by purchasing one of the new houses with their compensation payments, and they would not be asked to actually leave until they had keys to their new houses. In the end, DiCicco's power worked to the residents' advantage, because he could find the money and administrative power to accomplish this costly compromise.

The Kings lost their houses in 2004 to DiCicco's plan. But in an uncanny display of how much everything had changed, with her children watching, Dorothy proclaimed her support for the plan at a Philadelphia City Council hearing in 1999. She told me that DiCicco's gratitude during the meeting was palpable and that afterward, he gave her "a big hug and a kiss, and it made [her] feel good."[8] DiCicco went on to brag during his re-election campaign about how he spearheaded the redevelopment of Jefferson Square. The Kings, too, told me a few years later that they were proud of what they had accomplished.

* * *

Just before Christmas in 2001, seven households living along the 2100 block of N. Bodine Street in North Philadelphia received letters from the City of Philadelphia Redevelopment Authority (RDA) saying that the agency was considering taking their homes. Those seven families were actually much more like one family—most were related as uncles, aunts, and cousins—and they all had spent significant time on the block. The newest resident had been there for ten years, and more than half had been there for at least twenty. They had built their little community from a place that others had abandoned. Most had bought their houses from the city for a dollar and back taxes, after past owners had died or simply stopped paying.

Officials had begun their plans to take properties for the American Street parcels, including those on N. Bodine Street, with much more care for residents' fate than did those who initiated Jefferson Square's redevelopment. Decades before the takings, American Street had been the heart of Philadelphia's nationally enviable textile industry, but it had been devastated by deindustrialization. In the 1990s, residents demanded government resources for help in coping with enormous losses of jobs and people and building vacancies. Community leaders had long cautioned against displacing homeowners for the American Street project, and the Office of the Mayor, the Office of Housing and Community Development, the Philadelphia Industrial Development Corporation, and even the Department of Commerce all had objected to such displacements in the past.

Officials and community leaders came to accept the use of eminent domain as a necessary evil justified by the promised community-level benefits from land development and new jobs for neighbors, however. These areas had just a dozen privately owned houses in the middle of much larger expanses of vacant land. Few people would be displaced, and though they would inevitably mourn their losses, they would receive assistance in finding replacements. Thus, resident and business leaders cautiously approved takings of mostly abandoned property to create new local jobs and with the understanding that the displaced residents would be respectfully relocated.

The government moved forward in 2001, planning to give the American Street acquisitions unusual attention as a pilot project of both Mayor John Street's Neighborhood Transformation Initiative and the American Street Industrial Corridor Empowerment Zone.[9] It went after three large and mostly vacant areas: two areas comprising three acres each along the 1700 and 2100 block of N. American Street (including those on N. Bodine Street) and one area comprising three quarters of an acre along the 2501 block of N. American Street. Each parcel included a handful of privately owned, occupied housing. The officials viewed the displacements as justified by the much larger areas of vacant land that surrounded the parcels that were unlikely to be developed without being consolidated.

However, delays resulted from interagency disputes and individual incompetence, and compensation for relocations was insufficient and frustrating, in part, because of inflexible title and health-and-safety regulations. Community members were incensed by what they heard about disappointingly low compensation amounts and insensitive communication with displaced residents. Interagency disputes and individual incompetence stymied not only the handling of individual relocations but also the area's redevelopment, so taken land sat vacant for years.

Just over three years after the first letters from the RDA arrived, all of the N. Bodine Street residents were gone. Philadelphia government had displaced them as part of an effort to create a large parcel for new warehouse and light industrial operations along N. American Street; their houses on N. Bodine Street, just to the west, were in the middle of that desired parcel. Two families stayed in the neighborhood, but the others retreated about two miles northeast, where they could afford suitable homes with their median compensation payments of $41,000. For some, the new homes were closer to their adult children, but none of them was content with having been displaced. Instead, they were resigned to their own powerlessness and to the loss of something very dear to them. Most summarized the experience with some version of, "When the city comes, there's nothing you can do," as if what happened to them had been a foregone conclusion.[10] Despite all of the government's good intentions, the takings would be memorialized in residents' and officials' memories, and even on film, as what government should not do rather than what it should.

The story of Manuel Velez, the last homeowner to leave because of the American Street takings to consolidate three separate large parcels, epitomizes the displaced homeowners' discontent. Velez had cherished the N. American Street home that was taken from him. He had originally gotten the house by leaving little notes in the mailbox asking the owner to sell. At first, the owner did not respond, but Velez kept asking and waited for over a year until the owner succumbed. Velez installed a roof, internal walls, and windows in the house. The house may have looked to passersby as if it sat in an industrial wasteland, as it had only one neighbor and was surrounded by vast areas of vacant land. But to Velez, "Mejor del mundo era allá. Porque no había nadie ni atrás ni al frente ni a ningún lado mio. Vivía feliz allí. (It was the best in the world there. Because there wasn't anybody behind, in front, or on either side of me. I lived happily there.)"[11]

The area was peaceful, and he could use and protect the vacant land. On abandoned property next door, he had built a garage where he stored his truck. Although there had been dumping there, he had stopped it by fencing off half of the block. There was a vibrant, densely packed Puerto Rican neighborhood just a few blocks away, but N. American Street was quiet.

Velez tried just about everything to stop the taking, and his experience galvanized others not only to help him but to fight eminent domain across the city. Because he was on the 1700 block of N. American Street, the second site that officials pursued, he had a bit more notice about what was coming than the families on the 2100 block of N. Bodine Street did. At first, Manuel located houses just a few blocks north that he could move into, but officials said they did not pass inspection. One of the N. Bodine Street residents had gotten a new home in a subsidized development a few blocks away, but according to Velez, this was not an option for him. Officials surmised from the less than stellar condition of his current house that he would destroy a new one, he said, and he did not really want a house that felt like it was in a "project," anyway.

Velez took his case to court, hiring a lawyer who had fought others' eminent domain cases successfully, but Velez lost initially and on appeal. He then enlisted the help of Rosemary Cubas, his friend's wife, a nearby resident, and a former member of the American Street Industrial Corridor Empowerment Zone's leadership group. Cubas put the government on notice that Velez had help; she had a video camera ready and recording when the RDA's relocation worker visited to discuss his displacement.[12] The American Street takings motivated Cubas to found the Citywide Coalition to Save Our Homes, for which she sought and received help from the national campaign led by the Castle Coalition.[13] Velez marched in the streets with them.

In the end, though, all of this fighting did not seem to win Velez much. After years of trying and failing to find a suitable replacement house, he packed his belongings into a trailer and started sleeping at his daughter's house. In 2008, he finally bought a row house much farther north with his compensation money. He felt like he had to because the RDA would only release much of that money if he bought a new house that inspectors passed as safe and sanitary.

Velez had been in the row house only a few months when I first visited him there. He paced through the house like a caged animal, pointing out everything he hated. From Puerto Rico originally, he told me in broken but clear English that the sellers had "just plastered over" cracks in the walls, and he stomped on the carpet in disgust, saying it was clearly covering up problems with the floors. He brought me out to the back patio to show me a huge, possibly hundred-year-old nut tree about five feet behind his house, and he kicked at the cracks it had made in the concrete, saying, "This is very bad." He described his neighbors as dirty and loud, pointing out fifteen to twenty balled-up dirty diapers that were strewn around the backyard immediately next door. He pointed to the front of his neighbor's house and said, "You see every morning tons of trash, right there." The neighborhood felt crowded and noisy. "All night long, [neighbors are] fighting, talk[ing] real loud. You can't sleep over here." He kept imagining escaping back to Puerto Rico, where he was sure that the government would not interfere with his life as Philadelphia's government had done. The taking of Velez's home had left him livid, depressed, and perhaps even ashamed.[14] He concluded simply, "They make me move. I can do nothing. They got the power; I ain't got none."[15]

Despite these feelings of hopelessness, Velez continues to fight, and his story motivates others to do the same. Cubas's organization documented the losses suffered by Velez and others on American Street in more than one video.[16] And even though officials considered his case closed by 2008, Velez was still thinking that he "had to find a good lawyer," one who would see the horrendous condition of the house he was forced into and would help him sue the city—and maybe even the bank and Allstate Insurance, which had been involved.[17]

Five or six years after the so-called pilot project began, it seemed evident not only that individuals had been treated poorly, but also that the cleared land had created practically no good at all. Chaes Foods, a meat distribution business, had built a new warehouse on the 2100-block site. But the company had abandoned its old building just two blocks to the south and across the street, and none of the local residents I talked to knew anyone with a job there. On the 1700- and 2501-block sites, all of the old buildings were demolished. In 2008, around the time that I completed many of my interviews, there were plans in the works for new companies on the 1700 block, but both areas were home only to grass and weeds. When I visited in 2014, just before this book went to print, both areas still lay completely vacant.

* * *

The Jefferson Square and American Street takings were unusual because they received a great deal of attention, but not because takings for private reuse are rare in Philadelphia. In fact, they were just two of the hundreds of private redevelopment projects for which the city took thousands of private properties in the 1990s and 2000s. I found that Philadelphia took a shockingly large number of properties—over 4,000 in sixteen years—for new private ownership. And yet, the startling prevalence of these kinds of eminent domain cases was matched by how unremarkable they seemed to the people involved. Citizens lodged formal resistance very rarely—in under 250 of those cases. Far from raising controversy, most of the takings were generally treated by officials and citizens alike as the ordinary, routine work of government.

Typically, citizens approved of takings for new private owners without hearing any names, personal stories, or detailed histories. Officials usually could explain that the taken properties were empty lots in the city's most troubled neighborhoods. Land would be turned over to social services, nonprofit developers of subsidized housing, small businesses, or even residents, who could take advantage of abandoned land next door. A few details about the property's current condition and the government's plans were all citizens needed to know to decide whether the takings were legitimate uses of government power.

* * *

These very real and varied stories about eminent domain in Philadelphia present a mystery that current understandings of eminent domain and private property cannot solve. In discussing the standards by which Americans evaluate the legitimacy of government actions, activists and academics typically refer to concepts that would not predict most of the reactions to eminent domain described above. These stories, covered in more detail throughout the book, only make sense once we see property in a new way.

We need to understand that when many American citizens today claim that government should protect their property, they are demanding protection for their investments.[18] I introduce the conception of property as investment to explain the full spectrum of experiences with eminent domain in Philadelphia. The city's officials and citizens decided whether government acted appropriately in its use of eminent domain—and, thus, toward property—by evaluating whether government had sufficiently and equitably kept people's investments safe.

Although colloquial meanings of the word "investment" vary, I use the word to describe the sacrifice of value of any kind—money, time, labor, love, or relationships—in the hope of future benefits. To secure an investment, government needs, therefore, to protect the value that an individual holds in a property. Government should preserve or help that value grow over time. In addition, an individual's attachment of value to a property gives him or her a claim to the future of the community in which that property is located. Residents who demand a say in how a neighborhood will change and in whether particular changes will enhance or detract from the community's value justify this demand through their past sacrifices to the community. In other words, government is expected to protect investment at both individual and collective levels. Citizens whom I observed did not seem to expect government to provide guarantees for an uncertain future, but they did expect government to do what it reasonably could to protect their investments.

The Kings, Manuel Velez, and many others confronting eminent domain led me to discover this meaning of private property that I had not read about before: Citizens treated property as an investment of value that they expected government to protect. The Americans whom I observed and with whom I spoke deemed the government's taking of property to be a legitimate use of its power when the government appeared to be protecting investments.

The Kings' early opposition to and eventual approval of the government's taking of their homes make sense only when we understand that citizens equate property with investment and hold government responsible for keeping that investment secure. Once the government's plans for the Jefferson Square project seemed to respect residents' investments of their fortunes and lives, the Kings still did not want to give up their homes, but they considered it reasonable for the government to ask them to do so. Members of the family and others could sacrifice their older houses, turn over their compensation money, and get new homes in the same neighborhood. They saw this outcome as exactly the one they deserved if government was going to remake the place that they had seen through hard times.

The positive reaction to Jefferson Square resulted not only from judgments about what happened to individuals but also about the degree of control wielded by those most invested in the community. Indeed, it was crucial to the compromise agreement that residences would be located in particular places. Before this agreement was reached, the residents and officials battled over conflicting visions. Importantly, both sides defended their visions, and they sometimes critiqued the other side, by appealing to a generally understood expectation that government should protect collective investment. The sides eventually negotiated a new vision for redevelopment that, they all agreed, did just that. Thus, community-level understandings of investment protection motivated initial resistance and later support for the project.

The concept of property as investment similarly explains how citizens and officials framed support and resistance at different moments in the history of the American Street takings. Those takings began with a vision that, if realized, probably would have made government actions seem legitimate, if not desirable, to residents and officials. Early support for the takings rested on considered, credible promises to secure and improve the values of existing community investments without seriously harming individual investments.

No matter how reasonable the early vision for American Street seemed, however, later implementation produced results that were viewed almost universally as a catastrophic abuse of government power. The results experienced by Velez and others, as described above, would be indefensible regardless of the new development's benefits. Because the redeveloped land sat vacant for years, however, it became impossible to claim that the government had achieved sufficient community-level protection to justify individual sacrifices of any kind. Resistance emerged in response to multiple signals that government was damaging, not supporting, individual and community investments.

The principle that citizens expect government to protect property as investment also explains the vast majority of eminent domain cases that occur without such drama. In the uncontroversial cases, citizens and officials could discern that individual owners would lose little to no value. They confirmed that properties to be taken were empty lots in depressed neighborhoods and that the government's plans would secure neighbors' investments of many kinds of value without giving value to the undeserving. Citizens saw that the neighborhood residents and business owners would receive a benefit from the development of abandoned properties by nonprofit organizations and neighboring institutions, residents, and businesses. In contrast, many of the more rare, contested takings involved the transfer of occupied properties to for-profit developers planning market-rate developments. These takings were opposed because government seemed to threaten existing value, and though it might have improved neighborhood conditions, it was not clear that the beneficiaries were the ones who had sacrificed in the past.

Finally, Philadelphians evaluated the legitimacy of individual compensation arrangements by assessing how well they accounted for the investments lost. Even in this part of the process, which at first glance would seem most market-oriented and individualistic, officials and citizens expected government to respect more than just monetary value and individual interests. Government officials attempted to assess how much people had committed to their properties not only in cash, but also in labor and emotions. They also attempted to determine whether people had long-term attachments to their properties' neighborhoods, and they designed compensation accordingly. Officials and citizens expected different compensation for properties with similar market value, for instance, if one owner seemed to be a speculator or slumlord, another a responsible absentee investor, and a third a long-term homeowner. These standards and practices explain why a couple of the owners displaced in the American Street takings believed that they were compensated fairly. Miguelina de Jesus, Manuel Velez's neighbor, felt justly treated because the taking of her property provided her with the money she needed to move out of a neighborhood that had started to make her feel isolated and scared. Most observers thought that the last resident of N. Bodine Street, who was provided with a newly constructed house nearby, had been treated reasonably. Similarly, a demand for investment protection explains observers' sympathetic reactions to individuals who, unlike the Kings, objected to their compensation for the Jefferson Square takings.

My conception of property as investment helps to explain people's frequent view of takings for private redevelopment as legitimate—a recurring theme in this book that differentiates it from typical accounts of eminent domain. Although people may not view takings for private redevelopment as right, just, or desirable, they do often view such takings as legitimate. They treat the action as reasonable, under the particular circumstances. I report on which takings citizens consider appropriate, and which they oppose with expectations that others will join their cause. Legitim a practical judgment that an action is reasonably justified, and it is of practice, rather than philosophy or ideology.[19] As this study of g ment authority focuses on officials' and citizens' judgments regarding the legitimacy of government actions, rather than on what they think is right or wrong, it uses a much less stringent standard than social justice.

The thesis of this book—that the conception of private property as investment motivates demands on government, particularly with respect to eminent domain—does not explain every aspect of every eminent domain case. I do not deny that alternative concepts of property are useful or that various political, economic, and cultural factors affect officials' and citizens' actions and responses regarding eminent domain. Indeed, this book describes many such factors in detail, as well as alternative frames for understanding property that are available. My more modest claim is that officials and citizens correctly expect to garner support for their arguments regarding eminent domain by appealing to the idea that government is responsible for property as investment.

In this book, I share results from a rigorous study of citizens and officials grappling with eminent domain on the ground. This is the first comprehensive research on the full scope of eminent domain for private redevelopment in a contemporary city, Philadelphia. There, I watched how residents and business owners faced problems involving real people, buildings, streets, sidewalks, and trash in urban neighborhoods and decided what they could and should ask government to do in these complicated and changing circumstances. Local politicians and bureaucrats interacted with colleagues, constituents, and community leaders with varying ideas and interests as they made policy decisions that would affect all of them. Readers will learn how people who are very close to government operations and the places affected understand eminent domain. These stakeholders developed complex, nuanced opinions that—unlike the sound bites and easy summaries used to discuss eminent domain in the news—have yet to be understood.

The stories in this book are surprising not only because citizens sometimes view eminent domain as justified but because my conception of property as investment is not the usual way that activists and academics talk about eminent domain or private property in general. In my study, citizens demanded that government respect investments in property, rather than respecting more celebrated or derided ideas associated with private property, such as individual rights, markets, or economic growth. As I discuss in more detail in the book's conclusion, the conception of property as investment differs from these conceptions of property,[20] and it much more closely reflects critical hopes that property can serve progressive ends. By conceiving of property in an intuitive but as yet unarticulated way—as investment—citizens and officials resolved an apparent contradiction between the public good and private rights.

EMINENT DOMAIN: PRIVATE PROPERTY AND THE PUBLIC GOOD

The Public-Private Dilemma

The issue of eminent domain speaks to the very core of liberal democracy. A tension between public goods and private rights is written into the Takings Clause of the US Constitution's Fifth Amendment, which allows government to take "private property . . . for public use" if it provides "just compensation."[21] Throughout American history, US local and national governments have used their takings powers, which Americans call eminent domain, for various public uses. These have included dams to power mills in the eighteenth century; railroads in the nineteenth century; and highways, utilities, and urban redevelopment in the late twentieth and early twenty-first centuries. Similar government powers—whether called eminent domain, forced expropriation, or compulsory purchase—exist and have been used in almost every country that protects private property. And yet, because any taking threatens serious harm to individual rights, governments challenge liberal democratic ideals when they declare that public needs for transportation, infrastructure, parks, and economic development warrant taking private property. By pitting public use against private property, eminent domain presents an enduring challenge to liberal societies' foundational commitment to individual rights.

When governments take private property through eminent domain, they trample on private-property rights, citizenship rights, and one's sense of personhood, in the name of the public good. Some legal scholars who identify as libertarians, advocating minimal government intrusion on liberal rights, interpret the Takings Clause as creating protection for private property as a fundamental entitlement. By their interpretation, the "public use" and the "just compensation" requirements should keep governments from overstepping their authority. The Takings Clause, they say, should prevent governments from opportunistically transferring property titles or regulating control over private property through zoning, taxing, or conservation ordinances.[22] Other legal scholars, who may be more accepting of government regulation, nevertheless see takings as particularly damaging to citizenship or personhood rights. They argue that takings strip citizenship rights by allowing a majority to violate the individual's right to receive equal consideration in democratic decision-making.[23] Some also hold that takings of property such as family homes—where people have raised children, entertained friends, renovated rooms, and cultivated gardens—damage one's very notion of self.[24]

Although the public-private tension at the heart of eminent domain is timeless, news coverage suggests that its recent use for urban redevelopment is particularly troubling. Once relatively rare, stories about the issue increased gradually starting in the late 1980s and skyrocketed with a highly publicized 2005 US Supreme Court case, *Kelo v. City of New London, Connecticut*.[25] In a search of over 200 American newspapers, an average of 65 articles containing the phrase "eminent domain" appeared per year between 1980 and 1988. In 1989 alone, however, there were 175 such articles, and by the time Susette Kelo lost her appeal to the US Supreme Court to save her home, over 4,000 such articles were being published annually. With coverage of *Kelo*, the country experienced a commensurate rise in mass-media coverage of eminent domain generally. Figure 1.1 compares the number of articles containing "eminent domain" and the narrower set mentioning "Kelo" in American newspapers over time, as well as the number of sources publishing those articles.[26]

Most of that coverage probably painted eminent domain in an exceedingly negative light, as the articles, editorials, and letters in newspapers immediately following *Kelo* certainly did. In one analysis of nationwide headline news for the month after the ruling, three messages dominated: government power has expanded; homes are endangered; and local politicians are ready to fight to protect property rights. Voices of planners and urbanists defending the power of eminent domain were virtually absent.[27] A 2006 cover of *Parade* magazine highlighted the issue by asking, "Will the Government Take Your Home?"[28] A 2005 editorial report in *The Economist* was titled, "Hands Off Our Homes,"[29] and the headline of a 2006 *New York Times* story suggested that while *Kelo* was decided in favor of government, it was a "Case Won on Appeal (to Public)" in favor of property owners.[30]

The *Kelo* ruling provoked a national uproar. It authorized a local government to take private homes for planned economic development—in this case, a project anchored by a new Pfizer Corporation research facility. Justice Sandra Day O'Connor wrote in her fiery dissent that as a result of the majority's decision, "The specter of condemnation hangs over all property. Nothing is to prevent the State from replacing any Motel 6 with a Ritz-Carlton, any home with a shopping mall, or any farm with a factory." These sentences were more widely quoted than any part of the majority opinion written by Justice John Paul Stevens. Media coverage of seemingly similar takings in big cities and small towns across the country

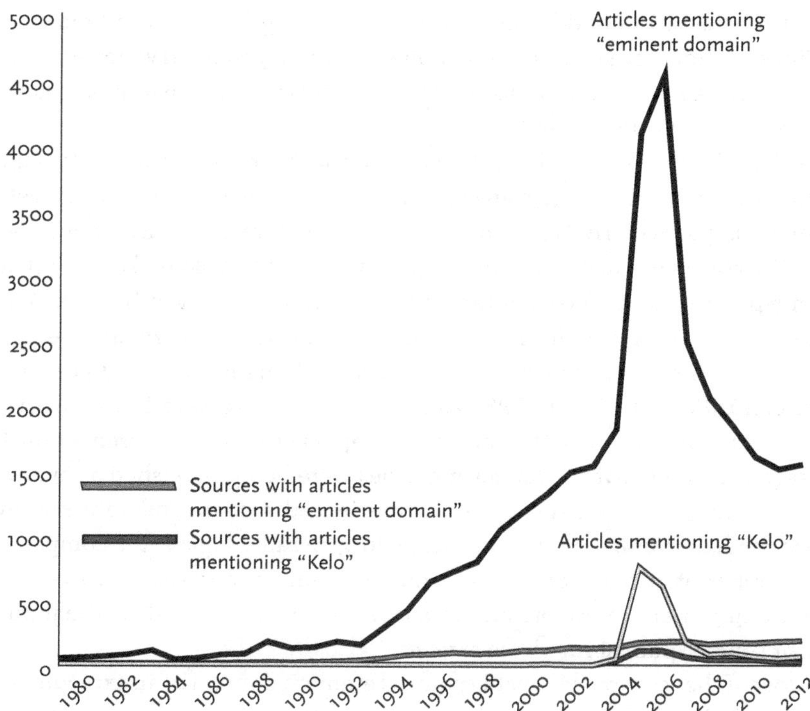

Figure 1.1:
National Newspaper Coverage of Eminent Domain and *Kelo*

made Justice O'Connor's warning seem even more dire. A few years earlier, authorities in Atlantic City, New Jersey had attempted to sacrifice three small businesses for the expansion of the Trump Plaza Hotel and Casino, but the courts stopped them.[31] After *Kelo,* owners of single-family homes finally settled a years-long lawsuit over threats that they would lose their homes to takings for new condominiums and town homes in Long Branch, New Jersey.[32]

Stories of working-class homeowners falling victim to wealthy capitalists and corrupt politicians via eminent domain also became popularized in mainstream entertainment. The innocent victim of government's overreach with eminent domain became a driving narrative in productions as diverse as the science fiction film (and the first movie to gross over $2 billion) *Avatar* (2009), the comedy movie *Be Kind Rewind* (2008) starring Jack Black and Mos Def, and the John Grisham mystery *Theodore Boone: The Activist* (2013). These stories of heartache cemented the notion that eminent domain for private redevelopment was everywhere—and everywhere it was, it constituted an abuse of government power.

Suspicion about the kind of eminent domain that this book is about—taking for urban redevelopment—is ubiquitous. According to public-opinion polls, Americans were more concerned about *Kelo* than about any other case before the Supreme Court. In a July 2005 national poll, 42 percent of respondents counted "private property rights" as one of the two issues in front of the court of greatest interest to them. This was the highest percentage of any issue and much greater than other "contenders, including cases involving parental notification for abortions by minors (34 percent), display of the Ten Commandments on public property (32 percent), and right-to-die laws (24 percent)."[33] Four different polls conducted in 2005 found that over 80 percent of the public disapproved of the *Kelo* decision, indicating that the decision was less popular than those in late twentieth-century cases about desegregation (including *Brown v. Board of Education,*), school prayer, abortion rights, and flag burning.[34] Moreover, unlike popular opinion on other controversial cases, popular opinion on *Kelo* was extremely uniform across most demographic and political lines. In state and national polls, disapproval for the ruling was nearly identical among Democrats, Republicans, and Independents and regardless of age, sex, education, income, and homeownership status.[35]

This consistency in the rancor for *Kelo* seems to suggest that the ruling might have violated core values, and private property is a strong contender, for at least one late twentieth-century national poll found that 74 percent of Americans said that they strongly believed that "[t]he right to private property is sacred."[36] In fact, a libertarian defense of property rights is one of the most commonly heard explanations for why Americans find recent eminent domain cases to be so abhorrent.

WHAT DO AMERICANS THINK IS SO WRONG WITH EMINENT DOMAIN TODAY?

The Libertarian Explanation

Mass-media coverage, academic scholarship, and my own conversations with colleagues, friends, and family suggest that Americans not only agree that cities' recent use of eminent domain is wrong, but also about the reason that it is wrong. According to these sources, US citizens believe that governments should never transfer property to new private owners. Americans sense that the taking of private property for new private, as opposed to public, owners is an atrocious act that violates the "public use" requirement of the Constitution's Takings Clause. (This was the most common argument in editorials following *Kelo*.[37]) Those who have fought to stop these takings have argued that when government takes property for a public highway, park, school, or utility, the taking is justified by the obvious "public use." In contrast, they say, the public does not gain ownership of and is denied access to property when it is transferred to a new private owner, such as for a housing development, retail center, hotel, or casino. Therefore, they contend, when government puts property into new private hands for the elimination of blight and economic development, the "public use" becomes suspect. By this logic, government should never transfer private property—especially not private homes—to new private owners.

I began this research because I suspected that something other than a disdain for private-to-private transfers sparked objections to cities' recent use of eminent domain. Previously, I had lived in neighborhoods in Norfolk, Virginia, and Tucson, Arizona, where city governments had cleared vast swaths of land in the 1950s and 1960s. Two or three decades after these clearings, I had encountered people who were much more ambivalent about urban renewal than critical academic and news accounts would have led me to expect. These people agreed that their neighborhoods had needed to change but spoke of their disappointment that takings had not led to the kinds of neighborhoods they deserved. My neighbor Maria Luisa Torres in Tucson, for instance, was quite matter-of-fact about having been pushed a few blocks away from her childhood home. Rather than longing for her old neighborhood, however, she mostly wished that there was a Burger King or another fast-food restaurant close by and regretted that there were few new businesses of any kind.

My suspicions that Americans actually hold more nuanced opinions about eminent domain was borne out by a closer analysis of polling data following *Kelo*. Most post-*Kelo* surveys that reported a majority disapproval of eminent domain for any private reuse had phrased the questions in quite biased ways. When more neutral phrases were used, the disapproval rating dropped by more than half, from over 80 percent to 40 percent, and when surveyors distinguished the kinds of properties to be taken and private developments to be supported, respondents showed significant variation in their opinions. In one poll, only 4 percent of respondents approved of the taking of homes for a shopping center, but 55 percent approved of the taking of vacant buildings for a shopping center, and 88 percent approved of the sacrifice of vacant and rundown buildings for a school.[38] As mentioned above, when I turned my attention to Philadelphia in 2006, I learned that thousands of Philadelphia properties were taken for new private ownership in the 1990s and 2000s, with no complaint from anyone involved. Officials and citizens seemed quite content with government taking vacant and often veritably abandoned properties and replacing them with new developments for affordable housing or with clean, useful expansions made by adjacent owners. This confirmed my suspicion that the widespread focus on blanket disapproval for eminent domain transfers to private owners was not telling the whole story.

The Left Explanation

Although I didn't generally find that Philadelphians disapproved of eminent domain because they opposed government transfers of property between private owners, they might have disapproved of it for another reason, which I call the left explanation. Left-leaning critics object to many takings because they benefit the rich and powerful at the expense of the poor and powerless. Indeed, this was the stand taken by such social justice organizations as the National Association for the Advancement of Colored People (NAACP), which publicly opposed recent eminent domain cases.[39] They argue that because eminent domain targets neighborhoods where the poor, racial minorities, and the elderly are most likely to live, it causes these groups to suffer disproportionately, even when it does not involve blatant discrimination.[40]

Governments' use of eminent domain often hurts the poor and helps the rich because it focuses exclusively on real property's exchange value and ignores its use values, according to left-leaning activists and academics. They claim that governments race against one another to secure outside capital investments in real estate, which they treat as a market commodity. But along with its exchange value—market prices—property is invested with such use values as shelter, identity, community, safety, and emotional sanctuary, left critics note. They emphasize that these values are vital to the well-being of poor and working-class people.

Governments' single-minded pursuit of economic growth causes them to practically abandon neighborhoods with low real estate prices, where the poor and working class live, according to left-leaning critics. They add that when neighborhoods do receive government resources, the result may be increasing rents and property taxes that force poor and working people to leave for less desirable locations. Eminent domain would not be abused as it is, many of these critics suggest, if governments stopped focusing exclusively on property's market value and recognized and secured its use values. Governments would act legitimately in their constituents' interests if and when they protected properties' use values—such as shelter, identity, and community.[41]

The left argument is invoked widely in public debates and scholarly work on cities, but I will show that it—like the libertarian focus on property rights—is ultimately incomplete as an explanation for popular reactions. I discuss the argument in more depth at the end of the book, but for now I will point out that, in most of the cases I observed, Philadelphians did not distinguish between property's use and exchange values. They expected government to protect both.

The Protection of Investment by Government

I argue that citizens and officials judge government policies by determining whether its actions protect investments in property. When they decide that a particular use of eminent domain protects investment, they judge government to be acting reasonably. When they decide that such a use threatens or damages investment, they judge government to be acting unreasonably. Ultimately, I argue, a notion of property as investment explains the everyday practices surrounding eminent domain (and other property policies) better than the more familiar libertarian or left arguments.

As noted earlier, I define "investment" as the sacrifice of any kind of value in the hope of future benefits. The first important characteristic of my conception of property as investment, which distinguishes it from the left argument about use and exchange value, is that it implies a pluralist position on the forms that value takes. Although the word "investment" sometimes refers to exclusively financial values, my use of the word invokes a wide variety of values, including money, social networks, material goods, wisdom, love, and skill. This pluralist position also reflects many popular uses of the word, such as investment of time and effort in raising children, learning to play an instrument, or building a physique. Similarly, people speak of investing emotional energy in sports teams, friends, and homes.

We know that people put all kinds of value into real property. They use money to buy, rent, and improve their properties, and they also use time, skill, and physical effort for improvements. They take advantage of social networks for support and advice about their properties, and they put furnishings and building materials into their properties. Finally, they put emotion into the decisions they make and into the time they spend with their properties. And as they sacrifice all these types of value, they expect to enjoy various types of value in the future.[42]

Even the most cursory examination of eminent domain in Philadelphia makes it clear that people consider many kinds of value in their judgments about which cases constitute legitimate government action. When

Philadelphia citizens grappled with eminent domain, they immediately considered the taking of some properties as legitimate, because these properties were abandoned, vacant, and almost completely lacking in market value, indicating that no one held any value in them at all. But citizens were much more cautious about properties that seemed to have any kind of current value, financial or otherwise. A property that could garner even a few thousand dollars on the real estate market, that was occupied, or even that encompassed a building was much less likely to be targeted by Philadelphia government—and if it was targeted, citizens were more likely to object.

A second feature that distinguishes property as investment from other understandings of property involves time.[43] For a commitment of value to be interpreted as an investment, by my definition, that commitment must last for a period of time. This factor differentiates my definition of investment from purchases in a market exchange, which begin and end once money is traded for an object. After a market exchange, the object could be resold immediately without causing people to characterize the original trade as anything other than a purchase. An investment, however, requires that a person hold value in an object for a period of time. An investment may yield continual returns—for example, the sense of security that someone feels each day while keeping a stock or a house, the satisfaction that a parent derives from watching a child grow, and the daily output from durable goods like washing machines and refrigerators. But the sacrifice of value, the connection between the person and the object, must endure. Rewards may also come in a moment long after the initial sacrifice of value, such as at the sale of an item or at child's school graduation.

Another brief look at evidence from Philadelphia, this time about compensation arrangements, illustrates the attention to long-term attachments in eminent domain policy. As citizens and officials distinguished owners who deserved more compensation from those who deserved less compensation, they used labels that referred, in part, to the longevity of the owners' attachments to their properties. Absentee owners who had spent a long time caring for or who stayed emotionally attached to their properties and intended to fix them up eventually were treated as if they deserved much more consideration than just market value. In contrast, absentee owners who were viewed as speculators and slumlords with no long-term attachments to their properties were treated as deserving the absolute minimum of market value. Similarly, homeowners who had lived in a house for a few years were treated as less deserving of special compensation than those who had lived in a house for a decade or more.

Perhaps the most important aspect of the conception of property as investment is that it emphasizes the social nature of property.

A conception of property as investment calls attention to how connected people's futures are. For example, property owners know that neighbors' behavior can affect the value of one's property over time. Homeowners who care for their properties by applying new paint, planting in a front yard, sweeping a sidewalk, and maintaining a generally social and lively space benefit their neighbors financially and enhance their sense of comfort and security. Conversely, those who allow a chimney to deteriorate, a roof to disintegrate, or trash to accumulate can harm their neighbors financially and in other ways. Moreover, much of the value of a place—and thus of a particular residence or business—derives from the social networks and organizations established there.[44]

Collective actions, including the building of organizations, can cause property to retain or lose its value. Investments in property motivate informal community organizing involving groups of neighbors, networks of sports teams or businesses, and church and school groups. Citizens invested in property expect a voice in government decisions about the use of nearby land, where a shed, a new park, or a toxic dump may be located. In addition, residents and businesses often struggle over municipalities' spending on trash collection, roads, schools, soup kitchens, and police. At the national level, the US government has affected property values through its policies involving credit, from mid-century redlining to present-day mortgage subsidies and the recent mortgage crisis. Thus, the conception of property as investment focuses attention on hopes about a collective future, encouraging political agreements and battles about how to control that future.

When property is treated as an investment to be protected, citizens want and expect government to provide insurance against the risks and uncertainties associated with the neighborhood's, city's, or larger community's future. They know that government activity has a major impact on how their neighborhoods change. Citizens want government to help prevent the abandonment of their areas and to provide these areas with services that sustain residents and businesses. Government can demolish dangerous buildings, prevent dumping, minimize opportunistic crime, provide good schools and parks, help businesses improve their facades, keep up sidewalks and streetlights, and collect the trash—or it can fail to do so. When citizens conceive of property as investment, they expect government to preserve and, perhaps, improve their properties' value in an uncertain future.

Although property and eminent domain are often discussed as individual stories, most of this book focuses on community-level decisions about neighborhoods' futures. And while property is owned by private entities, and two of the chapters analyze individual properties, the rest of this book tracks larger development projects that swept up over a hundred properties within them. This may seem an odd way to study property, but it makes sense because of how local governments generally work and understand property values to change. They generally attempt to influence large areas of space, not single properties. Too much theory about property and citizen expectations of government protection has focused on individual parcels, ignoring the political battles that involved entire neighborhoods and development projects.

Yet my conception of property as investment does not redirect all attention from individual to collective responsibility for property's value. Instead, it provides a unique solution to the public-private dilemma that eminent domain exposes by highlighting how public and private actions combine to impact the value of private property. Citizens using investment protection as a standard for government action know that, while an owner's own sacrifices make a property valuable, collectivities also have significant control.

A CITYWIDE STUDY

Although recent years have seen vociferous public debates about eminent domain for urban redevelopment, governments' actual use of these powers remains mostly a mystery. The 2005 US Supreme Court opinion in *Kelo,* which sided with the government and permitted eminent domain for economic development, sparked heated rhetoric and reform bills to limit eminent domain powers in almost all fifty states. But legislators and policy advocates lamented the dearth of scholarly data about the practice. "Information . . . Is Limited" was the disappointing title of the Government Accountability Office's year-long study, delivered in 2006 and meant to educate Congress on the topic.[45] In writing about eminent domain, legal and historical scholars have relied on sparse evidence from a few litigated cases and data about slum clearances undertaken a half-century ago.[46] Much of what is written about contemporary eminent domain, therefore, comes from activists and policy advocates who have positions on the issue that they want to defend.[47]

In this book, I do not offer my own conclusions or opinions about whether eminent domain for private development is right or wrong. I conducted my research to discover how citizens and officials involved in particular cases make tough decisions—not to decide how I would react if I were in their shoes. Although my conclusion discusses recommendations for reform that would make policy better reflect everyday experience, I neither unequivocally defend residents and property owners against government nor wholeheartedly endorse government actions against constituent opposition. Instead, I simply convey and make sense of the stories I observed.

Academic studies of urban redevelopment usually focus on single, controversial projects. Instead of examining only the cases that reach the courts and the news, I looked at the full variety of cases in a city. I compared all of these cases and dug into the histories and aftermaths of controversies to find out why cases developed opposition or acceptance. Of course, many of the instances of eminent domain that I observed evoked anger and dismay, but others enjoyed widespread approval. Because I share both what happened and what people thought about it, I move beyond simple reporting of existing policy to discuss what people want policy to be and why.

I studied every single actual and potential use of eminent domain in Philadelphia from 1992 to 2007. Within these parameters, eminent domain was possible in a wide variety of neighborhoods, but the relevant agencies and laws remained constant. In the next chapter, I explain how and why I selected Philadelphia as my case study. I chose the time period 1992 to 2007 because it was long enough to allow cases to complete an official process that can take several years, included two different mayoral administrations, and ended before post-*Kelo* reforms significantly affected law and practice. In order to understand policy routines that can be taken for granted, I studied and wrote an overview of the city's practices regarding eminent domain. I also completed a more thorough investigation of two mid-sized, controversial projects that offer insights into how, when, and why decisions about the legitimacy of government using eminent domain become difficult or well-received.

By designing my research as a case study of a city that includes devastated neighborhoods, thriving neighborhoods, and everything in between, I made it possible to generalize my findings to other cities at the neighborhood level. In a 2000 analysis of residential real estate markets, researchers labeled 62 percent of Philadelphia's residential areas as either devastated (36 percent) or distressed (26 percent). In many of these areas, there was no real estate market to speak of—any sales were at abysmally low prices, with habitable residences going for as little as $5,000 to $10,000. However, other Philadelphia neighborhoods were doing significantly better, with 25 percent labeled as transitional (moving up or down) and 13 percent designated as steady, high, or rising (see Figure 1.2).[48] Philadelphia neighborhoods also varied significantly by income, racial and ethnic makeup, and building stock. Though not as easily charted, political conditions varied across neighborhoods as well, due largely to the district councilperson's particular character. Thus, even when a city as a whole differs significantly from Philadelphia, some of its neighborhoods are likely to be similar to some Philadelphia neighborhoods. Nevertheless, limiting my research to Philadelphia enabled me to observe authorities operating under one set of laws and with one set of city and state agencies.

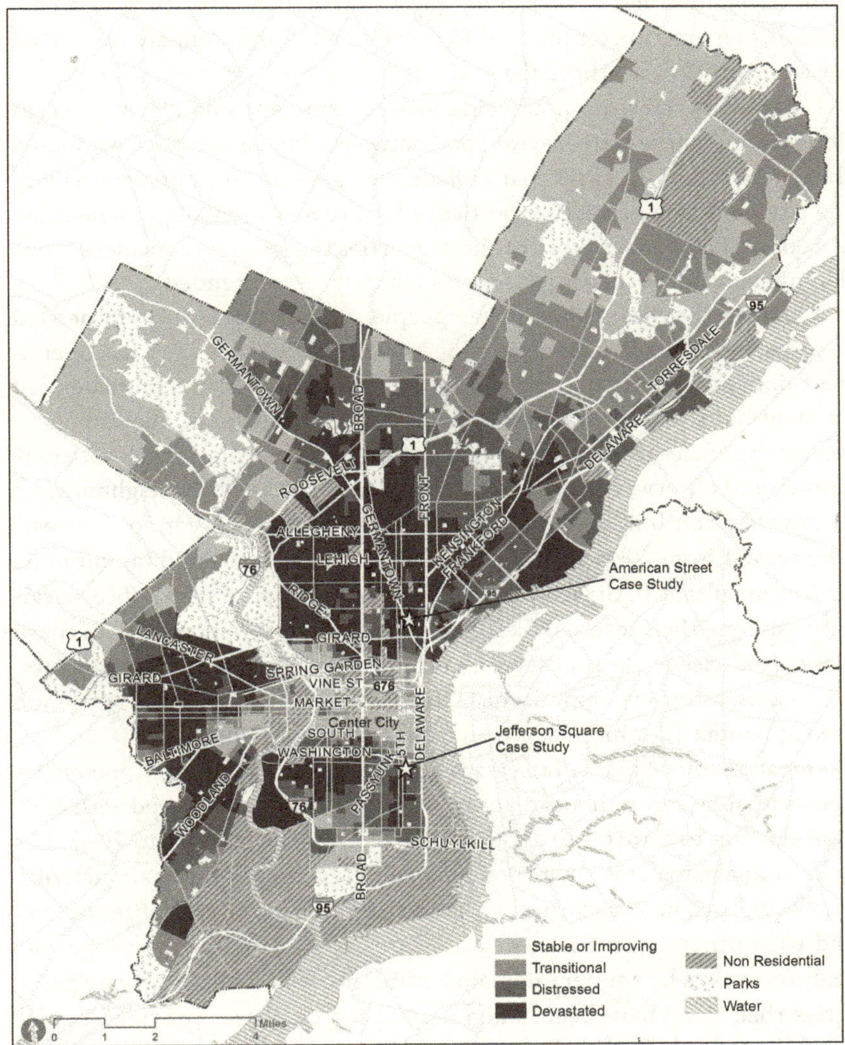

Figure 1.2:
Philadelphia Residential Neighborhood Conditions in 2000, Noting Case Study Locations
Source: Policy Solutions Group at The Reinvestment Fund, work conducted under contract with the City of Philadelphia.

By studying an entire city's practice and the long histories of medium-sized projects within that city, I avoided some pitfalls of urban-redevelopment studies focused only on large-scale conflicts. Many of these studies fail to investigate differences between controversial and uncontroversial projects and government's reasons for pursuing specific projects. I wanted to understand the full spectrum of possible and pursued cases of eminent domain to avoid bias caused by selecting only certain cases in one city or a few cases from different cities. By designing my research as a case study of a city, I could compare projects pursued to those avoided and compare those that raised controversy to those that did not.

I started by creating a citywide view of eminent domain practice in Philadelphia in the sixteen-year span between 1992 and 2007. I compared the eminent domain cases that Philadelphia government pursued to all of the city's existing private properties, which represented all possible cases of takings. I also analyzed all of the properties that the city considered condemning and all of the projects for which they were intended.

I combed the files, talked to the people, and analyzed the data needed to provide a rigorous overview of the breadth of Philadelphia's use of eminent domain for private redevelopment. The RDA, which administers all eminent domain for private redevelopment in Philadelphia, allowed me to work in its offices regularly for a year and a half to read files, speak with personnel, and observe their actions. The Office of the Mayor's Neighborhood Transformation Initiative (an anti-blight initiative of Mayor John Street, who served from 2000 to 2008) and The Reinvestment Fund (a nonprofit policy consultant to Street) also allowed me to observe their office activities, examine their internal files, and speak with their employees. In these offices and elsewhere, I observed and interviewed over 100 bureaucrats, politicians, attorneys, appraisers, business owners, activists, and residents. (See Appendix 1 for more detail on my research methods.)

I created an original database with information about every one of the approximately seven thousand properties that the RDA pursued with eminent domain to transfer to another private owner from 1992 to 2007. For help in analyzing this census of Philadelphia's eminent domain activity, I collected original data through archives, interviews, and observations and used others' quantitative data sets. To contextualize the properties that were taken by eminent domain within the city's 540,000 private properties that could have been taken, I analyzed databases provided by the RDA, the City of Philadelphia Bureau of Revision and Taxes (BRT), and The Reinvestment Fund (TRF).

I more closely examined two particularly controversial development projects, involving properties covered in my census, projects that raised significant public protest and controversy. These projects fell on what I call a "legitimacy boundary line," straddling perceptions as legitimate uses or abuses of government power. I analyzed the drawn-out politics involved in these projects, and the bulk of the book examines their long histories in order to elucidate the construction of legitimacy at the margins.

For these projects, I investigated what happened before, during, and after public conflict erupted, as well as what happened when there was little to no conflict at all. I researched how government workers, property owners, renters, and neighbors involved in particular cases determined, close-up and over time, what counted as legitimate government action. Although the conflicts seemed at first glance to be battles between David, the citizens, and Goliath, the government, I was surprised to discover that both projects enjoyed periods of local support or at least ambivalence. Shifts over time from support to resistance and vice versa reveal the complex foundations of government legitimacy.

Both of the projects planned for acquisition of over a hundred properties. They were in two different neighborhoods, one about a mile north and the other a mile south of the city center. As noted above, the projects were called American Street and Jefferson Square (their real names—they were in Philadelphia, after all). For the American Street project, located in lower North Philadelphia, government consolidated property on three different city blocks (two 3-acre sites and one 0.7-acre site) to make space for light-industrial and warehouse development. For the Jefferson Square project, located in upper South Philadelphia, government helped assemble properties in a five-square-block area for a new mixed-income housing development.

For these two projects, I reviewed all RDA files on the acquired properties and examined related documents kept by other organizations—for American Street, Philadelphia's Office of the Mayor's Neighborhood Transformation Initiative (NTI) and the Philadelphia Empowerment Zone (EZ), and for Jefferson Square, the Jefferson Square Community Development Corporation (JSCDC). I reviewed publicly accessible official documents and media coverage regarding the projects. Furthermore, I attempted to contact and interview all individuals whose property was acquired by the government for the projects, as well as many bureaucrats, politicians, attorneys, appraisers, business owners, activists, and neighboring residents involved in the projects. In all, I conducted seventy-one semi-structured interviews, averaging seventy-one minutes, related to American Street and Jefferson Square. Finally, I observed public meetings and employees working in the aforementioned organizations (except the JSCDC) between 2006 and 2008.

BOOK OUTLINE

My second chapter provides the context for my research on Philadelphia in the 1990s and 2000s by synthesizing national histories of urban redevelopment and eminent domain policies. Drawing on others' research, I describe local and federal urban-redevelopment politics from the modernist, progressive policies of the 1950s to today's neoliberal policies supporting private activity and resistance led by libertarian activists. Throughout this history, I consider how Philadelphia reflected national experience. The chapter concludes with a discussion of my choice to study Philadelphia and its consequences.

Chapter 3 offers a broad overview of Philadelphia's experience with eminent domain and presents my census of its eminent domain activity. The census allows a comprehensive look at which properties and development projects Philadelphia pursued with eminent domain, when it followed through with those pursuits, and which actions drew resistance. The chapter starts to demonstrate why and how the conception of property as investment explains practice.

Chapter 4 begins my discussion of the American Street project, probably the most hated eminent domain pursuit in Philadelphia's recent history. It describes the project's history, much of which has been forgotten since fierce resistance developed. This history illustrates how local residents and business owners might sanction takings when they see a carefully considered, plausible promise of neighborhood transformation with no damage to individual positions. In other words, they are inclined to accept credible promises to secure and improve the values of existing investments.

Chapter 5 explains how the American Street project shifted from enjoying cautious community support to becoming a local icon of eminent domain resistance when threats to investment protection seemed imminent. It details the litany of problems that stymied attempts to provide the previously anticipated results. The chapter demonstrates that just as residents support government programs that seem to protect community and individual investments, they also reject programs that seem to threaten those investments.

Chapter 6 turns to the early years of the Jefferson Square project, where residents initially reacted to the plans with loud opposition. It describes how politicians devised plans for the neighborhood's redevelopment in order to realize their own vision of neighborhood improvement. Because they assumed that few were invested in the area, they planned displacements without consulting or showing sufficient respect for the area's residents. This assumption was false, and the neighborhood erupted in opposition when the plans became public.

Chapter 7 follows how vociferous opposition shifted to strong support for the Jefferson Square takings—most important, from the homeowners who would be displaced. It demonstrates that residents can change their minds about takings in response to changing perceptions about whether those takings will support their investments. The chapter also shows that government can meet seemingly impossible demands to support investment through its takings—and that it can earn approval for doing so.

Chapter 8 discusses compensation for takings and how property represents an individual-level investment, as demonstrated by the experiences of individuals affected by the American Street and Jefferson Square projects. The chapter makes it clear that officials and citizens determine whether compensation is legitimate by assessing whether it matches the investment lost. They show concern that government respect two basic aspects of investment, as I define it: its pluralistic inclusion of many types of value and its enhancement of value with the passage of time. Officials and citizens alike believe that government should identify the investment held in a property and match it with a suitable replacement.

Chapter 9 concludes the book by discussing what my findings, taken exclusively from Philadelphia, imply about urban politics and the meaning of property in general. First, it discusses how and why the libertarian campaign to limit eminent domain and the cases it has brought to the public light have misrepresented everyday concerns about government control over land and buildings. In the chapter, I argue that public opposition to certain eminent domain cases does not reflect a wider sympathy with the movement to limit local government powers of eminent domain, zoning, taxes, or services, but rather a concern with a variety of ways in which government policies go awry in a neoliberal age when public power serves private interests. It further reflects on what urban and legal scholars might learn from this study of everyday encounters with property policy, suggesting that a conception of property as investment might be more subversive or progressive than existing ideas offered by progressive critics of property and capitalism. Finally, I use eminent domain as a lens for discovering a new social meaning of property at a time when reverence for privatization seems to have triumphed. The conception of property as investment, which emerged as governments turned to private solutions for public problems, ironically may transform and even undermine the private nature of so-called private property.

CHAPTER 2
The Policy and Politics of Urban Redevelopment

This chapter provides context for the Philadelphia stories to come by sketching a history, drawn from others' research, of US urban redevelopment policy from the late 1940s to the present.[1] It focuses on the structures of public policies, the support for and resistance to those policies, the use of eminent domain, and Philadelphia's similarity to or departure from national trends. This history concludes with a contrast between the recent and post–World War II national debates over eminent domain for urban redevelopment. This national history illuminates just how unique a time the turn of the millennium was for urban redevelopment policy and how that policy developed. It also helps to explain my selection of Philadelphia as the city for my study, which I discuss at the end of the chapter.

POSTINDUSTRIAL URBAN REDEVELOPMENT POLICIES AND THE RISE OF NEOLIBERALISM

The conception of property as investment and the recent public debate over eminent domain arose from a half century of postindustrial decline and urban redevelopment policies. Since the Great Depression (with a brief respite during World War II), manufacturing has dissipated from America's once proud industrial centers, leading to devastating losses in population and jobs. And since the 1950s, three distinct waves of urban redevelopment policies and politics—which I will call progressive, liberal, and neoliberal—have sought to save cities and particular urban neighborhoods from the vagaries of deindustrialization.

During the progressive era of the 1950s and 1960s, governments launched large-scale programs with dramatic visions for the renovation of dilapidated neighborhoods and housing, largely funded by the anti-poverty and housing policies of Presidents Truman and Johnson. Robert Moses's sweeping rebuilding of much of New York serves as a dramatic icon of this era, but so does the work of his nemesis, Jane Jacobs. During this period, resistance to top-down planning grew to be formidable. By the 1970s, governments had retreated from such bold policies by scaling down projects, incorporating bottom-up participation, and guaranteeing protections for displaced residents.

The 1980s ushered in a fiercely liberal approach to urban policies, among other policies. A reverence for small government prompted a full withdrawal of resources from city redevelopment and poor neighborhoods, not just a downsizing of projects or devolution of decision-making power. As the Reagan administration deregulated industry and retracted federal welfare programs more generally, its assistance to local governments to develop housing and support neighborhoods shriveled. Local governments led by Democrats, including some that had resisted large-scale projects of the 1950s and 1960s, pursued redevelopment. However, they secured federal support only for projects that promised downtown development of business districts. Resistance to these projects was much more muted and localized than opposition to earlier, large-scale urban renewal had been.

By the early 1990s, liberalism had begun to give way to neoliberalism. When Presidents George H. W. Bush and Clinton were in the White House, federal policies supported a generally more active role for government in urban property than during the Reagan era, but they targeted individuals rather than neighborhoods or cities. Local governments largely took a similar approach in their spending of national and local resources. In the 1990s and 2000s, neoliberal policies involved government in promoting private ownership, leading to the current mixture of a strong government hand and support for private ownership.

Modernist, Progressive Pursuit of the Public Good

In the late 1940s and the 1950s, federal and local governments began to treat the redevelopment of declining cities and neighborhoods as one of their core responsibilities, and they took a very particular approach to doing so. Governments leveled neighborhoods that they deemed unsafe and unsanitary. In their place, they planned, funded, and constructed major housing, commercial, and recreational developments. In municipal politics generally, progressive reformers at the time became emboldened by their technocratic expertise. They believed that by using calculations, diagrams, and reason, they could overcome political connections and corruption to make cities better places for everyone—especially the poor who were suffering in slums. This era saw the rise of the urban planning profession and planning commissions, which promised that technocrats could produce better and more equitable cities.

The Federal Housing Act of 1949 initiated "urban renewal" programs that would lead to massive slum clearances, demolishing tens of thousands of homes and businesses across the country, but especially in the postindustrial cities of the Northeast. The act also enabled the construction of thousands of units of new public housing. Federal resources joined with the progressive ethos to produce larger-than-life planners such as Ed Logue, who oversaw the federally funded clearance of the West End of Boston and much of downtown New Haven, Connecticut, and Robert Moses, who constructed highway, housing, and parks projects stretching from the Bronx to Long Island in New York.

During this era, local authorities that possessed both eminent domain powers and autonomy from elected officials were established. Indeed, in 1954, the US Supreme Court affirmed that local governments had the authority to remove blight using eminent domain, even if they took property that was eventually transferred to new private owners. In *Berman v. Parker* (1954),[2] the court denied protection to the owner of a productive small business in an area of Southwest Washington, DC that was slated for demolition. This demolition was planned as part of a project that would displace more than 5,000 people, 98 percent of whom were African American, to construct new housing. The court opinion explained that it followed judicial precedent in leaving it up to legislatures (in this case Congress, instead of a city council) to decide what counted as a public use. If the legislature determined that blight removal was a public use, the judiciary could not say otherwise unless another constitutional imperative justified judicial intervention. To the question of whether transferring property to new private rather than public owners violated the Takings Clause, the majority opinion responded, "... The public end may be as well or better served through an agency of private enterprise than through a department of government—or so the [legislature] might conclude. We cannot say that public ownership is the sole method of promoting the public purposes of community redevelopment projects."

In the 1940s and 1950s, many states, including Pennsylvania, passed laws enabling local authorities to use eminent domain for blight removal and private redevelopment. Like the US Constitution, the Pennsylvania

Constitution requires that eminent domain be for a "public use,"[3] and a state law passed in 1945 proclaimed that the redevelopment of blighted urban communities constituted such a use. This "Urban Redevelopment Law" created public bodies known as Redevelopment Authorities that were responsible for eliminating urban blight and were empowered to do so via eminent domain.[4] The law authorized local planning commissions to create a "redevelopment area," affirm that an area was blighted, and review a "redevelopment proposal" by the Redevelopment Authorities that detailed planned property acquisitions and relocations.[5] Finally, a "governing body" such as the Philadelphia City Council would hold a public hearing and approve the redevelopment proposal before the Redevelopment Authority could actually declare properties taken.[6] An "Eminent Domain Code" passed in 1964 refined the process of "condemnation" by detailing notice requirements, compensation principles, and litigation and appeals procedures.[7]

As in other American cities in the 1940s and 1950s, power in Philadelphia shifted to progressive reformers who pushed grand visions of reform and redevelopment. A new coalition of Philadelphia lawyers, bankers, business people, and civic leaders joined forces to replace corruption and patronage with professionalism and efficient management. Some members of this reform coalition were committed to large-scale urban planning and redevelopment and created organizations to enable it. The City of Philadelphia Planning Commission (PCPC) and Redevelopment Authority (RDA) were established in 1942 and 1946, respectively. In 1947, the glitzy and original Greater Philadelphia Exhibition, designed by a group including planner Edmund Bacon and architect Louis Kahn, attracted over 300,000 attendees to engage in creating grand visions for the city's future. In 1952, Democrat and reformer Joseph Clark took the mayor's office, after 100 years of control of Philadelphia government by the Republican machine. Another reformer, Richardson Dilworth, followed Clark from 1956 to 1962, and the office has since remained in the hands of Democrats. In addition, the city passed a new charter in 1951 and provided for the creation of a Philadelphia Commission on Human Relations that would fight racial discrimination and work to achieve interracial understanding.[8]

The City of Philadelphia pursued physical renewal as major industries that had begun to decline during the Great Depression continued to shrink after wartime production evaporated. Under the leadership of progressives, the city government initiated several projects that required eminent domain and drew on federal urban renewal funds. With the support of the PCPC (where Edmund Bacon was executive director from 1949 to 1970), the RDA oversaw the initiation of 31 federally assisted renewal projects between 1948 and 1962. Those projects were spread across six of the city's ten districts, covered 6 percent of the city's land area, and cleared 5 percent of the city's housing units. The city's renewal program during that time cost $223 million ($1.9 billion in 2013 dollars, with CPI conversion), with about half of the funds coming from federal grants. Those renewal projects, for which the progressives had high hopes, included residential clearance mostly in lower North and West Philadelphia; the creation of a new neighborhood called Eastwick in the Southwest; Center City residential development projects called Washington Square and Independence Mall; expansions of Drexel University, Temple University, and the University of Pennsylvania; and scattered residential renovation projects.[9]

Modernist Failures and Responses to Them

Just a few years later, in the late 1960s and 1970s, the urban-renewal policies of the 1950s and 1960s were viewed as even worse than simple failures. Not only had the progressives' grand visions often failed to materialize, but their plans had caused irreparable destruction. Hundreds of thousands of residents had lost their homes, and many of the displaced residents had nowhere to go because more affordable housing was destroyed than built. Researchers concluded that urban renewal caused a net loss of 50 to 75 percent of urban housing and that the loss of low-income housing was even greater, because some of the rebuilt residences were priced beyond the reach of poor families.[10]

In 1968, the Johnson administration found that three of the cities with the best reputations for their renewal programs had woefully failed to replace the low-income housing they destroyed. Between 1956 and 1968, Detroit had demolished 8,000 homes for urban renewal and had built 758 homes with federal programs; between 1952 and 1968, New Haven had cleared 6,500 homes for urban renewal and highways and had built 951 homes; between 1959 and 1968, Newark had displaced residents from 12,000 units and had created 3,760 units. The displaced residents had been provided with little in return.[11] They had suffered significant monetary, psychological, and community damage when their neighborhoods were sacrificed in the name of renewal that rarely happened—or that happened but benefited others.[12]

One reason that reconstruction failed was that public housing faced organized attacks, from the private housing industry (including the National Association of Real Estate Boards' leadership, which detested public housing) and local white, "not in my backyard" activism against public housing.[13] In Los Angeles, all existing homes in Chavez Ravine, over 300 acres with a small village feel at the edge of the city, were cleared by 1952 to create a 10,000-unit public-housing project. Before the construction of public housing began, however, the development elite went after the space and successfully tarred the project's promoter as a Communist;[14] instead of public housing, Chavez Ravine eventually hosted the Los Angeles Dodgers Stadium. Frank Wilkinson, former assistant director of the Los Angeles City Housing Authority lamented, "It's the tragedy of my life, absolutely. I was responsible for uprooting I don't know how many hundreds of people from their own little valley and having the whole thing destroyed." In Philadelphia, according to a 1963 analysis, the original clearance projects for which there were data had demolished 6,200 housing units and constructed only 3,400. Politicians eventually shied away from many of the planned public housing projects after clearing the land, once they faced vociferous neighborhood opposition at the sites.[15]

Of course, the burden of the government-induced destruction was not equally distributed. Mexican Americans lost their homes in Chavez Ravine. Across the country, poor and working-class people, mostly African Americans and non-white ethnic groups, suffered well beyond their proportions of the population.[16] Between 70 and 80 percent of those displaced by urban renewal were African American.[17] Among African Americans who were not directly displaced, many found themselves increasingly trapped in racially and economically segregated neighborhoods and cities. By the late 1950s, leaders of urban-renewal projects started to express regrets that they had targeted slum housing, for they had underestimated demolition costs, the scale of neighborhood problems, and resistance to the sites chosen for public housing while overestimating private interest in redevelopment.[18] Neighborhoods were changing due to factors well beyond their control.

Poor and non-white neighborhoods suffered in postwar American cities not only because of governments' slum clearance but also because additional federal policies and private action worked directly against their renewal. Many of these neighborhoods were sacrificed to make way for the burgeoning federal highway system. Subsidies for mortgages and infrastructure attracted middle-class and white families to the suburbs, while redlining and direct racial discrimination in housing finance and sales denied opportunities to non-white families.[19] As the effects of these policies mounted, it became painfully evident that governments had overwhelmingly failed to bring people and money to cities and neighborhoods that suffered from population and capital flight. Instead, they often had exacerbated problems originally caused by industrial decline.

In response to the harm inflicted by governments' modernist programs—and as part of the broader Civil Rights Movement—populist resistance to the programs mushroomed into a new political force in the 1950s and 1960s. Grassroots, neighborhood-based organizing with a decidedly oppositional and antagonistic stance toward government took off during this period. Saul Alinsky, who had founded a national organization for community organizing (the Industrial Areas Foundation) in 1940, moved to Chicago in the 1950s. There, he developed tools for poor African-American neighborhoods and shared them through his organization and writing. In a tumultuous time for the country at large, neighborhood-based activists demanded that governments stop implementing the results of top-down decisions and start listening to the people on the streets.[20]

Powerful voices to mobilize grassroots forces against local governments' urban renewal powers grew during this era. Jane Jacobs wrote what would become the most widely read critique of top-down planning, then and now, in response to Robert Moses's plans to subject parts of lower Manhattan to urban renewal.[21] James Baldwin renamed the 1949 Housing Act's "urban renewal" program "Negro removal" to call attention to massive, racialized displacement.[22] President Johnson's Kerner Commission reported in 1968 that grievances against inadequate housing, urban renewal programs, and a lack of community participation in planning helped cause the unrest and rioting that were sweeping across the country.[23]

As in other cities, Philadelphia residents organized to fight against racialized displacement, the splitting of neighborhoods by highways, and the devotion of resources to downtown and park projects. Residents and small-business owners resisted clearances for Independence Mall and surrounding Drexel University and Temple University in the 1950s; along South Street and Pine Street in the 1960s; and around the University of Pennsylvania, Chinatown, and Market Street East in the 1970s. This mostly oppositional organizing stopped some projects, most notably clearances in Chinatown and along South Street.[24] These political victories were somewhat hollow, however, as many residents left voluntarily over the long struggles, and neighborhoods suffered.[25]

Nevertheless, Philadelphians developed grassroots political strength through these struggles. By the 1970s, community-based activist organizations, including a strong squatters' movement, emerged to fight racial discrimination and build self-help resources for the poor.[26] The Philadelphia Council of Neighborhood Organizations, a coalition of 250 neighborhood groups formed in 1975, demanded the distribution of federal money to housing and neighborhood programs instead of downtown redevelopment. The North Philadelphia Block Development Corporation, formed in 1976, focused on getting redevelopment money to the predominantly black residential areas of western North Philadelphia.[27]

As local governments faced resistance and acknowledged their own failures related to "slum clearance," their goals started to shift more to downtown development, residential renovation, and industrial and institutional development. Philadelphia was exemplary in this regard. Leaders had watched downtown projects build successfully on private investment while attempts to redevelop the most devastated neighborhoods just outside downtown faced a myriad of problems, including a failure to attract new private money.[28] In lower North Philadelphia, for example, government had cleared 10,000 housing units (85 percent of all of those demolished in the city), but private redevelopment was rare.[29] In 1957, Philadelphia officially changed its renewal policy to focus less on the wholesale, publicly financed rebuilding of the worst areas—the kinds of plans that did not seem to be working and had been drawing protest.

The RDA shifted funds and priorities from residential clearance to new programs for residential preservation (restoration rather than rebuilding), industrial development, institutional expansion, and focused economic growth in Center City. The change could be seen in the disposition of land that the agency acquired. In the early 1950s, 80 percent of the land secured for renewal had stayed in public and institutional hands, and much of the planned redevelopment had been public housing. As priorities shifted in the late 1950s and early 1960s to more strategically entice private development, however, 90 percent of the land acquired was transferred to private owners.[30] Indeed, Neil Smith's well-known critique of how "American gentrification has been actively planned and publicly funded" focused on Philadelphia's downtown renewal of the 1960s, beginning with Society Hill.[31] The term "gentrification" was coined in 1964 in London to describe spotted private redevelopment of older urban cores, but also to flag the deleterious displacement of the poor that could result from the successful economic and physical redevelopment of a city's center.[32]

In the 1960s, federal policies responded to widespread criticism but continued to fail in their efforts to protect poor neighborhoods and poor urban residents. President Johnson's Model Cities (1966) and Community Action (1964) programs scaled down redevelopment project sizes and moved away from the sweeping plans of the 1950s. They shifted money from slum clearance to social services and homeowners' repairs, and they instituted community-level decision-making in distributing federal money. The Johnson administration also created the Department of Housing and Urban Development (HUD) in 1966 to overcome earlier administrative problems. Still, many of the hopes for these reinvented programs and new anti-discrimination laws were plagued by implementation problems.[33] The Fair Housing Act of 1968 created formal protections against discrimination on the basis of race, religion, and other protected classes in the renting, selling, financing, and insuring of housing, but its enforcement was weak, and discrimination in housing continued in force.[34]

By the mid-1970s, as anti-discrimination policies mounted, they were increasingly enforced and started to show results. The Equal Credit Opportunity Act of 1974, the Home Mortgage Disclosure Act of 1975, and the Community Reinvestment Act of 1977 attacked geographical discrimination in private residential lending. The Uniform Relocation Assistance and Real Property Acquisition Act of 1970 guaranteed substantial compensation when residential tenants and homeowners faced displacement as a result of a federally funded project. It also required that any public housing units demolished would be replaced by new housing units, and it established guidelines to ensure community participation in federally supported redevelopment planning. Although this protection for displaced people emerged only when displacements slowed dramatically, it and many of the other protections mentioned above are still in force today and impact government's current redevelopment policies.

The 1970s was a transitional decade for urban policy in that it saw the federal government cede control over its own support for cities to local authorities, thus lifting the federally enforced focus on redevelopment. Although formal rules instituted under Presidents Nixon and Carter still required disbursement of federal funds to low-income communities, they also gave local governments the leeway to ignore those requirements, so many cities diverted federal assistance to higher-income areas. In 1974, Congress created the Community Development Block Grant (CDBG) program, which replaced urban renewal and survives today. The program provided resources for an array of neighborhood needs, including infrastructure improvements, social services, and business development, and stipulated that a portion of that money be spent in low-income neighborhoods. CDBG passed as part of President Nixon's "new federalism" plan to give local governments increased authority over how they spent federal money.

Local governments often redirected money away from poor neighborhoods despite federal requirements to do otherwise. Cities used these funds primarily to help with their general operating expenses, and some local policy advisors promoted a strategy of triage, using the funds to boost transitional areas that might be saved primarily by private investment. (Political leaders failed to make these policies public, perhaps sensing that their diversion of funds from the poor would have provoked strong resistance.)

In addition, because CDBG determined the distribution of federal funds through a formula based on city population, it drew federal resources away from industrial cities and to Sun Belt cities instead.[35]

The shift in focus was evident in Philadelphia, where one could see replacement of large-scale eminent domain with increased interest in downtown development and small-scale renovation in outlying areas.[36] Into the 1970s, Philadelphia was "banking" abandoned private land in the hopes of consolidating larger parcels for future development.[37] Although the city continued to acquire land in outlying neighborhoods through eminent domain, it did so less aggressively than before. Local government policy became more cautious, not only because of a political or philosophical shift, but also because of a resource deficit. By the 1970s, postindustrial city governments had lost their capacity to accomplish almost anything at all. Many faced dire fiscal crises—most famously, New York almost defaulted in 1975—and, as a result, they pulled back from programs aimed at human welfare, neighborhood development, and physical redevelopment.

Federal Government Retreat and Local Invention of Public-Private Partnerships

As a free-market philosophy took hold in the national government of the 1980s, policy changes significantly reduced municipal access to federal resources. Following liberal ideals, the Reagan administration significantly retreated from all kinds of support for local government, including most redevelopment projects other than those supporting central business districts. In conservatives' attempt to "free" private individuals and corporations to act without undue influence from government, they defunded and dissolved almost all prior federal housing and community development programs except CDBG.[38] These actions actually followed the recommendation of a Carter administration task force, which argued that because the US economy had become "deconcentrated, decentralized, and service-based" as the "cities of the old industrial heartland . . . los[t] their status," the federal government should facilitate that change rather than fight it. "Ultimately, the federal government's concern for national economic vitality should take precedence over the competition for advantage among communities or regions," according to the task force.[39] The Reagan administration asserted that "the private market" should allocate funds and could do so more efficiently than government administrators. It recommended that cities become competitive and "concentrate on increasing their attractiveness to potential investors, residents, and visitors."[40] The federal government, according to the administration, should support particular places only insofar as they were crucial to national economic growth but otherwise should leave them to their market-determined fates.

In the face of these federal cuts, municipalities did not end their attempts to develop their locales, but they did create new ways of doing so while working more cooperatively with private developers. By the late 1970s, cities were beginning to recognize that innovative deal-making between city hall and mall developers was showing strong signs of success in risky undertakings such as the Faneuil Hall Marketplace in Boston and Pike Place Market in Seattle. In the 1980s, such public-private deals proliferated. As opportunities for retail development dried up in the suburbs, city governments attracted developers by offering land and parking facilities; building streets, sidewalks, and parks to supplement shopping centers; and crafting tax incentives to get profit-sharing deals and secure anchor developments. To name just a few, Harborplace opened in Baltimore, Embarcadero Center in San Francisco, South Street Seaport in New York, Gallery II in Philadelphia, and Copely Place in Boston.[41]

Large cities attempted to "revitalize" dying downtowns not only with shopping malls, but also with convention centers, museums, aquariums, and sports stadiums.[42] One pair of scholars declared an "arms race" for convention business, as cities built 100 convention centers between 1970 and 1985. The race also extended to sports stadiums: After New York's 1957 loss of the Dodgers to Los Angeles, other cities strove to avoid similar fates by offering numerous incentives to existing and potential local teams. Some cities even built stadiums without any commitment from a team at all.[43] The mid-1980s ushered in a new trend of cities building casinos to draw new tourist dollars. New Orleans was the first big city to open a casino, in 1992.[44] Local governments became more creative in their partnerships with private entities and even secured federal support for central business districts' anchor projects. Funds usually came from the only urban program passed by the Carter administration, Urban Action Grants (1977). By the 1980s, except for these large building projects, the tool of eminent domain for urban redevelopment mostly sat on the shelf collecting dust, with one well-known exception. In what was both a vestige of the past and a foreshadowing of the future, General Motors convinced Detroit to level an entire neighborhood, Poletown, displacing 4,200 people, for the construction of a new plant and the jobs it would bring.[45]

Successful redevelopment and the unintended effects of government policy revealed their Janus-faced nature through growing urban inequalities. Even as national economic conditions began to improve in the 1980s, cities' downtown development efforts produced uneven results across cities and across neighborhoods within cities. Baltimore was exemplary, for as it celebrated its unprecedented successes in commercial waterfront developments, poverty in the neighborhoods next door only worsened. Its first African-American mayor remarked in 1987 that the city had gotten "much prettier and much poorer" in the prior twenty years.[46]

City governments contributed to the expansion of neighborhood inequalities within cities in the late 1970s and 1980s. They abandoned some of the social priorities of earlier years, focusing less on housing the poor and giving more resources to office and residential developments that mostly benefited the well-to-do. Gentrification—in the form of increased rents and retail prices and coercion from landlords, rather than by government bulldozers—spread in the 1980s, affecting more and more cities and neighborhoods across the country.[47] By the late 1980s and early 1990s, when downtowns boasted successful commercial development, much of that development was physically defended from poor areas. In 1990, 40 percent of the census tracts in the nation's hundred largest cities were considered "poverty tracts" (compared to 27 percent in 1970), where over 20 percent of the residents were poor. Fourteen percent of these tracts (compared to 6 percent in 1970) were found to suffer from "extreme poverty," defined as poverty rates of over 40 percent.[48] As a result, William Julius Wilson named the concentration of poverty in particular neighborhoods as the major problem of the late twentieth-century American city.[49] Racial segregation between blacks and whites has somewhat moderated since the 1970s, but socioeconomic segregation increased dramatically from the 1970s through the 1990s.[50] As urban inequalities increased in the late 1980s and early 1990s, violent crime rates soared.[51]

Philadelphia's increasing neighborhood inequalities mirrored the promise and the problems of other cities in the 1980s. In the late 1960s, the city government began redeveloping the eastern edge of Center City into Penn's Landing, a recreational and tourist attraction. In the 1970s, high-income "urban pioneers" had settled in noticeable numbers in the Center City neighborhoods of Rittenhouse, Queen Village, and Fairmount.[52] By the 1980s, Center City's Society Hill had become upscale, and other downtown projects were considered development successes.[53] The West Philadelphia, working-class, African-American residential neighborhood called Black Bottom was gone; it had been replaced by the University of Pennsylvania's expanded campus.[54] In many other neighborhoods, into which many of the displaced had moved, an increased concentration of poverty and unemployment and the rise of crack cocaine wrought devastation. The North Philadelphia area called Kensington, once a blue-collar working-class neighborhood, became one of the most notorious havens for cocaine and heroin.[55] It was so riddled with abandoned buildings and social problems that it earned the colloquial nickname, "The Badlands."[56]

As resources in Philadelphia became scarce and neighborhood conditions more dire, political and residential relations became more competitive—and often violent. Mayors focused on law-and-order issues, and City Council members became more possessive of their turf. Mayor Frank Rizzo, an Italian law-and-order politician with unabashed racist overtones to his policies, reigned from 1972 to 1980. Across the city, when African Americans moved into predominantly white low-income neighborhoods with high job losses, older housing, and greater resident longevity, they faced violent resistance and mass demonstrations. In 1986 alone, the Philadelphia Commission on Human Relations received complaints about over 300 interracial "incidents."[57] Even Philadelphia's first African-American mayor, Wilson Goode (1984–1992), managed to exacerbate racial tensions and neighborhood malaise when he directed the city to send a helicopter to bomb the house of a black-power organization in a residential West Philadelphia neighborhood. Not only this dramatic incident but also the more mundane everyday policies showed how Mayor Goode and other mayors of the era were beholden to contradictory demands from the poor constituents who had elected them and from downtown elites.

At the same time, the rise to power of Goode and other African-American politicians reflected the political incorporation of individuals and organizations who had previously engaged in politics of resistance. In the late 1960s and early 1970s, minority politicians such as Maynard Holbrook Jackson of Atlanta, Coleman Young of Detroit (both elected in 1973), Walter Washington of Washington, DC (1967), and Carl Stokes of Cleveland (1967) were winning mayoral elections in large cities for the first time. The incorporation of previously organized opposition extended beyond the mayors' offices to grassroots organizations. Many of those who had fought earlier renewal efforts became involved with newly formed community development corporations that secured government funding to accomplish neighborhood economic development and housing construction.[58]

As fiscal crises and federal policies shriveled resources for all but the most business-oriented downtown developments, newly elected African-American leaders were becoming indebted to downtown developers, but they were also beholden to their African-American and poor constituents. In Philadelphia, Goode's policies reflected this dilemma. He promised to get resources to outlying neighborhoods by directing at least half of the city's federal CDBG money to predominantly black North Philadelphia. However, he also supported downtown development by continuing to implement a decades-old plan for a convention center to take up five Center City blocks.[59] Harold Washington, elected as the first African-American mayor of Chicago in 1983, pursued many of the programs that business leaders wanted, such as economic development downtown. But he also pursued goals that were based on concerns for racial justice, such as the development of outlying areas, even when doing so alienated business elites.[60]

Despite the growing inequalities among urban neighborhoods and across race and class lines, opposition to government policy was mild in the 1980s. The new political incorporation, combined with governments' increasing reliance on public-private partnerships, stunted organized resistance. Little political opposition formed to stop governments from supporting the public-private partnerships and their development projects. In fact, African-American and Hispanic residents from poorer sections of cities often lent support to such plans, for they wanted jobs and shopping centers. The residents who did voice opposition were often professionals critical of the project designs or costs, or ideological conservatives who opposed the use of government power for private undertakings.[61] Both types of opposition were quite localized in the 1980s, but in the 1990s, the latter group of libertarian-minded critics would coordinate their efforts and build national strength in reaction to yet another shift in federal policy.

A Neoliberal Combination: Strong Government and Support of the Private

The 1990s and the Clinton administration ushered in a reinvigorated role for the federal government in urban development, but with programs geared toward privatization rather than publicly controlled planning. A Republican-Democrat consensus formed around neoliberal ideals: a combination of big-government efforts (which the Reagan administration would have abhorred) and support for private markets (which earlier progressives would have reviled). Rather than targeting specific neighborhoods or cities for support, federal policies funneled resources to individuals and businesses. The federal government creatively promoted increased private ownership with an apparent faith that other social goods would follow.

In 1993, Congress made an experiment in the tax code, the Low Income Housing Tax Credit, permanent. The credit sends funds through a complicated matrix of for-profit corporations, banks, nonprofit developers, and other private organizations to produce low-income housing. Since its inception, it has been responsible for more units than direct federal subsidies.[62]

Also in 1993, the Clinton administration's Empowerment Zones/ Enterprise Communities (EZ/EC) program became federal law, taking a free-market approach to the rejuvenation of urban areas. (The ideas underlying the EZ/EC program were actually birthed during the Reagan administration and were instituted by many states during the 1980s.[63]) The Clinton program created "enterprise zones" free of tax and regulation, and it provided tax credits to businesses for hiring employees and locating in designated communities. The program also spent funds on services related to employment—such as education, job training, and child care—and required strategic planning and community partnerships.[64]

Beyond EZ/EC, the Clinton administration transformed federal housing programs so that the federal government would support privatized services. After Republican attacks on HUD, the agency reinvented itself, mostly by providing vouchers for private housing to replace public housing. HUD also initiated a HOPE VI program, which funded replacement of concentrated public housing with a more scattered mix of privately and publicly owned new homes. Of course, the largest federal policy supporting housing had become tax deductions for home mortgages, which supported mostly middle- and upper-income families.[65] The George H. W. Bush and Clinton administrations also dedicated federal resources to providing low-income families with the credit they needed to become homeowners, charging Freddie Mae and Fannie Mac with making their home mortgage programs more accessible to these families. In sum, the neoliberal champions of the 1990s made it government's responsibility to expand private ownership and business enterprise to new people and places—in particular, to poorer people and neighborhoods.

In the 1990s and 2000s, local governments also deferred to private interests to guide public decision-making and resource distribution. Rather than fashioning their own grand designs, as they had in the modernist period of the 1950s and 1960s, or turning only toward downtown, as they had in the more economically liberal 1980s, they tried to provoke and respond to private interest in neighborhood development, wherever and however it occurred. Municipal governments synthesized big government and private interests by creating menus of different policies for places with different kinds of private activity. In the 1990s and 2000s, as gentrification was becoming a familiar phenomenon, pro-gentrification policies in particular became extremely popular. One gentrification scholar commented, "... The general trend was unmistakable: in country after country, and city after city, more and more public policies began to encourage the kind of investment, subsidy, and planning processes that have long been understood to reinforce gentrification pressures."[66]

During the same era, governments showed a renewed willingness to use eminent domain—but usually in response to requests from private developers that had designed their own projects. In New York, government used eminent domain so that Bruce Ratner (Forest City Ratner Companies) could build a Nets stadium and new housing on Brooklyn's Atlantic (Navy) Yards site and Columbia University could expand its northern Manhattan campus by seventeen acres. In a case that led to a landmark Supreme Court decision (see discussion later in this chapter), Susette Kelo and owners of fourteen other properties went to court after the City of New London used eminent domain to acquire 115 private properties to implement a 90-acre redevelopment project anchored by a new Pfizer Corporation facility. And Atlantic City, New Jersey pursued properties so that Donald Trump could expand his casino's footprint.

While continuing to support private development where they sensed private-sector interest, governments also responded to private disinterest—in part, by pursuing vacant-land management. New organizations like the Land Bank of Genessee County, Michigan (encompassing the city of Flint) formed to help whole cities and counties cope with the debilitating vacancy problems associated with long-term depopulation. Across the country, not only new land banks, but also nonprofit organizations and existing government agencies invented stewardship programs for privately owned vacant land. They took responsibility for cleaning, maintaining, and acquiring abandoned properties on an unprecedented scale. They demolished buildings and cleaned, leveled, and even fenced and mowed the grass on vacant lots, whether they owned them or not. They sometimes, but not always, took over titles as well, either by foreclosing on properties because of delinquent taxes or through eminent domain. When they did take ownership of the land, the term "land banking" referred to their intent to hold on to it for a while because there was little private interest in it, at any price.

In some cities, overall shrinkage or downsizing became a principal goal of long-term, comprehensive planning.[67] Between 2002 and 2005, the City of Youngstown, Ohio developed a plan for a "smaller, greener, cleaner" city.[68] Debates about how and whether Detroit should plan for a "shrinking," "right-sized," or "ungrowth" future hit the national news in 2011.[69] Of course, city governments were not always so prescient. Flint became notorious, in part through the movie *Roger & Me,* for having thrown away $13 million on public subsidies for a Hyatt Regency that closed a year after it opened and $100 million on an AutoWorld museum that closed six months after opening.[70] Whether or not they were correct in their predictions, cities instituted policies along a continuum, according to their assessments of an area's future growth or decline.

The administration of Philadelphia mayor Ed Rendell (1992–2000) exemplified how 1990s city governments shifted away from directing downtown development to respond more broadly to private activity. Although he used eminent domain to complete a decades-long effort to construct a downtown convention center, Rendell also secured HOPE VI and EZ/EC resources to subsidize the development of privately owned housing and businesses well beyond Center City. The city also established a side-yard program to transfer ownership of abandoned properties to owner-occupant neighbors, who would presumably care for them.[71] And in the late 1990s, the New Kensington Community Development Corporation partnered with the Philadelphia Horticultural Society and the City of Philadelphia to create a "vacant land management program" for cleaning, fencing, and maintaining abandoned, vacant land.[72]

Mayor John Street (2000–2008), a former squatter-activist and city councilman, followed Rendell. He took office with a promise to spread the city's increasing wealth and, in particular, to devote government resources to repair blighted neighborhoods beyond Center City. He spent his first two years in office enlisting the City Council's support for a $500 million anti-blight program to be funded by local bonds. The "blight" label recalled postwar renewal policies, and Street's administration would use the laws passed fifty years earlier to get authority to use eminent domain when necessary. Critics worried aloud whether Street would repeat the displacement debacles and development failures that plagued earlier "slum clearances."

Street distinguished his program with a new title, the Neighborhood Transformation Initiative (NTI), and a different strategy. The program called for government to minimize displacements when demolishing buildings and acquiring property titles, ensuring that no more than a few hundred of the thousands of affected properties were occupied. In contrast to earlier programs' focus on slums, NTI promised something for every neighborhood. Wealthier neighborhoods might need sidewalks and street lamps; poorer neighborhoods might need demolition of dangerous, vacant buildings. Finally, the program would be financed and controlled locally, so that federal regulations would not endanger local priorities. (In reality, federal money would influence NTI's implementation indirectly by funding affordable housing projects proposed by local development corporations, and then supported by NTI.) Street received significant praise for the first, intentionally visible step of his program, the removal of 60,000 abandoned cars from Philadelphia streets. Criticism mounted, however, when the program's more intensive undertakings—the building demolitions, lot cleanups, and property acquisitions—showed underwhelming results.

My study period spanned the administrations of Mayors Rendell and Street, so I researched local policymaking during the neoliberal era. I studied the daily life of eminent domain in a city that, in broad strokes, reflected a national trend in which governments increasingly directed policy around enticing private action. Local governments shaped policy by what they anticipated private actors would do and could be encouraged to do. To some onlookers' chagrin, little organized opposition challenged the growing reliance on and support of private activity for redevelopment in cities across the country. In fact, one group of such observers—committed libertarians—reacted to the dearth of resistance to private-public cooperation by developing a campaign against eminent domain in the late 1990s and early 2000s. The campaign eventually reached the US Supreme Court with the *Kelo* case and immediately drew national attention. Thus, this book covers the time period before the legal reforms that followed the post-*Kelo* debate, a time when the libertarian campaign against eminent domain was planted and grew.

Libertarian Resistance to Contemporary Eminent Domain

The circumstances behind the *Kelo* case exposed just how much the national and local politics of property policy had changed over fifty years of urban redevelopment policy. Over the past half-century, the US Supreme Court has heard only two cases about eminent domain for urban redevelopment, both of which reflected the policies and politics of their times. In both *Berman v. Parker* (1954) and *Kelo v. the City of New London, Connecticut* (2005), the court allowed local governments to move forward with eminent domain for private redevelopment, ruling that legislatures, not the courts, could determine what constituted a public use. And yet, the ways in which governments used that authority in the two projects behind these cases were quite different.

Berman involved a plan to clear a huge area and replace it mostly with public housing, whereas *Kelo* involved a plan to raze a much smaller number of functioning buildings for new development anchored by the Pfizer Corporation. In the 1950s, the District of Columbia displaced over 5,000 people, 98 percent of whom were African American, to make space for the construction of new housing, with at least one third of the units preserved for low-income residents. In the 1990s, New London targeted 113 properties for economic development—not housing.

The cases' contrasting racial overtones highlighted an additional change in the politics of resistance. Sam Berman, the plaintiff in *Berman*, was an

African-American businessman who objected to the planned clearances. His race served as a strong reminder of African Americans' disproportionate suffering from urban renewal programs. Susette Kelo, the plaintiff in *Kelo*, was white, and her race may have helped activists mobilize support for the fight against eminent domain. The public-interest group supporting her wanted to represent a libertarian, rather than a racial justice, case that showed eminent domain could threaten white Americans as much as anyone else.[73]

Libertarians, not racial or social justice organizations, led the national anti-eminent domain campaign in the early 2000s. Eminent domain became an important part of libertarians' larger attempt to preserve and expand the progress toward liberal values made in the 1980s. They applauded Reagan's liberal downsizing of government but revolted over Clinton's and George W. Bush's expansions of government activity, even if those resources would flow to and through private entities.

Libertarians were building their organizing power in the 1990s when they began leading a new national fight to restrict eminent domain. In the struggles against 1950s and 1960s urban renewal, libertarian political advocacy groups did not take center stage in the free-market critique of the "federal bulldozer" as a distortion of market incentives.[74] By 1990, libertarian public interest groups had materialized, with significant force. In 1976, Charles Koch and two partners founded the Cato Institute (previously the Charles Koch Foundation, began in 1974), and it had grown to become one of the most influential American think tanks.

The libertarian public interest law firm, the Institute for Justice (IJ), emerged with other conservative, libertarian organizations and made eminent domain one of its core issues. In 1991, the Koch Family Foundations provided start-up funding to help found IJ, which would focus then and now on fighting for economic liberty, educational choice, property rights, and the First Amendment.[75] IJ has largely used litigation to mobilize public sympathy around its larger goals; it began its eminent domain challenges with a case against Donald Trump, which it won in court,[76] and in 2002, created a spin-off organization, the Castle Coalition, to manage a broader public campaign for property rights, focusing on "eminent domain abuse."[77] The IJ hit the jackpot with *Kelo*. It turned the unambiguous loss in the majority opinion, accompanied a fiery dissent, into a win for their larger organizing plans.[78] In the week following *Kelo*, the IJ announced that it would spend $3 million, half its annual budget, to "combat eminent domain at the state and local level."[79] In the 1990s and 2000s, therefore, this fierce advocate for libertarian causes had taken over leadership from the left in the fight against eminent domain, and by showcasing many white, working-class victims in small cities, they mobilized a new constituency for the struggle.[80]

However, mobilizing support from traditionally liberal constituents such as poor black residents of inner cities has been one of IJ's key and quite original strategies since the libertarian organization's inception. IJ founders surmised that fighting for liberal-seeming constituents would improve their chances of winning in court, as well as their public profile and reputation. According to a historian of conservative legal organizations, "representing traditionally liberal clients had the potential to transform the identification of civil rights with liberalism," which "IJ leaders calculated [would make it] possible for conservatives to gain a hearing on a wide range of issues."[81]

Indeed, national-level racial and social justice organizations lent support to the libertarian resistance to eminent domain, although they did not lead the fight. Left-leaning organizations objected to eminent domain in the 1990s and 2000s for one of the same reasons that libertarians did—an aversion to the capture of government power by big business—but their reasons diverged from there. Simply put, libertarian organizations object to bold government interventions in private control, while left-leaning groups invite such interventions but demand that they promote social justice and avoid deepening social inequalities. Governments continue to target predominantly poor and African-American neighborhoods with eminent domain,[82] and many left-leaning individuals and organizations object to what they view as eminent domain's victimization of the poor and racial minorities. It is indeed possible that statistical discrimination has replaced direct discrimination. Because redevelopment is only technically justified where officials can point to physical conditions that are at least somewhat problematic and thus show potential for improvement, poor and working-class neighborhoods are at greatest risk. The disproportionate suffering of poor people and people of color from eminent domain thus makes many left-leaning scholars and activists add their voices to the national fight against it, but this does not mean that they support a broader libertarian agenda.

In fact, left-leaning scholars have expressed significant ambivalence about eminent domain because they consider it government's responsibility to ensure that neighborhoods are livable and that housing is decent. They grant that improving poor neighborhoods might indeed require significant government intervention and that takings may even be justified at times.[83] This dilemma has made local politics about some development projects extremely complex, as social justice organizations take surprising positions in support of new developments that displace long-time residents. For example, the fight over Brooklyn's Atlantic Yards development was particularly protracted because local leaders of eight community groups eventually took the side of the redevelopers, after signing a community benefits agreement ensuring the construction of affordable housing; job training and hiring of local residents; and assistance with local schools, community facilities, and small-business development.

Citizens judging government at the turn of the millennium faced a very different political and geographic landscape than they did in the 1950s. Governments assumed a very different stance about their role in urban development: they acted as if they could and should nudge, rather than direct, private action. Although overt racial discrimination was reduced dramatically, neighborhood inequalities and the concentration of racial minorities and the poor had greatly increased. And to make political positions even more complicated, despite increased inequalities between the rich and the poor, the wealth of those at the bottom had improved. Thus, owning a home had become possible for the first time and constituted the most significant source of financial wealth for America's lower- and middle-income families. In sum, American citizens confronted a new combination of increased overall wealth and larger inequalities. They owned real property in greater numbers, and that property constituted a greater proportion of household wealth than ever before. And finally, they had over a half-century of experience in watching governments attempt to guide redevelopment under threats of continued urban decline. At this unique historical moment, citizens and officials judged government and understood private property in the particular way that I explore in this book.

PHILADELPHIA AS A CASE STUDY

To understand how American citizens conceive of property, I designed a rigorous study of eminent domain in a single city—Philadelphia. This was a strategic choice that would ensure that my findings were nationally salient.

Urban Americans' shared history and conceptions of property made me confident that some findings from Philadelphia could be generalized to other cities. As we have seen, various US cities have weathered the same economic and social trends, along with the same changes in federal community-development and housing programs. Moreover, Americans share a historical commitment to the ideal of private property and a more recent sense of outrage at eminent domain abuses.

To be sure, despite common national political cultures and federal policies, cities' eminent domain practices might look very different. Indeed, getting to know eminent domain in Philadelphia does not provide insight into the volume and character of eminent domain in other cities as a whole. Though deindustrialization traumatized practically all of urban America, the experience across cities and neighborhoods over time has been extremely uneven. Similarities of size, built environment, politics, economics, and laws affect the degree to which another city's or neighborhood's eminent domain practices reflect Philadelphia's. To some extent, neighborhoods across cities may be more comparable than neighborhoods within them, so findings about eminent domain in one Philadelphia neighborhood are likely to reflect the character of eminent domain in a similar neighborhood of another city. Overall, the character of Philadelphia's eminent domain practice probably looks a lot more like those of distant Chicago or nearby Baltimore than those of Camden, New Jersey, the small, struggling city right across the river, or New York, the large, thriving city just a hundred miles away.

I selected Philadelphia, in part, because its intermediate economic and demographic position among American cities at turn of the millennium made it potentially more representative than many other cities. In relation to other postindustrial cities seeking to spark redevelopment, Philadelphia was an intermediate city in terms of size and networks, as well as the ways in which it was changing. While New York and Chicago had become "global cities" because of their financial and knowledge-economy power, Philadelphia could be considered at best a "second city."[84] Its trade and information networks were ranked at a qualitative level below iconic global centers and yet at a level above many smaller cities, like Camden (New Jersey), Flint (Michigan), or Allentown (Pennsylvania).

Philadelphia's population indicators have rested comfortably in the middle range of postindustrial cities. Consider population change over the long durée of postindustrialization. Between 1950 and 2010, Philadelphia lost a quarter of its population. This loss was considerably less serious than those of Detroit, St. Louis (Missouri), and Youngstown (Ohio), which dropped almost two-thirds in the same time period. Yet Philadelphia failed to achieve the growth of Columbus (Ohio), or Indianapolis, which approximately doubled their populations between 1950 and 2010, or New York, which also managed to gain residents. Philadelphia also has something of an intermediate status with regard to race and nationality, with a 2000 population that was 45 percent white and 9 percent foreign born. (See Tables 2.1 and 2.2 for statistics for postindustrial cities selected for the variety of population sizes.)

Philadelphia's signs of economic strength have also stood in the middle range of postindustrial cities of comparable size, with its 2000 poverty rate amounting to 185 percent of the national rate. By contrast, the 2000 poverty rates in Detroit, Cleveland, and Flint were over twice the national rate, while the poverty rate in Camden was three times the national rate. At the low end, Indianapolis's poverty rate was about equal to the national rate, and New York, Chicago, and Boston had poverty rates at about 150 percent of the national rate.

In 2000, median household incomes in Philadelphia were about 73 percent of the national level, and comparable to those of Detroit and Baltimore. Smaller cities had even lower median household incomes, with Camden, Youngstown, and Cleveland at 56 percent, 58 percent, and 62 percent of the national median, respectively. But the larger cities of New York, Chicago, and Indianapolis all had higher median household incomes, at between 90 and 95 percent of the national median.

Philadelphia was also in a middle ground in the sense that it faced an uncertain future, between anticipated growth or decline, at the turn of the millennium. For decades, the city had been hemorrhaging residents and jobs, and housing prices had been dropping. In the early 1990s, the city faced such a dire fiscal crisis that its escape from bankruptcy was not a foregone conclusion. And yet, by 2000, population declines started to slow, and economic conditions improved. In the early 2000s, there were indications that the population might even stabilize or increase slightly and that real estate prices were rising. Philadelphia's rate of population loss was decreasing, almost to zero—the city's population decreased by 13 percent, 6 percent, and 4 percent in the 1970s, 1980s, and 1990s, respectively.[85] Although housing prices had been only 61 and 62 percent of the national medians in 1970 and 1990, and dropped to 50 percent of the national median in 2000, they had climbed to 79 percent of the national median by 2010.[86] Local rents had remained fairly equal to national prices in 1990, 2000, and 2010.[87]

Philadelphia's turnaround in population and housing prices was by no means guaranteed to persevere, however, and the fact that wealth and poverty remained stubbornly low presaged continuing problems. The city's poverty rate remained fairly steady, at 155, 185, and 175 percent of the national rates in 1990, 2000, and 2010, respectively.[88] Its median household income was 82 percent of the national average in 1990 but only 73 and 69 percent of it in 2000 and 2010.[89]

Philadelphia's position on this borderline between growth and decline was well suited for this study because it rendered the city's judgments about eminent domain less predictable than those of more clearly growing or declining cities. The booming real estate markets of New York and Boston, for example, seemed to predict that almost any use of eminent domain

Table 2.1. POPULATION CHANGE IN NORTHEASTERN CITIES BETWEEN 1950 AND 2010

	1950[1]	2010[2]	Change (1950–2010) (%)
United States	150,697,361	308,745,538	105
Cities of 2010 population over one million			
New York	7,891,957	8,175,133	4
Chicago	3,620,962	2,695,598	-26
Philadelphia	**2,071,605**	**1,526,006**	**-26**
Cities of 2010 population between 500,000 and one million			
Indianapolis	427,173	820,445	92
Columbus	375,901	787,033	109
Detroit	1,849,568	713,777	-61
Baltimore	949,708	620,961	-35
Boston	801,444	617,594	-23
Cities of 2010 population between 100,000 and 500,000			
Cleveland, OH	914,808	396,815	-57
St. Louis, MO	856,796	319,294	-63
Allentown, PA	106,756	118,032	11
Flint, MI	163,143	102,434	-37
Cities of 2010 population under 100,000			
Trenton, NJ	128,009	84,913	-34
Camden, NJ	124,555	77,344	-38
Youngstown, OH	168,330	66,982	-60
Long Branch, NJ	23,090	30,719	33
New London, CT	30,551	27,620	-10

[1] National: US Bureau of the Census, "1950 Census of Population: Volume I Number of Inhabitants," p. 1–3, https://www.census.gov/prod/www/decennial.html, accessed November 24, 2013; all cities other than Long Branch, NJ and New London, CT: US Bureau of the Census, June 15, 1998 (internet release date), "Table 18. Population of the 100 Largest Urban Places: 1950," http://www.census.gov/population/www/documentation/twps0027/tab18.txt, accessed June 18, 2013; Long Branch and New London: US Bureau of the Census, "1950 Census of Population: Volume II Characteristics of the Population," p. 30–9; p. 7–7, https://www.census.gov/prod/www/decennial.html, accessed November 24, 2013.

[2] US Bureau of the Census, 2010 Census, "State and County Quick Facts," http://quickfacts.census.gov/qfd/states/, accessed November 24, 2013.

within those cities would draw fierce controversy. Conversely, the devastated expanses of land in Detroit and Youngstown were likely to make eminent domain much more acceptable there. Differences in opinion about whether and when to use eminent domain were more likely to occur in Philadelphia, where conditions were middling and the future uncertain, than in Flint or New York, where the city's future trajectory, for good or for ill, seemed clear.

Table 2.2. INDICATORS OF ECONOMICS, RACE, AND NATIONALITY IN 2000, SHOWING PHILADELPHIA'S INTERMEDIATE STATUS

	Economic Characteristics							Race and Nationality	
	Median Household Income	Individuals Below Poverty (%)	Median Value of Owner-Occupied Homes	Median Gross Rent	Home Ownership (%)	Unemployment (%)	Workforce in Manufacturing (%)	White (%)	Foreign Born (%)
U.S.[1]	$41,994	12	$119,600	$602	66	4	14	75	11
Cities of 2010 population over one million[2]									
New York	$38,293	21	$211,900	$705	30	6	7	45	36
Chicago	$38,625	20	$132,400	$616	44	6	13	42	22
Philadelphia	**$30,746**	**23**	**$59,700**	**$569**	**59**	**6**	**9**	**45**	**9**
Cities of 2010 population between 500,000 and one million									
Indianapolis	$40,154	12	$98,500	$567	59	4	14	69	5
Columbus	$37,897	15	$101,400	$586	49	4	9	68	7
Detroit	$29,526	26	$63,600	$486	55	8	19	12	5
Baltimore	$30,078	23	$69,100	$498	50	6	8	32	5
Boston	$39,629	20	$190,600	$803	32	5	6	55	26

Cities of 2010 population between 100,000 and 500,000									
Cleveland, OH	$25,928	26	$72,100	$465	49	6	18	42	5
St. Louis, MO	$27,156	25	$63,900	$442	47	7	12	44	6
Allentown, PA	$32,016	19	$76,900	$541	53	4	20	73	10
Flint, MI	$28,015	26	$49,700	$476	59	8	23	41	2
Cities of 2010 population under 100,000									
Trenton, NJ	$31,074	21	$65,500	$604	46	6	9	33	14
Camden, NJ	$23,421	36	$40,700	$522	46	8	15	17	9
Youngstown, OH	$24,201	25	$40,900	$401	64	6	18	51	2
Long Branch, NJ	$38,651	17	$135,300	$727	42	5	8	68	20
New London, CT	$33,809	16	$107,900	$592	38	5	12	64	10

[1] National data from US Bureau of the Census, Census 2000. "Tables DP-1–4, Geographic Area: United States," http://censtats.census.gov/data/US/01000.pdf, accessed November 24, 2013.

[2] All city data from US Bureau of the Census, Census 2000, Demographic Profiles: 100-percent and sample data, http://www.census.gov/census2000/demoprofiles.html, accessed November 24, 2013.

While we wouldn't necessarily expect acceptance or rejection because of Philadelphia's intermediate economic conditions, there are several reasons that we might expect eminent domain to be particularly open to criticism in Philadelphia, namely political fragmentation, political corruption, a Quaker heritage, and neighborhood parochialism. The city has a history of political fragmentation that might make citizens less willing to accept or trust government authority in the name of a public good. As the city's tax coffers and federal funds dried up in the 1980s, city council members became less cooperative and more competitive to ensure that their districts got their share of a shrinking pie.[90] District Council offices have become veritable "fiefdoms" (according to interviewees), cooperating with one another only to the extent that each traditionally grants the others authority over what happens in its territories. (Philadelphia City Council has ten district members and seven at-large members.) When issues concerned more than one district, fights were much more likely to erupt among council members over getting their share, as happened with Mayor Street's Neighborhood Transformation Initiative. Moreover, lack of cohesion in the local Democratic Party contributes to fragmentation among executive agencies, commonly referred to as acting like "silos."[91]

Philadelphia's reputation for political corruption might also have a negative impact on citizens' willingness to accept politicians' use of eminent domain. Although reformers have repeatedly attempted, sometimes successfully, to clean up Philadelphia politics, their celebrations often have been followed by new evidence of continued dirty dealings. Pennsylvania had the country's fifth highest rate of federal convictions for public corruption between 1976 and 2010, and over half of those convictions were in the eastern district, with Philadelphia as its population center.[92] In the wake of a recent controversy over a collapsed Center City building, the former Licenses and Inspections Commissioner called the department a "political back-water where money walks" and that must be freed from "political chicanery."[93] According to a news reporter, the Philadelphia Police Department is "reeling from repeated allegations of corruption [and] acts of admitted corruption."[94] Indeed, in the 1980s, the FBI's ABSCAM investigation of bribery put three City Council members (the president, the majority leader, and another councilman) in prison. Councilman Leland "Lee" Beloff was also sent to federal prison for trying to extort a developer and a builder, the latter to get a free luxury apartment for his mistress. In the 1990s, Councilman James Tayoun went to prison for tax evasion, mail fraud, and racketeering, and in the 2000s, Councilman Richard Mariano went to prison for taking bribes. As I write these words in August 2013, Pennsylvania state senator Vincent Fumo, from Philadelphia, has just finished four years in federal prison and is beginning six months of house arrest for 137 corruption convictions.[95]

Finally, Philadelphia's cultural traits made me suspect that its residents would be less likely than others to trust government's use of eminent domain. Outside the city, Philadelphia is probably most well known for its Quaker heritage and neighborliness—traditions that run counter to any rabid search for financial profit.[96] Its "City of Brotherly Love" moniker is confirmed by the countless greetings of "How ya doin'?" encountered on a walk through most neighborhoods. As I couldn't help but observe when I lived in Philadelphia for five years, Philadelphians also characterize themselves as unusually attached to their neighborhoods, many of them rarely leaving and frequently expressing pride in their few blocks of the city. Indeed, Philadelphia has an unusually high percentage of homeowners—in 2000, its homeownership rate was higher than that of any other city (other than Youngstown and equivalent to Indianapolis and Flint)—suggesting that Philadelphians have a particularly strong commitment to their houses (see Table 2.2). This neighborhood attachment may be due, in part, to the domination of Philadelphia's landscape by row houses. Row houses pack residents together tightly and push them to collect on the public sidewalk and street, which may create some of the real and imagined community orientation of neighborhood life.

Despite the city's political fragmentation and corruption, neighborliness, and attachment to place, and neighborliness, Philadelphians actually endorse a vast majority of the city's uses of eminent domain. To demonstrate and begin to explain this surprising endorsement, I now turn to my census of the thousands of eminent domain cases in turn-of-the century Philadelphia.

CHAPTER 3
Rhetoric Without a Cause

Beyond Libertarian and Left Cries of Abuse

When they cry abuse in battles over eminent domain, people generally justify their anti-government positions by appealing to a libertarian (i.e., classical liberal) ideal about the sanctity of private rights or to a left-oriented ideal about protection of the poor against profit-seeking developers. However, it is necessary to look beyond these familiar ideals to understand how Americans judge instances of eminent domain as legitimate uses or abuses of government power. Although familiar ideas reflect conflict rhetoric, they do not tell us how some cases of eminent domain become contested while many others are accepted. I call appeals to these familiar ideals "rhetoric without a cause." Unfortunately, such after-the-fact appeals are often mistaken for the actual causes of conflicts. The arena of post-conflict rhetoric is the wrong place to search for the reasons behind how, when, and why conflicts emerge, and it is a terrible place to stop the investigation.

This chapter begins to unveil additional justifications for government's eminent domain powers by sharing a comprehensive view of how eminent domain works generally—how, where, and for what kind of redevelopment government officials take properties. In it, I present a summary of all of the eminent domain cases that happened in Philadelphia over a decade and a half (the properties that were actually taken) and compare them to the full universe of potential cases (each and every privately owned real estate property in the city). Viewing the city as a whole clarifies how citizens and officials treat government legitimacy in the broad context of what is possible. What emerges is a full picture of eminent domain in daily practice—including the common and the rare, the unremarkable and the uncontroversial—that helps us understand how government earns legitimacy. I do not overlook, ignore, or replace the images of abuse in the courts and the news. Instead, I place those cases in the context of a more general practice.

Most people assume that there is virtually always significant opposition to governments using eminent domain for private development. The case that reached the US Supreme Court as *Kelo v. City of New London, Connecticut*, for instance, drew massive, national attention, most of it negative. And yet, in many cases in Philadelphia, citizens and officials support this policy in practice. Given the disgust for the cases that we generally hear about, it is hard to understand how and why so many cases of eminent domain for private reuse are uncontroversial. If every case of eminent domain that you have heard about in the news infuriates you, you are not alone.

And yet, literally thousands of cases of eminent domain for private reuse would infuriate almost no one, but to date, there has been very little public awareness about these cases. This chapter begins to fill a gap in public information, and it shows how Philadelphia's everyday practice differs dramatically from the stories that most of us are used to hearing. Indeed, from the early 1990s through the first decade of the 2000s, the government of Philadelphia took thousands of properties for private reuse. Most of these cases never hit the news or provoked court battles, and none reached the US Supreme Court. When we look at a whole universe of cases, rather than the headlines in the news, we can see problems with the conventional ways of understanding what motivates judgments about eminent domain.

Even the briefest glance at Philadelphia's general practice shows that everyday evaluations of eminent domain clearly differ from those that are based on the tenets of the recent libertarian-led movement against eminent domain. If most Philadelphians agreed with libertarians' property-rights logic, they would be particularly repulsed by government transfers of private property to new private owners, and this practice would never gain support. And yet, as mentioned earlier, the city violates property titles in this way regularly, prompting few objections from citizens.

A closer look at the kinds of properties taken and the plans for their redevelopment reveals that left-leaning demands for use-value protection also fail to make sense of how officials decide which takings to pursue and how citizens react. If they used standards proposed by left-leaning pundits and academics, the poorest citizens would demand that government avoid supporting real estate prices and instead protect the use values that property can provide, while the middle class and wealthy would support the pursuit of exchange values. However, in the vast majority of cases that government pursues or avoids, no one makes a clear distinction between use value and exchange value. Furthermore, if we impose the use/exchange value distinction, we see that government policies promising to respect and support both use and exchange values and meeting resistance when either is put at risk.

In fact, an overview of everyday practice sheds light on alternative concerns about the just distribution of value. To be sure, citizens and officials demand that government work to alleviate poverty or, at least, not exacerbate economic inequalities. But concerns that those who are invested in property reap the rewards of government action are even more salient in eminent domain policy. Citizens and officials base their decisions on the need for government to assist those who have invested value in their properties by caring for them and demonstrating a commitment to keep doing so.

THE EVERYDAY AND THE EVERYWHERE

The City of Philadelphia Redevelopment Authority (RDA) expropriated almost one of every hundred privately owned properties in the city between 1992 and 2007. During this period, the RDA Board began the process of taking almost 6,880, or 1.3 percent, of the city's 540,000 private properties,[1] and it completed the process for 4,320, or 0.8 percent, of those properties (see Figure 3.1). The difference between the pursued and taken represents properties that the RDA dropped from consideration before condemning, often because the RDA or developer purchased them instead. Because many owners probably sold to the RDA once they got word of the threat of a taking, it makes sense to think of the real number of properties acquired through the takings power as somewhere between 4,320 and 6,880—about 1 percent of the city's private properties. In all, finding that the city has taken approximately 1 percent of its private properties in sixteen years suggests that the practice was a somewhat regular, rather than exceptional, undertaking.

And yet, very few of these property takings met any official resistance. Owners of only 240 of the 4,320 (6 percent) taken properties lodged any kind of official contestation, through litigation or revestment. Condemnees (the official word for occupants and owners who lose property to eminent domain) filed litigation, protesting either the taking itself or the amount of compensation, in 160 cases. Revestment, meaning that the RDA gave properties back in response to an owner's objection, occurred in another 80 cases.[2] Of course, these measures fail to count other forms of protest,

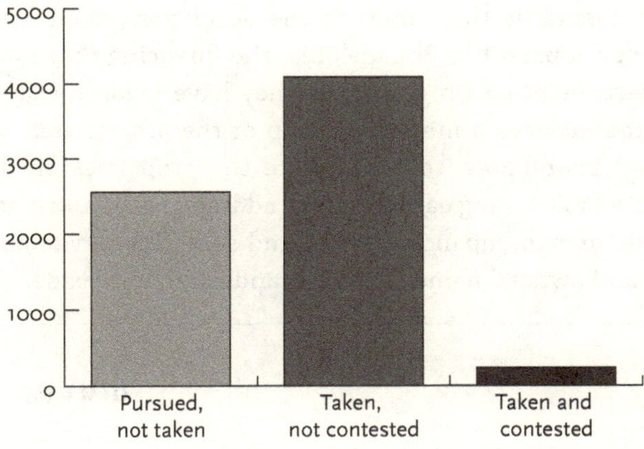

Figure 3.1:
Philadelphia Properties Pursued for Eminent Domain, 1992–2007 (of 540,300 Total Privately Owned Properties Citywide in 2000)

such as telephone calls, letters, and statements at public hearings. Still, if every case of eminent domain for private redevelopment should reek of illegitimacy because of a commitment to property rights as sacred, formal opposition in 6 percent of cases seems surprisingly low.

DISTINGUISHING THE ACCEPTABLE FROM THE UNTHINKABLE

An overview of which properties were taken and why clarifies how officials distinguished plausible eminent domain targets from unthinkable targets—and how the high frequency/low controversy combination was possible.

The official pursuit of a property starts rolling when an RDA employee called project manager writes a memo asking RDA Board members to consider a preliminary approval. When the RDA Board passes a related resolution, the potential taking then moves on to other administrative and legislative bodies for consideration. The early memo characterizes targeted properties, their neighborhoods, and plans for redevelopment (see Figure 3.2 for an example of such a memo). The RDA's designation for the neighborhood where the takings will happen, which by law it calls an "urban renewal area," heads the memo (the line starting with "RE:"). Sometimes, the memo will also offer a description of current physical, social, and market conditions in the neighborhood, as well as plans for redevelopment in the immediate area. Regarding the future plans, the memo usually includes a few paragraphs on what kind of redevelopment has been proposed. The memo often mentions the names of the developers, their history with the RDA or development in Philadelphia, the financing they have secured for the project, or other progress that they have made toward the project. The memo includes a minimalist map of the project area, within the neighborhood boundaries, to note where the properties are located. It also includes a table listing each property address, with information about building structures, occupancy, zoning, and sometimes even about delinquent taxes and owners' names. Officials and citizens consider all of these

ITEM II (b)

Memorandum

REDEVELOPMENT AUTHORITY OF THE CITY OF PHILADELPHIA

Date: November 6, 2002

To: Members of the Board

From: Herbert E. Wetzel

Board Meeting Of:
November 12, 2002

RE: New Kensington & Fishtown Redevelopment Area
New Kensington & Fishtown Urban Renewal Area
Fourth Amended Redevelopment Proposal
Fourth Amended Urban Renewal Plan

This is to request approval of a resolution authorizing the preparation of the Fourth Amended Redevelopment Proposal and Fourth Amended Urban Renewal Plan for the New Kensington & Fishtown Redevelopment Area, New Kensington & Fishtown Urban Renewal Area.

There are a total of fifty-three (53) properties covered by this request, which includes acquisition for two (2) different projects. The two- (2) proposed projects are described below. These projects will need to come before the Board at a future meeting for approval.

Open Space Management Program, Phase 4
Fifty-two (52) properties will be acquired in the New Kensington-Fishtown Urban Renewal Area to be used as sideyards, recreation areas, and supplemental open space by residents and businesses in the community. This is the fourth phase of the New Kensington Sideyard Program that focuses on systematic acquisition and reuse of vacant derelict property. The acquisition cost of this project is estimated to be $279,892 and will be paid by the Office Housing and Community Development

Frank Spezzano & Jan Morgen
One property will be acquired on behalf of Mr. Spezanno and Ms. Morgen, who own an adjacent structure. The vacant property will be rehabilitated for residential use. The construction cost is estimated to be $40,000. The acquisition costs for this property estimated to be $80,959 and will be paid by the developer.

A fact sheet, property list, acquisition map, and resolution are attached.

Prepared by: Lynda McClary
Approved by: Michael Koonce

Figure 3.2
Selected Pages of Sample Memo from RDA Staff to the RDA Board for Consideration of a Taking

ITEM II (b)

FACT SHEET

NEW KENSINGTON & FISHTOWN REDEVELOPMENT AREA
NEW KENSINGTON & FISHTOWN URBAN RENEWAL AREA

I. PURPOSE

There are a total of fifty-three (53) properties covered by this request, which includes acquisition for two (2) different projects. The two- (2) projects are described below.

Fifty- two (52) properties will be acquired in the New Kensington-Fishtown Urban Renewal Area to be used as sideyards, recreation areas, and supplemental open space by residents and businesses in the community. This is the fourth phase of the New Kensington Sideyard Program that focuses on systematic acquisition and reuse of vacant derelict property. The acquisition cost of this project is estimated to be $279,892 and will be paid by the Office Housing and Community Development

One (1) property will be acquired on behalf of Mr. Spezanno and Ms. Morgen, who own an adjacent structure. The vacant property will be rehabilitated for residential use. The construction cost is approximately $40,000. The acquisition cost of this property is estimated to be 80,959 and will be paid by the developer.

A. CLEARANCE/ACQUISITION (See the attached spreadsheet)

II. AREA DATA

Present Use	Number of Properties	Proposed Reuse
R-9A	3	residential/related
R-10	28	residential/related
R-10A	15	residential/related
C-1	1	residential/related
C-2	5	residential/related
G-2	1	residential/related

III. RELOCATION INFORMATION

None of the properties in this request are occupied. No properties require relocation assistance.

IV. ESTIMATED COSTS

The estimated cost of acquisition for this proposal is $360,851.

Figure 3.2 (Continued)

ITEM II (b)

V. SUMMARY DATA

	OSMP	MARL	TOTAL
Lots:	52	0	52
Buildings:	0	1	1
Total Parcels:	**52**	**1**	**53**
Buildings to be Demolished:	**0**	**0**	**0**
Residential Relocation:	0	0	0
Commercial Relocation:	0	0	0
Total Relocation:	**0**	**0**	**0**

Figure 3.2 (Continued)

ITEM II (b)

PROPOSED ACQUISITION LIST

PROJ.	House#	Dir	Street	OWNER	BLDG /LOT	OCC/ VAC	ZNG
MARL	925		Marlborough Street	John Dougherty	Bldg	Vac	R10
OSMP	2412		Amber St.	Emmanuel F. & Anna R. Hansen	Lot	Vac	R10
OSMP	2414		Amber St	Joseph L. & Clara Hormer	Lot	Vac	R10
OSMP	2205		Blair St	Michael Heston	Lot	Vac	C-2
OSMP	2207		Blair St	Joan Sutton	Lot	Vac	C-2
OSMP	2318	E.	Boston St	John E. Boyle	Lot	Vac	R10A
OSMP	2313	E.	Cabot St	City	Lot	Vac	G-2
OSMP	2220		Coral St	Henry Allen	Lot	Vac	R10A
OSMP	2222		Coral St	John & Margarite Dougherty	Lot	Vac	R10A
OSMP	2474		Coral St	Edward & Elizabeth Fisher	Lot	Vac	R10A
OSMP	1306		Crease St	Kushin Construction Co.Inc	Lot	Vac	R10A
OSMP	1308		Crease St	Barrett Develop. Corp	Lot	Vac	R10A
OSMP	2200	E.	Cumberland St	Joseph & Suzanne A. Stock	Lot	Vac	C-1
OSMP	2128	E.	Dauphin St	Grace Gettler	Lot	Vac	R10A
OSMP	2130	E.	Dauphin St	PHDC	Lot	Vac	R10
OSMP	423	E.	Flora St	Thomas & Helen Croyden	Lot	Vac	R10A
OSMP	1771		Frankford Ave	Denneth Sofronski	Lot	Vac	R10
OSMP	2012-14		Frankford Ave	Ina Schwartz	Lot	Vac	C-2
OSMP	2016		Frankford Ave	Robert Buchanan	Lot	Vac	C-2
OSMP	2018		Frankford Ave	Thomas C. Tompkins & Roscoe Knight	Lot	Vac	C-2
OSMP	2418		Frankford Ave	Robert & Rosemary Kurz	Lot	Vac	R10
OSMP	2420		Frankford Ave	Fed Polonia S&L Assoc.	Lot	Vac	R10
OSMP	2422		Frankford Ave	Robert & Rosemary Kurz	Lot	Vac	R10
OSMP	2424		Frankford Ave	Robert & Rosemary Kurz	Lot	Vac	R10
OSMP	2426		Frankford Ave	John Aitchison	Lot	Vac	R10
OSMP	2428		Frankford Ave	City	Lot	Vac	R10
OSMP	2451		Frankford Ave	Florentino & Mecedes A. Caba	Lot	Vac	R10
OSMP	2453		Frankford Ave	Tri-State Corp	Lot	Vac	R10
OSMP	2610		Frankford Ave	Henry J. Chybinski	Lot	Vac	R10
OSMP	2612		Frankford Ave	Florence Alexine Wnek	Lot	Vac	R10
OSMP	2614		Frankford Ave	Florence Alexine Wnek	Lot	Vac	R10
OSMP	2616		Frankford Ave	Henry Chybinski	Lot	Vac	R10
OSMP	2618		Frankford Ave	Henry Chybinski	Lot	Vac	R10
OSMP	2620		Frankford Ave	Henry Chybinski	Lot	Vac	R10
OSMP	2046		Hagert St	Albert & Florence Tanghe	Lot	Vac	R10A
OSMP	2103	E.	Hagert St	City	Lot	Vac	R10
OSMP	2105	E.	Hagert St	City	Lot	Vac	R10
OSMP	2107	E.	Hagert St	City	Lot	Vac	R10
OSMP	2109	E.	Hagert St	City	Lot	Vac	R10
OSMP	1900	E.	Lehigh Ave	St Albans Check Cashing Corp	Lot	Vac	R10A
OSMP	2032	E.	Lehigh Ave	Joh Cordell		Vac	R10
OSMP	2028		Martha St	City	Lot	Vac	R10
OSMP	128		Melvale St	Frank J. Hild	Lot	Vac	R10
OSMP	2201	E.	Norris St	George I. & Gilda M. Tumolo	Lot	Vac	R10A
OSMP	1218	E.	Oxford St	Harcourt Builders Dvelopers Inc.	Lot	Vac	R9A
OSMP	1228	E.	Oxford St	Nicholas & Genovepha Zwarczuk	Lot	Vac	R9A
OSMP	1230	E.	Oxford St	Charle T. & Dolores M. Cahill	Lot	Vac	R9A
OSMP	8	E.	Palmer St	Debeek	Lot	Vac	R10
OSMP	256		Richmond St	City	Lot	Vac	R10
OSMP	2074	E.	Sergeant St	Jos R. Benson	Lot	Vac	R10A
OSMP	253	E.	Thompson	Betty Maebuis	Lot	Vac	R10A
OSMP	2208		Trenton Ave	Stella Brzycki	Lot	Vac	R10A
OSMP	2323	E.	York St	Richard A. & Dorothy Anderson	Lot	Vac	R10A

Figure 3.2 (Continued)

different characteristics as they easily accept some proposals, treat others as unthinkable, and carefully consider some that fall in between.

In the most common types of cases that won approval—what we might call the prototypically legitimate case—government condemned vacant, abandoned lots in a devastated neighborhood for the construction of affordable housing by a nonprofit developer or the expansion of an existing residence, business, or institution onto an adjacent property. If we conjure up the mirror image of such a taking—a prototypically illegitimate case—we see government pursuing a set of primarily occupied properties in a stable neighborhood for a for-profit developer to construct market-rate housing or a stand-alone commercial operation. Notably, this image exists only as a hypothetical possibility, as the Philadelphia government rarely, if ever, pursue such a case.

Officials decide whether to pursue takings by considering the kinds of properties to be taken and the kinds of developments that will result. The most routine eminent domain practice demonstrates an understanding of property as investment, and it explains how so many Philadelphia properties could have been taken with so little resistance. Citizens and officials most commonly justified takings, first, by verifying that little to no value would be lost by the existing owner and, second, by confirming that future plans for the property would secure the investments of many kinds of value by neighbors.

Current Devastation and Abandonment: No Threat to Value

Because government officials understand property as investment, they have viewed the pursuit of property in which the owner seemed to have invested no value as a legitimate government action, and they have moved forward with these pursuits accordingly. In other words, government could be justified if it took an owner's property title without hurting an investment. These officials reasoned that government could take the titles of such properties—for example, an empty lot in a devastated neighborhood—without hurting an investment, and citizens generally agreed. Indeed, one of Susette Kelo's lead attorneys from the libertarian Institute for Justice told me that he understood popular sentiment as such. He said, "There's not a whole lot of opposition for taking the truly abandoned properties."[3] He explained that his organization had not taken on some of Philadelphia's cases and probably did not even know about most of the takings in Philadelphia because they did not involve properties in which the owners had invested.

Abandoned properties in run-down neighborhoods seem to have little to no value to anyone in their current state. The owners, if they are even around to notice, may experience the value of such properties as nothing more than sources of additional property taxes and, perhaps, headaches. Worse, neighbors who still value the neighborhood are likely to be bothered by noxious uses such as dumping and drugging that abandoned properties invite. When such a property is threatened with eminent domain, its neighbors are unlikely to think that the government is stealing. Instead, they reflect that by simply getting the property into the hands of someone who values it, government can protect their own investments in their homes and their communities. Government often gains approval when it takes a property in which an owner has little invested at all and invested neighbors stand to gain from the taking.

The first indicator that a property title had little value at all to the owner, but potential value if transferred to someone else, is the poor condition of the neighborhood. Indeed, local officials started their eminent domain process by demonstrating neighborhood "blight," largely because state laws allowed or required them to justify a taking in this way.[4] (Seventy-eight percent of the property takings in this study were justified by designations of areas as blighted; 22 percent were justified by designations of individual properties as blighted.) To be sure, vague blight definitions in legal doctrine allowed planners to apply the designation almost anywhere, but Philadelphia officials generally adhered to the restrictive spirit of the law. For instance, a downtown hospital's request for a condemnation to expand their campus did not even make it to the Philadelphia City Planning Commission's formal review process because, as one planner put it, the "hospital was fishing" for a justification in an area that did not deserve a blight designation.[5]

Overall, Philadelphia restricted eminent domain to its most problematic neighborhoods. Over four of every five (84 percent) properties taken were located in neighborhoods that would have seemed completely devastated to an outsider, though just more than one in three (36 percent) of the city's residential neighborhoods qualified as such (in an independent study conducted by The Reinvestment Fund, described in Appendix 2). Almost all of the rest of the takings happened in neighborhoods doing a little better but still with extremely poor conditions. (Fourteen percent of taken properties were in "distressed" neighborhoods, which accounted for 26 percent of the city's neighborhoods.) Thus, 98 percent of all taken properties were located in neighborhoods with very serious problems, although only 62 percent of the city's neighborhoods qualified as such. The remaining taken properties, a mere 2 percent of the total, rested in the city's remaining neighborhoods

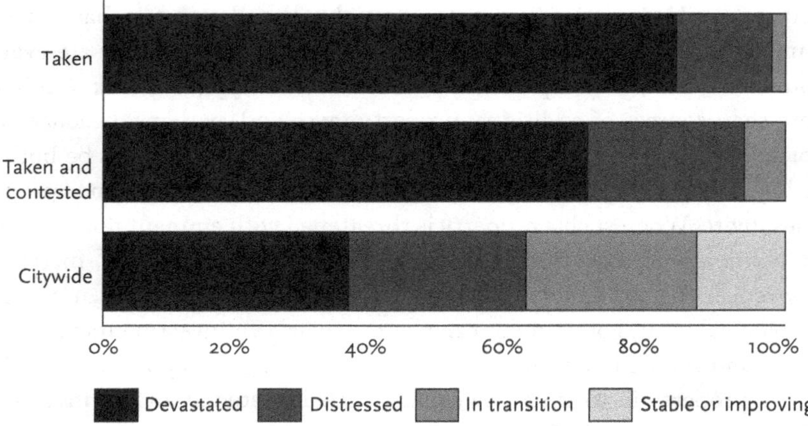

Figure 3.3:
Neighborhood Conditions of Taken, Taken and Contested, and Citywide Properties

identified as "in transition," and practically no properties were taken from "stable" or "improving" areas (see Figure 3.3).

Not only did government concentrate its takings in the neighborhoods with the worst conditions, but it faced more resistance when it moved into neighborhoods with better conditions. Owners were more likely to object to takings in neighborhoods with fewer physical problems and higher market prices. A property taken in the neighborhood with the (objectively) worst conditions—the areas I am calling "devastated"—was the least likely to draw formal resistance. Takings of property in the neighborhoods just one category better were much more likely to be litigated or revested. And a property in the best of the neighborhoods—"stable" and "rising"—targeted for eminent domain was the most likely to be contested.

The second indicator that an urban property had no value to an owner but potential value to invested neighbors—and, thus, that it was ripe for a taking—was that it remained unoccupied and undeveloped. When considering whether to pursue properties, officials largely avoided actually displacing people. When Mayor Street faced public concern about early plans to acquire 5,000 properties under his anti-blight program, he repeatedly stressed how few of the properties considered were occupied. Indeed, RDA Board members seemed much more careful about taking occupied than vacant properties. Watching their public meetings, I noticed that they often passed resolutions putting forward vacant properties in a perfunctory way but scrutinized the taking of occupied properties more carefully. When occupied buildings were pursued for condemnation, they were usually justified as "collateral damage" of larger projects comprised mostly of vacant land.

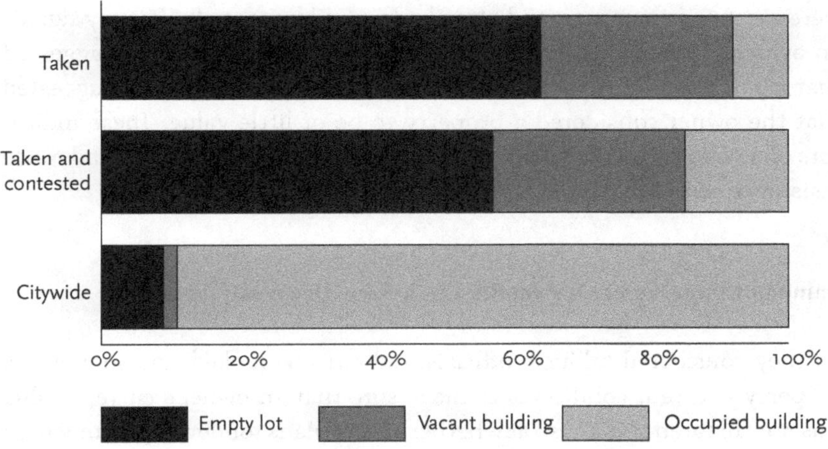

Figure 3.4:
Property Conditions of Taken, Taken and Contested, and Citywide Properties

The vast majority of properties taken between 1992 and 2007 were vacant. A full 92 percent, or 3,990, of the over 4,320 properties taken for private reuse were vacant. In contrast, about 11 percent of the city's 540,000 private properties were vacant (see Figure 3.4).

When a parcel lacked any building at all, it was even more likely to be taken. Indeed, 2,760, or 64 percent, of the 4,320 properties taken were empty lots. By contrast, only 9 percent of properties across the city were estimated to have been empty lots in 2000. Thus, most properties taken were not only unused but also undeveloped.

Contestations of eminent domain provide additional evidence that the taking of an occupied building raised much more suspicion than the taking of a vacant building or lot. Government was twice as likely to encounter formal opposition for taking an occupied property as for taking a vacant one. Takings of only 5 percent of empty lots and vacant buildings were litigated or revested, while takings of occupied buildings had an 11 percent chance of being opposed in those ways.

Special attention to occupied properties throughout the official process, the public discussion of vacancy when officials defended policy, the extreme discrepancy between the vacancy rates of taken properties and all of the city's properties, and the infrequency of opposition to taking vacant properties made me recognize that the importance of vacancy to government legitimacy could not be overstated.

To some extent, the low frequency of resistance to takings overall was due to the fact that most properties taken were in devastated neighborhoods, were vacant of occupants, and often had no buildings at all. Vacancy signals an owner's lack of care or concern, and a lack of development suggested that a parcel was even less valuable. Together, these conditions suggested that the owner considered a property to be of little value. These indicators of an owner's lack of value drew government's taking power and made resistance very unlikely.

Imminent Improvement: Benefits to Those with Investments

As they considered takings, officials and citizens looked not only at the property's current conditions to make sure that an owner's current value was not threatened but also at whether future plans for development would improve the value of others' investments. Although Pennsylvania law did not require takings to be justified by any particular kind of future development, such plans factored importantly into official decisions. Philadelphia officials evaluated the 4,320 taken properties as part of approximately 400 distinct projects, with various levels of precision about the intended redevelopment.

Specific development plans were preferred to no future plans at all, for they provided a stronger guarantee that real improvement would result from a title transfer. To be sure, officials sometimes acquired properties without any specific plan for redevelopment, and some advocate this approach because it allows government to assemble scattered properties into larger parcels and to react reliably and quickly to interested developers. Still, officials tended to avoid this practice, called "land banking," because they understood that taking property without promising specific improvements was politically dangerous. Only 13 percent of the project proposals in the period I studied were for unspecified future plans (see Figure 3.5). Officials' aversion to land banking, evidenced by these numbers and data from interviews and archives, suggests that they felt the need to demonstrate that real improvement—new housing, a cultivated yard, or a renovated business or institution on a previously vacant property—was imminent. Cathy Califano told me that local residents often resisted government plans to assemble large parcels of land in the absence of businesses committed to buying and building on those parcels.

> There was some concern that neighborhoods felt. They were questioning..., "Why was the city land banking land? What are they going to do with that in the future?" There were some concerns [about] land banking. There was a diversity of perspectives, [but there were concerns] that land banking tied up real public

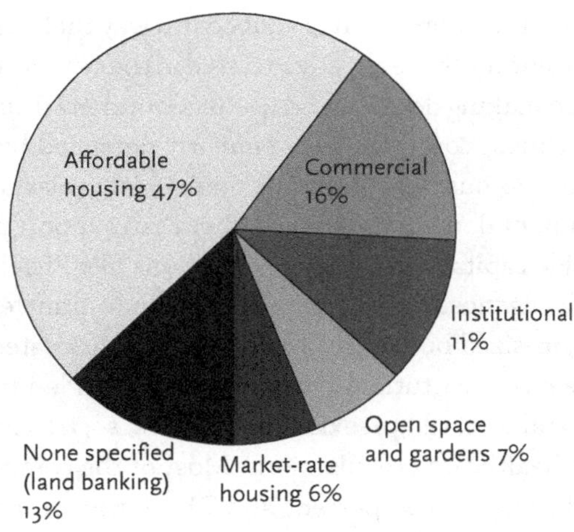

Figure 3.5:
Types of Redevelopment Projects Planned for Taken Properties

> resources in property that doesn't have... specific projects tied to it. [Some neighborhood people thought] [t]hey should only be doing real projects.
>
> Cathy Califano, EZ Economic Development director[6]

(As I mentioned in Chapter 2, many cities have established entities whose sole purpose is land banking, as a way of dealing with vast amounts of abandoned property. During my research, Philadelphia had no such agency. Here, the phrase refers to one way that the RDA distinguished its different eminent domain pursuits.)

The majority of plans for takings (87 percent of projects) were not for land banking; rather, they anticipated that particular redevelopment projects would improve values, and affordable housing constructed by a nonprofit developer was, by far, the most common kind of project that won support for eminent domain. One nonprofit director explained to me that the need for land for affordable housing made her accept the use of eminent domain as reasonable, even in rare cases when it displaced homeowners and tenants. She said, "There's a tension there in getting the land for... affordable housing.... And so for us, we kind of can't come out in a pure line around eminent domain, because for us it feels like a necessary part of the process."[7] Affordable housing projects accounted for 47 percent of the total projects, and nonprofit developers were behind 72 percent of them.

Although affordable housing projects were most frequently planned for taken properties, commercial and institutional projects of a particular kind were also common. They were often described in a way that emphasized their improvement of value for those already invested in the city and neighborhood, by cleaning up and making derelict land useful. Commercial and institutional projects, the next most common, were similarly defended by their value to existing residents and business owners. Commercial projects accounted for 16 percent of eminent domain projects. Rather than support plans to attract and benefit outside capital from huge corporations like Pfizer, Wal-Mart, or Ritz-Carlton, officials mostly used eminent domain to transfer properties to small- and medium-sized businesses that were already located in the neighborhood and the city. Institutional projects, which made up 11 percent of the projects, generally served preexisting churches, social services, community centers, and healthcare organizations. Most of the commercial projects and institutional projects—58 percent and 71 percent, respectively—were expansions into vacant lots that abutted current operations.

By giving taken properties to adjacent owners or nearby neighbors, government rewards those who have already invested in the place. This practice of awarding invested neighbors was evident as officials helped commercial and institutional operations to expand. It was also the impetus for a whole program for residential side yards. Expansions of homeowners' properties into adjacent parcels accounted for a large number of taken properties. (They were treated as a single project of the "open space/gardens" category, itself accounting for 7 percent of total projects.) Of course, all of these expansions into neighboring lots—yards, open space, garden projects, and commercial and institutional building—promised, like any new use of vacant land, to give value not only to the new owner but to neighbors, whose surroundings would improve.

Market-rate housing projects, which comprised 6 percent of the redevelopment projects for takings, can also adhere to a logic of investment. In these projects, those who buy the housing invest by putting down the sales price to commit to a risky neighborhood, and this is a basic market transaction. They have not been there for any length of time, and therefore, the only thing they get from government is the opportunity to buy. (Remember that none of these properties is in a neighborhood with a stable market.) However, the beneficiaries who justify these projects are usually the neighbors who will be rewarded by the cared-for properties nearby. Officials are more hesitant to support and citizens are more likely to resist market-rate housing and some commercial projects because they breed suspicion that government is motivated more exclusively by market or growth ideals. But it is because some of these projects can be interpreted as supporting investment that they happen at all.

BEYOND LIBERTARIAN AND LEFT EXPLANATIONS

Challenging a Commitment to Property as Rights to Control

When faced with the dilemmas faced by real properties and neighborhoods, the general public clearly does not share libertarian protestors' view that it is always wrong for government to put private property in the hands of new private owners through eminent domain. If it did, the thousands of Philadelphia properties taken for private redevelopment between 1992 and 2007 would have provoked significant opposition. But as we have seen, owners formally resisted in only a few hundred of the thousands of cases that occurred. Despite rhetorical appeals to property as a right once controversy erupts, this conception of property did not help Philadelphians decide which cases they found objectionable.

Citizens and officials accepted that eminent domain was justified when government turned an abandoned lot in a devastated neighborhood over to a private developer. These kinds of takings, the ones that are most common, almost never make the news—perhaps because journalists understand that audiences will judge them as reasonable. Yet, such cases are no more or no less takings of private property to transfer to another private owner than the cases that have raised so much ire. Thus, we need to recognize that simply describing a property as having been effectively ignored by its owner, who lets it sit vacant and uncared for in a neighborhood inundated by problems, can suggest that it deserves less protection. When a government takes such a property for private reuse, it meets much less objection than when it takes a cared-for and lived-in house or business.

To be sure, property-rights advocates, when faced with the reality of these neglected properties and benevolent redevelopment projects, might quickly acknowledge that these are not the kinds of properties or reuses that they are talking about when they object to eminent domain. But this lack of concern about the taking of certain kinds of properties for certain kinds of redevelopment projects is an important finding that we must understand. The ease with which property-rights advocates accept some takings for private reuse tells us that a principle of property rights does not explain what motivated its champions to object to certain cases, even though their rhetoric attributes their objections to a violation of property as a set of rights. The easy acceptance of *some* takings of private property for private reuse demonstrates that an appeal to the sacred nature of private property as rights to control land and buildings cannot even explain the actions and concerns of its own proponents. In their approach to property in these cases, even property-rights advocates do not expect government to treat property as a right.

To be clear, I am not arguing that anyone should judge particular cases of eminent domain differently. Instead, I am arguing that sometimes we are mistaken about our own reasons for objecting to certain cases. The evidence from Philadelphia suggests that when people explain that they object to eminent domain because they sense a violation of property as a private right, they often give us an inaccurate analysis of their reasons. When they use the language of property rights to defend furor about eminent domain for private reuse, they appeal to a yardstick of legitimacy that even the most vehement property-rights champions are not using to decide when government abuses its powers. Therefore, other principles or ideas must explain when government goes wrong. Citizens and officials must employ additional or alternative sets of criteria to determine government legitimacy.

Benefits for the Invested, Without the Exchange-Value/Use-Value Distinction

By identifying government as a protector of value rather than property title, left-leaning observers of urban politics come closer to accurately identifying what citizens and officials expect from government with respect to property. Philadelphia officials justified decisions with indicators that a taking of a property title would actually preserve and improve many kinds of value of land and buildings. Most of the time, however, they did not distinguish between use value and exchange value. Instead, they distinguished between the invested and the un-invested and attempted to ensure that their actions benefited the former, rather than the latter.

In the vast majority of cases, indicators of use value and exchange value overlapped entirely, making it impossible to distinguish between objects that hold one kind of value but not the other. These were not the critical categories that helped Philadelphians decide when and where government is justified in pursuing eminent domain. In general, use value and exchange value are so deeply intertwined in urban properties, neighborhoods, and development plans that it is misleading for us to separate the two. Indeed, if we force this distinction, as in these plans for the use of eminent domain, almost any modern plan for urban redevelopment is justified by creation of both use value and exchange value and its risk to neither. And it would be difficult, if not impossible, to say which type of value is being most supported by actions that invariably affect both.

There may be a fine line, or no line at all, between justifying eminent domain as a tool to alleviate a neighborhood's problematic physical and social conditions and as a way to support real estate prices. A determination that a neighborhood is "blighted," which has been used to justify takings for many years, for example, usually requires some evidence of substandard, undesirable, or unhealthy physical or social conditions. Though laws defining blight rarely, if ever, say anything about market prices, the physical conditions they include map onto low market prices and even onto an absence of market transfers at all (because prices are so low). Indeed, Philadelphia's Mayor Street demonstrated how fluid the line between market and physical conditions is as he sold his program for neighborhood revitalization to Philadelphia voters. Originally, he promised a sweeping "anti-blight" program, but later he renamed it the Neighborhood Transformation Initiative (NTI) to emphasize that the city would direct resources of different kinds to all kinds of neighborhoods, from the most desperate to the thriving, across the entire city. In the renamed initiative, neighborhood conditions would justify what kinds of programs would make sense, and those conditions were discerned by an analysis of real estate markets, which was really a combination of physical, social, and price indicators. The technical analysis of market conditions included not only sales prices but also several different signs of physical and social conditions, such as vacancy and demolition rates, building ages and conditions, and household credit profiles. But neighborhood conditions are only the very first standard—and never the only standard—that officials use.

Officials and citizens use an investment logic to evaluate whether government action is warranted in the cases they judge routinely. A combination of property vacancy and neighborhood desperation suggest that a property, in its current condition, holds close to no value to anyone at all, so a forceful transfer will hardly damage the value of an individual investment. Vacancy, the most important indicator that a particular property can be taken legitimately, signals a lack of current value without making the use/exchange distinction. The fact that an owner is not using a property suggests directly that it holds little use value to him or her, but also that selling or leasing it would bring a low price compared to that of a habitable building. Moreover, vacant properties are understood not only to disturb physical conditions in the neighborhood by drawing noxious uses but also to decrease properties' market values significantly.[8] The transfer to a new owner who will use and care for the property for almost any new kind of use will help to improve neighbors' investments in their properties.

The desperation of the neighborhoods, the owners' abandonment of the properties, the nonprofit status of the developers, and the anticipated benefits of the new development all create expectations of improvement and few worries about harm to anyone. These few indicators show that nothing of value will be destroyed and promise that new value will accrue to those who deserve it because they have already invested in the place. Such cases are easy to contemplate and are uncontested.

Plans for the future of taken properties display a concern for the improvement of value through use, and the new use creates exchange value. The most common type of project supported by eminent domain is affordable housing, which might seem to primarily promise use value. However, even in this case, when use value is created, exchange value is, too. Most contemporary affordable housing projects are explicitly intended not only to provide shelter for the poor but also to support the market value of properties and the neighborhoods in which they sit. New residents will buy and rent this housing on a "private" market but at subsidized rates. Many of these programs are designed to increase homeownership, and though new owners may buy at a below-market price, they also may choose to cash out several years later. Thus, like any other kind of development, affordable housing projects built on vacant property are expected to improve a neighborhood's physical, social, and market conditions.

Similarly, in commercial and institutional expansions as well as residential side yards, use and market value are both at stake. Adding a significant amount of land to any property is almost guaranteed to increase its market value. And as a result of either of these kinds of expansion, as in any new use of vacant land, the neighborhood's physical and market conditions are likely to improve.

To be sure, eminent domain policy reflects a concern for just distribution, and sometimes this means goods for the poor. This is evident in the support for affordable housing, which reserves benefits for low-income families. In addition, one might argue that by focusing government resources in poor neighborhoods, benefits are being targeted to poor residents. Still, the neighbors who benefit are the ones who stay there. Those who remain invested in the place reap the rewards of government action.

Residential, commercial, and institutional expansions, when supported through eminent domain, are also justified by the distribution of benefits to particular constituents. But poverty does not qualify the homeowners for yards next door or qualify businesses and churches for the opportunity to expand their operations. When the new owner is the next-door neighbor, the most direct benefits of the transfer go to people and organizations who have been caring for that exact spot and, thus, deserve more than others to receive those benefits.[9] Thus, the most proximate caretakers of property seem to secure some of the greatest benefits from government's eminent domain powers, and neighboring owners are rewarded with better physical conditions and higher prices. (Of course, if prices become significantly higher, renters lose, but in the neighborhoods where most takings happened, drastic price increases were not anticipated.)

LOOKING FOR LIMITS TO GOVERNMENTS' EMINENT DOMAIN POWER

There is a deep national anxiety about whether property rights restrict government's use of eminent domain at all, especially when it is justified by a city's need for growth. The City of New London's sacrifice of decent homes for an economic development plan, sanctioned by the Supreme Court in *Kelo* (2005), led opponents to conjure up hypothetical images of the most outrageous cases they could imagine—and to show that these cases were legally permissible. In her dissenting opinion, Justice O'Connor suggested that government could replace a Motel 6 with a Ritz-Carlton, and activists attempted to get local government to take the home of Justice Stevens to make the point that even it was in danger. These possibilities screamed caution about a dangerous slippery slope in the law of eminent domain. And yet, the cautioners needed to use hypothetical examples to create such fear and outrage because they could not find similarly egregious real-life examples. Despite the warnings of judges, journalists, and activists, my research shows that in at least one large city, the taking of functioning businesses and homes for higher-intensity development is actually quite rare, and officials generally avoid cases that would so readily strike most Americans as an abuse of government power.

The public alarm about a limitless pursuit of economic development results in part from a failure to observe and understand how officials actually make decisions about when and where to take property. This chapter has illustrated how officials and citizens distinguish quickly between patently illegitimate and legitimate pursuits. In the everyday, routine world of policymaking, officials rely on simple categorizations and brief descriptions of neighborhoods, properties, and redevelopment projects to help them determine when it is appropriate to use eminent domain. Often, eminent domain passes through the administrative processes with little question, hundreds of properties at a time. Partly because of general agreement about their legitimacy, the bulk of cases flow so smoothly that they often seem unremarkable. In these cases, politicians and bureaucrats prepare the resolutions, stamp the papers, pass the bills, and continue on with little notice about particular cases. If the cases sometimes imagined by eminent domain's opponents were to be pursued, they would strike most officials and citizens as obviously and clearly unacceptable. Therefore, individuals rarely propose that government attempt them, and if they do, officials often reject the proposals right away. Eminent domain patterns in Philadelphia suggest that something has limited governments' economic-development pursuits.

Evidence about routine practice provides a stark contrast to fears about governments careening out of control in pursuit of economic development and endangering all Americans' property rights to benefit the greediest developers with the deepest pockets. In the decades prior to *Kelo,* Philadelphia government took a large number of properties for private redevelopment but rarely caused alarm by doing so. In the prototypical case, officials condemned a set of vacant lots and buildings in distressed neighborhoods, usually to transfer to a nonprofit developer to construct subsidized housing for poor families. Officials also often gave vacant properties to adjacent residents, business owners, and institutions to expand their homes and operations. In cases like these, property owners rarely lodged protests, and public controversies rarely, if ever, emerged. Officials almost never pursued the taking of an occupied home or business in a stable or growing neighborhood so that a for-profit entity could construct market-rate housing or a new commercial endeavor.

I have argued that these patterns defy explanation by the more familiar libertarian and left protests against eminent domain. I have also described how these routines can be understood as reflecting a logic of property as investment that government is expected to protect. However, it took more than this overview of the taken-for-granted routines to convince me that this logic of investment lay behind citizen judgments of government legitimacy. Indeed, I needed to see how citizens and officials distinguished between use and abuse in cases that they considered harder to judge, or at least around which consensus was hard to develop. I needed to look closely at controversial cases to see how participants justified and critiqued government action more explicitly and thoughtfully than they do in the routinely accepted or avoided cases.

In the next five chapters, I turn to conflict-ridden cases: real-life (rather than hypothetical) cases in which citizens cried loudly of government abuse. In studying these cases, I investigated not only how the government's opponents justified their opposition after the conflict developed. I also investigated how the case developed enough support for government to pursue it in the first place, despite signs that resistance would follow. Why were individual properties with value put at risk? How were corporations and individuals with no previous local commitments allowed to get these properties? How and when did they become the objects of protest, and when did they not? It is through contested cases like these that people fight to define the standards for legitimate government action and determine how they should be applied. And thus through these cases, it becomes clearer what it means to say that urban Americans appeal to a logic of investment when they judge government protection of property.

CHAPTER 4

American Street I

From Badlands to Promised Lands

A LEGITIMACY BOUNDARY LINE

Imagine a line that distinguishes legitimate from illegitimate government action. The majority of eminent domain cases that Philadelphia pursues rest comfortably on the legitimate side of that line and win approval easily. Generally speaking, these are takings of vacant properties in devastated neighborhoods for the development of affordable housing by a nonprofit developer or for the expansion of a residence, small business, or institution into adjoining property. By contrast, officials almost never even consider the cases that would rest most clearly on the illegitimacy side of the line. These would be takings of occupied properties in stable or thriving neighborhoods for housing or commercial developments to be sold on an open market.

The cases that stir conflict are those that fall on or very near what I call the legitimacy boundary line because their particular combinations of neighborhood projects, properties, development projects, and developers make their legitimacy hard to judge. Though in the heat of conflict, controversial cases can seem obviously illegitimate, they are actually boundary cases. They are not the most egregious examples of what government *could* do with its eminent domain powers. Instead, they are the most egregious examples of what government *does* do. Cases that draw resistance are unique because they are both contested *and* thinkable.

In these cases, the routine classifications uncovered in the last chapter do not indicate clearly how the action will be received. These eminent domain pursuits often contain mostly vacant properties but also some occupied ones. These projects often occur in neighborhoods that are not the most devastated and might even be located close enough to new developments and denser populations that hopes for improvement without drastic measures like eminent domain are reasonable but far from certain. Moreover, they might involve for-profit developers or construction to be sold partially but not exclusively on open markets. In short, the classifications that typically indicate clear legitimacy or illegitimacy give mixed signals.

Government officials pursue these takings cases because they imagine that they *might* end up on the legitimate side of the boundary line. Protests and after-the-fact project failures can make it seem that judgments of abuse must have been obvious all along, and to be sure, some people will have objected from the beginning. But controversial cases are actually the ones that people find hard to pin down as legitimate uses or illegitimate abuses of government power.

These government actions become thinkable only through careful consideration by officials and citizens. Simple descriptions about properties and redevelopment plans can fail to provide clear signals about legitimacy. In these cases, instead of relying on broad categories (like vacancy or nonprofit status), officials, residents, and other constituents take the time to make detailed evaluations. If and when these cases appear to be legitimate, careful consideration of details trumps the routinely employed categories. In these cases, officials and citizens close to the planning consider what they know about the particular developers involved, about the people or companies whose properties will be taken, and about the neighborhood's potential.

Officials promoting a boundary-line project hope that others in government and their constituents will come to accept the action as an unfortunate last resort. At best, as these cases move through the planning and implementation process, those who accept them as legitimate might describe themselves as hopeful that such an unfortunate act might solve difficult problems. But until they can look back and breathe a sigh of relief about what was accomplished, they are likely to remain deeply skeptical that hoped-for results will be achieved by this dramatic action.

In boundary cases, people's conclusions about the effects of government action are more careful and contested than usual, but they still appeal to the conception of property as investment. When officials and citizens move forward with these cases, they generally do so with cautious hope that, all told, the government action will have preserved and improved investments as well as any other potential approach might have.

But legitimacy is precarious in boundary cases because it is so difficult to figure out exactly what kind of impact government action will have on investments. It is unclear how much a taking will actually harm individual investments, and there are reasons to anticipate that it will not. It is unclear whether the project will improve neighborhood conditions, and there are reasons to expect that it will. It is unclear whether government inaction will lead to less favorable results than those anticipated to result from eminent domain. In these cases, there are multiple and contested understandings of current conditions and varied and uncertain predictions about short- and long-term futures.

This chapter introduces a boundary case—American Street—that became an icon of illegitimacy in Philadelphia. Of the several thousand takings that Philadelphia pursued in the 1990s and 2000s, a dozen of those caught up in the "American Street takings" became locally infamous as symbols of eminent domain abuse. When I started my research, all of the Philadelphia officials I asked about eminent domain told me about the American Street takings and described them as a debacle. Many said they were wrongheaded from the beginning, and it was easy to predict that they would become a government embarrassment.

Indeed, public accounts of the American Street takings reflect many of the stories that have hit the national news in recent years, in that residents describe being bowled over by an economic development project that they had no part in planning. Officially, the American Street takings were planned to alleviate neighborhood blight and to provide jobs for neighborhood and city residents. Poor Puerto Rican residents were told to forfeit their family-like communities and homes they had lived in for decades. Residents protested these takings at Philadelphia City Council hearings; they marched in the streets; they told their stories in the newspaper and on film.[1] The American Street takings motivated neighborhood resident Rosemary Cubas and others to form the Citywide Coalition to Save Our Homes to fight eminent domain in other Philadelphia neighborhoods and to connect with the Castle Coalition's national campaign against eminent domain to receive assistance and to join the fight.[2] And yet, the resistance failed to stop the takings.

In investigating the American Street takings, I expected to find nothing but political corruption at worst, private capture of government at best—but I found little evidence of either. After careful research, I concluded that the most devastating, accurate case that one could reasonably make against the American Street takings would be of government incompetence and a naïve yearning for a remaking of an industrial area. But I get ahead of myself. I will cover the breakdown of this case into utter failure in the next chapter.

In this chapter, I look back to the time before this project seemed so easy to dismiss. In fact, it was touted by Mayor Street as a pilot project of one of his major campaign promises and as a goal of one of the first federal Empowerment Zones. Street and other officials knew it was risky (thus, they called it a pilot project), but they promoted it because they expected it to earn, not lose, points with voters once they saw the results.

This chapter examines a forgotten period in the American Street takings, demonstrating how the project became thinkable as residents, business owners, and government officials became cautiously optimistic that taking property would actually protect investments. During this early planning for the American Street takings, evidence mounted that they could be justified. Eminent domain plans grew from efforts made even years before these takings were on the table. Residents and business owners had been working to improve a neighborhood struggling with major problems caused by abandonment by factories, property owners, and, many would argue, even government services.

In the first section of the chapter, I describe neighborhood conditions in the decades preceding the takings. Outsiders mostly bore witness to a sad and dramatic decline in the physical and social conditions of an area once revered for industrial production as factories and workers moved out and drugs moved in. Insiders lamented these changes, but they also understood the neighborhood as a source of refuge, strength, and community for Puerto Ricans who had fought for the right to be there. The second section of the chapter charts how residents and small-business owners met the neighborhood's challenges with self-help strategies. They became increasingly organized and made demands that government pitch in to help. The last section of the chapter goes into significant detail about how government's efforts culminated in plans to use eminent domain to assemble three large parcels for commercial redevelopment.

In the final section of the chapter, I explain how community representatives and government officials developed skeptical hope that the consolidations of three large parcels could be a promising addition to other work that community members and government officials had already been doing to protect the value of the neighborhood. Officials who thought the takings were warranted convinced neighborhood residents and business owners, as well as other government officials, that it was possible and even likely that investments would be protected and improved through the takings. Officials promised to protect displaced residents' individual investments through careful and generous relocation plans, and they promised to improve collective investments by creating new uses for abandoned land and providing local jobs. Many accepted the trade-off, tentatively believing that government would preserve and improve investments by taking property titles.

VIEWS OF THE NEIGHBORHOOD

A boundary case developed along N. American Street, at the southern end of a Philadelphia area that was infamous for its crime, drugs, poverty, and general desolation. The larger neighborhood's widely known and depressing nickname, the "Badlands," seemed to say it all. In his news program *Nightline* in 1995, ABC's Ted Koppel featured the "Badlands" as a scourge on the nation. Just a year earlier, a columnist for the *Philadelphia Inquirer* titled his first novel *Third and Indiana,* a reference to a corner just seven blocks north of the first large case of eminent domain on American Street.[3] The novel followed the development of a child who, struggling with the madness of his surroundings, sneaks out at night to paint the silhouette of a body on Philadelphia's main thoroughfare each time the violence near him claims another soul.

The neighborhood's problems were manifest not only from individual stories of pain and loss, but also from the statistics summing up the average experience of residents. The area's poverty level was about 45 percent in 1990 and 2000, six times the national average and over double the city's average. A paltry 5 percent of the adult population had graduated from college. The median market value of an owner-occupied home was less than $30,000.[4] These numbers spoke clearly of hardship.

The physical appearance of the southern end of N. American Street, where eminent domain was eventually used, suggested more of a wasteland than a badland. The area looked neglected, deserted, and discarded. The estimated housing vacancy rate of around 10 percent only accounted for the houses still on the market. Many owners had simply abandoned their buildings to the forces of nature, and as they deteriorated and became dangerous, the city tore them down. Many of the vacant buildings that were once industrial plants stood as huge monolithic portraits of devastation. By the 1990s, almost all of those large buildings were either empty or gone, and environmental contamination filled what was left. Some warehouses operated, especially food distribution businesses, but "pipers" (slang for crack addicts) inhabited other warehouses that had been vacated when industries left the city decades earlier. Where workers' housing had once stood, directly adjacent to the factories, there were now occupied as well as empty row-houses and vacant lots. Many of the blocks on either side of the major street looked better—just a street or two away, there were some blocks of densely packed, occupied row houses in varying conditions. Yet other blocks that had once been similarly dense with houses were pockmarked with lots laid bare by building collapses and demolitions. Illegal dumping on the sixteen acres of vacant land along the corridor in the

Figure 4.1:
N. American Street, 1500 Block, Looking Southwest (2009)
Source: David Gehosky

late 1990s and squatting in the vacant buildings were constant problems.[5] Much of the empty land became mini-landfills and urban weed farms. (See Figures 4.1–4.3.)

Vince Dougherty, director of the Mayor's Business Action Team of the Philadelphia Department of Commerce, described the neighborhood this way:

> It was abandoned, unused, falling apart, homeless people, drug addicts were in there, the pipers were all in there. And they run out like rats in the night and rob people and then go back and get hits of drugs. Don't forget how bad this area was.
>
> Vince Dougherty, Director, Mayor's Business Action Team, Philadelphia Department of Commerce[6]

The people who lived and worked in the area in the 1990s intimately knew the problems associated with the Badlands reputation. Whether they had come to the area recently or decades earlier, they experienced neighborhood poverty and abandonment firsthand. Residents felt the sting of trying, and failing, to find jobs there. They watched neighbors move to better areas, leaving their houses to slowly but surely disintegrate. Many feared that thieves would take whatever they kept in their homes. They felt

Figure 4.2:
N. American Street, 1500 Block, Looking Northeast (2009)
Source: David Gehosky

Figure 4.3:
N. American Street (in background), 2100 Block at 200 Block of W. Diamond Street, Singh Tire Center Owner and Employee (2009)
Source: David Gehosky

inundated by the trash that mounted in the properties left vacant, much of it dumped there by people from elsewhere. One resident who had brought up her children in a house right on N. American Street told me about its sad state by the late 1990s, after they had moved out: "I liked my house, but I did not like the neighborhood, because there were no houses around it. It was empty, and everybody was throwing trash and the rats were coming around there, and it was very bad."[7] Business owners also worried about crime and recoiled at the mountains of trash around them. Even if they were not personally bothered, many thought that the neighborhood's physical condition and reputation made potentially worthy employees unwilling to apply for and accept jobs there.

Many Philadelphians set the neighborhood's contemporary sad state inside a larger narrative of loss because they remembered a more vibrant, pleasant N. American Street. This neighborhood was famous well before it became known as the Badlands, and its reputation was positive. It was famous for being the economic center of a vibrant and growing city throughout the first half of the twentieth century. N. American Street had been the pride of the city's industrial age. The heart of Philadelphia's textile industry was located on a single mile stretch of N. American Street, a dirt strip over one hundred feet wide with rail tracks down the middle. A century ago, factory workers—Eastern Europeans, Puerto Ricans, African Americans, and others—lived in brick row-houses alongside these centers of production. The empty buildings and spaces of N. American Street spoke to many in Philadelphia of the economic vibrancy that had once been there.

For many of the existing residents and business owners of the American Street area, however, the problems of the Badlands told only part of the story. They also experienced their place of home and work as a refuge from greater ills and as a source and symbol of strength. As American Street had lost its factories and many residents over the decades, some businesses and residents had stayed behind. Though most big industry had vacated the area, some businesses remained and others came anew. At the turn of this century, 450 businesses operated along and near American Street. They were relatively small—just 10 percent with more than twenty employees—and mostly clustered on the east-west streets at the north and south end, where pedestrian traffic was heaviest.[8]

New residents came from Puerto Rico and other parts of Philadelphia. In the 1960s and 1970s, some arrived as they retreated from urban renewal and gentrification a few miles to the west. As they came, ethnic battles over

Figure 4.4:
Norris Square Park, East of N. American Street (2009)
Source: David Gehosky

resources ensued.[9] Puerto Ricans fought for the place against white racism and built a new enclave there.[10] Resident Iris Torres remembered:

> All the white people that surrounded the school hated the blacks and the Spanish-speaking people who went there... In the late 70s... all hell broke loose, and there was violence in the [Norris Square] park, twenty-four/seven because the Latinos were coming, and the Latinos were going to stay.
>
> Iris Torres, Resident and CLI Member[11]

By 2000, Puerto Ricans outnumbered residents of other racial and ethnic backgrounds. Almost ten times as many individuals identified as Puerto Rican near American Street as in the city at large (55 percent vs. 6 percent), and between one-third and three-fifths as many American-Street-area residents compared to city residents identified as white, black, or Asian. With all of the problems that the area offered, it also offered a space for these people to create and maintain their homes and businesses. (See Figures 4.4–4.5.)

Residents and business owners came and stayed in the American Street area for different reasons—some of them came because the land was cheap, others followed their friends and family, and still others came because the open space made them feel good. Whatever the reason for their arrival,

Figure 4.5:
Residential Area East of N. American Street (2009)
Source: David Gehosky

they managed life and work there. Sometimes they worked to stop the problems caused by the broken-down buildings, needles, thieves, rats, and trash. Other times, they turned what others would see as problems into opportunities. They put their time, their labor, their emotions, and their money into the place. These people who lived and worked in the neighborhood, and who devoted energy to improving it, would become involved in actions and discussions meant to influence the neighborhood's future.

CREATIVELY PROTECTING INVESTMENTS FROM THE INSIDE

Well before anyone in government seriously pursued taking homes and businesses along American Street for redevelopment in the 1990s, residents and business owners employed various self-help strategies to improve their houses and neighborhood. Residents helped themselves and each other to create homes they could live in. They put time and labor into making homes out of buildings that wealthier people would have avoided.

Most of the homeowners who would later be targeted by eminent domain had created their homes from abandoned and dilapidated properties a decade or more earlier. Many had taken advantage of extremely low prices to acquire the properties in the first place. On the block where takings later became the most controversial, Claudina Pantoja had rented her house for $30 a month in the 1960s, and by the 1990s, she paid $60 a month. Several of her neighbors rented from the same owner. When he died in the 1990s, no one took interest in collecting rent or caring for the properties in his name. For several years, Claudina and her neighbors continued to live there without paying rent. Eventually, they too secured titles to their homes from the city, for prices between a dollar and a few thousand dollars to cover back taxes.[12] At the other end of the block, Sonia Ortiz decided to move into the neighborhood after she found out about an opportunity to buy a vacant shell (walls and a roof but little more) for a dollar from the city. Sonia's father told her about the building, saying that it had been a two-bedroom house and—with new windows, plumbing, electrical, drywall, and more—it could be again. She and her two young kids moved in as soon as her father and uncle had installed a kitchen and bathroom. She lived there for ten years, cleaned up the yards around her, and acquired a next-door lot from the city, too. She showed pride in what she and her family had accomplished. After describing the extensive repairs, she said, "When people passed by, they said that I had the best house in the neighborhood."[13]

As described in Chapter 1, Manuel Velez was determined to get a house in the neighborhood—a particular house that probably looked like a wreck to almost anyone else. He dropped little notes off and occasionally knocked on the door at a house on the 1700 block of N. American Street. Eventually the owner fell on hard times, succumbed, and sold it to him. Velez explained that he did not have to pay much because:

> No tenía rufo arriba. They didn't have a roof. No walls, no había nada adentro, you know? Yo le puse toda a la casa. La hice... Se anadaba como si no tuviera, se andaba tapando. Esposa con nenes chicititos. Y asi andaban tapando el agua... con plástico. No tenía rufo la casa. Nada. Las paredes, ni ventana tenía. Yo hice la casa. I make the house. (The house didn't have any roof or walls. It had nothing inside, you know? I put everything in the house. I fixed it all myself. I made the house myself. They were living there without any roof, covering up with a tarp, with plastic. There was a woman a little kids living there. The house had no roof. Nothing. Neither walls nor windows. I remade the house.)
>
> Manuel Velez, Condemnee on 1700-block site[14]

Residents and business owners also improved what lay beyond their property lines. People who lived and worked in the area cleaned the space around them and even fenced property that they did not own to prevent dumping. Ortiz remembered, "When I first moved there the lot on my right-hand side was so full of trash... and we cleared all that... I mean, that trash was sitting there for years!" One nearby resident followed up her description of the neighborhoods' problems of drugs and dumping by saying, “Neighbors started chipping in and cleaning up the neighborhood.”[15] This involved picking up trash from the sidewalks and Norris Square Park, but residents also took more drastic measures. Another resident, Tomasita Romero, explained problems even on her more densely populated street, which was not targeted by eminent domain: “At the end of the block, people come and dump and dump.... They come at night and just dump it. So this is a never-ending fight”[16] (see Figure 4.6). She helped initiate gardening on several vacant lots, claiming control over land that wasn’t legally hers by putting up a fence. She explained:

> Little by little people moved away and the houses were left unoccupied and they got old and the city couldn’t care less. So, houses got demolished. I live on Second Street. Behind my house is almost a whole block with no houses. Trucks then [came] at night and unload[ed] whatever they didn’t want,... and that was terrible. Cars [came] in at night, prostitution and everything. So, my neighbors and I ... got together and fenced that space... I figured if I just put a fence up it would stop them. I had to take control because no one else was going to do it for me. I couldn’t be afraid to say, “This is my house, and you don’t do that around here.”
>
> Tomasita Romero, Neighborhood resident and informal community leader[17]

Figure 4.6:
Community Garden Established in Vacant Lots along N. 2nd Street (2008)
Source: Debbie Becher

Figure 4.7:
N. American Street, Home of Manuel Velez and Adjacent Lots Used for Truck Storage, on 1700-Block Site Targeted for Eminent Domain (2008)
Source: Debbie Becher

One large family living a block off American Street commandeered a group of lots the width of about five row homes. When I was walking there in 2008, the fenced-in area had a large vegetable garden, a chicken coup, and several yard chairs. You would have to either look up the titles or ask the people using the lot (and living in the house adjacent to it) to find out that they did not legally own it. The yard they had cultivated was even featured in a local paper, and they were proud.

A few blocks to the south, at 1700 N. American Street, Manuel Velez fenced off half of his block, between his house and the street to the south (see Figures 4.7 and 4.8). He told me how and why he did this, before his block became part of the second site targeted by eminent domain:

> Allí me tiraban la basura. Me tiraban perros muertos, gatos muertos. Pondrían allá. Y yo fui a la ciudad, yo fui allá al RDA, "Mira yo quiero poner una fenza porque me están tirando perros muertos, todos los animales muertos." Y

Figure 4.8:
N. American Street, Fencing of Abandoned Land in Foreground, Truck Storage and Home of Manuel Velez in Background, 1700-Block Site Targeted For Eminent Domain (2008)
Source: Debbie Becher

> entonces yo vine, compre un alambre, y puse un cerco, que todavía esta el cerco allí.... La fensa que puse pegaba de la esquina, del Cecil B. Moore hasta el rancho mio. Para salvar la basura, para salvar que tiraban cosas muertas y todo.... Sí funcionó. Yo la puse alta, poca alta. (I had a problem with people coming into my yard and dumping trash and dead dogs. I went down to the city and talked to RDA and asked if I could put up fence and stuff, and then I put up some wiring and put up a fence around that's still there to keep people from throwing their dead dogs.... The fence I put up went all the way around, from the corner at Cecil B. Moore to my house, so that it would block off people from throwing dead things and all there.... It worked. I put it up high.)
>
> Manuel Velez, Condemnee on 1700-block site[18]

Residents of N. Bodine Street, on the first site that was condemned (the 2100-block site), shared similar memories about how they had cleaned the vacant land, gardened and played on it, and found peace on their little block with seven residences. Aida Cartegena described it to me:

> Everything was empty lots. We cleaned all that too. So we had all those empty lots and we fixed [and] cleaned the lots because the people over there would

> consider us... family. I was the Block Captain from the block. We had it real nice and clean. We had flowers; we planted trees. It was like seven houses, but it was always real nice and clean. No problem. My kids grew up there.... When summer time came,... everybody came out with a grill. So everybody cooked. We were like a family. I mean, there were always drugs in the area and people that got busted but then they will bother another block. I mean, the cops did not have to go down there, practically.... That was a quiet block and nobody had problems. Once in a blue moon, you could see a cop in our block, usually passing by.
>
> Aida Cartegena, Condemnee on 2100-block site[19]

Residents found ways to create a sense of safety in a larger neighborhood and city that they knew posed dangers. They would try to limit opportunities for theft around them. They did what they could to ensure that houses on their blocks with any valuables (e.g., copper pipes) did not stand vacant long enough for opportunistic crimes. Some of them vigilantly watched what was happening on their block. They felt personally responsible for preventing burglaries of their neighbors' houses. And many residents attributed the safety they felt either to their own watchfulness or to the attention of their neighbors.[20]

They explained to me that for these reasons and others theirs was a nice block, even though there were problems in the larger neighborhood.[21] For some, the vast amount of vacant space actually created a feeling of safety, for they thought that it served as a barrier that anyone attempting to harm them would have to cross.[22] Claudina Pantoja, 2100 block resident, told me, "In front of us, there was only a lot. It was empty, so you felt free because there was nothing there."[23] In a response to my question about liking the area around his 1700 block house, Manuel Velez responded, "Mejor del mundo era alla. Porque no había nadie ni atras ni al frente ni a ningun lado mio. Vivía feliz alli. (It was the best in the world there. Because there wasn't anybody behind, in front, or on either side of me. I lived happily there.)"[24]

For many, especially on the 2100 block of N. Bodine Street, the combination of space and close-knit relationships among the few residents made a terrific combination. Jasmin Pantoja, the daughter of condemnee Claudina Pantoja, explained, "Because there were only like six or seven houses on the block and no neighbors, it was a pretty peaceful place... hardly [any] cars passed; nobody tried to break in.... It was a nice neighborhood... not [a] nice neighborhood, but [a] nice block. Plus, they had the other lot next door where they planted and stuff."[25] Ana Rivera remembered, "Bodine [the little street west of N. American Street where residents on the 2100-block site lived] was a calm place, there weren't problems. If the kids wanted to play outside they were more calm. There wasn't danger for them or anything."[26] Sonia Ortiz, just down the block, said "Where I lived, it was very quiet and my kids were not exposed to any kind of drug activities"[27] (see Figures 4.9 and 4.10). Wanda Ocasio recalled the same block as "the best," adding,

> El mejor neighbors que había. Éramos todos Puertorriqueños. Only seis casas había.... Vivíamos todos allí, compartíamos todo allá igual que familia. Nunca tuvimos problemas. Ninguna.... Y era bueno porque el gobierno nos dio un lot y nosotros hacíamos like a garden a little garden.... El gobierno nos dio un lot. Tu sabes que lo usáramos para sembrar.... Podíamos cerrar la calle. Porque estaba pequeñas. Teníamos dos bombas, porque en este tiempo. (The best neighbors that there were. It was all Puerto Rican. Only six houses there.... We all lived together and shared everything together just like family. We never had any problems. Not one.... And it was good because the government gave us a lot where we made a little garden where we used to plant things.... We could close the street because it was small. We had two fire hydrants that we could open, for the hot weather.)
>
> Wanda Ocasio, Condemnee on 2100-block site[28]

Wanda had seven chickens, four rabbits, and such a prolific garden that she could share eggs, tomatoes, pumpkins, and more with her neighbors, and they shared with her. She especially remembered getting peaches from Claudina Pantoja's tree. After Wanda had told me details about the process of losing her house, she reflected, "Era bueno mi bloque. (It was good, my block was good.)" Asked if she was sad about being displaced, she replied, "Sí. Yo creo que con los que habla tambien te diga lo mismo. Era tremendo. Aunque la casas eran pequeñitas, tremendo bloque. (Yes. I think that everyone will tell you the same. It was a tremendous block. Even though the houses were really small, it was a tremendous block.)"

Technically, if observed from the outside, residents fencing and using other people's properties amounted to trespassing or squatting on land to which they had no right. Practically, however, this kind of activity was not only accepted but welcomed, for it improved the environment for all of the neighbors. Moreover, there was no free-for-all, with people grabbing up whatever property had been abandoned. Almost always, people cared for and fenced land directly adjacent to property they owned or rented. Their use of the abandoned property seemed an extension of investments they had already made. If they ventured beyond their own property, they

Figure 4.9:
N. Bodine Street. Sonia Ortiz's House, 2100-Block Site Targeted for Eminent Domain, circa 2001
Source: RDA File

Figure 4.10:
N. Bodine Street, Looking North from Sonia Ortiz's House (at the South End of the Block), 2100-Block Site Targeted for Eminent Domain, circa 2001
Source: RDA File

Figure 4.11:
Neighbors Enjoying N. Bodine Street and Vacant Space, on 2100-Block Site Targeted for Eminent Domain, circa 1990s
Source: Wanda Ocasio, Condemnee

sometimes did so in the name of a larger community group and wider access, mostly for the purpose of community gardening. In all, a lack of security and care for the neighborhood's land led residents and business owners to help themselves, solve problems, and create opportunities.

These informal forms of cooperation sometimes led to more formal organizing for the neighborhood's improvement. Two longtime residents established relationships with the local city councilperson, when they visited regularly to discuss governments' impact on the neighborhood and to get help. Walt DeTreux, former chief of staff for City Council Member Richard Mariano (District Seven), told me that he considered Iris Torres and Tomasita Romero neighborhood leaders because:

> These women were the ones that everybody listened to, everybody followed.... They were the boss.... Anytime they came to us and complained about any issue, we would follow up on it.... We would respond. I mean, they were good ladies. They were really good people. And they would get our attention.
>
> Walt DeTreux, Former Chief of Staff, City Council Member Richard Mariano, District Seven[29]

In the 1980s, Tomasita Romero, Iris Torres, Eugenia Burgos, and others organized to actively fight drug dealing. They formed United Neighbors Against Drugs (UNAD). Eugenia Burgos, an informal community leader and former member of the American Street Empowerment Zone Community Trust Board (ASCTB), explained to me,

> I was always active, and when I came here I saw all the things that needed to be done, and I saw the effort of the few people that [were] involved at that time. I just had to be part of it. I wanted to make some changes.... [I] started organizing. I participated in... UNAD. We organized in the corners that were heavily infested with drugs, and we stopped drug activities at nighttime.... We established a relationship with the police district. And as we saw the need growing, we had to get involved in many things—not only in the aspect of violence and drugs, but also [in] trying to find a way to support the folks already here. We tried to organize our own housing [and] education.
>
> Eugenia Burgos, Informal community leader and former American Street Empowerment Zone Community Trust Board (ASCTB) member [30]

Residents increasingly organized themselves to make demands on government to do something about neighborhood problems. Torres and Romero organized formally at first as UNAD and later with the nascent Norris Square Neighborhood Project (NSNP), which focused on cultural and environmental education. In addition to these community-based nonprofits, several others formed in the 1970s and 1980s to advocate for residents, encourage and control revitalization, provide social services, and build community. As in other neighborhoods across the city and nation, many of those organizations formed initially with an adversarial relationship to government but later professionalized and shifted to a more cooperative stance. Two groups in the area formed to pursue lawsuits against government and banks for neighborhood neglect;[31] others, including UNAD and NSNP, formed in the 1980s with an original focus on community development and a more solicitous approach to government officials from the beginning.[32] Since then, the number of organizations has grown immensely, and several created or became community development corporations that construct residential and commercial buildings.

Residents were not alone. Business owners pursued improvement strategies and organized themselves to demand government assistance. Small businesses that stayed and new ones that arrived initiated their own self-help and government-focused strategies, and they built ties with resident leaders. Tomasita Romero, a resident and informal community leader, told me that while she has no taste for politics, she eventually found herself at community meetings hosted by business owner Sid Haifetz, who encouraged her to speak up and complain. Speaking of herself and Iris Torres, she added,

> I owe him [for what] he instilled in us. We were afraid to open our mouths even in small meetings, and we used to go to these huge meetings with people from the city and hide behind each other so that they [wouldn't] ask us any questions. And now she watches me. She says, "Tomasita, now you can't shut up!" . . . Now I have to speak out [about] the things I like and the things I don't like. . . .
>
> Tomasita Romero, Neighborhood resident and informal community leader[33]

A core group of business owners founded the American Street Business Association in 1979. The Association claimed 150 members in 2002. Many business owners wanted a more vibrant and dense business district. Surveyed in 2001, business owners reported concerns about property deterioration, vacancy, illegal activity (drug dealing, especially, but also prostitution in certain areas), and personal and property security, as well as problems with short-dumping, street trash, graffiti, and the "negative appearance of junk yards." They said they wanted employees and customers from outside the area to feel safe coming to their buildings. Many reported employing local residents, but others cited trouble finding qualified employees from the immediate area.[34]

By the late 1990s, when officials would propose taking occupied properties to consolidate large areas of mostly vacant land, the American Street Business Association and several resident organizations had built strong foundations and had forged ties to one another and to government officials. At the same time that residents and businesses were working to change the neighborhood, government officials were making their own efforts, sometimes in communication with the grassroots leaders. Most notable were several formal moves in 1993 and 1994: the formation of a cross-agency American Street Site Assembly Program, the award of state Enterprise Zone funds for the area, and the designation of the "American Street Industrial Corridor" as one of the first federal Empowerment Zones.

GOVERNMENT INITIATIVES FOR IMPROVEMENT

A String of Government Programs

Within Philadelphia government, individuals and agencies had different opinions about what to do along American Street, and they approached the area with disparate and sometimes conflicting programs. Officials remembered the street's industrial past, and some hoped to enable its resurgence as a job center in a new economy. They envisioned new light manufacturing and warehouse operations attracted to a location conveniently close to downtown and the highway. As early as the 1970s, local officials identified this section of N. American Street as a problem that government needed to address and as a place with great potential. First, the newly formed Office of Housing and Community Development (OHCD) and, next, the Commerce Department worked to rejuvenate the area for business; by the late 1970s, they collaborated with the longtime business owners for the same goal. Together, they visualized American Street as a vibrant, modern industrial corridor.

They thought that creating a safe environment and obtaining property ownership (often called "site control") would be necessary first steps. Jim Hartling, who formed his own urban-redevelopment consulting firm called Urban Partners in 1980, recalled that when he was in charge of economic development for OHCD in 1978, he knocked on doors along American Street to ask residents to sell their scattered homes to make way for large sites for industrial development. Though he did not get far, he thought he was doing the right thing, telling residents, "You're living on a block with meat slaughtering and stuff and you're the only house. If you want to get out, we'll buy you out.'" Although Hartling stayed only peripherally involved in American Street over the next few decades, he reflected back and said, "What you're seeing right now is...the most current aspect of 25 years of public policy, longer than 25 years of public policy. I mean, we were assembling [land]...back almost 30 years ago."[35]

Vince Dougherty, of the Department of Commerce (director of the Mayor's Business Action Team), made the strip his cause and became known as the "czar of American Street,"[36] Dougherty invited the recognition. He filled his office with memorabilia of his efforts. When I interviewed him in 2007, a floor-to-ceiling adaptation of a US flag with "American Street" printed across it hung behind his chair, and photos of ribbon-cuttings and capital improvements surrounded us. By the 1980s, the boosters of an industrial American Street could boast of some signs of success. New facilities were built and opened by Honor Foods, Truck Parts, Cogan and Gordon, and American Metal Moulding.[37]

Employees in the Commerce Department worked to gain support from other departments, in part through official declarations of plans for an industrial American Street. In October 1997, for instance, they secured a land-use study of the "American Street Industrial Corridor" from the Philadelphia City Planning Commission. The findings revealed that the area (between Second and Third Streets, Girard and Cambria Avenues) was dominated first by vacant land and second by warehouse distribution centers.[38] Cathy Califano, the Empowerment Zone's former Economic Development director, explained that from her point of view, by the early 2000s, the different agencies had come to a

> policy agreement where we shouldn't have residential property right on the industrial corridor.... This was not overtly said. But it's a place where people are raising children at the same time there's a scrap metal yard seeping like heavy metal into the soil. So that's not a very good combination of land usage.... To make the corridor uniformly industrial, you had to relocate some of the families who were there.
>
> Cathy Califano, former Empowerment Zone Economic Development Director[39]

General declarations of support by no means cemented cooperation. In the 1990s, other agencies planned to support a new school and Boys Club along American Street, while the Department of Commerce fought to preserve the area for industry. The OHCD funded affordable housing projects that were supported by community groups as well. As long as this housing was not on the blocks directly adjacent to American Street, residential and similar developments posed no problem for the light industrial vision. Indeed, those planning for the large-scale land assembly for light manufacturing and warehouses would propose a green buffer zone between these operations and residential blocks.

Internal communications and private admissions of doubt repeatedly exposed agency fragmentation over whether government should reserve American Street itself and the blocks directly adjacent for industrial development and whether agencies were taking concrete actions to do so. Eugenia Burgos, an informal community leader and former ASCTB member, explained how this fragmentation affected people who were trying to make something useful from the land:

> One thing that I question[ed] as a city worker... was that... we had given some of those properties to people for a dollar, and a... short time after we had to turn around and buy those properties, and I said, "Why are we giving properties [away]?"... I kept on raising the question, "Why are we processing this if we know that those parcels are going to be needed and are going to be taken?"
>
> Eugenia Burgos, Informal community leader and former ASCTB Member[40]

Many people in city government were skeptical that American Street could ever become the kind of industrial corridor that the Commerce

Department imagined. A planner at the Philadelphia City Planning Commission told me, for example, that he thought the plan for businesses to locate there was "disingenuous" because it was unlikely to happen.[41] High-level officials at the City of Philadelphia Redevelopment Authority, the agency responsible for processing the property takings, expressed similar reservations. Dougherty found himself constantly fighting these misgivings. In a March 1998 e-mail exchange with his colleague, he complained about the general lack of cooperation on this project by writing, "This is my semi-annual @(!*@^(!)(^%#!#%@!_*@!%!+ session (on this particular subject, that is)."[42] In January 1998, after Dougherty found out that OHCD had funded a housing project along the corridor, he complained in a memo to his supervisor:

> You know as well as I do, once a project gets to this point, one would have a better chance of survival standing in front of a speeding Metro liner than standing in the way of the project. What I am suggesting is that OHCD needs to notify us at the very beginning of proposed projects in the American Street area. It seems to me, that when OHCD was approached by someone looking to do a project in the American Street Enterprise Zone, and American Street Empowerment Zone, by an industrial site, on G-2 land, one of these things should have triggered alarms at OHCD to notify the Commerce Department. This is certainly not the first time this has happened.
>
> Vince Dougherty, Director, Mayor's Business Action Team, Philadelphia Department of Commerce[43]

Small business owners along American Street helped to access resources for the light industrial development in the area. In 1993, business owners from the American Street Business Association lobbied Governor Casey and won the area a state Enterprise Zone designation. As part of that award, the state dedicated $25 million for a five-year land assembly project.[44] To manage that money, Dougherty formed the American Street Site Assembly Program, to be guided by a committee of local business owners and government agency representatives.[45]

Soon, with support from both resident and business leaders, city officials accessed federal money to follow the state funds they had already secured. Several resident and business leaders became interested in the Clinton administration's new federal Empowerment Zone (EZ) program. They convinced then-Mayor Ed Rendell to apply for the first round for what they called the American Street Industrial Corridor.[46]

Guillermo Salas, the head of a nearby community development corporation, the Hispanic Association of Contractors and Entrepreneurs (HACE), recalled how the application process involved grappling with insecurities and disagreements about what the area should and could become:

> I was part of the planning of the Empowerment Zone application for HUD funding back in '95. . . . American Street was very bottom-up. It's to the credit of government and this community. There was a recognition that community people living in the area needed to have a voice in what goes on there. Now there's different views and opinions with different people as to what it should be. You know, some people are pro-retail. . . . I don't know how retail can be supported on American Street, given the competition surrounding us with retailers. And so I just believe that it should be maintained as an industrial base. Now we'll never get the factories back. That's a misnomer. But to the extent you can get employers, maybe wholesalers, distributors of products that can create jobs. . . . I do believe that the corridor should maintain sort of an industrial job base.
>
> Guillermo Salas, President-Cofounder, Hispanic Association of Contractors and Entrepreneurs (HACE)[47]

In 1994, Philadelphia became one of the six cities nationwide to win an EZ designation, and the award was divided among three areas. Twenty-nine million dollars were dedicated to the American Street Industrial Corridor.[48] Land assembly, the goal I follow here, would become one small tool in a wide range of EZ strategies for redevelopment.

From the moments when they first decided to join forces with government to improve neighborhood conditions, resident leaders showed a healthy skepticism that government power, once unleashed, might be directed against their wishes. They showed concern about maintaining control over any government initiative, especially the EZ, which would focus so much attention on their small area. Rosemary Cubas, a resident activist who would later lead opposition to the property takings, expressed her doubts. She perceived the EZ as a "double-edged sword," with the potential to hurt residents as much as it helped them.[49]

Cubas and other residents founded the Community Leadership Institute (CLI), with EZ funding, to build residents' leadership capacities and to keep the EZ in line.[50] To be sure, federal EZ legislation required significant community oversight. In 1995, EZ staff boasted the involvement of a wide variety of businesses and resident advocates and managed community-wide elections of an oversight body called the Community Trust Board. Philadelphia seemed to do a much better job of making community oversight happen than many other sites around the country, yet the extent of resident control over the EZ would remain a contested issue throughout the program's life and the property takings.[51]

Toward "Aggressive" Land Assembly

One of government's redevelopment strategies was to consolidate multiple small parcels of land into larger ones for warehousing and light industry. This land-assembly effort supplemented a number of ways in which officials nurtured N. American Street's rebirth. Early on, they paved what had been an extremely wide dirt road with railroad tracks down the middle. They cleaned up environmental damage from old industrial uses. They also enforced building codes to force owners to care for properties and zoning codes to encourage commercial development. They recognized, however, that new light-industrial and warehouse development could not happen on fragmented, small pieces of land. Dougherty and others heard commercial developers complained that in order to develop the kinds of buildings that government envisioned, they needed bigger parcels than any one owner had. Officials understood this need for land assembly as a result of changes over time in building construction and use. They heard from developers that warehouse operations would need space for truck entry and parking, for instance. Similar issues plagued residential development, for Philadelphia's row-house lots are often no more than 16 feet wide—much smaller than the typical parcels used for new construction.

At first, the group overseeing land assembly pursued what they called "lowest hanging fruit," or properties that they could get with few legal or political hindrances.[52] They foreclosed on tax-delinquent properties. This put properties up for sale at sheriff's auctions, where the city easily won the bids for them, as few others showed any interest. They also purchased what they could from willing sellers. They even used eminent domain for vacant, abandoned properties, an act that few considered politically dangerous. Officials thus started consolidating smaller parcels to make them more attractive to redevelopers, through means that they thought of as "conservative," meaning that they were politically uncontroversial.

When eminent domain was used with little fanfare as part of the "conservative" land-assembly effort, government rested, in my terminology, squarely on the legitimate side of the boundary line. Owners of vacant properties were sometimes impossible to locate, making a voluntary sale impossible. Tax bills mounted, but had not accumulated enough to make foreclosure an option, under Pennsylvania law. (This usually happened with vacant lots because their tax bills were so low.) Thus, at the request of the Commerce Department, RDA and other officials transferred ownership of these properties to the city and gave the court compensation to hold in the event of the former owner's appearance. It seemed that taking these properties to eventually give to other private owners who might use them could do little harm and was likely to improve neighborhood conditions. To the extent that it sparked any reactions at all, this "conservative" approach garnered support from others in government and from community members. Purchases of property from owners, forced auctions and bidding for vacant tax-delinquent properties, and takings of abandoned properties did not seem to harm the value of anyone's investments in the acquired properties and promised to improve the value of neighbors' investments. The absence of protest over these takings, as well as the lack of mention of them by anyone other than government officials in interviews, helps confirm that community members judged them to be legitimate.

Officials engaged in land assembly knew, however, that they needed to avoid displacing anyone from an operating business or inhabited residence if they wanted other agencies to offer unequivocal support for their work. In other words, they knew that the occupancy of a property signaled that the use of eminent domain approached and crossed the legitimacy boundary line, and thus would create political backlash. Officials considered taking occupied property to be an "aggressive" approach to land acquisition, and in the early 1990s different agency heads had explicitly prohibited the "American Street Site Assembly Program" from using it. As early as 1993, the American Street Site Assembly team suggested the west side of the 2100 block as a potential parcel for acquisition, but initially held back because it was dotted with occupied private properties.

Without forcefully taking occupied properties, those promoting the area's redevelopment were left with practically nothing to offer businesses that might locate there.[53] Once the cross-agency team had acquired all the property it thought it could under this "conservative" approach, it still had no single parcel larger than one acre. This was not even close to the three acres that businesses said that they required for the kinds of operations planned for the area. Several lots could be consolidated and made available as large parcels for industry if they took a more "aggressive" approach, condemning occupied housing and businesses.[54]

During the 1990s, as other agencies resisted forcing any residential displacements, especially without the promise of a specific development project, officials at the Department of Commerce became increasingly frustrated about their lack of progress. Dougherty wrote in a 1997 memo to his supervisor, Duane Bumb:

> Almost every developable site left on American Street has a smattering of occupied residences. In one case, five occupied structures prevent us from creating a 2.5 acre site. From the beginning of the Site Assembly program, we knew we would have to deal with this issue at some point. We have reached that point!

> We either have to deal with this issue now or shut down the program for lack of sites. Bill feels that this is a policy issue that Steve needs to handle with the Housing Cabinet. Key questions are: Do we want to do this? Who does it? (PIDC [Philadelphia Industrial Development Corporation] absolutely refuses to get into this!) How do we do it? (Buy out? Condemn? Urban Renewal? Replacement Housing?) Where does the money come from? One key part of this that Steve needs to be aware of is that RDA and OHCD have been hesitant, to put it mildly, to move people out without a project in hand. This, once again, becomes a never-ending case of "which comes first. . . ."
>
> Vince Dougherty, Director, Mayor's Business Action Team, Philadelphia Department of Commerce[55]

This plea did not seem to be enough to push anyone with the power to do so to tell Dougherty to condemn occupied properties.[56] Within a year, however, things had changed.

A confluence of events in the late 1990s and early 2000s made it seem possible that government would gain more intergovernmental and broad public support for what once seemed unthinkable: the displacement of American Street residents. Most important, in 1998, a new, pressing incentive emerged in the form of a small, local business that wanted to build there and provide jobs. Reline Centers of America, an automotive brake company, had sold its land just south of the area to a residential developer and begun looking for a place to build an expanded facility. The owner started talking to the Department of Commerce about relocating its operations to one of the least populated large sites along American Street. At the time, large areas were identified on the west side of the 2100 and 1700 blocks that had eight and seven occupied and privately owned homes, respectively.[57] The Department of Commerce asked other departments to consider "pilot" condemnations to assemble these large sites. It took two years before anyone moved forward with the idea publicly.

In 2000, three major government programs coalesced around the plan to create three-acre sites on these two blocks and another three-quarter acre site on the east side of the 2501 block, all requiring condemnation of privately owned and occupied residential properties[58] (see Figure 4.12). The cross-agency American Street Site Assembly Program, led by the Commerce Department, was the major proponent of the idea and offered intimate knowledge about parcel ownership. The Empowerment Zone also got behind the plan, and it had financial resources and community connections. Mayor Street had just taken office after campaigning on a major anti-blight program that would involve condemning occupied property across the city. His nascent Neighborhood Transformation Initiative (NTI)

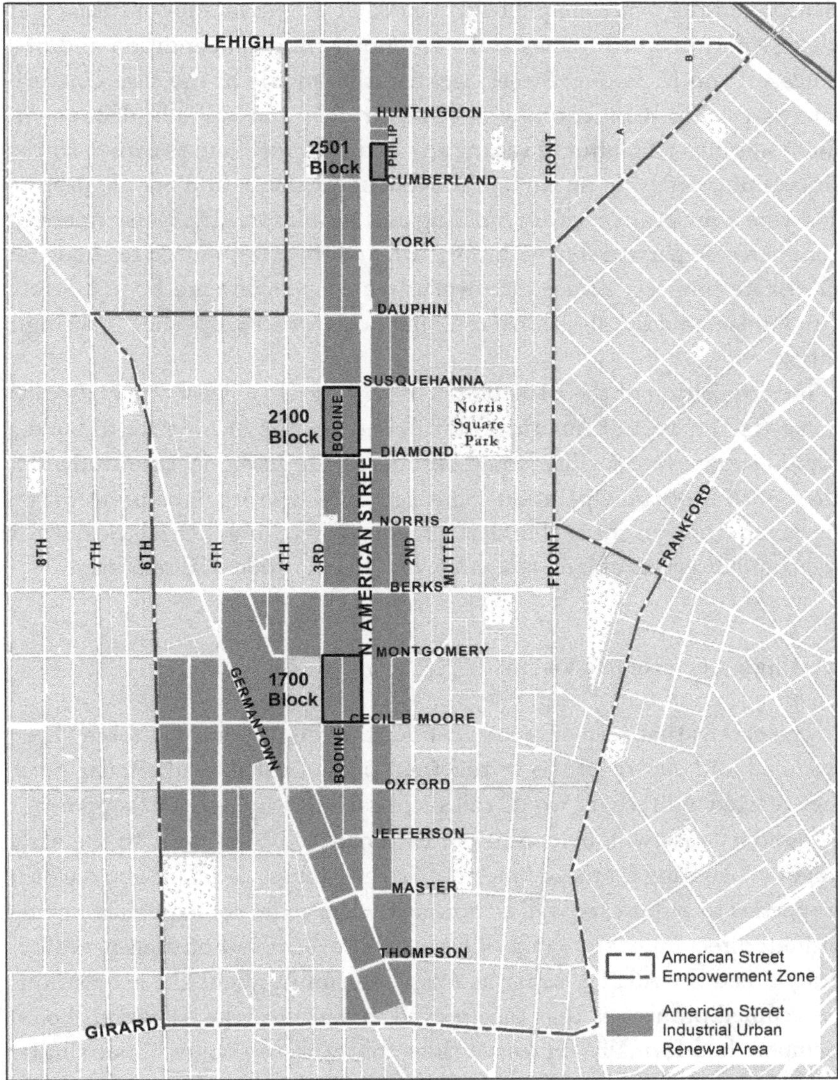

Figure 4.12:
American Street Takings Sites and Surrounding Areas
Source: Al B. Parker

had power to fight interagency fragmentation. NTI also created public discussion and possibly a greater public tolerance for the necessity of limited relocations.[59]

In late 2000, the 2100 block became an "early action site"—an NTI pilot project. Two thirds the seventy-two parcels on the block were privately owned, and the rest were publicly owned. Of the private properties, eight were owner-occupied homes and were mostly in good condition and in a single row on N. Bodine Street, right in the middle of the site. One private parcel was a functioning auto-repair shop but was tax delinquent. There was also a handful of vacant and occupied row houses owned by the Philadelphia Housing Authority. The remaining public and private properties were a multistory vacant building and vacant lots. The Department of Commerce, in partnership with the PIDC and the RDA, moved to condemn all private property across just over three acres, eliminate Bodine Street through the middle, and transfer all publicly owned properties to a single entity.

The acquisition of the 2100 blocks of N. American Street and N. Bodine Street (to the west of American) for Reline Centers of America to build a 60,000-square-foot facility would become a "site assembly case study." EZ director of Program Operations Santiago Burgos wrote, "The project is an ideal case study for the NTI in that it requires grappling with all the hurdles and complex issues of land assembly, reuse, and residential relocation."[60]

Creating a Compromise Vision

To the extent that residents knew about these new plans for taking both occupied and vacant property together, or had considered similar ones, they reacted with what I would call skeptical hope. Indeed, any support for a boundary case will, by definition, be tentative or hesitant. In the early stages of planning for these American Street takings, decisions about which properties to acquire, as well as how and when to do so, happened mostly without direct input from resident leaders. Government officials never formally asked the ASCTB, as far as I can determine, about the acquisitions of occupied properties that they moved forward to take. However, Board members had formally expressed their concerns and hopes about similar initiatives, and some members had individually known of and offered tentative assent to the plans.

When they considered the use of eminent domain, Community Trust Board members were extremely concerned about displacements. They reluctantly supported the development of a ball field, which required only a handful of relocations. Nevertheless, in discussions about takings, they were vocal about their expectation that relocations should be extremely limited in number and that people being displaced should be treated well. No matter what the planned end use, one EZ staff member told me, in general, "The Board... always said it was against the idea of acquiring land in a way that dispossessed people unless it was absolutely necessary."[61] When its consideration of the ball field first introduced the potential for relocations to the Board in 1995, one member asked for assurances that communication would be initiated early on with those to be relocated in order to secure their "buy-in" to the project.[62] When relocation was sporadically mentioned for different projects over the years, Trust Board members requested similar assurances that the number of relocations would be minimal and that communication and compensation for relocated residents would be responsible and humane. Neighbors to an area taken in 2002 and 2003 confided similar sentiments a few years later. They told me that they certainly feared that their own houses were at risk and did not want to be forced to move. But whether or not they thought they were the ones who would face the loss, they worried about condemnees being treated fairly.[63]

At the same time, residents and their leaders were extremely interested in development that would bring good, local jobs. One Board member explained to me, "I supported that [the 2100 block acquisition] only because I saw the importance of bringing jobs because the neighborhood is dying. And it needs to be revived, and if we don't bring jobs we are going to die."[64] Thus, her willingness to sacrifice scattered residences was only justified if the development actually provided local jobs. People who lived close to targeted properties voiced similar attitudes. One woman, who lived directly across the street from a block that was cleared for a new warehouse, had knocked on some doors to organize her neighbors against the takings in 2002 or 2003. She said that she found neighbors to be generally happy about what they thought were plans for new housing, and they were eager to see a local factory providing jobs.[65]

A simple government promise or vision that jobs would come was not enough. Residents and their leaders expressed a healthy skepticism about whether government could guarantee the results it hoped for from the condemnations. Skeptics understood that despite policymakers' best intentions, government acquisition of land takes much longer than anticipated—stretching beyond the hoped-for six months to one, two, or more years—although businesses operate on a tight timeline. They worried that once the residential displacement and land acquisition were complete, businesses would be long gone. In addition, they knew that market and other policy conditions change so quickly that the same businesses willing to build one day may not be interested six months or a year later.

Moreover, even if light warehousing and industrial companies would build there, these critical observers claimed, government could not ensure that they would offer jobs to people from the immediate neighborhoods.

Residents' past experiences suggested that employees might come from elsewhere.[66] To the extent that it existed, support for eminent domain thus rested on specific expectations about future relocations and development.

Residents and leaders were clear about the conditions under which taking occupied properties would be acceptable. Existing residents and business owners would need to experience benefits from the new improvements. Because displacements would cost individuals a great deal, they would need to be rare. Residents and business owners who were displaced would need to be treated with respect and compensated for the investments that they lost.

Once they started pursuing acquisitions, staff members in the Commerce Department and the EZ promised to attend to all of these concerns. Representatives of the Commerce Department assured detractors that a functioning business was planning to take over one of the blocks they were acquiring and that several others had shown interest in the other blocks.[67] City staff members demonstrated that the number of relocations was extremely small compared to the size of the parcels to be consolidated and reused. And though communication with specific relocatees would have to wait until particular properties were identified, staff members reassured resident leaders that it would happen in a timely and respectful fashion. The government representatives said the RDA would administer a legally regulated relocation process that guaranteed communication and fair compensation.[68]

The consolidation of properties on three sites—not just the original 2100-block site—became a pilot study of Mayor Street's Neighborhood Transformation Initiative (NTI), with the help of the American Street Empowerment Zone. The agencies were piloting how government could responsibly and carefully relocate residents for redevelopment and earn popular approval for doing so. They identified three areas along American Street on which they could assemble two three-acre sites and one three-quarter-acre site from several smaller ones if they sacrificed just over a dozen occupied properties. To create three large sites for redevelopment, government would combine publicly owned properties with an equal number of properties that it would force from private ownership. In all, government agencies expected to take 109 privately owned properties spread across the three sites. Ninety-eight of the properties were vacant, but thirteen were occupied residences and three were occupied businesses (see Table 4.1).

One of the three-acre sites, at the 2100 block, would be pursued first and under a tight timeline so that it could be sold to Reline Brakes for its relocation and expansion. Required approvals were given by the RDA Board,

Table 4.1. PROPERTIES PLANNED TO BE TAKEN FOR AMERICAN STREET LAND ASSEMBLIES

Site	Area (Acres)[1]	Number of Properties	Property use 2001–2002[2]			
			Empty Lot	Vacant Building	Business	Residence
2100 block[3]	3.2	57	48[4]	1	1	7
1700 block[5]	3.0	31	25	0	2	4
2501 block[6]	0.7	21	19[7]	0	0	2
Total		109	92	1	3	13

[1] City of Philadelphia Board of Revision of Taxes, "Property Information," http://www.phila.gov/brt/propertyinformation/Pages/default.aspx, accessed March 31, 2009. Area calculated from property searches.

[2] Herb E. Wetzel (RDA) to (RDA), Memorandum Re: North Philadelphia Redevelopment Area, American Street Industrial Corridor Urban Renewal Area, 1st Amended Redevelopment Proposal, 1st Amended Urban Renewal Plan September 30, 2002; Memorandum Re: North Philadelphia Redevelopment Area, American Street Industrial Corridor Urban Renewal Area Redevelopment Proposal March 21, 2002; Memorandum Re: North Philadelphia Redevelopment Area, Model Cities Urban Renewal Area, Twenty-Eighth Amended Redevelopment Proposal, Twentieth Amended Urban Renewal Plan September 20, 2001.

[3] Including the 2100 block of N. Bodine Street, the 200 block of W. Diamond Street, and the 200 block of W. Susquehanna Avenue.

[4] Fourteen lots that were already publicly owned are included in this count. Several additional parcels on the site owned by the Philadelphia Housing Authority were to be combined with these and are not included in these counts.

[5] Including the 1700 block of N. Bodine Street and the 200 block of Cecil B Moore Avenue.

[6] Including 2502-32 N. Philip Street and 211-17 W. Cumberland Street. (These are compound addresses.)

[7] Thirteen of these lots were already owned by the city and would be consolidated with the other eight privately owned properties.

the Philadelphia City Planning Commission, and the City Council between September and December 2001. The official process to acquire the other two sites, at the 1700 block and the 2501 block, would begin a few months later. As promised, RDA officials began preparations for the relocations almost as soon as the takings began their way through the official approval process.

PERCHED AT THE BOUNDARY

Plans to pursue the American Street takings were officially launched in 2000, at a time when the outcome was extremely hard to predict. At that moment, no one could guarantee whether this project would be seen as a prized exhibit or a devastating debacle of government intervention.

Although government officials had generally avoided the forceful acquisition of occupied properties until the late 1990s, residents and planners had generated a cautious optimism that if government forced limited relocations in the middle of mostly vacant land, it could bring new, local jobs. When Reline Brakes expressed a desire to build on the 2100-block site and even signed a contract promising to do so, residents and officials gained confidence that the sacrificed land would be quickly redeveloped by a business that would employ locals. When the Mayor's Office assumed leadership and promised to oversee the official process, community leaders felt somewhat assured that forced dislocations would be few and that residents and business owners would be treated respectfully and compensated generously. With these promising new developments, they imagined that the taking of a few occupied properties, dotting a much larger swath of vacant land, might bring clearly desirable improvements without causing significant harm.

At the point when officials planned to move forward with the American Street takings as a pilot project to demonstrate the responsible use of eminent domain, it seemed possible to many of those most closely involved that moving forward, even at the cost of people's homes, might be the right thing to do. It seemed possible that this drastic approach might make many people better off and would avoid serious harm.

It seemed possible, in other words, that by taking properties, government could help neighbors achieve changes they wanted and protect their investments. As a group, neighborhood residents and business owners could potentially enjoy the cleaned-up development and regular care of new owners on large sites, most of which had previously lain vacant and collected trash. As a group, locals could benefit if new jobs became available for them. Individually, a dozen residents and business owners would have to make the unfortunate sacrifices of their homes and businesses, but they might be cared for and compensated well enough that eventually they would feel almost whole in their new locations.

But these optimistic outcomes were by no means guaranteed. Would the neighborhood actually see new businesses developed, would those businesses create local jobs, and would the relocated residents receive fair treatment?

CHAPTER 5

American Street II

From Promises to Protests

Although the last chapter showed how the American Street project initially inspired skeptical hope in officials and citizens alike, it was in fact, a boundary project—and one headed for disapproval as a violation of individual- and community-level investment. By describing the specifics of that trajectory, this chapter will emphasize an often overlooked point: Here, the apparent abuse of eminent domain was not caused by clearly reprehensible intentions or behavior. Once failures become evident, observers sometimes say that officials should have known that their plans would end up hurting neighborhood residents and businesses. These observers may even conclude that officials never intended to deliver on their promises and that corruption, rather than concern for the neighborhood, drove them to pursue the takings. But, as we shall see, a boundary project's promises can turn into disappointments even without officials engaging in such reprehensible behavior.

Because details are so crucial to the evaluations of boundary cases of eminent domain, historical contingencies—chance, circumstances, or simple luck—determine their legitimacy. Countless unpredictable problems with project implementation can happen, challenging the promised protection of investments. Interagency disputes and other bureaucratic difficulties may slow or derail projects. Delays in property acquisition and communications with owners may disrupt plans. Businesses set to redevelop property may experience unexpected downturns, dashing their hopes for expansion. When officials fail to adjust or account for these challenges, they can doom a project's success.

Historical contingency is everywhere, of course. But in a case that rests close to the boundary line, its impact is much more likely to transform the project's legitimacy.

Despite its official presentation, the American Street project was a borderline case from the beginning and, thus, was vulnerable to the aforementioned pitfalls. Project advocates labeled it a pilot project for Mayor Street's NTI because they were experimenting with increased political risk by relocating residents. The optimism they expressed concealed their knowledge of potential pitfalls and opposition, their knowledge that this really was a borderline case. Indeed, as the project moved forward, community residents and business owners became increasingly fearful that the promises on which cautious support had rested would not be realized. And as the takings were implemented, they started to damage, rather than protect, investments. In the span of just one year, many small and large mishaps within government but outside the project boosters' control destroyed the hopes on which public support rested. Unfortunately, officials did remarkably little to adjust their plans in response to these mishaps.

In the face of a looming project with increasingly terrifying results, residents and business owners became enraged, and they protested. As unfortunate events accumulated, hope for government assistance turned into cries against government intervention. The protests won some concessions but ultimately failed to stop the takings, and the project left an enormous scar on Philadelphia government's reputation with respect to eminent domain.

Ultimately, government failed to deliver on each of the two important tenets of earlier acceptance of its takings plans. First, it missed the mark on protecting individual-level investments. Government initiated personal, thoughtful communication with the displaced families about what was going to happen much too late, if at all, and it seemed to offer very little compensation for their losses. In addition, rumors spread through the neighborhood that many more homes were at risk of the government bulldozer. Second, government failed to provide collective-level improvements. Officials' efforts to draw new development and local jobs to the cleared sites were frustrated, and for a long time, there was no evidence of *any* new development that had justified the individual-level sacrifices. Support for the takings dissolved as optimistic plans unraveled, and it became clear that government action would harm rather than support individual and collective investments.

RELOCATING RESIDENTS: RESPECTING INDIVIDUAL INVESTMENTS

Government Plans

The American Street takings were a planned experiment in taking occupied properties, to be sacrificed because of their location within a larger area of vacant parcels. Could government account for homeowners' investments of time, money, labor, and emotion while taking their property titles? Although the answer that eventually emerged was a resounding no, in the beginning, government had mechanisms in place that, if they had worked, might have earned it praise. Its plans called for forcing very few residents out and giving those residents significant help through the transition.

Project managers expected a professional, regulated, and tested set of practices to ensure the respectful relocation of displaced homeowners. "Relocation workers" of the RDA would guide residents through the process, help them find new places to live, and deliver government compensation. Federal guidelines for compensation set minimums for decent, though not generous, treatment of relocated residents. They call for owners to receive an appraiser's estimation of fair market value of their properties and additional money to cover the gap between that amount and the cost of comparable homes. Renters are usually offered a sum to cover the difference between the old rent and the new, more expensive rent, for three-and-a-half years. (Compensation is discussed in detail in Chapter 8.) For those interested in subsidized housing, relocation workers puts dislocated residents at the top of Philadelphia Housing Authority waiting lists that otherwise take years to climb. Government also pays residents' and businesses' moving, utility start-up, and settlement costs. No one thinks that displacement is easy, but government workers imagined that the official process would mitigate the pain.

When I spoke with them, RDA relocation workers acknowledged that displacement is always hard, especially in the beginning, when people first learn that it is happening. But they also emphasized that for many, the final result is positive, allowing renters to become owners or helping owners move into better houses. Maria Reyes, a relocation technician who fought against the American Street takings before she was hired by the RDA, told me how she came to see the process after managing it from the government side:

> I know my first approach with my clients in relocation is really bad.... I go to your house. Knock, knock, knock [makes the sound with knuckles against the desk]. "The city wants your house." And it's really bad. And it's really bad because the

people have been there for fifty years, their memories, their kids grew up there. And I know it's really bad. But I've seen the outcome in so many cases.... The outcome is good. Because even though the city is taking your house, the city has some program or some assistance [so] you know.... This doesn't look that bad at the end.

Maria Reyes, RDA Relocation Technician[1]

Shortly after official approvals were set in motion for the first of the areas to be assembled along American Street, RDA staff members began to give the occupied residences and businesses the special attention they had promised.[2] At this point, there were few signs that the plans for limited, careful, and respectful relocation of residents—plans on which the project's legitimacy rested—were in danger. However, it soon would be clear that typical administrative procedures did not protect residents of the American Street area from a harrowing experience filled, first, with dramatic uncertainty about who would be pushed out and what they would get and, later, with serious disappointment with compensation.

The Unraveling

Problems with the plans for respectful relocation accompanied the government's first direct contact with targeted residents. Community leaders had already been informed of the relocations, and a newspaper announcement had listed the addresses, but RDA officials initiated direct contact with targeted property owners and occupants on the 2100-block site by sending form letters in late December, 2001. Those letters signaled disregard rather than care (see Figure 5.1 and Table 5.1).

The letters were full of bureaucratic jargon. They were titled "Model Cities 28," which meant nothing to people outside a few agencies. They stated that the RDA was "considering" acquiring the owners' properties, not definitely planning to take them. Moreover, the letter's main focus was on a property appraisal, not about the taking itself, compensation, or the more general redevelopment plans. These letters might have alerted residents that something was afoot, but they said little about what would happen and when and how residents might be affected.

Though the RDA staff members considered these letters official notification that the city was likely to use eminent domain, residents did not interpret them in that way. To some residents, their letter looked like just one more of the countless, though not particularly important, notices about redevelopment efforts of the Empowerment Zone, the Enterprise Zone,

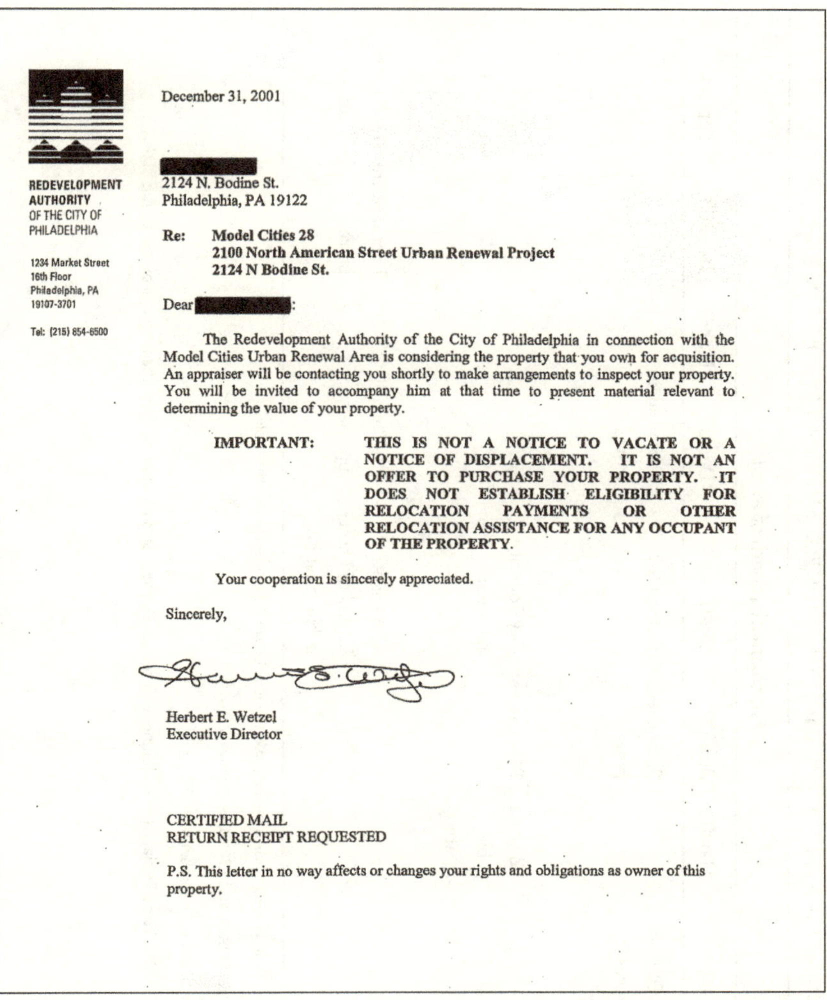

REDEVELOPMENT AUTHORITY OF THE CITY OF PHILADELPHIA

1234 Market Street
16th Floor
Philadelphia, PA
19107-3701

Tel: (215) 854-6500

December 31, 2001

[redacted]
2124 N. Bodine St.
Philadelphia, PA 19122

Re: **Model Cities 28**
2100 North American Street Urban Renewal Project
2124 N Bodine St.

Dear [redacted]:

The Redevelopment Authority of the City of Philadelphia in connection with the Model Cities Urban Renewal Area is considering the property that you own for acquisition. An appraiser will be contacting you shortly to make arrangements to inspect your property. You will be invited to accompany him at that time to present material relevant to determining the value of your property.

IMPORTANT: **THIS IS NOT A NOTICE TO VACATE OR A NOTICE OF DISPLACEMENT. IT IS NOT AN OFFER TO PURCHASE YOUR PROPERTY. IT DOES NOT ESTABLISH ELIGIBILITY FOR RELOCATION PAYMENTS OR OTHER RELOCATION ASSISTANCE FOR ANY OCCUPANT OF THE PROPERTY.**

Your cooperation is sincerely appreciated.

Sincerely,

Herbert E. Wetzel
Executive Director

CERTIFIED MAIL
RETURN RECEIPT REQUESTED

P.S. This letter in no way affects or changes your rights and obligations as owner of this property.

Figure 5.1:
First Letter Sent to Owners and Occupants on 2100-Block Site

the American Street Business Association, or local community development corporations. When I spoke with them years later, many condemnees did not recall the letter at all. Those who did said that they did not really know what to think about it. They were either not worried or simply resolved to stay put.

Elizabeth Segarra, a volunteer with the Community Leadership Institute, which later fought the American Street takings, told me that the people displaced from the 2100-block site "only got one [letter]. And only a few

Table 5.1. IMPLEMENTATION AND NOTIFICATION TIMELINE FOR AMERICAN STREET TAKINGS

	Approximate month of event[1]							
	Sep-01	Dec-01	Mar-02	Jun-02	Sep-02	Dec-02	Mar-03	June-03	Sep-03
Proposal 1[2] 2100-block site—Model Cities Urban Renewal Area (URA)	RDA passes	City Council approves[3] First letter sent		Second letter sent	Taking filed[4]	First resident moves			
Proposal 2 Creation of American Street Industrial Corridor (ASIC) URA			EZ hosts public meeting	RDA passes	City Council approves				
Proposal 3 1700-block and 2501-block sites—ASIC URA					RDA Passes[5] EZ and CLI host public meetings[6]	City Council approves		First resident moves[7]	First taking filed[8]

[1] If the month noted in column is not exact, the event is put in closest month by date and the exact month is noted below the table.

[2] Proposals 1, 2, and 3 were RDA Board resolutions 16797, 16909, and 17023, respectively.

[3] City Council hearings were on December 5, 2001, June 5, 2002, December 9, 2002.

[4] August 2002. As required and outlined by law, when the RDA files a Declaration of Taking with the court, the title is transferred from the previous owner to the RDA.

[5] October 2002.

[6] October 2002.

[7] July 2003.

[8] August 2003.

of them got it. And if you read that letter, you wouldn't even understand it yourself. It wasn't fair. Some of them put it in the shoebox. Others forgot."[3] Perhaps residents could not imagine that the city would actually take and demolish their houses.[4] In 2008, as Sonia Ortiz looked at the initial letter she received about her house on Bodine Street, she reflected on it. She said that she would not have thought it had anything to do with her. She didn't know what "Model Cities" was. She knew the city was supporting development along American Street, but not on Bodine (one short block to the west). And the letter just said something about an appraiser, so "I didn't really take it seriously."[5]

As you read this story in a book with details about eminent domain—pulled together for you to focus on in one sitting—it may be hard to believe that people would disregard a letter from the city that even implied a taking was in the works. But the nonchalance with which residents sometimes read these letters makes sense. Little bits of information had trickled down to these residents over several years. Neighbors might have mentioned something about what was happening while they carried on the business of their daily lives, while they were making dinner for their families, dealing with crying kids or their own headaches, or just going to and from work. Since I studied this case, I started to notice how I disregard letters from the city about plans to change zoning, traffic, or some other important facet of the area surrounding my own house every now and then. I do not respond if I think the plans are for something to happen far into the future and thus unlikely to happen at all. I do not mean to disregard them; I just plan to deal with them later, when I have more time, but that time rarely if ever comes. Thus, it is reasonable to think that residents of the areas targeted in the American Street takings would have basically ignored these letters about a possible condemnation and an impending appraisal.

The confusing effects of this letter, or lack of any effect at all, were exacerbated by unrelated delays in the project, which put off more specific communication with residents for months. RDA officials planned to follow the initial letter quickly with another one naming a specific dollar amount from the appraisal and a personal visit from a relocation worker. If this had happened, residents would have at least been more clearly informed that these plans were moving ahead. Instead, RDA relocation workers and project managers were stalled for six months as the RDA lawyers and accountants haggled with those of the Philadelphia Industrial Development Corporation (PIDC), the agency paying for the takings, over the contract between the agencies.[6] In mid-January 2002, RDA appraisers made estimates about real estate value without going inside the buildings or communicating with property owners at all.[7] Steps to accomplish the takings and notify condemnees halted there.

The delay confirmed the suspicions of those who dismissed or misunderstood the first letters by suggesting that nothing was really happening. As the RDA's relocation process for the 2100-block site became stalled by negotiations over funding, which would continue until the summer, no one visited the residents designated to be displaced. The residents' next opportunity to see government in action was during the process related to the acquisitions of the other two areas. The official approval and notification process is too complicated to detail here and, more important, too messy for laypeople (and often for the most intimately involved bureaucrats) to follow. Nonetheless, this messy process prompted a public meeting. The first acquisitions of the 2100-block site had been approved as part of the Model Cities Urban Renewal Area (URA), which covered much of North Philadelphia. (An "Urban Renewal Area" must be officially designated by City Council before the acquisition of properties for urban redevelopment.) Because of delays associated with the larger Model Cities URA, Commerce and EZ staff members decided to create a smaller American Street Industrial Corridor URA, to facilitate the second and third land assemblies (the 1700- and 2501-block sites). In anticipation of the required public notice for the City Council hearing on this action, the EZ held a public gathering in the neighborhood on March 7, 2002 (see Table 5.1). Yet again, government missed an opportunity to inform residents about who would be displaced and what they would get.

When they did hear from officials, residents learned little of what they really needed to know. Government workers did not clarify whose property would be condemned. At their own public meeting meant to inform the neighborhood about the upcoming plans, officials of the American Street EZ and the RDA avoided discussions about specific properties. There is no evidence that either city officials or community leaders who cohosted a March 2002 meeting with about seventy attendees talked specifically about the sites planned for acquisition that would cause displacement: the 2100-block site, which had already been approved for condemnation by City Council, or the 1700- or 2501-block sites, which would be officially proposed over the next few months. According to an outline they prepared for the meeting, officials discussed plans only "in very broad strokes" for the development of American Street as an industrial area with a green buffer surrounding it.[8]

Moreover, speakers emphasized that the official step that City Council was about to take, the creation of an "urban renewal area, does not automatically trigger condemnation of all parcels within that area" and that another process would be necessary for specific acquisitions. This was true, but it left out the very real plans to condemn specific parcels, which were already making their way through the earlier stages of the administrative process.[9] Indeed, a packet from the informational meeting stated, "There are no current projects that would require anyone to move" (see Figure 5.2). By withholding information about who would be displaced and how, officials allowed people to imagine that losses would be greater than they ever

Questions & Answers...

About the American Street Industrial Corridor
Urban Renewal Area

Why create an Urban Renewal Area in the American Street Industrial Corridor? There are over 7 acres of vacant, tax delinquent land along the American Street Industrial Corridor and over 40 employers with 925 employees along the Corridor. The City hopes to continue to bring new companies to the area and convert the vacant land into productive use. Creating an URA is a way of preparing the area for future development. If successful the URA will attract new businesses to the area. The URA also defines the area for proposed industrial use.

What kind of industries are you trying to bring? Light manufacturing and service businesses.

How will you ensure that these industries are environmentally safe? Businesses interested in relocating to the area must comply with local, state and federal environmental and health standards.

How will you ensure that jobs benefit community residents? Businesses must agree to hire community residents in order to take advantage of the tax incentives and financial products of the Empowerment Zone.

Is there a process to hire community residents? The EZ will work with existing neighborhood organizations to promote job openings at new companies that locate to the American Street Industrial Corridor.

How will I be affected? You will benefit from the expected new development that will come to the neighborhood. At this point in time, the City has no specific plan to acquire properties in the area. If the City decides to acquire properties, there will be a separate process.

More...

Figure 5.2:
Two Pages of Information Packet from the EZ Public Meeting, March 2002

Q & A continued...

Will I have to move? Creating the URA does not require anyone to move. Only a small number of the properties in the area are residential and occupied. The City is focused on developing the vacant land. There are no current projects that would require anyone to move.

What are my rights? You have the right to testify before City Council on the proposed legislation. You also have the right to participate in public hearings when the Redevelopment Authority reviews proposed projects. If in the future a proposed project overlaps with your property you will have the right to financial compensation and housing services.

What are my obligations? If in the future a proposed project overlaps with a property that you own, you must sell your property to the RDA. If you are a tenant, you must relocate within a reasonable period of time.

What is the relocation process? The City is focused on developing vacant land. There are no current projects that would require anyone to move. However, if in the future a proposed project overlaps with a property that you live on, the RDA and City Council will hold public hearings for comments. The RDA will notify you and explain the steps involved in the process.

When will these changes occur? Once the designation is approved there will be no immediate noticeable change. Changes will start to occur once new businesses are attracted and/or new development projects are implemented.

Will my taxes go up? No, taxes will not go up as a result of the designation.

Where and when will I be able to have input into decisions? Residents will have the opportunity to ask questions and voice their opinions about the redevelopment proposal at City Council hearings prior to adoption of the proposal.

***

Figure 5.2: (Continued)

intended, that the scope of the takings was grander than planned, that more homes would be lost, and, therefore, that even more damage would be done to their investments.

Not only did people not know who would be displaced, they could not get clear answers about how the displaced would be compensated. At public meetings, officials talked about how compensation worked in general, but reminded people that individual situations differ. Worse yet, the compensation arrangements did not become clearer once redevelopment workers contacted targeted residents again.

When RDA staff members did finally work directly with individual residents to figure out how to assist them and compensate them through the transition, the contact raised more fears than it settled. The communication started with another letter that sparked confusion and anger. The RDA sent owners of occupied homes on the 2100-block site what it calls "offer letters" in July 2002.[10]

These letters would become notorious symbols of government's disregard of the displaced families, especially because of the $20,000 amount mentioned as compensation. Even though, technically, the letter provided accurate details about compensation, practically it suggested what seemed like a ridiculously low amount for the loss of a home. Beyond the $20,000 figure, the letter provided few other insights into what would happen to residents. (Almost all properties had the exact same appraised value; this often happens because the RDA performs drive-by "mass appraisals.") I found no one who argued that the houses were worth more than $20,000 on the real estate market, but everyone I talked to claimed that this was not enough compensation for losing one's house.

Anyone familiar with RDA practice might know that the letter's mention of "additional benefits" in the sentence following the $20,000 figure could be significant. Residents could and would, in most of these cases, get more than double that amount once the process was complete, but they did not know or even suspect this at the time they received these letters. Moreover, the few sentences about compensation amounts were embedded in many paragraphs of legalistic disclaimers. In all, the letter created an impression of a government interested only in meeting its own legal requirements, not in caring for residents losing their homes. At some point, another letter written with a similar emphasis on legal correctness, rather than practical clarity, may have also been delivered to occupied homes. It had no date, name, or address to identify for whom it was intended, and I found no record of it in the RDA files related to these owners, but in 2007, Sonia Ortiz, one of the relocated residents, showed it to me from her scrapbook.

When relocation workers finally visited homeowners of the 2100-block site personally three to four weeks following the offer letters, they asked for a lot of information, but gave out very little, thus failing to allay confusion and frustration. RDA workers were documenting individual situations to create more specific estimates of compensation, and this would take time. To make matters worse, some owners spoke mostly Spanish, but the RDA had no relocation specialists with that skill or professional translators to assist them.[11] As the official process marched on, the RDA sent residents another letter about a month following the in-person visits (mailed on September 3), listing all of the documents needed to "determine eligibility" for relocation benefits. This letter, like the others, probably only increased worries about what residents would receive for their losses. At this point, residents surmised that they stood to lose a great deal. They would lose their homes and be paid a paltry sum. No one was even showing them the consideration of explaining in person what was happening.

The Re-evaluation

Opposition coalesced around a sense that residents' individual investments were being destroyed. As just described, compensation amounts initially presented clearly failed to account for the value of homes. Also, the dozen families who were told that they might be displaced could not get clear information: about if or when the takings would actually happen or precisely what compensation would be awarded if they did happen. In addition, many started to suspect that officials would actually go after many more than the originally targeted homes. Residents came to believe that not just a dozen families but hundreds of people would be subject to the same disregard.

When I spoke with residents affected by the American Street project, some of them used the word "investment" in describing what the project had threatened; others talked about all of the time, labor, and money they had put in their homes, without saying "investment." One man who lost his house on the 2100 block of Bodine Street complained, "After we bought it, I invested a ton of money in the house—new windows, new everything—thinking that we would live the rest of our lives there. We wouldn't have invested all that money in something that wasn't ours. And then it was that the city told us we had to move."[12] Ana Rivera, a condemnee from the same block, protested,

> It's not good that they take people from their own homes, who have years there, with kids that were born there, the grandkids are there.... If I were in government? I'd think first about people, the people who live there. First I'd think [about] that. The time that they had there, the houses that were theirs. There, all the houses were ours. They weren't houses that owed anything to a bank. All were owned. That one thinks, the people that had more than twenty, thirty years there in their little houses, that expect that one day they'll die, and that they'll die in their places that they'd been for so many years, those are the things that bother and that hurt.
>
> Ana Rivera, Condemnee on 2100-block site[13]

Whether they used the word or not, people responded to a concern that the financial, labor, and other value they had invested in residences would be lost. Sonia Ortiz, the woman who told me that the first RDA letter had not made her worry that takings on the 2100-block site were on the way, became seriously concerned after the public meetings in March 2002, as word began to spread about government's plans. In May 2002, before the "offer letters" mentioning $20,000, and before opposition to the takings began organizing, she wrote a letter of protest to the RDA to say that it should cease its plans because she had "lived here for nine years. I've invested much money on my property, and much hard work.... I will appeal this matter to save my house and neighborhood, even if it means hiring a lawyer"[14] (see Figure 5.3).

Ortiz told the government bluntly that the taking was wrong because it did not respect her investment. Unlike the owners of the vacant lots

Sonia Ortiz
2104 N.Bodine Street
Philadelphia, PA 19122
(215)739-4385
May 02, 2002

To: Redevelopment Authority & Model Cities Urban Renewal Project
1234 N. Market Street 16th Floor
Philadelphia, PA 19107

I Sonia Ortiz who live at 2104 N. Bodine Street do not agree on selling over my property. I've lived here for 9 years. I've invested much money on my property, and much hard work.

The Empowerment Zone Program came to my neighborhood with the intention on revitalizing my community not to tear houses down. There are plenty of empty lots in the city of Philadelphia where you could construct your "industrial site". The reason you are targeting my neighborhood is probably because is in North Philly. I know that you would never do this to a middle class neighborhood.

My opinon is that the Redevelopment Authority should reject the offer you're getting from outsiders who want to take over my property. I will appeal this matter to save my house and neighborhood, even if it means hiring a lawyer. I expect a response from you pertaining to this issue.

Please use the mailing address or phohe number provided in order to communicate with me.

Sincerely,

Sonia Ortiz

Sonia Ortiz

Figure 5.3:
Letter Sent to the RDA from Sonia Ortiz, Protesting the Takings, May 2002

throughout the city, she had put time, money, and effort into her property. Moreover, Ortiz contrasted her investments with those "outsiders"—businesses with no prior local ties or commitments—to whom, she imagined, government was illegitimately giving her property. Because of her history of investments, she suggested, she deserved greater protection.

Residents of the second site being assembled, the 1700-block site, made similar statements in public testimony to City Council later the same year. Daralia Rodriguez lived in a house around the block from her parents' house; both houses sat within the area government planned for acquisition. She assured Council members that her family was not against progress but added that they did not want to sacrifice their "quality of life or financial investments."[15] She recounted how they valued her parents' house in particular. Her father had bought the house forty-six years earlier because the address had the same number as his winning lottery ticket. "It's old, but it's ours," she said. "It's our house."[16] Now that she and her parents were losing their houses, she said, she expected the city to treat them fairly and provide just compensation.

The pitifully low amount that people heard was being offered in compensation screamed of government's failure to respect resident investments. The notion that government had sent homeowners a letter to announce the condemnation and offer them $20,000 in compensation became a widely known symbol of government's outrageous mishandling of the displacements. Guillermo Salas, who had been a member of the government-community advisory team for the project and an early supporter of the plan, told me that he was offended when he heard about these letters. His expression of bewilderment matched that of several other interviewees:

> Well, the concept [of acquisitions of a few occupied homes for a large industrial parcel] is good. *But you just don't come to those families and give them a $20,000 check and say, "Go away."*... And so the result of that was the community got riled up. There were meetings. There were demonstrations.... You just don't tell people pack up and go. Go where? So you get $20,000. What in the world can you afford today with $20,000? [Emphasis added.]
>
> Guillermo Salas, President-Cofounder HACE[17]

Salas's exasperation is indicative of the kind of turn that a boundary project can take when plans unfold in unexpected ways. He had been extremely involved in and supportive of redeveloping American Street to host light industrial and warehouse operations. And yet, he was appalled and spoke out against the project when he learned that the residents to be displaced received letters mentioning $20,000 in compensation. Eugenia Burgos, a neighborhood resident who had been generally supportive of the city's efforts at redevelopment for several years, expressed similar dismay at government officials' general failure to communicate:

> It was a shame, because they didn't handle the things the way they should. What they did is they made the neighborhood totally against them. I look at things like when you work... in partnerships, you don't come in and tell folks you have got to do this and you have got to do that and you don't have anybody there to explain why.
>
> Eugenia Burgos, Informal community leader and former ASCTB member[18]

The problem was not only the low compensation amount; it was that residents did not know what was going to happen. They were not sure who would be displaced and when or—though the $20,000 figure was widely discussed—how much compensation the displaced residents would get and when. As they invested in their homes, they expected security in two senses: first, counting on returns such as shelter and community with a high degree of certainty; and second, the security of knowing that they could keep their houses was itself a return on investment. The city's lack of information threatened their security in both of these senses. At the December 2002 City Council hearing on the second site, the daughter of a resident (Manuel Velez, discussed in Chapter 1) complained fiercely about how little government officials had told people. Milagros Velez said that her father had not known anything about the takings plans until October, when he heard what was happening through the "grapevine" and neighbors. She pled:

> In order for residents to be willing to move, we do want to know what we're going to get.... We're not going to want to move if they're not going to tell us what we're going to get.... *They were all of a sudden like just sent a letter that said, "Oh, you got a couple of months to move, and we're offering you $20,000."*... We want someone, anyone, to set up meetings with us... because we don't know anything, and we're like lost out in space. [Emphasis added.]
>
> Milagros Velez, Daughter of 1700-block site condemnee[19]

Confusion led neighborhood residents to look for help outside government. The woman who would eventually lead the effort to organize people against the takings was introduced to the issue when a resident of the 2100-block site presented one of the letters to her and pleaded for assistance because she did not know what was happening. Estabania Massa, a 70-year-old widow, approached Rosemary Cubas as she was leading an unrelated neighborhood meeting on community lending. Massa waved a copy of the RDA letter in the air. She said (in Spanish) that she was going to lose her house and begged Rosemary Cubas for help. Cubas recalled, "I thought she was crazy.... She told us that she had to move, that the city was taking her house. She kept repeating over and over again that she'd gotten a letter that she couldn't understand, but that the government was coming to take away her home."[20]

Cubas knew that something had gone drastically wrong with the EZ's plans to involve community leadership in redeveloping the area. Though Cubas had initially supported the EZ, served on its advisory Community Trust Board, and even participated in discussions about using eminent domain, she had always expressed caution. For reasons independent of the takings, Cubas became severely disenchanted with the EZ—she had fought with it for several years about the follow-through on its early promises to develop indigenous political leadership. At the time Massa approached her, Cubas had just learned of the EZ's final decision to deny funds to her initiative. Cubas, therefore, was probably not surprised by the callous treatment that Massa described. Moreover, Cubas worried that government's efforts to remake the neighborhood without resident leadership would extend beyond the three areas along American Street. Cubas responded to Massa's plea by mobilizing residents to fight the city.

Neighbors came out against the takings when they feared that huge losses, many more than officially planned, were at stake. Cubas and others called people to public meetings by telling them that their large neighborhood, including the densely packed areas, were at risk. Cubas recruited about 200 residents to come to a first, "urgent community meeting" in October 2002. The Community Leadership Institute (CLI), the organization over which Cubas had fought with the EZ, hosted the meeting. She knocked on doors and passed out flyers that said, "Your home may be in danger of expropriation.... We must unite and fight this, just in case they are heading in our direction."

Another flyer read simply, "If you own a property within the surrounding American Street business corridor, you should do everything possible to attend this meeting. United We Stand. Divided We Fall." On November 4, Cubas held another community meeting, during which she and others assessed the positive and negative aspects of the EZ's October 24 meeting. They praised city staff for gathering over 300 people to attend the meeting and starting this "long overdue communication," for the carefully designed meeting format and detailed content, for the Spanish translation, and for good interaction between staff and community members after the meeting. They criticized EZ staff, however, for failing to answer most of the questions posed by residents or answering them in "misleading ways." The flyer summarizing this response concluded, "The most important demand of residents was not dealt with and needs to be pursued: Stop all condemnations, rezoning, and relocations until impacted residents and other residents have been informed and involved through a Planning Commission community planning process" (see Figure 5.4). Elizabeth Segarra, who became a volunteer for the anti–eminent domain effort called the Citywide Coalition to Save Our Homes, recalled being recruited:

> She [another resident] knocked on my door and she said, "You know that your home can be the next taken through this project. Come to this meeting. We're having this meeting tonight and we're having all these neighbors organized because you have a right to stay if you want to stay." So I started attending the meetings.
>
> Elizabeth Segarra, CLI Staff Organizer[21]

Fears mounted, and hundreds of residents responded to what they thought were threats that government would clear many more occupied homes than officially targeted. Rumors spread that the city aimed to acquire an area four blocks wide and several blocks long (much bigger than the new American Street Industrial Corridor Urban Renewal Area). Some thought this was for industrial development; others said it was for a new highway or widened road right down Second Street, the heart of Norris Square's heavily Puerto Rican residential community.[22] (Locals referred to the neighborhood as Norris Square Park.) Cubas and others described the threat of eminent domain as facing the entire neighborhood, not just the few blocks being condemned.[23] Califano, the EZ Economic Development director, thought that "Rosemary [Cubas] fell prey to misinformation and used that at times to exacerbate the problems of fear and anxiety."[24] At public meetings, Cubas showed a map outlining official plans for sidewalk and landscape improvements to depict the area she said the City planned to condemn and demolish,[25] and she protested to City Council about a list of properties to be taken for gardens as if homes were at stake.[26] Walt DeTreux, the former chief of staff to Council Member Richard Mariano, told me that Cubas exaggerated the project's threat to the community:

> You know I understand it. I understand it. But it was a problem for one or two people that Rosemary made into . . . some big community crisis. Because if they're taking his house, next they're taking your house. She was telling people there

was . . . a tree-planting plan. They were going to plant trees on Second Street. She told them that this plan [determined] the different houses they were taking.

Walt DeTreux, Former Chief of Staff, City Council Member Richard Mariano, District Seven[27]

While DeTreux seems to have minimized the opposition to the plan (by citing one or two families instead of over ten for whom "it was a

Assessment of the Special Called American St. Empowerment Zone [ASEZ] meeting with Community Residents on 10/24/02, 6pm, St.Boniface School Cafeteria

Positives

- It appeared that over 300 persons attended
- Community resident participation was thoughtful, plentiful, on varied subjects and fairly well disciplined
- The ASEZ agreeing to have this meeting with the community was a very good start at long overdue communication
- The format and most of the content of the meeting was good & showed a lot of effort--- 1) the Power-point presentation on ASEZ funded projects with funding distribution; 2) having the ASEZ staff/Board Members and representatives of different City agencies present [Commerce, City Planning Commission, Licenses & Inspection.... and the head of OHCD for this area, Ms.__________, to answer questions], 3) map clarifying what is the American St. Industrial Corridor Urban Renewal Area within the ASEZ; 4)invitation & applications for residents to apply to serve on the ASEZ Board, 5) providing the **City of Phila Bill # 020279, introduced May 2,2002 by Councilmen Mariano and DeCicco which establishes the American St Industrial Corridor Urban Renewal Area**
- Translation at least to Spanish –the largest language group, was good.
- Interaction between agency people and the community after the meeting was pretty good

Negatives

- **Most of Concerned Residents of ASEZ questions were not answered or answered in misleading ways. Demands were not addressed. Examples include:**
  - Although we were given the names of members who are now on the ASEZ-Community Trust Board, we did not get the number of community residents [which we know is very few], "community representatives" was substituted, which misrepresents the reality
  - Although we were told that ASEZ funds have already been allocated the reality that there is still $7.6 million in a Funding Stream [a form of endowment for the community] and how that will be/can be spent and who really has power over this was not explained.
  - No one really explained who is pushing for the American St Industrial Park. Instead we were told that certain areas have been in industrial use for decades and that many organizations and agencies support the revitalization of these long standing industrial areas to attract employers to the neighborhoods and create jobs for residents. **We were not told that the 6 occupied houses on the 2100 Block of Bodine are zoned residential and are being targeted for industrial use. Nor were we told that the 50 parcels –5 of these presently occupied by families--- were**

Figure 5.4:
CLI Response to EZ Public Meetings Held in October 2002

being requested in the City Council last Thur October 31, 2002, FOR INDUSTRIAL USE? And what would neighborhood organizations answer if asked if they are behind the take over of occupied homes and residential land for conversion to industrial. The residents spoke loudly against the introduction of the large land intensive warehouse operations that offer few jobs and a multitude of nuisances such as rats with food processing/distribution operations.

- Although we were given the amount of residents hired vs non-residents -- -180 retained residents since 1997 among the 567 new jobs created, we were told **some jobs** resulted EZ loans to non-profit organizations. At the meeting residents inquired the job & salary levels of these jobs but were told they did not know.
- <u>We received misleading answers</u> to "Why when the ASEZ is ¼ mi from homes selling at $250,000 and up should such attractive land be used utilized for more industrial rather than residential?? The answer says the land being target for industrial revitalization ....has been in industrial use for decades. This **IS NOT TRUE: examples: The 2100 Block of Bodine St where 6 homes occupied by families is being taken by Eminent Domain is being taken for eventual use. Additionally the 50 properties ---5 of these lived in by families---- being requested in the City Council last Thurs October 31, 2002, ARE RESIDENTAL AND ARE BEING REQUESTED FOR INDUSTRIAL USE?**

<u>The most important demand of residents was not dealt with and needs to be pursued</u>: STOP ALL CONDEMNATIONS, REZONING, AND RELOCATIONS UNTIL IMPACTED RESIDENTS AND OTHER RESIDENTS HAVE BEEN INFORMED AND INVOLVED THROUGH A PLANNING COMMISSION COMMUNITY PLANNING PROCESS.

Figure 5.4: Continued

problem"), it may be hard to understand how these activists, with seemingly very good intentions and strong community histories, would have misled their neighbors about the city's plans so much more dramatically. According to at least one colleague who had great respect for Cubas, she reportedly denied that she was the source of rumors about plans for much larger scale acquisition or that she knew who was.[28] Indeed, most of those who named Cubas as the source of the rumors also talked about her with deep respect. Eugenia Burgos, an informal neighborhood leader and former member of the ASCTB with Cubas, said that even though Cubas had misled neighbors,

> She was a wonderful person and a great committee worker. I had a lot of respect to her but she worked with what she had. She was given that information, and she felt that it was her responsibility to let folks know.... Sometimes when you work within the system you learn to not trust.
>
> Eugenia Burgos, Informal community leader and former ASCTB member[29]

Elizabeth Segarra, a CLI staff organizer, responded to my question about inaccurate information in a 2007 interview:

> We didn't give bad information.... We were learning [to the best of] our knowledge, and we were notifying people correctly. And even though we were still in the process of learning [about] eminent domain... I don't think we ever gave people false information.... There were 5,334 properties they were taking, and out of those [were] 240 occupied homes, and we notified people [of] that.[30] Also, there were places that the city said was vacant, and there were buildings there. So that was true. And everything that CLI [the Community Leadership Institute] said, we have evidence of everything we said to people... to back us up. So we're doing good. And yes, they're probably saying that we're giving false information to people because they want us to look like the bad people. Because people are upset with us, of course. We start some process, and we rally, and we make some noise. For a little organization that [had] two staff, we [had] a lot of impact.... I think we have evidence to back up everything that we said.
>
> Elizabeth Segarra, CLI Staff Organizer[31]

An urban planning professor who met Cubas in 2005 thought that the learning process Segarra describes above may explain what EZ staff called the spreading of misinformation. He thought that Cubas and others working with her recognized that there was an important "process of discovery." He explained that they were poor people trying to figure out how to navigate the system, and Cubas offered guidance. People with CLI, he said, had to figure out how they could even find out what was happening to anyone and their property and if they had a voice in the process.[32]

Official responses to the crisis did little to quell fears of widespread displacement. EZ staff members responded to what they dubbed as a "misinformation campaign" by Cubas and CLI about the scope of the takings by holding meetings of their own and personally visiting residents in the 1700- and 2501-block sites.[33] Residents were unlikely to trust them at this point, and, as mentioned earlier and continues to be evident from the evasive language in materials mailed to residents after the meetings (see Figure 5.5), officials continued to evade requests for specific information in large meetings.

However, community leaders used unofficial channels to alleviate their own worries about widespread takings, and they calmed the neighborhood panic. Tomasita Romero, a leader on community efforts about drugs, gardens, and children, went directly to her District Councilperson's office when Cubas told her the city was coming for the neighborhood.[34] DeTreux, former chief of staff to the councilperson, remembered that he told Romero

AMERICAN STREET INDUSTRIAL URBAN RENEWAL AREA

What happens if one lives within the Industrial Corridor Urban Renewal Area? NOTHING, unless a project is planned.

How do I know if a project would be planned?
The City will support projects on:

- Sites with frontage on American Street not being used by an existing business;
- Blocks with a large amount of vacant land and that would allow for the creation of a parcel of at least one acre;
- Areas that do not disrupt solid, healthy residential blocks or businesses; and
- Areas that minimize the amount of relocation required.

What happens if one lives in area for which a project that requires relocation is planned?

- Owners and tenants will receive notification that their property is being condemned and that they are entitled to certain relocation benefits;
- Owners will receive a letter informing them that they will be contacted by an appraiser;
- Owners have the right to request an appraisal, at the City's expense, that covers both the interior and the exterior of their house;
- Owners are entitled to receive relocation benefits that will enable them to purchase a comparable property anywhere within the United States, or to become tenants;
- Tenants are entitled to relocation benefits to enable them to find comparable rental housing or opt to become home-owners; and
- Owners and tenants are entitled to assistance to pay for their moving expenses.

ÁREA DE RENOVACIÓN URBANA INDUSTRIAL DE LA CALLE "AMERICAN"

¿Qué sucede si uno vive dentro del Área de Renovación Urbana Industrial? NADA, a menos que un proyecto haya sido planificado.

¿Cómo sé si un proyecto será planificado?
La Ciudad apoyará proyectos en:

- Terrenos con frente hacia la Calle "American" que no estén ocupados por industrias;
- Bloques con gran cantidad de parcelas baldías y que permitan la creación de terrenos de al menos una cuerda;
- Áreas que no afecten bloques residenciales sólidos y saludables o industrias existentes; y
- Áreas que minimizen la cantidad de re-ubicaciones requeridas.

¿Qué sucede si uno vive en un área para la cual un proyecto que requiera re-ubicación ha sido planificado?

- Propietarios e inquilinos recibirán aviso de que su propiedad esta siendo condemnada y de que tienen derecho a ciertos beneficios de re-ubicación;
- Propietarios recibirán carta informándoles que serán contactados por un tasador;
- Propietarios tienen el derecho a requerir una segunda tasación, pagada por la Ciudad, y que cubra tanto el exterior como el interior de la vivienda;
- Propietarios tienen derecho a beneficios de re-ubicación que les permitirá comprar una propiedad comparable en cualquier lugar en los Estados Unidos, o a convertirse en inquilinos;
- Inquilinos tienen derecho a beneficios de re-ubicación que les permita encontrar vivienda de alquiler comparable, u optar a convertirse en propietarios; y
- Propietarios e inqulinos tienen derecho a asistencia para pagar sus costos de mudanza.

The Philadelphia Empowerment Zone: Making Revitalization a Reality.

Figure 5.5:
Information Mailed from EZ in November 2002 to Attendees of Public Meetings Held in October

and another local leader, "'Nobody is taking your home.' . . . I had to explain it fifteen times, more for reassurance. It's not that they didn't know it. They knew it. But she [Cubas] would get them worked up."[35] Another resident leader and city employee, Eugenia Burgos, asked RDA officials she knew about the alarming gossip and was reassured by their confirmations about which properties were actually being taken.[36] Romero, Burgos, and a few others shared their confidence that government plans were actually limited to the three officially announced sites and would displace 13 families and 3 businesses from private properties.

The community residents, rallied by warnings of major clearances, went home once the rumors appeared to be false. Meetings drew tens of people instead of hundreds. The plan to relocate the few residents on the three sites along N. American Street was much less objectionable than the rumors that many more were in danger. A core group continued the fight against eminent domain along American Street and spread their campaign to other neighborhoods, but their numbers had dropped dramatically.

Despite the opposition's quick reduction in size and government's continuing intention to take the land, the public attention did force bureaucrats to improve their treatment of displaced residents. As mentioned earlier, two of the leading EZ staff members dropped their other responsibilities to personally knock on doors and talk, in Spanish when necessary, to the residents being relocated from the 1700- and 2501-block sites. They wanted to prevent the confusion to which the 2100-block residents had been subjected, and their attention and advocacy more than likely resulted in slightly more compensation. After one relocated resident (the same woman who had alerted Cubas to the takings) complained of significant construction problems in the older house she had bought as a replacement, RDA officials did something atypical: They found resources to cover the repairs, even after they had settled with her over compensation.[37]

It is very likely, in fact, that the increased attention to the larger plan to take properties along N. American Street led the RDA to provide more generous compensation to those relocated about one year later in the process. (See Table 5.1 for timeline and Table 5.2 for compensation details.) A comparison of compensation for twelve homeowners displaced by the three land assemblies makes it clear that, on average, those relocated later (from the 1700- and 2501-block sites) received more money than those relocated earlier (from the 2100-block site). If we consider the median situation, homeowners relocated for the second set of takings received about $17,000 more than those displaced by the first taking ($58,319 vs. $41,149). Note that even the lower amount that owners on the 2100-block site received is more than double the $20,000 first offered for the real estate alone. This is because the full compensation amounts are a sum of what officials dub "real estate compensation" and "relocation benefits." In real estate compensation, the median family on the 2100-block site received $22,000 ($2,000 more than the original offer), yet the median owner on the second pair of sites received $13,000 more: $35,000. Residents of the first block also received much less in relocation costs, calculated as the difference between real estate compensation and the cost of a comparable house (up to $22,500), direct moving expenses (between $700 and $1,600), and utility-transition costs. Median compensation for relocation benefits was $19,149 and $28,218, respectively, for the different sites.

All of these families used their compensation to buy new houses.[38] As a result of the differences in compensation, the houses that the first set of relocates purchased were worth approximately $13,000 less than those bought by the second group (median prices of $47,450 and $60,000, respectively).[39] Most families had no mortgages on the house they owned before and successfully avoided taking on new ones. They stayed in North/Northeast Philadelphia but were mostly unable to relocate in the same neighborhood if they wanted to; instead they traveled about two miles away from their old homes and farther from the center of the city.

Table 5.2. RELOCATION RESULTS FOR HOMEOWNERS

	2100-Block Site 7 Homeowners[1]			1700- and 2501-Block Sites 5 Homeowners		
	Median	Min	Max	Median	Min	Max
Time (years)						
Move in until first notification[2]	22	10	40	10	2.5	30
First notification until move out	2.25	1	3.25	.75	.67	4.75
Money						
First offer for real estate compensation[3]	$20,000	$20,000	$20,000	$30,000	$15,000	$45,000
Final real estate compensation	$22,000	$20,000	$27,000	$35,000	$15,000	$45,000
Final relocation compensation	$19,149	$3,000	$35,545	$28,218	$1,942	$50,468
Final total compensation (real estate and relocation)[4]	$41,149	$25,000	$54,545	$58,319	$35,233	$95,468
Balanced credit or debt[5]	($12)	$15	($8,153)	($3,490)	($655)	($32,567)
New loan amount[6]			$47,900	$2,000		$30,000
Sale price of new house[7]	$47,450	$34,000	$87,900	$60,000	$34,000	$64,900
Distance (miles)						
From condemned to new house[8]	2.0	0.3	4.8	2.2	1.9	5.7

[1] Two residents formally treated as tenants by the RDA are included in my calculations. In both cases, figures include compensation both to the formal owner and occupant.

[2] Approximate number of years occupied house before 2002.

[3] Amount in first written letter for just compensation for real estate, not including relocation benefits.

[4] Amount received as both real estate compensation and relocation expenses, including moving and incidental costs. Does not include in-kind compensation before or after settlement or subsidies leveraged through other government and nonprofit programs. This amount is not necessarily the sum from the two rows above, for it represents the real total compensation of an individual while the amounts reported in the two lines above could refer to different individuals.

[5] Amount of credit or debt attached to house title erased (balanced) at settlement. For example, the median debt erased on properties with relocatees in the last two sites was $3,490. This debit/credit was paid off. Any amount rolled over into a new loan above and beyond the amount of debt previously attached to the title is represented in the next row.

[6] Three of seven condemnees took out new loans, so the median is zero.

[7] One person, not included in the calculations for this row, did not buy a new house but moved in with a relative instead.

[8] Calculated with directions tool on www.maps.google.com as walking distance.

Figure 5.6:
Manuel Velez, Displaced from the 1700-Block Site, at his New Northeast Philadelphia Home (2009)
Source: Debbie Becher

To be sure, the wide variation in individual compensation and relocation experiences also resulted from differences in the physical conditions of the forfeited houses, the debts connected to those houses (mortgages and liens for utilities, for example), the replacement houses, and displaced residents' particular interactions with RDA officials. Although the majority began and ended with no mortgages, two families moved from homes where they had mortgages (of $32,000 and $3,600) to homes that were completely paid for, and two took on new mortgages, which accounted for the largest new debt in each group ($47,900 and $30,000). In addition, two owners who had mortgages increased them by a few thousand dollars (from $32,000 to $34,000 and from $4,200 to $9,500).[40]

Commenting on what they had heard and seen about others' compensation amounts and new houses, most of the condemnees from the 2100 block of N. Bodine Street concluded that staying longer and fighting made a difference. As I discuss in Chapter 8, which focuses on compensation, one of the 2100-block owners ended up in a house worth much more than the sales price reflects, because the RDA arranged for him to purchase a newly constructed home just a few blocks away that was federally subsidized for low-income buyers. Indeed, he had been very vocal about his protests, and he managed to be the last one remaining in his old house, before he succumbed to the forced relocation. Even two single women who had horrifying stories of what finally pushed them out—a break-in in one case and an enormous factory fire next door in the other—lamented that they had not stuck it out longer to get greater compensation and, possibly, even to keep the taking from happening at all. And yet, Manuel Velez, the resident who fought hardest against his displacement (see Figure 5.6), also received one of the lowest compensation amounts, and no one stopped the takings.

REDEVELOPING LAND: RESPECTING COLLECTIVE INVESTMENTS

When her family on the 1700-block site had heard about the revitalization of American Street years ago, Daralia Rodriguez testified to the City Council, they had been excited because they thought they would benefit. Once they realized they would have to leave, excitement turned to disappointment that they would not be there to enjoy the changes.[41] Little did she know that, almost a decade later, few improvements would be evident for anyone to enjoy.

Although residents resisted the American Street project primarily to fight individual losses, an additional and lasting sense of frustration stemmed from the fact that the project never delivered on its promises of community-level improvement. The project's harm to the individual investments of residents and business owners had been justified by plans to enhance collective investments by bringing new jobs for local residents and caring for previously vacant land. The project's legitimacy rested on a promise of basic, collective improvements that had not been fully realized several years after areas were cleared.

The promised improvements appeared much too late, were too meager, or failed to materialize at all. Development took over five years to begin on the first site, the 2100-block site, and it was only accomplished by a company that moved from two blocks away, leaving another old building vacant. By 2008, when I talked to many of the displaced residents, the two other sites had been completely cleared, but no development had occurred on them. These failures to redevelop or to create local jobs disappointed just about everyone.

If the neighborhood's redevelopment had happened, it might have served the people who had already invested there. Neighbors ask government to encourage improvement, or at least stability, for their benefit. They say, for instance, that those who come and stay during the hard times deserve improvements, and they should be the first to benefit, but in the end, the boosters of the American Street project could not provide these benefits.

Government Plans

As we saw in Chapter 4, the commitment by a local business, Reline Centers of America, to build on the 2100-block site had made wary politicians and administrators overcome their reservations about taking occupied properties. The American Street Site Assembly Program had already acquired much of the vacant property, but Reline's interest helped convince others that a handful of residential displacements was politically feasible. Herb Wetzel, RDA executive director, and Cathy Califano, EZ Economic Development director, presented the plan for the first, 2100-block site, to City Council in 2001 as well-considered and broadly supported. Califano justified the project to the City Council in this way, "This is the first site-assembly project of its type on N. American Street, and the success of this project is critical to the overall redevelopment of the area.... This business will build a 30,000 square-foot facility, retain thirty existing jobs, and create thirty new living-wage jobs for Philadelphia residents."[42]

The acquisitions, Califano claimed, would also "restore land that is currently [occupied by] tax-delinquent, dilapidated buildings and turn it into productive use." Moreover, she said, "Both the area businesses and the community development corporations were consulted about this project, and all hope that it will result in the attraction of new jobs."[43] No one expressed opposition or even doubt at this meeting, during which City Council considered and passed approval for the taking of properties for the 2100-block site.[44]

The Commerce Department researched Reline's history to ensure that it had the capacity to fulfill its promises. Then, they signed a contract. Reline promised to build and provide jobs; government promised to provide land in a timely manner so that Reline could move when it lost its existing facility. If these plans were realized, takings on the 2100-block site would likely have earned at least some approval from local businesses and residents.

Commerce and EZ officials expected to find businesses to develop on the two additional sites (the 1700 and 2501 blocks) once they consolidated land ownership. The 1700-block site, like the 2100-block site, would provide a single parcel of more than three acres. The 2501-block site would be much smaller, but it would also require a much smaller sacrifice, of only two resident families. Commerce employees expected to ensure that any business receiving land would provide what constituents demanded. The department would screen interested businesses based on their ability to provide the physical development and jobs. And the new cross-agency political will to assemble large sites suggested that the Commerce Department might succeed in fomenting development where it had failed in the past.

In addition to using eminent domain, officials used zoning rules, infrastructure construction, and cleanup efforts to retain existing light industrial businesses and attract new ones. For instance, the Commerce Department had been getting support for the enforcement of industrial zoning to prevent new residential development that worried business owners, for their truck traffic and noise would surely become a nuisance if residents were nearby.[45] EZ and Commerce officials also designed and sought funding for a widened entry at the south end of American Street, off Girard Street, so that trucks could easily access the area from Interstate 95. In addition, after business owners requested large-scale cleanup operations and more serious efforts toward vacant-land management in a 2000 survey, government financed a Pennsylvania Horticultural Society program called Philadelphia Green that had gotten its footing in this area.[46] Neighborhood leaders identified abandoned, vacant lots for local contractors to clean, seed with grass, surround with a low wooden fence, and maintain to, according to the program director, "make a nice, clean look in the community. And nobody can . . . hide your drugs in turf."[47] These measures promised to complement land acquisition by making the area inviting for warehousing and light-industrial operations that would improve land care and hire locals.

The Undoing

Just as plans for respectful relocation unraveled, so did hopes for swift and beneficial redevelopment. First of all, it took several years before government even took what officials call possession of the 2100-block site, the land-assembly site with the earliest hopes for redevelopment. The RDA filed the "Declaration of Taking," legally making it the owner of the properties in August 2002, several months after originally planned.[48] It was another two years before all of the occupants had moved out. Second, officials fell short of fulfilling hopes that they would create an inviting business environment by using zoning restrictions and constructing a new road-entry. In the 2000s, a few private developers convinced the zoning board to approve variances that allowed them to build housing.[49] In addition, plans to widen the southern access to the strip and better connect Interstate 95 to American Street only limped along. By 2008, no drills had hit the pavement, no asphalt or concrete had been poured to reshape the intersection, and it did not look likely that any would for at least a few more years (see Table 5.3).

The most significant delay in the takings was caused, as mentioned earlier, by a conflict between the RDA and another agency, the Philadelphia Industrial Development Corporation (PIDC), over a contract holding the latter responsible for paying for costs of acquisition. Before the RDA will actually condemn a property, it requires a signed contract from the entity paying the bill. Negotiations between the RDA Legal Department and PIDC over this issue stopped the project from moving forward for several months.

These intergovernmental problems delayed making the properties available to the company committed to redeveloping them, and this had enormous ramifications: the most important being that the delay helped make Reline Centers of America lose interest. Sometime in late 2002 or 2003, before the city could finalize the sale of the 2100-block site to Reline, the company decided to move to a smaller location in Northeast Philadelphia. The taking had dragged on longer than expected, and Reline determined that business was not going as well as planned.[50]

The rush for the first area, the 2100-block site, evaporated once the interested company that sparked the pursuit moved to the suburbs. After Reline pulled out, the RDA continued to move occupants out and demolish buildings. The area did not become level and vacant until three years after the RDA had anticipated having it cleared. It took another two years for the RDA to completely consolidate the property title so that the full parcel could be transferred to a new owner.[51]

The Commerce Department pursued other business owners who had expressed interest. Officials began discussions with one company that did not work out,[52] then with a distributor of chicken wings that did (Chaes Foods, also known as C&C Poultry).[53] Before giving Chaes Foods access to the site, Commerce hosted several discussions between the company's owners, community leaders, and neighborhood residents.

Finally, in early 2008, Chaes Foods opened a new 50,000-square-foot warehouse for operation, but the long-awaited new development was a mixed blessing at best. When Chaes Foods moved into the 2100-block site (see Figure 5.7), the company vacated its older building just two blocks away (see Figure 5.8). The 1900 block of N. American Street, which Chaes Foods previously occupied, became vacant.

Officials also struggled to find a business committed to redeveloping the second three-acre site at the 1700 block. As early as 2003, government had acquired all of the property titles it pursued, and three of the four displaced families vacated their houses soon thereafter. Yet, officials in the Commerce

Table 5.3. AMERICAN STREET PROPERTIES' USE AND OWNERSHIP PREVIOUS TO TAKINGS (CIRCA 2001), PLANNED FOR, AND REALIZED SUBSEQUENT TO TAKINGS (BY 2009)

Site[1]	Area (acres)	Use 2001–2002	Planned Reuse	Owner 2009[2]	Use 2009
2100 block	3.2	48 lots 7 residences 1 business 1 vacant building	Reline Centers of America	Chaes Foods (March 2007)	Processed meat warehouse
1700 block	3.0	25 lots 4 residences 2 businesses	Unspecified industrial	Yishai Kidar (1700 N. American St. LLC) (Jan. 2008) and the RDA	Lot
2501 block	0.7	19 lots 2 residences	White Oak Ice Company	RDA	Lot

[1] See notes for Table 4.1 for details about site addresses, area, and use 2001–2002.

[2] Dates purchased from government are in parentheses.

Department failed to secure a business commitment to redevelop the area quickly. In 2004 and 2005, two different interested buyers asked for and received "land reservations" from Commerce for the parcels, but they never produced the development plans required to secure the land from government. In 2005, Commerce officials began negotiating with Yishai Kedar, with whom they would eventually sign a contract to build a combination office/warehouse space, to include room for his heating and cooling and real estate companies, on the site. The final resident to leave, Manuel Velez, stayed in his house alone on a vast amount of open space for several years, until 2007, when officials finally evicted him because they thought new construction was about to begin.

The 1700-block site still lacked any redevelopment by 2009, and even then, Kedar's planned construction of office/warehouse space would take up only a portion of the cleared area. Just when Commerce officials thought that the RDA could sell the land to Kedar, another stumbling block emerged: Somehow, officials had missed a sliver of land that made the title company unsure if the RDA officially owned, and could thus sell, the whole property. The RDA had to initiate another takings process for the newly

Figure 5.7:
2100-Block Site after Takings, New Chaes Foods Warehouse and Passerby on N. American Street, Previously Site of N. Bodine Street Homes (2008)
Source: Debbie Becher

Figure 5.8:
1900 Block of N. American Street, Left Vacant by Move of C&C Poultry (a.k.a. Chaes Foods) to 2100-Block Site (2009)
Source: David Gehosky

discovered parcel. To keep things moving forward, the RDA and Kedar split the land sale and development into two stages. By early 2008, the RDA settled with Kedar for a portion of the land on the southern side (without the surprise properties) and expected to convey the rest for the construction of 35,000 more square feet of industrial space and offices later. As my research ended in 2009, Commerce's prime booster of American Street's industrial redevelopment, Vince Dougherty, was expecting Kedar to begin building on the southern portion soon and was projecting neighborhood benefits. In the end, he said the project will "retain twenty-five jobs and create an additional ten to fifteen jobs... Mr. Kedar committed to make every effort to hire from the neighborhood."[54] And yet, the site was still completely empty five years later, in 2014, when I visited it as this book went to print. (See Figure 5.9.)

Even without any hold-up in acquiring the properties on the smaller, 2501-block site, officials could not boast of specific plans for redevelopment there in 2009. The Commerce Department was repeatedly disappointed by companies expressing interest but not following through. After a few companies dashed hopes this way, one seemed more likely to work out. In 2007, a snow-plowing and industrial cleaning business called Mr. Spotless planned to build a 10,000-square-foot facility to

Figure 5.9:
1700-Block Site of N. American Street, from South End Looking North, Previous Location of Manuel Velez's House Still Vacant after Takings (2014)
Source: Debbie Becher

store equipment and chemicals. Commerce pursued an agreement with the owner until the summer of 2008, when Mr. Spotless lost a major contract and officially withdrew its interest. When I spoke with Dougherty in 2009, he admitted his doubts about the 2501-block site by reporting, "We are discussing how to move forward with this site especially given the economy." At this time, though others were, Dougherty was still not declaring this site, or the project as a whole, a failure.[55] However, this site too remained empty in 2014, when this book was published. (See Figure 5.10.)

The Re-evaluation

Onlookers would not wait forever to judge that the redevelopment plans for the three sites along American Street had produced only larger, cleaner, and more vacant lots. Although in 2009 Dougherty still anticipated that more businesses might come, community members had become sadly disappointed as they watched the land languish for years after residents had been pushed out. They were ready to declare government's failure to provide promised improvements.

Even in the first few years, when there was nothing at all to show but cleared space, officials and residents were unreservedly disappointed. The

Figure 5.10:
2501-Block Site, Looking Northwest Toward N. American Street, Still Vacant after Takings (2014)
Source: Debbie Becher

RDA project manager for these takings called what happened the "worst case scenario," because people who were dislocated would see the vacant space and want to say to government, "Well, you took my house for no reason at all. You took my house. There is no project here. Why did I go to all this heartache for you not to have a project there?"[56] Elizabeth Segarra, a neighbor who stayed involved in the anti-eminent-domain organizing, gave a similar evaluation: vacant land only made people angrier about the displacements. She told me:

> And this was in 2002. We're already in 2007. That was five years ago. And they still haven't built anything in that land. You know how pissed off I would have been if they took my land and they still didn't build nothing in my land? That's hard to swallow when they drive by and they see that.
>
> Elizabeth Segarra, CLI Staff Organizer[57]

From Segarra's perspective, the sight of vacant land exacerbated the sense that the takings were wrong. It reminded people who knew what happened that people were pushed out, and it confirmed that nothing of benefit *to anyone* resulted.

When development did happen, it elicited a small amount of praise, or at least ambivalence. I talked with people just six months to a year after the new Chaes Foods (C&C Poultry) warehouse had opened on the 2100 block. Although no one mentioned that a warehouse and a parking lot were particularly attractive or inviting, at least one neighbor referred to the building, the mowed grass, and the fence as cleaner and nicer than the vast amount of abandoned space and trash that were there before the takings began. But she also complained about the noise from the trucks; she said, "Now, we're dying because at two o'clock in the morning it makes so much noise. The factory opens at two o'clock in the morning and wakes us up."[58] Just two blocks away on N. American Street, however, the property that Chaes Foods had left vacant looked much worse than it had. Instead of an operating business, weeds grew through the windows of an empty, old brick building, in the cracks of the parking lot, and through the surrounding barbed-wire fence. But even if Chaes Foods had not left another large lot abandoned, its new building on the 1700-block site would not have been enough. No one had suggested that seeing the land looking better constituted sufficient justification for tearing down occupied homes.

A desire for new, good jobs for neighborhood residents made the takings seem reasonable to some, but in 2009, there was still little assurance that such jobs would materialize. Chaes Foods added few, if any, local jobs that community residents knew about. Dougherty at Commerce told me that Chaes Foods had reported adding sixteen new jobs by the end of 2008 and was expecting to hire more workers soon.[59] But neighborhood residents did not have this information, nor did Dougherty claim that the new jobs went to locals. As one resident and community leader told me, this kind of benefit is extremely hard to track and thus unlikely to provide any assurance to neighborhood residents that they have won something.[60]

Residents had been skeptical from the beginning about whether new business development would help them, and this skepticism continued after they set their eyes on the new operation. Another community-organization leader—Luis Mora, executive director of the American Street Financial Services Corporation—told me that resident suspicion stems from a sense that outsiders will not hire them. He said residents think that "[t]hose people [business owners] do not participate in the community. They are outsiders. The owners are not from the community, and they do not live in the community. So there is always this suspicion that it is not really benefiting the community."[61]

Indeed, residents said that they knew, from experience, that businesses along American Street would not hire from the neighborhood. Community representatives had complained about this at meetings of the ASCTB, the EZ's advisory board.[62] As I spoke to one resident, she pointed to "the strip"

(American Street) and said that they don't give jobs to "us"—probably meaning poor people and, more specifically, the poor Puerto Ricans who lived there.[63]

Ethnicity and class signaled who would get jobs and who would not. No one seemed to think that poor Puerto Ricans, the majority in the surrounding residential areas, would get these jobs. These residents shared a memory of Asian owners hiring other Asians, not Puerto Ricans. Indeed, one of the women who lost her house on the 2100-block site told me how infuriating it was to her to see that "the Chinese" (the owners of C&C Poultry) were the ones who redeveloped her land. Another person who lived on the street facing the new development told me he was quite sure that no one who lived in the neighborhood worked in the warehouse. To explain how he knew that, he raised his hand and pointed an index finger to the parking lot. He said the fact that we couldn't see any old cars was evidence enough that people like them, low-income people, weren't working there.[64]

Others cited even more direct evidence that the new warehouse was not hiring locals, and they were angry about it. They knew of people who had applied for jobs and had been rejected. This confirmed their suspicions about the city's inability to make deals with companies that would provide jobs for *them*. One neighbor told me that her 32-year-old son applied for a job at the warehouse three times after he was laid off from his construction job. Each time, he was told that they were not hiring.[65] Sonia Ortiz, who had moved a few miles away after she was displaced from the 2100-block site, kept her eye on whether jobs for locals had materialized, and she was disappointed. She told me:

> I had my cousin go around because he lived down there and he [sent] his application since they opened, and they always say they are not hiring. So, it just shows you that it just moved from one place to the other, kept everybody there and never brought new jobs to the neighborhood. I wish I could sue them because they misled us. They lied to us.
>
> Sonia Ortiz, Condemnee on 2100-block site[66]

CONCLUSION: FALLING ON THE WRONG SIDE OF THE BOUNDARY LINE

This project lost support because it failed to fulfill expectations that government could protect residents' investments. Investment is about change over time, and an investment logic draws attention to how government action affects change. Five to six years after government officially started these American Street takings, it looked pretty clear that the takings had made things worse, not better. The takings damaged, rather than supported, both individual- and community-level investments.

The American Street takings sat precariously on the legitimacy boundary line from the beginning, for the quick signals used to judge routine cases were mixed. There were some very basic signs that opposition would emerge. Occupied housing, not just vacant land, would be sacrificed. The fact that this project involved taking occupied homes is what made officials consider it a pilot project for political success in the first place. Moreover, the property would be given to a for-profit company for commercial operations, rather than to a nonprofit developer of housing. Looking back, the American Street Empowerment Zone executive director thought that the commercial development and lack of a local nonprofit sponsor made these takings a "hot-button" issue.[67] The RDA's deputy executive director and former executive director similarly told me that neighborhood folks might have supported housing, but "[w]e were acquiring properties strictly for commercial development, and I think we may have gone a little far."[68] Although these elements of the plans warned that citizens would disapprove, other aspects of the project suggested that government's efforts would be welcomed. The projects would address massive amounts of vacant and abandoned property ripe with problems, and promises of swift redevelopment would benefit neighbors with improved physical surroundings and new jobs. Moreover, officials planned special attention from representatives of several agencies and the Office of the Mayor to assure a smooth and respectful relocation process and prevent interagency delays. A commitment from a responsible and familiar small business owner to develop quickly and hire locally substantiated promises of benefits that had eluded Commerce in the past. However, as officials moved forward, a collection of contingent events destroyed hopes that government would protect individual and collective investments by taking properties along American Street.

A series of small, unpredictable, concurrent events ensured government's failure. Badly written letters, fights between agency lawyers over a contract guaranteeing financing, ups and downs of small businesses, and the timing of a conflict between the EZ and a community leader over support for a community-based effort were just some of the happenings that cemented the project's disappointments. Little things had effects beyond their immediate consequences, and they built on one another. Together, these events ensured that there would be no protection for individual or collective investments.

Looking at the American Street takings as history, it is very tempting to say that hopes were misplaced from the very beginning. And many do say that officials should not have risked these takings and that citizens should not have supported them, for the damage done to investments was guaranteed from the beginning. It is certainly possible that such critics are right in this case. Perhaps, given more evidence from research that others might complete about the greater political and economic context in which these officials intervened, we might conclude that they were foolhardy to ever imagine that their optimistic plans would come to fruition. I was, in fact, inclined to make such a judgment when the project along American Street was the only one I had examined.

However, after I looked into another project just a few miles away that followed a very different trajectory, I changed my mind. I came to understand the American Street takings as no less of a government failure but to see that failure as much less of a foregone conclusion from the very beginning. I came to understand initiatives like the American Street takings as boundary projects that can earn legitimacy when I bore witness to another unlikely success story that ended in a very different way. The next two chapters follow another set of takings that displaced even more families and seemed patently illegitimate when first publicly announced, but later could boast widespread approval.

CHAPTER 6

Jefferson Square I

Competing Visions of Investment Protection

Although disputes about investment protection are common to all eminent domain controversies, the specifics of those disputes can vary widely. The two previous chapters showed that resistance to the American Street project arose from government's failure to meet agreed-upon standards for investment protection. Had the project met those standards—minimal and respectfully handled relocations, the creation of jobs for neighborhood residents, and the cleanup of trash-strewn vacant land—it may well have won widespread approval. In other cases, however, resistance arises not because of implementation problems but because of fundamental disagreements about what constitutes investment protection.

This chapter turns to one such case—the Jefferson Square project in South Philadelphia. Local politicians worked with the neighborhood's hospital owners and nearby community leaders to design a redevelopment plan requiring eminent domain, and they thought this plan created a win-win situation. In their eyes, comprehensive revitalization would improve the area, and current residents and businesses would be thankful for the positive changes. First District City Councilperson Frank DiCicco got behind early plans for a massive redevelopment of three hundred properties. By 1998, designs were drawn up to provide the local hospital with a new parking lot and to improve area housing. Sixty new homes would be constructed to sell to low- and middle-income buyers. Many existing homes would be significantly rehabilitated for first-time buyers with below-median incomes. Moderate improvements would be made to some owner-occupied homes (without changing ownership).[1] This bold, government-assisted redevelopment plan, DiCicco thought, would not harm anyone who had been truly dedicated to the area. The change would, he imagined, assist invested community residents by improving the area physically and by bringing in new, caring homeowners. DiCicco, elected in 1995, hoped that this transformation would eventually become one of his signature, highly praised accomplishments.

Jefferson Square's redevelopment included many indicators from both sides of the boundary line. Many signals lent the plans easy legitimacy points: plans for the construction of affordable housing by a nonprofit developer in an area with low real estate prices, high vacancy rates, and poor building conditions. But other characteristics would challenge its legitimacy: the displacement of residents and business owners, the construction of housing to be sold at market rate, improvements for a for-profit commercial operation, and a location that rested close to where the real estate market had been rising. On its face then, Jefferson Square was easily identifiable as a boundary case, whose legitimacy would likely be contested.

From the moment they heard about it, many local residents thought that the Jefferson Square Revitalization Plan would destroy, rather than protect, their investments and thus should be resisted. Residents first started to form a concrete desire that government keep its hands off their neighborhood when they sensed that they were being pushed out. That moment was the morning that JoAnn King, mentioned in the book's first pages, saw a large orange sign on her front door. Though neighborhood decline had been difficult, residents strongly preferred being left alone to the power-brokers' vision, as they understood it: that they would be pushed out so that outsiders could reap the benefits of their neighborhood. Thus residents developed a different vision of how government could protect investments and act legitimately: it could stay away and let them continue to manage as they had been.

RESIDENTS' VISION OF SELF-HELP AND GOVERNMENT ABSENCE

In the late 1990s, in the South Philadelphia area called Jefferson Square, many residents imagined a hands-off government as the best form of protection for their investments. When residents received tidbits of information about early revitalization plans, those tidbits suggested that their investments would be wiped out. The government's plan was to send several families with long roots away and to rebuild the neighborhood for others—outsiders with no prior connections or commitments to the neighborhood.

In other words, residents discerned that government was seriously endangering the value they had sacrificed in the past and the security they expected to enjoy in the future. If government was going to act with such careless disregard, being left alone seemed a much better, secure alternative. They protested that "[t]his plan is being imposed on the community," and thus had no neighborhood support.[2] Thus, as residents learned of government plans, they developed an opposing view. If they could have posted their own sign at the neighborhood border for government to read, it might have said, "Keep Out." Perhaps residents expected that government would act this way because it had done so for many decades.

Sudden Government Attention to Building Conditions

Signs that government was really doing something in the late 1990s to stem the neighborhood's decline contrasted sharply with previous experience, as locals had gotten used to taking care of an area that government had abandoned to larger social and economic forces. DiCicco created plans for Jefferson Square's revitalization in the 1990s and was not alone in showing concern about the neighborhood's decades-long decline. The councilman had grown up a few blocks away and lamented the changes he witnessed over the years. Managers of Mount Sinai Hospital shared the councilman's distress. The hospital was built in the 1920s and 1930s,[3] and it served as an important local employer (though it had changed owners several times). In the 1980s and 1990s, Mount Sinai employed approximately 400 to 500 workers. But it struggled to survive, and by the late 1990s, it was only using a portion of its large campus (see Figures 6.1–6.4).[4]

Many of the residents, who had lived in the area at least since the 1950s, 1960s, and 1970s, recalled times when it had been much more vibrant: filled with markets, pawn shops, gaslights, grocery stores, drug stores, and cobblers' shops. One of them shared with me that she thought that it was "basically just a nice neighborhood,"[5] and another said simply, "I loved it."[6] The area declined in ways that residents could not control. As the waterfront began to slow down, Peggy King Brookins, one of JoAnn King's sisters told me, jobs and then "most of the people that were Irish and Italian... began to move outside the city."[7] Residents recollected that the predominantly African-American neighborhood had been more racially mixed in earlier years, comprised mostly of Italians and African Americans, but also Koreans.[8] To be sure, thoughts of that older racial diversity evoked fond memories of mutual interest and tolerance as well as sour remembrances of conflicts over respect, public space, gang rivalries, and racial

Figure 6.1:
Overview Just North of Hospital, Facing North toward Downtown
Source: JSCDC (circa 2000)

Figure 6.2:
Mount Sinai Hospital, Mostly Vacant in 2009
Source: David Gehosky

segregation. Shirley Corbin-Nelson, another of JoAnn's sisters, remembered the family moving from downtown to a "well kept... little street" in the early 1960s.

Shortly thereafter, however, owners began to abandon their houses. "The houses started deteriorating, and the neighborhood just started going down, down, down," Corbin-Nelson said.[9] Some homeowners died and left their houses to their children, who chose not to live there and sold them. Over time, whites moved out, and when new people moved in, they were usually black.[10] At some point, it felt like people generally stopped moving in and were only moving out.[11] Buildings either remained and stayed vacant or were demolished, leaving small open lots where homes had once been. As many residents left, those who remained watched drugs and prostitution come in and ruin streets they had once enjoyed.[12]

Although US Bureau of the Census data on the area as a whole may not be very representative of what it felt like to be on certain blocks, they are suggestive of a downward trend that resisted the more recent citywide trend of improvement. In 1990, the area had a median household income of $21,204 and a median owner-occupied housing value of $45,533, amounting to 86 percent and 92 percent of citywide medians, respectively. But in 2000, the area had a median household income of $21,912 and a median

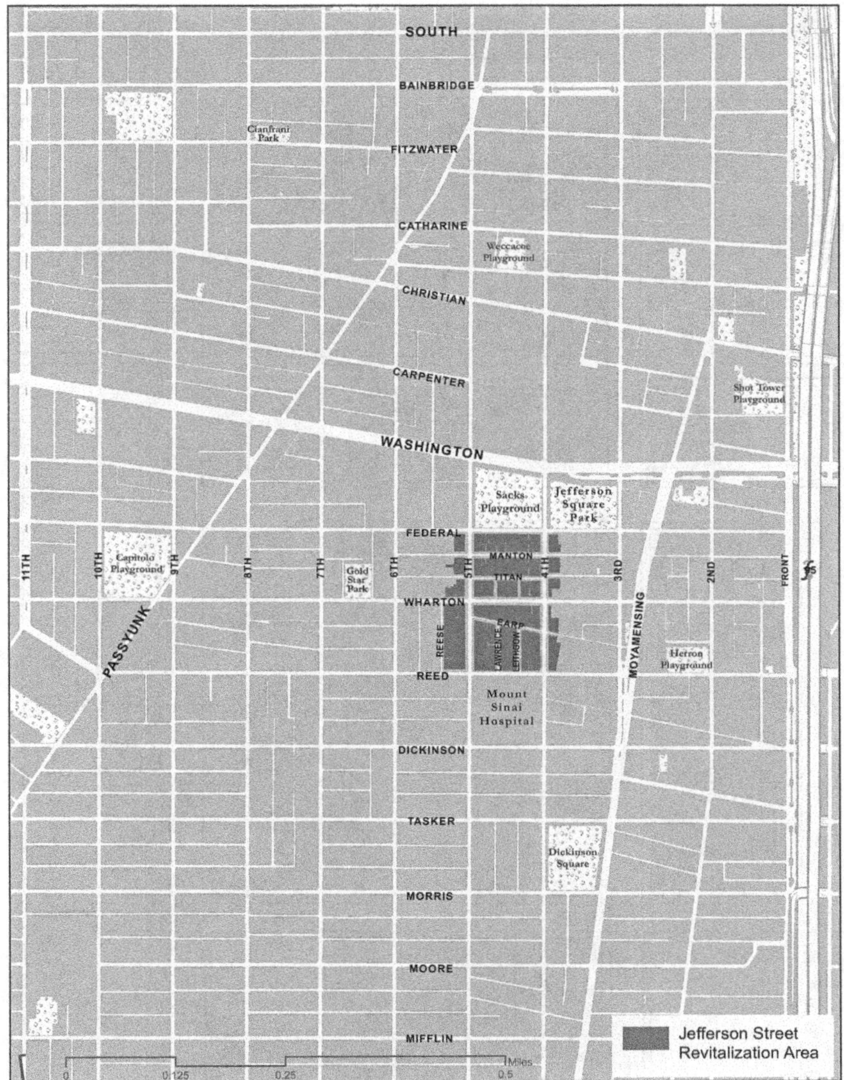

Figure 6.3:
Jefferson Square Revitalization Area in Context
Source: Al B. Parker

owner-occupied housing value of $48,000, amounting to 71 percent and 80 percent of citywide medians, respectively.[13]

Despite these conditions, many people—both longtime residents and newcomers who saw the neighborhood as an opportunity—continued to

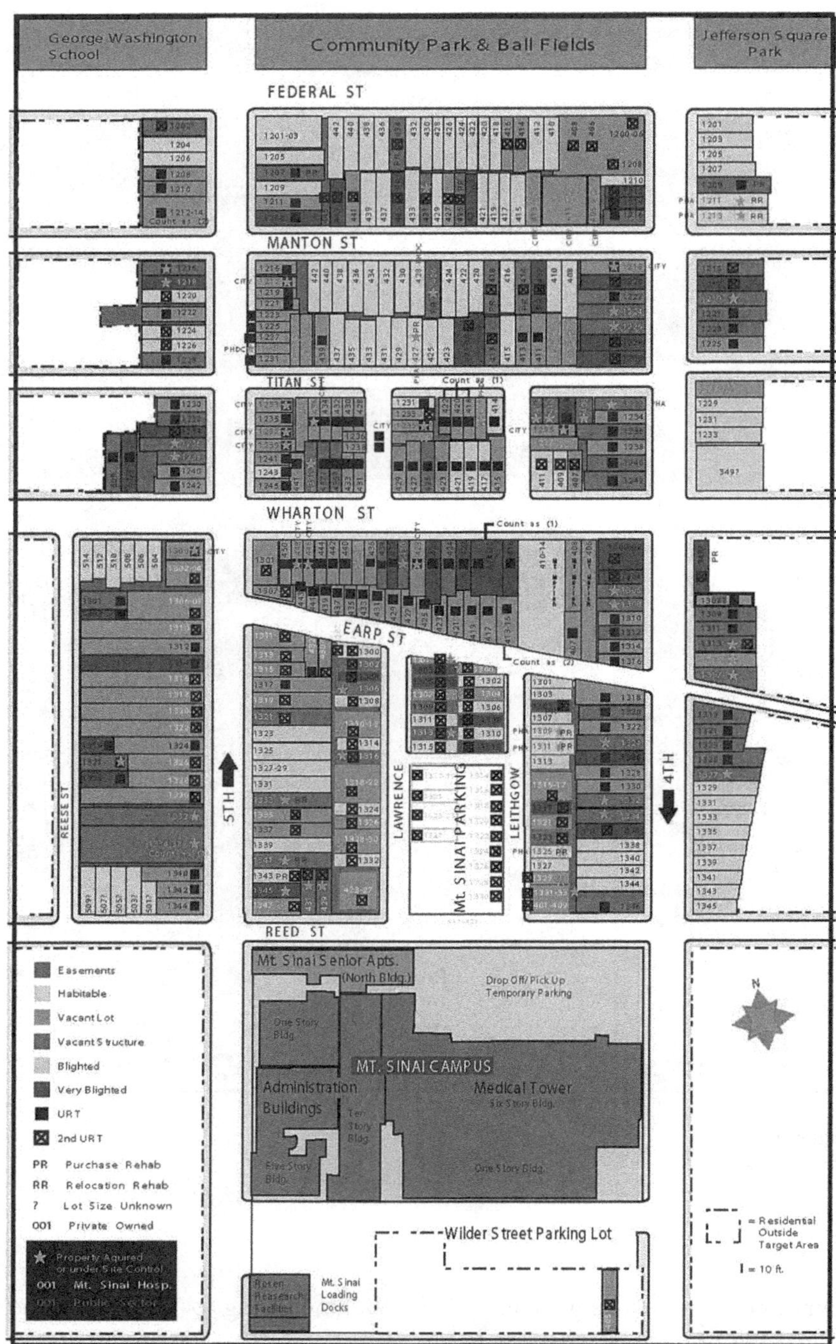

Figure 6.4:
Conditions as Seen by JSCDC Prior to Redevelopment, December 2000
Source: JSCDC

invest in Jefferson Square. Rather than passively accept the neighborhood's decline, they put money, labor, and effort into their individual properties, local churches, and neighborhood recreation programs. And they expected to reap future benefits from these sacrifices.

Some residents invested in their individual properties. Dorothy King and Richard King, Jr., slowly bought properties from many of the people who left the neighborhood, and they either gave the properties to their adult children or kept them to rent out. Dorothy took advantage of "white flight as blacks moved in," according to a community organizer who later worked with her. "Everybody sort of wanted to move to New Jersey.... And so they bought these properties that nobody else wanted."[14] Jefferson Square homeowner Sam Holbrook said that, for decades, he had maintained his own home while watching owners of rentals (where rents were subsidized by government) let their buildings fall into disrepair.[15] Thus, as others had abandoned properties, these residents invested their time and money in them. They kept buildings occupied, and sometimes in good condition, helping themselves and preserving general neighborhood conditions.

Residents often invested in the neighborhood's public spaces as well. They pushed drug-dealers off the streets and took those streets over with their own parties. One neighbor to the redevelopment told me that he and others like him had always made sure that kids did not sell anything on *his* block: "If they wanted to do drugs, they did not do them down here where we could see them."[16] Peggy King Brookins remembered her mother keeping the same kind of watchful eye over her block.[17] As others left, the remaining residents built a sense of community. As noted earlier, the Kings gave their block the nickname of King Street; they told me that others called it by the same name.[18] In addition, they fondly remembered throwing an outside birthday party for Dorothy King every July.[19]

This self-help approach to neighborhood care made sense when government did little. For many years, even decades, residents had witnessed little identifiable government action to stop the neighborhood's decline. They had heard about ideas for government-sponsored improvement, but had rarely, if ever, observed those ideas produce tangible results. Residents did not necessarily think being left to fend for themselves against difficult social, economic, and demographic changes beyond their control was the optimal or even just thing for government to do, but they had gotten used to it.

A resident recalled occasional meetings about ideas for redeveloping the neighborhood as "so preliminary that there was no point of getting terribly excited, until they presented something.... They were talking about this for two decades. You couldn't do anything until they pitched you something real."[20] DiCicco offered a similar account in 1999, remarking, "With all due respect to some of my predecessors, many of them had a plan that never came to fruition for one reason or another."[21]

In the late 1990s, government signaled that it was making a drastic departure from its prior, inattentive approach: Residents received a warning that government was going to force them out. According to many residents, the orange signs posted on the front door of JoAnn King's house and other properties on January 31, 1998—declaring the buildings dangerous, condemned, and uninhabitable—marked the beginning of government's redevelopment effort.[22] They signaled that government was really moving forward with a serious plan and sounded a terrifying alarm. Someone with power in government stood ready to strip them of everything they had given to their homes and neighborhood and their future plans. The meaning of the posters seemed clear: "Get out," a blunt and harsh message that government was pushing people out.[23] Shirley Corbin-Nelson remembered, "The big—you know the big orange signs were placed on doors . . . said they had to move."[24]

To many, the signs seemed a devious attempt to scare residents into running away and to ensure that they demanded nothing in return. Officially, signs from the Philadelphia Department of Licenses and Inspections (L & I) declared buildings dangerous and thus uninhabitable. They made it clear that owners who wanted to keep their houses would be required to spend thousands of dollars on them—a striking rise in the cost of homeownership. Residents interpreted this as a scare tactic: owners were meant to capitulate and sell before government made them pay fines for violations.

Residents knew that someone in government was coming after them, even if they did not know why. Citing building-code violations was not eminent domain, but something more insidious: a well-known strategy to terrify poor people—and most often poor black people—out of an area that others wanted, quietly and without any compensation at all. Residents also knew that L & I typically ignored dangerous and unlawful building conditions. The meting out of building-code violations and dangerous-building designations was not an impersonal, objective bureaucratic process in Philadelphia. It was much more haphazard and reactive to particular requests. Whoever targeted the buildings, they assumed, was trying to get them to leave and was using government force in an underhanded, illegitimate way to do so.

The orange signs suggested that the people who, in contrast to government's inattention, had lavished attention on the place, were going to lose. They suggested that government was ripping the future away from people who were most attached to the place, and who had the greatest expectations of enjoying it in the years to come.

Confusion by Design

The orange signs created deep insecurity. Residents reacted to them with fear and anger, but for the most part initially expressed curiosity. Government had demonstrated a lack of respect for residents' investments by plunging them into confusion about the future of their homes, a primary source of stability. Residents developed a general sense that they were being forced out, but they received little other detailed information about government plans. For over a year, their most consistent reaction to the news of government's plan was to want more information about what to expect.

First, residents asked questions. Peggy King Brookins said that one of her mother's initial responses to the signs was wonderment:

> I remember the day that they came and put the orange stickers on the doors and she [my mother, Dorothy King] went out. After she actually looked out the window and saw the stickers on as far as she could see them, and then *she went out and saw them and started reading them and wondered what was going on*. [Emphasis added.]
>
> Peggy King Brookins, family member of condemnees[25]

Church and settlement house leaders remembered the phone calls from people wanting to know what these signs were all about. What did it mean to find a notice on your door saying no one can live there? What was going to happen? Were the bulldozers coming right away? Who was trying to get them out? Why did this only happen on a few blocks and to some buildings, not others?[26] Johanna Bauman recalled:

> One young woman... called me up one day and told me that her mother had come home from shopping and there was a big orange sign on her door saying "keep out," and can I please come and help her figure out what's going on.... Another woman... called me up, and she had come downstairs and found somebody had put a big orange poster on her door saying "keep out."
>
> Johanna Bauman, United Communities Southeast Philadelphia Community Organizer[27]

It took much more than a few telephone calls to find out what the government had planned, where and when those plans were to be implemented, and by and for whom they had been created. For quite a long time, residents could squeeze very little information from government officials.

Residents persisted, and turned to whomever they could think of to find out about government's plans and who was behind them. For example, Johanna Bauman, quoted above, said that the first thing she did for residents was to call L & I and demand answers to their questions. But no one at L & I would say why those particular signs had been posted. When residents finally lured the L & I commissioner to a meeting, she mostly focused on what the signs meant procedurally.

The commissioner apologized for mistakenly having posted signs only meant for vacant buildings on occupied homes. Her inspectors reportedly thought all of the buildings on which they posted signs were vacant. She did not, as residents wanted her to, talk about the larger changes to the neighborhood behind the sudden attention to these buildings. No matter how many times she was asked, the L & I commissioner would not explain the details behind why specific houses were being condemned at this specific time.[28]

Eventually, DiCicco was revealed as the power behind the plans, and residents learned of the plans' official name, the "Jefferson Square Community Revitalization Plan." This new knowledge gave them a target for their questions, but not necessarily answers. When they finally did get answers, they were not the answers they wanted to hear.

One of the crucial pieces of information that residents demanded, but could not get, was about how the displaced would be treated. At one of the first public hearings on the issue, residents and their allies showed up in large numbers. They insisted on knowing who was being displaced and how they would be cared for. They wanted answers about compensation and relocation for individual people in the footprint of the plan, whose investments seemed in the greatest danger. Noel Eisenstat, the executive director of the RDA, and DiCicco continued to frustrate residents by evading specific answers to their questions.[29]

Although the general statements that residents heard early on about caring for relocated residents were unobjectionable, the lack of detail was extremely disconcerting and led residents to believe that their losses would not be compensated in any meaningful way. It seemed that there were plans for displacement and vague recognition of needs for relocation assistance but no specific arrangements for assisting the displaced. The dearth of detailed information about relocations left residents to conclude that government was not giving their individual investments the consideration they deserved.

Residents also asked about the planned community-level improvements that officials thought justified the dislocations. Until they saw the designs, residents could not evaluate whether they would consider the proposed changes improvements at all or whether benefits would accrue to those with investments. When residents finally learned the basic elements in the redesign of their neighborhoods, they did not see much to like (see Figure 6.5).

"Someone Has to Hurt"

Residents vehemently rejected government's vision for an expanded hospital parking lot on the exact spot where occupied houses then stood. They also became outraged at the idea for housing to attract new, middle-class residents to the neighborhood. Given these designs, the planned beneficiaries, at best, had not invested in the place themselves; at worst, they had contributed to the area's decline.

The government planned community-level benefits for the non-invested rather than the invested. Residents discerned that not only were those who had given so much to the place to be "wiped out," but the benefits were meant for an entirely different class of people. Residents heard DiCicco say that they had to move out because people with more money were going to move in. At a City Council meeting, Dorothy King protested that the latter group consisted of the same people who had cut ties to the neighborhood years earlier:

> Years ago people moved out of this vicinity. It wasn't good enough for them to live in. They moved out, to Strawberry Mansion, the suburbs. Those big houses out there, they're tired of them, and they want to come back in the neighborhood.... They feel it's getting too convenient for black people. They want to move back now.... [We] have the movies down there for our kids three blocks away. It's too convenient for us now. *But we lived through the bad part. We want to live through the good part.* [Emphasis added.]
>
> Dorothy King, Condemnee[30]

In contrast to the people who left the neighborhood to enjoy the suburbs, she said, to the public listening at City Council chambers, those who had sacrificed so much to remain attached to the neighborhood were the ones who deserved to benefit from any government action. A neighbor similarly

G. WASHINGTON SCHOOL
5TH STR
COMMUNITY PARK & BALL FIELDS
JEFFERSON SQUARE
FEDERAL STREET
APTS
REMAIN
EXIST. ALLEY
MANTON STREET
ONE WAY
TITAN STREET
WHARTON STREET
CHURCH
REESE STREET
5TH STREET
4TH STREET
MT. SINAI HOSPITAL
PARKING SPACES = 144
REED STREET
MT. SINAI APARTMENTS FOR SENIORS
MEDICAL TOWER
MT. SINAI HOSPITAL

accused the government of destroying what residents had built to benefit an outsider, a private developer with "no history in South Philly" to "make a better profit," a developer who did not care about what would be destroyed.[31] Or even more bluntly, a commercial property owner charged, "This is not a plan that you want to rehab the neighborhood. It's a land grab. Someone gets money out of the deal."[32] Though government handing out benefits to outsiders was incendiary enough, there were more offensive signals about the redesign to come.

It seemed that on a few blocks, practically no benefit would come at all. A parking lot could not possibly offer a community more value than the homes it would replace. Thus, residents saw an even deeper disrespect for their investments than in the plan for higher-class housing. When residents learned that a parking lot was slated for the block that some called King Street, they were enraged.[33] Mary Black, another of JoAnn's sisters with a house in the target area, told a news reporter, "I just can't see how I would have to leave to make room for parking."[34] The idea that their homes were being sacrificed for a parking lot clearly suggested that officials did not respect their homes and community as valuable—it seemed that government valued pavement more than homes. Jeremey Newberg, hired initially by DiCicco and State Senator Vince Fumo to manage planning and development for the revitalization plan, told me after it was all over:

> At first, we really screwed up, because we proposed just wiping out [the area] between Fourth and Reed... essentially... to make additional parking for the hospital, thinking that we could get another operator for the hospital. That was the dumbest decision I ever made in my life, and I got skewered!... It wasn't going to work in the community.
>
> Jeremey Newberg, Capital Access President, Jefferson Square Project Manager[35]

PROPERTY LEGEND		
192 HOME OWNERSHIP UNITS (INCLUDING EXIST. HOUSING)		TOTAL
RH (MN)-	CANDIDATES FOR RESIDENTIAL REHAB PRELIMINARY ESTIMATE	96
TW -	NEW TWIN UNIT (COUNTED PER RESIDENCE)	76
ROW -	NEW ROWHOME ADD-ON	1

Figure 6.5:
Early Design for Jefferson Square (Scheme 8, May 1999)
Source: Kramer+Marks Architects

If there was any benefit to the parking lot, new owners of the defunct hospital building would reap the rewards. The hospital's owners had initiated the neighborhood planning years earlier and were involved in the design for the parking lot. But Mount Sinai's new owner, Allegheny Health, Education and Research Foundation (AHERF), closed the hospital's doors in October 1997 before filing for bankruptcy in July 1998.[36] Allegheny had two prospective buyers for the Mount Sinai properties, but neither their purchase of nor their plans for the complex were certain. As residents looked at the parking lot on the plan, they knew that the hospital was not operating, and despite DiCicco's and Newberg's claims that any company interested in occupying the hospital buildings would demand such parking space, no one knew if anyone would actually open the hospital again. Parking, therefore, was only an imaginary necessity for a business that did not exist.

Moreover, after doing some careful research, residents learned that the hospital that had once anchored the neighborhood with employment had also severely, if unintentionally, contributed to its more recent decline. Over the years, it had bought forty-five surrounding land parcels, with the intention of developing them. Instead, it demolished dilapidated buildings, left the land empty and the remaining buildings vacant, and held onto the land while waiting to redevelop. By the late 1990s, the hospital was the largest landowner (beyond its own campus) and the most significant contributor to the blight that justified redevelopment. If the parking lot provided any benefit at all, giving the owners of the hospital (even new ones) such an improvement would reward the institution for damaging the neighborhood.

In the face of this devastating proposal to wipe out their investments in favor of higher-class housing and a parking lot, residents easily concluded that government neglect would be preferable to government intervention, and they fought for government to go away. At the first City Council hearing on the plan, populist-leaning City Councilperson David Cohen spoke four times of how he disapproved of "uprooting people from their homes" and received applause each time. At one point, he said, "To uproot people out of their homes to provide a parking space—[*Applause*] is something I think people ought to go back to the drawing board [to change]."[37]

Residents complained that DiCicco would not listen when they told him that his design was untenable. Dorothy King told City Council:

> Our Councilman Frank DiCicco... said that they was going to build townhouses where our houses [are]. He told me to my face, he said, "Mrs. King, Leithgow Street and Lawrence Street is completely out." Leithgow Street is where I lived forty years. He said people come into the neighborhood with money and he said that they wanted grass for the kids to play. I said, "Councilman DiCicco, what about my

kids who was born and grandkids who was born and raised in the street?" He said, "Mrs. King, Someone has to hurt." That's what he said, "Someone has to hurt."

Dorothy King, Condemnee[38]

After hearing DiCicco's a position that "someone has to hurt"—and knowing that the "someone" was her family—Dorothy King fought DiCicco, to keep his vision from making any progress.

A COUNCILMAN'S VISION OF GOVERNMENT-ASSISTED REVITALIZATION

When DiCicco was first elected in 1995, he hoped to improve struggling neighborhoods in his South Philadelphia district, including Jefferson Square, an area he designated and named after Jefferson Square Park. During his first years in office, he quickly made progress on significantly detailed plans for this neighborhood. DiCicco convened numerous public meetings, formed an advisory group of mostly professionals, and created a new nonprofit, the Jefferson Square Community Development Corporation (JSCDC), to advocate for and carry out the plans.[39] He used his connection with State Senator Vincent Fumo, who had helped him get elected, to develop the plans[40] and to secure funds for redevelopment. By the time the project was complete, Senator Fumo had drawn down $1.5 million dollars from the state for it (although Fumo's largess looked especially suspicious afterward, when he was sent to prison in 2009 for convictions on 137 counts of corruption).[41]

In 1999, when DiCicco presented his plan for approval by the full City Council so that eminent domain could be used to support it, he pronounced that "[t]his was my plan. This was part of my vision. So I take full responsibility."[42] To be sure, Mount Sinai Hospital had called leaders together to plan for redevelopment before DiCicco was elected.[43] But when the company that owned the hospital declared bankruptcy and closed the hospital's doors, DiCicco strengthened his own resolve to pursue change and took over. Mount Sinai's closure, he said, left him "two battles to fight": the rehabilitation of homes and the vacancy of the hospital facility.[44]

DiCicco's vision diverged dramatically from residents' hands-off view of government; it involved a strong and active government hand in neighborhood change. DiCicco defended his vision with similar broad principles, appealing to the idea that his plan would respect investments in the neighborhood. Although many residents disagreed, from DiCicco's point of view, the neighborhood's redesign would benefit precisely those who had poured value into it.

Benefits for the Invested

The councilman claimed that his plans responded to constituent demands for government to reverse the neighborhood's decline. Existing and former residents had been saddened to watch the neighborhood go "down and down and down."[45] Residents and businesses in the area had continued to invest their time, money, and more to the area, and DiCicco believed that his involvement would support their efforts. The fact that attempts to get government involved in the neighborhood's transformation actually began before DiCicco came to office in 1996 supported this view. Managers of Mount Sinai Hospital had invited city officials to help them stop the deterioration in their vicinity. They thought that the neighborhood had started to deter patients and visitors and, thus, hurt their business. Fred Druding, Sr., executive director of the nearby Weccacoe Development Association, attended early meetings about the issue and told me that Mount Sinai administrators "knew in order for them to survive they had to do something about the surrounding area because people don't want to go there."[46]

The hospital owners, later joined by DiCicco, targeted a specific five-block area that they viewed as the most problematic pocket in a larger area of better conditions. The first written report said that this area had "the highest concentrations of vacant lots and blighted structures and general devastation."[47] Plans drafted in 1997 designated an area for redevelopment where over half of the properties were already vacant.[48] According to these early counts, Jefferson Square would fully redevelop 266 properties, 111 of which were occupied (155 were vacant lots or structures) and renovate approximately another forty occupied and ten vacant structures.[49] DiCicco could have thought that he was responding to demands from within the neighborhood. For example, a woman who moved across the street from the area in the 1990s recalled what it looked like to her: "There were these very large houses that were basically derelict. I think one of them had people living in it. And they had garages on our street which were mainly breeding places for cats."[50]

DiCicco and other supporters defended their bold plan by saying that they could make redevelopment happen where others had failed. They argued that their plan might actually materialize, precisely because it was bold. Jeremey Newberg wrote in a 1997 memo that the design was "ambitious and costly because it proposes the transformation of a neighborhood."[51] Newberg emphasized that the plans—unlike either unsuccessful private efforts or plans from officials and community leaders that people had watched "collect dust"—offered a uniquely dramatic redesign and an unusual combination of public and private-sector resources. Even the hospital owners with whom DiCicco collaborated had drawn up their own plans and had bought forty-five land parcels to redevelop, but had only left the area with more, instead of less, vacant land.[52] Supporters of DiCicco's plan adamantly denied that they hoped to achieve this success with and for outsiders; instead, they said the neighborhood's transformation would benefit, first and foremost, the people who had invested in the neighborhood only to be disappointed by its deterioration.

DiCicco, in fact, had personally requested that the city post those orange condemnation signs, and he had thought that doing so would respect individual investments. He had intended the notices to help, rather than hurt, existing residents. Residents were right to think that government officials were trying to scare owners into selling, but they were wrong about which kinds of owners the officials were trying to scare. DiCicco intended the posters to frighten speculators into selling cheaply, before they got word of any redevelopment plans. The signs were supposed to frighten only the absentee owners who let their buildings fall apart and lie vacant. Rather than alarm residents, he wanted to use government power to rid the neighborhood of vultures who preyed on the them. Residents' confusion, he might have argued, arose from government's mistake in distinguishing speculators from residents. These signs are not typically used on occupied buildings. The signs intended for vacant buildings mistakenly went up on occupied homes, including the home of JoAnn King. Indeed, it is often hard for officials to tell whether buildings are occupied, especially when people are living without utilities. To be sure, the Kings do not believe that anyone could have thought that JoAnn's house was vacant; it did not have that appearance, and the utilities were on, they said.[53] But even if the L & I inspectors knew the houses to be occupied, DiCicco might still have approved the postings because he thought the owners were absentee landlords.

The more complete official strategy for land acquisition reserved harsh tactics like the orange signs for speculators, who bought property but otherwise refused to lift a finger or spend a dime to care for it. If the signs had worked as DiCicco intended, they would have treated people precisely according to what they had invested in their properties, by holding those who treated the property as a simple contract, for which they paid a market price and abided by the written rules, as just that kind of owner. By enforcing building codes with speculators, government could hold them accountable to the law and prevent them from getting more than the market value of the property. The signs were one of many coercive tactics reserved for the least invested owners. The power brokers readily admitted that they were trying to push people out, but they argued that the owners they were pushing to sell would lose nothing that they deserved by doing so.[54]

As they planned to acquire properties for the redevelopment, DiCicco and others devised different strategies for different kinds of owners, distinguishing between those who were more or less invested in the neighborhood and treating them accordingly. Everyone would be asked to sell, but government would treat the unwilling in different ways. Owners of multiple, vacant, or rental properties, as well as short-term speculators, warranted different carrots and sticks from government. Most important, coercive tactics—increased building-code and tax enforcement—were reserved for these kinds of owners (although the revitalization plan mentioned eminent domain as a last resort for all owners).[55] Thus, from the beginning, officials intended to make sure that speculators, slumlords, and primarily financial investors in particular got no more than the money they had put into their properties. They intended to treat caring homeowners—who had invested more than the money to buy the properties—more gingerly.

DiCicco's early plans stated clearly that residents and business owners, with more invested than absentee owners, would receive more resources and more careful treatment. Whereas officials planned to use primarily coercive tactics to pressure absentee owners into selling, they planned to offer homeowners and business owners benefits or incentives instead. Officials intended to present homeowners and business owners with inducements such as relief from property taxes and tax liens. Residents who chose to remain in the area directly surrounding the new development would be offered services to improve their houses, including substantial rehabilitation. Government would give those threatened with displacement—those with houses in the footprint of planned redevelopment—opportunities to buy new homes at discounted prices, and they would receive relocation assistance. One of the first drafts of the official plan even mentioned how careful the people managing the redevelopment would need to be with any residential relocation:

> The JSP [Jefferson Square Plan] Management Team is very aware of the fact that many people who have remained in the neighborhood are long time residents who are wary of any project proposals that have any similarity to 'Urban Renewal' efforts of two decades past. Special effort and sensitivity will be given to understanding and meeting the needs of this group of residents.
>
> *Jefferson Square Master Plan Phase I—DRAFT*, February 1997[56]

The plan also said that the owners of houses in the area slated for demolition and rebuilding would be "offered a fair market sale price and/or re-location services, as well as first right to purchase one of the new houses developed."[57]

Despite his apparent intentions to respect residents' investments, DiCicco grossly underestimated how invested many residents were. He unabashedly talked about how there was a lot of cleaning up for government to do. DiCicco and others supporting the revitalization plan were ready, even eager, to rid the neighborhood of owners who let their buildings fall into disrepair and remain vacant, and many residents would have supported such a change. But DiCicco inadvertently lumped many of the caring residents in with others he might have more pejoratively labeled as slumlords and drug users. As one of the community organizers who worked closely with residents remembers it, DiCicco first advertised his vision with statements that went something like, "'This is a lousy neighborhood. There's drugs. It's a mess. Houses are falling down. It's at the edge of Center City. I can turn this neighborhood around. I can attract in investors. I can make this a nice neighborhood.'"[58]

In a crucial misreading, DiCicco thought, from what he could see on paper and by driving down the block, that the Kings would not be very attached to their properties. DiCicco seems to have assumed, at first, that the Kings were absentee owners. In the first Master Plan, the "Acquisition Strategy" lists "Anna, Dorothy, Joan, or Richard King" as a "small investor" with seven properties—more than any of the six other owners who were listed this way, to be treated similarly.[59] As an outsider with little knowledge or understanding of the people living in the neighborhood that he planned to redevelop, DiCicco interpreted the names on paper and the poor conditions of the housing as signs that owners did not care and were not committed to their houses and neighborhood.[60]

Worse yet, DiCicco was using redevelopment to rid the neighborhood of drugs, and he did not necessarily identify the right houses or families as the ones supporting the drug trade. When I asked Fred Druding, Sr., who had helped with redevelopment planning in the mid-1990s, what issues were involved, he responded,

> ... Probably the same issues that remained for Jeremey [Newberg] ... [including] a lot of drug activity in that area at that time. Some of the people were against the plan because we were disrupting their business.... They came to meetings and they would just object to things.... They try to disrupt details of any plan or they could delay it.... Basically, it was ... two key families and they own several properties also in the area at that time. So they would want more money for their homes and issues like that.
>
> Fred Druding, Sr., Weccacoe Development Association Director[61]

Johanna Bauman, the community organizer who worked with residents, told me that she thought DiCicco had wrongly assumed that at least one woman was a "drug kingpin" and thus treated her without the respect an older woman in her home deserved.[62] Indeed, in the formal plan he submitted to City Council in 1999, DiCicco justified his renewal plan, in part, by the area's "pervasive drug activity," and it is quite likely that he did not know exactly who was responsible for it.[63]

DiCicco told me that he was wrongly accused of believing, as a white, middle-class Italian, that all the neighborhood's mostly poor, black residents were dispensable. He said later that residents' early impression of him as simply pushing out poor black people was mistaken. "I think I was being looked at as someone who had no regard for the people who were living there who happened to be black, and I was the white guy who was going to gentrify the neighborhood," he said. DiCicco denied the accusation that he had implicated everyone in the area with the drugs and the dilapidated housing. He said that, yes, he knew that there was a drug problem, and he wanted to respond to requests from some residents for help in stopping it, but he does not think he ever said that everyone there was involved in it. He emphasized instead that he was trying to rescue the neighborhood for the residents who had tried their best to be stewards.[64]

Despite general statements that they would treat displaced residents carefully and considerately, officials failed to provide more detailed accounting of how this would happen.[65] Perhaps they were foolishly optimistic to believe that most residents would want to leave if given the resources to do so. Officials' hopefulness about the extent of voluntary participation may have allowed them to overlook how they barely addressed the costs of relocation in the project budget.[66] Someone at the RDA noticed the oversight and scrawled questions beside the statement about relocation costs not being included in the budget: "Approximate #? Residential? Commercial?"[67] Thus, at first DiCicco and his allies planned to respect the individual investments of homeowners, but only in the abstract. Indeed, one of the JSCDC Board members offered this vocal support at the earliest City Council meeting on the topic: "As long as a comprehensive relocation package is made available . . . , the [JS]CDC will have gone a long way in minimizing the impact of the plan . . . . If the plan includes a comprehensive relocation package, . . . then the result would be win-win."[68] Project boosters did not know or would not admit that their failure to conduct careful planning would seriously challenge the trustworthiness of their more general statements of protection for displaced residents.

Councilman DiCicco expected the primary beneficiaries of government's intervention to be people invested in the neighborhood: those who lived and worked on properties directly adjacent to the proposed redevelopment.

Figure 6.6:
428–432 Earp Street, Vacant Lots (Foreground) Taken for Jefferson Square
Source: JSCDC (circa 2000)

Like other proponents of anti-blight programs, DiCicco argued that his actions were meant to prevent harm to bordering areas with social, economic, and physical problems. If intervention can stem decline in the most problematic areas, the argument went, benefits will accrue to those neighbors who otherwise would watch helplessly as conditions worsen around them (see Figures 6.6–6.8). At the first City Council hearing on the Jefferson Square plans, DiCicco said:

> When I was campaigning, . . . I spoke to . . . my concern for blighted areas . . . on the fringe of or within stable communities, communities that had been maintained, homes that have been occupied by families for three, four generations. . . . My concern was that something needed to be done before this blight would continue any further.
>
> Frank DiCicco, First District City Councilperson[69]

One of the first written plans defended the attempt to turn the neighborhood around for the existing residents who cared. It mentioned demands made by locals at a 1996 community meeting: homeownership development, vacant-lot cleanup, building on community diversity, and housing for a range of incomes.[70] Indeed, those driving the redevelopment had invested a great deal in the neighborhood themselves and stood to benefit. Mount Sinai Hospital, which first convened meetings, had been operating for decades and employing neighbors for generations. DiCicco himself had

Figure 6.7:
1306 S. Leithgow Street, House of Shirley Corbin-Nelson, right; House of JoAnn King, left. Taken. Both Relocated to New Jefferson Square Houses.
Source: JSCDC (circa 2000)

grown up in the neighborhood and had recently bought a house six blocks away,[71] so his personal history and attachment to the neighborhood motivated his concern for its future. "I'm familiar with what this neighborhood was, what it is, and I have a vision for what I'd like to see it become in the future," he said at a City Council meeting.[72] Similarly, Fred Druding, Sr., who helped draw up the plans, felt a strong attachment to the project because he had grown up in a house in the center of the target area. Thus, the improvements were intended, DiCicco insisted, to benefit many of the very people who had given so much to the neighborhood in the past and intended to stay there into the future.

To be sure, DiCicco and his allies considered their boldest move to be the design for market-rate housing to sell to middle-income homebuyers. Like previous visions for redevelopment,[73] DiCicco's vision included the construction of new homes, the rehabilitation of old ones (approximately seventy-four new and twenty-six rehabilitated houses), and require some

Figure 6.8:
1302 and 1304 S. Lawrence Street, Owned by Mount Sinai, Taken for Jefferson Square, Vacant on Right, Tenant Occupied on Left
Source: JSCDC (circa 2000)

demolition and relocation. On about half of the area targeted, however, instead of new row-houses to mirror the building type already dominating the city's landscape, a development of lower-density twin houses (two houses sharing a single wall) that had side yards, backyards, and driveways would be constructed. DiCicco and his project manager Jeremey Newberg believed that this kind of structure would attract first-time and "move-up" homebuyers with low and moderate incomes who preferred South Philadelphia but could not find housing there that suited them. According to Druding, Sr., this vision departed from the initial vision of a row-home development discussed at the earlier hospital meetings because DiCicco and Newberg learned that interested buyers "wanted something with a little bit of ground. They didn't want to have just that front door and concrete pavements in front of them."[74] At first, the proposed houses had an anticipated sale price of $70,000 to $89,000, and they were expected to sell to families with incomes between $25,000 and $60,000. The new houses were concentrated in a three-by-three block square bounded by Federal and Reed Streets, and Fourth and Seventh Streets; the area outside those boundaries would see rehabilitation of existing rental and owner-occupied units.[75]

DiCicco believed that attracting outsiders—middle-class homebuyers—was necessary to make change possible. He said that he did not expect to hand out government resources to outsiders; unless they received subsidies for housing because of their low income, newcomers would pay market price for their housing. In the early plan document, Newberg and DiCicco proclaimed:

> The Plan is a departure from typical housing programs where government subsidies are targeted to households earning low- and very low-income. The Jefferson Square Plan is a mixed-income project designed to serve households who have the financial means to live somewhere else but will choose Jefferson Square out of preference rather than only financial need.
>
> *Jefferson Square Master Plan Status Report*, June 4, 1997[76]

Testifying to City Council, Newberg defended a mixed-income housing plan against claims that they were pushing out the poor, saying:

> We're not about a gentrification project; we're about a revitalization project. But to do this you need to avoid reproducing housing that exclusively serves very low income people. We are not doing "either or." We are doing "and both."
>
> Jeremey Newberg, Capital Access President, Jefferson Square Project Manager[77]

DiCicco said at the Council meeting that his invitation to outsiders to join the neighborhood was a necessary element of any plan that would be successful. By settling there, higher income homeowners would give benefits to the already invested, not the other way around. He was inviting outsiders in, only to the extent that they could help the place for insiders, the people who already lived and worked there. The neighborhood, he thought, needed more people to care about it and to bring their money into it.

At the same public forum, a resident serving on the JSCDC Board, emphasized a need for someone to use the hospital grounds behind his house:

> I am alarmed at what may be perceived as a project aimed at kicking out poor and defenseless, often minority, families to create housing that they cannot afford. My position is, who can afford to continue with the conditions as they are? I find it disturbing that these are conditions, at least during the twelve years I've lived in them, which have gone unchallenged for generations. Where is the chorus of concerned parties when drug deals are open air and permitted round the clock?

There are in fact neighbors who feel imprisoned inside their own homes, afraid to enter and leave because they know that saying anything or doing anything to end these decrepit conditions would be dangerous.

Kirk Brown, JSCDC Board member and neighbor[78]

Responding to Diverse Perspectives on Community Improvement

DiCicco defended his plan as having incorporated requests voiced by residents. From the beginning of his involvement, he claimed, he had opened dialogue and had done his best to make the design respond to community concerns. Many neighborhood members, he said, shared his vision for the neighborhood's redevelopment. Like Kirk Brown, other residents and community leaders spoke out publicly in favor of DiCicco's efforts. Most prominent was the Reverend Carl Fitchett, who had been the preacher at Mount Moriah Temple Baptist Church for nineteen years. The church was in the redevelopment area, although the plans did not call for it to be torn down. A 1998 newspaper article quoted him as supporting the project: "I've seen the plan, and I can see how it can really, thoroughly upgrade the neighborhood without really damaging the neighborhood. We need those townhouses he's talking about.... You maintain the community as it is to a degree, and you add on affordable housing, a tax base, a viability."[79]

These public statements of approval from residents and community leaders supported DiCicco's claim that he had developed a plan that at least some existing community members judged legitimate and desirable. Moreover, DiCicco denied claims that he had operated in a secretive manner. He pointed out that he had consistently held open meetings in the neighborhood to discuss redevelopment plans. The 1997 planning document mentioned resident requests made at such a meeting: to increase homeownership rather than rental opportunities, clean up vacant lots, build on community diversity, provide housing for people with a range of incomes.[80] Although the article in the *Philadelphia Inquirer* appeared after conflict had erupted, the news that there was a plan in the works had been public much earlier. Despite complaints that DiCicco had conceived the plan in secrecy, he and Newberg had held a community meeting about the plan in September 1996 that had been advertised by about 800 flyers and attended by fifty-seven people.[81] A community newspaper covered the story after a 1996 meeting—well before the condemnation signs on front doors alarmed residents—and described planning of

> an ambitious, long-range revitalization of the neighborhood.... What role should a hospital play in a community, aside from providing medical care? The leaders of Mt. Sinai Hospital, Fourth and Reed Streets, and the surrounding Greenwich Square community intend to hammer out an answer as they begin to plan an ambitious, long-range revitalization of the neighborhood they share.... All parties met last week with Mayor Rendell, who has expressed great interest and willingness to help. But the key to getting the plan rolling and to seeing it through to the end will be the support of Mt. Sinai Hospital, the largest employer and property owner in the area, community leaders say.... The South Fifth Street Renaissance Project will focus on housing and neighborhood beautification.
>
> Frank Lewis, *South Philadelphia Review*, 1996[82]

Residents may not have heard of this or other meetings, but even if they had, they would no doubt be reluctant to later admit it, for this admission would lessen their credibility when they claimed to be stunned by the blunt, harsh signs of the plan moving forward. However, they also could have known about government's long-range planning and still have been unconcerned, until they saw the drastic signal that something was really happening.

DiCicco suggested that any appearance of lack of concern for resident views resulted from residents' difficulties conveying a unified voice. He expressed frustration in his attempts to respond to diverse resident views about what should happen in the neighborhood. To be sure, from some residents, he had heard that his design to remove homeowners to put up a parking lot was fatally flawed and that he should abandon it. From other residents and leaders, he had heard that his vision was sound. The community organizer who came to assist residents who wanted to stay affirmed the wide diversity of reactions to DiCicco's plans. She remembered:

> You had the whole spectrum. I mean some people were [saying], "I just want to get out of here and be able to sell my house for a whole lot of money so I can go to New Jersey," [while others said,] "I just want them to go away and leave us alone."
>
> Johanna Bauman, United Communities of Southeast Philadelphia Community Organizer[83]

In response to a question posed at a City Council hearing by a representative of the St. John's Leadership Team (a resident group that Bauman helped form, discussed in Chapter 7), DiCicco said:

> One of the problems I've experienced is that there were no groups of people that came on [to] speak for the... people in the community. I really need to get a better understanding of who is really speaking for them, because when we do individual discussions, we are then accused of undermining community by pitting one neighbor against the other.... It would be helpful to me to know who it is we should speak to when we have these discussions rather than have four or five different discussions and everybody all over the place and I get accused of not giving enough information out, which I've been accused of for the last two years. You have to come together.... Make some decisions.... Who you want to speak for you?
>
> Frank DiCicco, First District City Councilperson[84]

DiCicco thus complained that there was no official neighborhood-based organization. He suggested that with so many different ideas about what should happen, it was impossible to come to any agreement about what people desired and deserved. A lack of neighborhood organization and a cacophony of voices on how to proceed stymied his efforts to make government responsive.

CONCLUSION

In the late 1990s, DiCicco and his allies developed an optimistic vision for Jefferson Square's transformation that they thought would benefit those who had invested there. To redevelop the area, they would need to encourage the departure of residents who did not have a strong desire to stay. The plan's supporters also would strip slumlords and speculators—owners who had extracted value from, rather than invested in, the neighborhood—of properties they would rather hold on to, although these owners would receive compensation for their financial losses. The orange signs condemning dangerous buildings would push out speculators and slumlords at reasonable prices. Committed renters, homeowners, and more caring investors would be approached about selling voluntarily, and if they needed to be forced out, they would receive more generous compensation and relocation assistance.

While caring adequately for those who lost property, the redevelopment would benefit neighbors by bringing physical improvements and new, caring owners. Newly constructed homes with yards and garages would attract homebuyers. The proceeds and other financing would subsidize purchases and rehabilitations for lower income families. As a result, those attached to the neighborhood would benefit. The project boosters imagined this as a neighborhood redevelopment that protected investments and, thus, as an appropriate government undertaking.

When residents learned that the impending redevelopment was going to sweep them and everything they had invested away, many demanded that government take its plans elsewhere. They argued publicly and loudly that government should keep its hands off what they had so carefully created and cherished. Over many decades, as government had largely sat still, they had given their time, emotions, labor, and tolerance to a neighborhood that had deteriorated around them. Government inaction would not necessarily have been their first choice, but they had come to expect it and learned to manage their properties in its absence. Once they felt attacked, their tacit acceptance of government absence turned to vehement insistence upon it. A group of residents who wanted to stay developed a strong vision about what government should do: get out and stay out. Over just a few years, government officials and long-term residents had developed entirely different views of the right thing for government to do, although both understood their visions as appropriately protecting investments.

Once the revitalization hit the neighborhood grapevine and local news as a government takeover, it rested on the illegitimacy side of the boundary line. To observers, this looked like a classic, compelling case of a government abrogating its duties, and the opponents of the project publicized the signs of its illegitimacy. Government was going to strip people of houses and a neighborhood they had lived in for decades. The victims were poor, African American, and relatively powerless people with a history of being pushed out of neighborhoods that wealthier white people began to find desirable. Indeed, the development of market-rate housing would hand over the land to people who could afford to buy it, and none of the people who already lived in the neighborhood had that kind of money.

Although DiCicco and others wielded the political and financial power needed to move forward with the project as planned, they would not have won a battle for public approval. Few would have predicted what actually happened instead.

This project soon overcame the challenges to its legitimacy. In just a few more years, the Jefferson Square project won approval from many, including those who had most vociferously attacked it. In the next chapter, I describe how this improbable turnaround happened.

CHAPTER 7

Jefferson Square II

Legitimacy Through Reconciled Visions

The outcome of the Jefferson Square project demonstrates how an eminent domain case that began on the legitimacy boundary line can gain a firm footing on the legitimacy side of that line. In the last chapter, we saw that the project's advocates and opponents initially held vastly differing opinions about how it would affect investments. DiCicco thought that his bold revitalization plan protected investments, but to many residents, being pushed out of the neighborhood for middle-class outsiders and for the half-vacant, bankrupt hospital complex to have a larger parking lot showed their investments no respect at all. In 1999, residents told a compelling story of underhanded moves to push them out for a pittance. On the land where their houses once stood, wealthy outsiders would buy new houses. And worse, an asphalt parking lot would become their only memorial.

This chapter explains how Jefferson Square's revitalization transformed from a plan evoking cries of government abuse to an accomplishment hailed as a symbol of good government. Political power on both sides of the issue forced them to collaborate on a creative and reconciled vision for investment protection. Impressive financial and administrative resources allowed this vision—unlike the original vision for the American Street project—to be implemented successfully.

DiCicco and his resident opponents were compelled to negotiate by one another's political power. The councilman's power drew residents to meet with him when they might otherwise have stayed home, believing that the project was just another planning exercise that would lead to nowhere. For their part, residents fiercely opposed to redevelopment displayed enough political power to force the councilman to listen. Residents were able to assert their opposition to the project by organizing important allies from their families, neighborhoods, and local institutions, and forming the St. John's Leadership Team. DiCicco responded to the residents by opening discussion on key parts of the plans, and residents offered to compromise with him for fear of losing the fight completely.

After fights became negotiations, the sides forged a shared vision of how Jefferson Square would be developed, how the project would be financed, and what would happen to the people who lived there. In fact, before these negotiations began and at the height of the conflict, no one had even proposed the ideas that eventually sealed the compromise. To be sure, this project remained close to the legitimacy boundary. The new plan retained elements to which community members had objected, such as clearing occupied housing and businesses for market-rate housing. However, it also included a generous and secure relocation package and called for housing where the parking lot had been envisioned. Both sides accepted the new plan, with its added provisions for the protection of individual and collective investments, as legitimate.

For government to retain legitimacy for this project, implementation had to reflect what was in the plans, which required impressive resources. Because officials were actually able to secure these resources, their implementation reflected earlier promises, and residents and politicians alike proclaimed a once doomed plan to be a resounding success.

POLITICAL POWER OUTSIDE THE NEGOTIATING ROOM

The signs that had terrified Jefferson Square residents also motivated those residents to actively and energetically oppose the project. These signs were important because they warned of the gravity of what faced them, and they did so relatively early, before City Council had given its legally required approval for the takings. Unlike the letters that galvanized American Street area residents with the mention of $20,000 after the plans had passed City Council, the L & I signs went up before the Jefferson Square plan made it to City Council. In Jefferson Square, therefore, very early in the planning process, the signs sounded an alarm to residents that government-led change was really happening.

The magnitude of DiCicco's and his allies' power further impressed residents and convinced them that if they did not push hard, they would certainly be squashed. Residents realized the need to fight power with power.

They realized that they would have to mobilize themselves, and their allies, to make a difference. Peggy King Brookins recalled:

> They [the people on the JSCDC board] were pretty prominent people. . . . I believe that was when I realized . . . had we not been persistent, they would have been very instrumental in having the project go the way they wanted it to go because they had always been connected politically. . . . I saw who we were dealing with and heard what they were saying, and I then realized that . . . we needed everybody we could get to confront them.
>
> Peggy King Brookins, Co-chair St. John's Team and Family member of Condemnees[1]

Brookins did not assume that DiCicco could carry out his vision alone. But the additional power that he mobilized created reason for worry. If she and her family members did not fight hard and amass some of their own powerful allies to help, they would certainly lose. Thus, the more signals DiCicco sent that he could make his plan reality, the more that residents opposed to his plan felt the necessity to organize themselves.

Residents secured their own powerful allies: professional community organizers and a legal-services attorney. Just before the L & I signs went up, Johanna Bauman of United Communities had been knocking on doors and meeting with local leaders and residents to find out what issues might inspire community organizing. She had been hired by the nearby settlement house to help adapt its programs to the immediate surrounding area.[2] Bauman had thus unwittingly introduced herself to residents as a resource just before the storm. During her effort to learn about community issues, she met another trained organizer, David Funkhouser, who would also become a crucial resource to residents. He was the new pastor at Saint John's Episcopal Church and had been strategizing about how to make his church more relevant to the neighborhood.[3] Bauman and Funkhouser quickly realized that DiCicco's revitalization plan was a perfect opportunity for organizing the neighborhood and that they could help.[4]

Residents opposing the plan recognized the need for expertise. JoAnn's sister Shirley Corbin-Nelson said that people with more education and experience with these kinds of issues knew who to go to and what to do. She remembered, "We did not know what to do. And, you know, with them, they spoke a lot better. They have more education on things like that." Moreover, Bauman and Funkhouser seemed to be the right leaders for them. Shirley said, "For some reason we stayed with St. John's. We had confidence in Johanna and Father David."[5] Soon, they also enlisted the help of Irv Ackelsberg, managing attorney of Community Legal Services of Philadelphia. He agreed to become the group's lawyer and attended countless meetings between DiCicco and residents.

The residents who led the effort to change DiCicco's plans said that they could not speak strongly enough about the importance of those professionals' guidance to the project's turnaround. Shirley remembered, "We wanted to picket. [Jo]hanna said no. That's not the way.... [We were ready] to put our gloves on and fight.... [Jo]hanna said that is not the way you do it."[6] Instead, she said, Bauman encouraged residents to do a lot of "footwork," talking with neighbors, politicians, and other city officials. Bauman set up the meetings, and she and Funkhouser would go along. Bauman recalled, "I think pretty much how to proceed came from me. I think people really had no idea. They enjoyed meeting with figures of authority in the city."[7] Together, they took their case to individual City Council members. June Cairns, Bauman's supervisor at United Communities, said that they tried to help the residents communicate with the politicians: "It was really important for them to be able to tell their story to the council so that the council would understand what we were asking for."[8] They visited a business owner who was interested in the abandoned hospital building and who, they believed, was behind DiCicco's request for a parking lot; Bauman instigated this meeting, too.[9]

Residents also mentioned how important it was to have Ackelsberg on their side as an attorney. Steve Honeyman, to whom Bauman's position as an organizer was connected, brought in Ackelsberg. Ackelsberg thought that residents primarily looked to him to tell them when they could feel comfortable that DiCicco would be accountable for his promises. Indeed, residents hesitated to agree to the compromise plan because it seemed too good to be true. Ackelsberg assured them it was possible and helped to ensure that the major tenets of the plan were mentioned in the City Council bill authorizing eminent domain.[10] To get power, residents thus pursued and found allies with the knowledge and skills to guide their efforts.

Additional personal allies sustained residents. Peggy King Brookins, who became a vocal leader, stayed involved because her family was threatened, even though she had moved to Germantown in North Philadelphia years earlier. Neighbors who did not even know the residents also became involved, first out of empathy for their powerlessness and later because of personal connections. Gina Caruso, the woman who took on a co-leadership role with Brookins, lived near the project but had not known any of the people targeted. Typically, Caruso avoided South Philadelphia politics, which she characterized as usually involving "yelling sessions" about disputes begun long ago. But this time was different. She said:

> I knew who was yelling at whom and why, and it wasn't just the usual screaming.... But this time, people were angry at what was on the table. The anger wasn't going back to Italy or South Carolina. The anger was about what was on the table.
>
> Gina Caruso, St John's Co-chair and Neighbor[11]

Caruso made a point of stopping my interview questions, which she thought were too focused on the political reasons that people were involved. She wanted me to understand that she and others stayed with the process because they had developed friendships. Other people talked about similar motivations. Kathy Furber, one of the less publicly visible yet crucial participants, had moved to the neighborhood only recently and came to the church and the organizing effort because she did not know many neighbors and wanted to feel connected.[12] Residents also spoke of the attachments they forged with allies as deeply personal, even familial. Dorothy King said in her testimony to City Council:

> We didn't know which way to turn. And if it wasn't for St. John's Leadership Team, I don't know where we would have been today. [*Applause*] They helped us. For what they've done, I can't explain. We didn't know where to turn. They came to us like a family.
>
> Dorothy King, Condemnee[13]

This collection of allies developed political power by coalescing as a single entity with a unified voice. They called their group the St. John's Leadership Team, after the church where they met and whose pastor offered guidance, and they claimed to represent residents who wanted to stay. To be sure, developing any kind of new vision across this diverse spectrum of interested parties would be extremely challenging. Even the people who wanted to stay in the neighborhood did not necessarily talk to one another, much less agree on what alternative would be acceptable. For instance, Virginia Nelson Holbrook, who had grown up there, and her husband Sam wanted to stay, but they did not intend to participate in the organizing to make it happen. They told their lawyer what was happening and trusted that he would look out for them, but they coordinated little with other neighbors.[14] Other residents who kept their wishes to themselves but eventually sold when they thought they had a good offer attended residents' meetings, but they had a very different agenda from the ones who wanted to stay. This became clear to others only after they sold their properties.[15]

Even with continued differences among residents, the St. John's Leadership Team made it more difficult for DiCicco to argue that diversity of opinion prevented him from responding to community concerns or to divide residents by conducting only individual negotiations. When DiCicco expressed his hesitation about negotiating with the group at the risk of offending others, Father David Funkhouser admitted the delicate balance they would strike, but nonetheless implored the councilman to treat the group as a legitimate negotiating partner:

> I just want to make clear that the St. John Leadership Team... really cannot claim to represent every person in the community. That's not the point of this. The St. John's Leadership Team has undertaken to try to pull together the community and to address these issues.... It is our hope... that in good faith we... can work with Councilman DiCicco and other persons to address our concerns and to come to some mutual agreement about what is really best for the community.
>
> David Funkhouser, Pastor St. John's Episcopal Church[16]

Indeed, even as Funkhouser made this remark about speaking for residents, people in the community were still fighting over that claim. The King family publicly tagged those claiming leadership on the issue for the other side as traitors and enemies. They were especially hard on Reverend Fitchett of Mount Moriah Temple Baptist Church. JoAnn's sister Shirley recalled that Reverend Fitchett "had told us, 'You all might well go ahead and move... because the city is going to make you move.'" They asked him rhetorically, "'Why is that, Reverend? Whose side are you on?'" They embarrassed him by calling out, "Judas!" to him in a crowded public meeting, and reveling in the subsequent laughter.[17]

By June 1999, DiCicco recognized that he had reached a stalemate with this strong-minded group of residents who refused to be swayed by his vision. He even admitted this publicly and agreed to stall implementation in order to host more meetings. Residents had publicly embarrassed DiCicco by challenging the project's legitimacy. DiCicco tabled the resolution he proposed to the City Council, although he had already ushered the plan through several formal hurdles, including passage by the Board of the RDA and the Philadelphia City Planning Commission. He vowed at the City Council hearing about the bill to step back and "work with every person, either individually or collectively, to see that you are all made whole and that no one gets the short end of the stick in the negotiation process."[18]

His project manager Newberg reiterated, "We will take whatever time is needed to manage the relocation process with sensitivity and dignity."[19] Of course, this was not their first promise to open community dialogues,[20] but the agreement to halt progress for the sake of more meetings was new. DiCicco temporarily stopped his attempts to have the city acquire occupied properties through voluntary sales or eminent domain,[21] and he agreed to initiate a new, sustained dialogue with community members and with the St. John's Leadership Team.

Johanna Bauman, the first professional organizer to work with residents opposed to the revitalization, explained the real effects of residents' new power:

> We took it to the point where... basically everything had stalled. We'd had meetings with enough people and made enough noise and gotten things into at least the community papers.... We started making enough noise that I think there was some pause in terms of well, we're not going to be able to just come in here, condemn the houses and take them and do whatever we want. We're obviously going to have to come up with a better plan.
>
> Johanna Bauman, United Communities of Southeast Philadelphia Community Organizer[22]

The balance of political power not only forced this temporary standoff and new meetings but also made negotiations toward a compromise at those meetings possible. Residents did not imagine themselves omnipotent, and they had to cede power to the other side. In fact, people kept coming to these meetings for the same reasons they began the fight: because they felt they stood to lose a great deal if they did not. Residents continued to worry about what a councilman backed by the powerful Fumo would do if they stopped fighting, and they worried that a stalemate could not last. The trained community organizers helped them to conduct a "power assessment" and concluded that DiCicco and his allies were too big to fail completely. DiCicco came to the meetings himself personally, rather than sending a representative, and they took this as a sign of the possibility of serious communication and negotiation.[23] They kept attending with the hope of such negotiation, and eventually it happened.

RECONCILING VISIONS INSIDE THE NEGOTIATING ROOM

The negotiations between DiCicco and residents took place during a long series of sessions in Saint John's Church. When meetings at the church began, residents and DiCicco seemed unlikely to break their deadlock. The first sessions are remembered more as yelling periods where anger flared than as discussions or negotiations. Residents were unwilling to negotiate with DiCicco and Newberg because the officials seemed intransigent on the issues that residents found most objectionable: the replacement of their homes with a parking lot and the lack of guarantees about housing for relocated residents.

At some point, DiCicco's approach and then residents' approach began to change. Residents who were there believe that DiCicco started to view and treat them as invested homeowners who cared about the neighborhood and wanted to stay there. Residents and their advocates think that DiCicco became willing to reconsider his design and relocation plans when he learned to respect them and to take their demands as homeowners, their claims to the neighborhood, more seriously. Later, DiCicco publicly admitted, "It was a learning process for me.... I had a vision for a community that is very close to where I lived.... Maybe I was a little bit slow or derelict in my presentation to the community, so I apologize for that." He told me that during the negotiations, he learned that the residents were more attached to their houses than he had realized. "I began to understand that they felt like, 'Even if we have a hole in the roof, it's our castle.' That's what I came to understand," he said.[24] DiCicco began to understand that residents were invested in their dilapidated homes and in a rundown area.

DiCicco emphasized to me that, while his understanding of the residents' needs changed, he had always regarded them as constituents whose wishes should be respected. He wanted the record to show clearly that he never intended to displace residents against their will. Even in his original vision, he was not planning to just create middle-class housing and ignore the existing residents. Instead, he seriously misjudged what the residents would want, and what they would think they deserved. He said, "It was a very blighted, desolate, two-and-a-half-block area that had stability on both sides.... If I could stabilize it... I just thought they would understand. They would take the money, go to senior housing, and move elsewhere."[25]

The residents became open to compromise once DiCicco agreed to build something other than a parking lot, which they had regarded as an insult to their investments. To residents, the striking of the parking lot signaled that, rather than destroying value, the change might create a collective improvement.[26] With the suggestion that new housing might be built where their houses then stood—even if it was not for them—residents became more willing to discuss how to make development plans work. The fights turned into discussions as speakers turned down their volume and people listened to one another. Ackelsberg, the attorney helping the St. John's Leadership

Team, described the change in the tone of the meetings succinctly: "I think that distrust . . . gave way to a spirit of cooperation."[27]

Despite the cooperative atmosphere emerging around planning agreed-upon collective improvements, residents remained opposed to the initial plan because of individual-level arrangements for those to be displaced. A second significant and concrete shift on DiCicco's part, therefore, took place when he recognized that he had to develop a generous and specific plan for individual displacement. Vague promises about taking care of the residents who lost their homes had made residents recall similar promises government had made thirty to forty years earlier. Although they had been told that the poor would not be pushed out of their neighborhoods closer to downtown by takings or by taxes, they had been forced to move nonetheless. DiCicco told me:

> I was saying "I'm not doing this to displace you." I came to understand, later, that was not enough, because I was not giving them any substantive answers about what I was doing to make them not have to move. . . . I didn't want to push them out, but I didn't have a plan.
>
> Frank DiCicco, First District City Councilperson, 2009[28]

Therefore, in addition to planning for housing in the space where these residents lived, DiCicco and Newberg set to work to guarantee acceptable relocation assistance. For a while, they had tried but failed to find a financially viable way to relocate these residents into new homes in the revitalized area or a very nearby location, at no extra cost to them.

The watershed moment, from DiCicco and Newberg's point of view, came once they figured out how to meet the residents' demands with a design, construction, and finance plan that they could turn into a reality. They figured out a practical way to plan and pay for housing that allowed residents to stay in the project footprint if they wanted to do so. In this redesigned plan, displaced residents incurred no financial costs; they would only have to surrender their current homes for keys to new ones. The market prices of the new houses would be more than $100,000 above—and as much as $200,000 above—what their existing homes were worth. Yet through subsidies that the officials would raise, any homeowner who wanted to stay in the area could get a "self-amortizing mortgage" for the difference between the price of a new house and the compensation for their old one. They would get title to the new house, and this mortgage would pay itself off over fifteen years if the family stayed in residence.

As enticing as these arrangements sounded, they were not enough to win resident support. Especially because the resources sounded unusually reasonable, the residents who were to be displaced demanded assurances that those promises would be met. DiCicco and Newberg offered to allow residents to move into new homes in the exact same location as their existing ones, but residents decided against it. Of course, staying at the same address would have required residents to move out while the new houses were being constructed, then move back in once they were completed. This surely would have been inconvenient, but the main problem for residents was security. By moving out before the new homes were built, residents would risk that something would fall through and they would never get the new homes they were promised. They would be more comfortable if they could see the new houses and had the deals in hand *before* they packed their things. In the end, these residents decided that security was more important than the piece of ground they had come to know.

DiCicco and Newberg agreed to divide the construction into stages. During the first stage, new homes would be constructed on vacant land. Then, residents would move, just once, from their existing homes to new ones a few blocks away. Only in the second stage would construction in the area where people had been living begin. Thus, the revised plan allowed residents to trade some of the emotional and other values they attached to their exact location for security about the future. In this way, residents chose security over sentimentality.

In December 1999, the two sides announced that they had come to an agreement and presented City Council with a revised design for redevelopment and a detailed relocation plan for residents. Peggy King Brookins spoke for some of the residents to be displaced, commenting:

> Our initial meetings were indeed tense, but we were able to overcome the tense atmosphere so that we could begin to work with the real issues regarding this relocation process. During the summer, they produced a plan which shows a lot more concern for the community than its original draft.... Thank you, Councilman DiCicco, for working with us and agreeing to allow us to be part of your decisions regarding what happens to our community.
>
> Peggy King Brookins, St John's Co-chair, family member of condemnees[29]

DiCicco similarly expressed appreciation for the cooperative effort and hope that in the future "we're going to have something that we can all be proud of."[30] Finally, Councilman-at-large David Cohen, who had so vehemently opposed the plan in June, offered his congratulations as well: "I want to commend all the parties. I understand that under Councilman DiCicco's leadership, all of the parties have been very busy at work, and I'm hoping that today, we can see an end to it, with all parties fully satisfied that their rights are protected forever."[31]

Residents also garnered security by requiring unusually detailed written declarations from DiCicco in the City Council bill authorizing the use of eminent domain. Cohen's reference to "forever" may have hinted at concerns about whether residents' approval would endure as the plans were implemented. Indeed, St. John's Leadership Team insisted that very specific relocation plans be included in the bill. The RDA authorities resisted, saying that state law prohibited such detail in the bill and that the relocation agreement should remain a separate document. Ackelsberg testified, to the contrary, that specific language in the Jefferson Square Plan needed to be included in the bill,[32] to provide residents the assurance that they needed. DiCicco offered his word, saying "I will assure you that there'll be no deviation from this."[33] Brookins explained that DiCicco's word and the sides' trust and faith in each other as individuals were not sufficient: "We're confident that, in all sincerity, the promises that have been made in the plan are those things that you and the developer intend to do. But, you know, stuff happens, and we need that assurance in writing ... preferably in the ordinance."[34] They received the highly unusual written declaration that they asked for, as the City Council bill referred directly to the relocation plan they had created and required compliance with it.[35] In addition, they got an even more unusual document detailing relocation arrangements: a contract signed by DiCicco, representatives of the JSCDC, and representatives of the St. John's Leadership Team.[36]

In the end, the residents and government officials agreed publicly to very specific plans and provisions for contingencies. Not only was the construction staged so that residents would not give up their houses until their newly constructed houses were finished and keys were in their hands, but they also had a written contract with DiCicco, witnessed by the entire City Council, that laid out the arrangement's details. A city planner who witnessed the process told me just how unusual and enticing to residents this must have been: "That was probably one of the best carrots.... In other areas, the development plans are not as clear and concrete as this one."[37]

Given how arduous the struggle was to come to this agreement, I wondered if there could have been an easier way. Could DiCicco have had more foresight and offered a similar plan from the beginning? Would residents have preferred this? When I asked Steve Honeyman, a professional organizer who assisted the resident group, he said the struggle itself was part of the positive result:

> Communities are based on a certain level of undescribed sense of ownership, sense of stake ... this is another thing I sort of got from Saul Alinsky [writer and founder of 1970s community organizing], that happiness lays not in finding happiness, but lays in the journey.... Only the means can justify the end.... The end cannot justify the means. So, whatever you say that he comes up with that

> is better for the community, actually in my world view it cannot be better for the community because the community was not at the table to think about.
>
> Steve Honeyman, Eastern Philadelphia Organizing Project Director[38]

Peggy King Brookins agreed that the fight was almost more important to her satisfaction than the new houses. When I asked her if she would have preferred the results without the battle, she said no:

> One of the most important things that I learned was that you could fight City Hall and win. And that if you do fight, if you do not win, you can at least say that we tried to do it. And you could have gotten something out of it, something more out of it than you would have, had you not fought for it.
>
> Peggy King Brookins, Co-chair St. John's Team and Family member of Condemnees[39]

As Honeyman and Brookins both emphasized, engaging in the process made residents and their allies proud. In addition, the final results would never have been realized, or even imagined, without this process. Both the fierce conflict after the orange signs were posted and the more cooperative negotiations that followed were necessary to generate the ideas that led to an agreement. The people in the negotiating room did not build models or standards for redevelopment generally; they envisioned unique solutions for this particular neighborhood, and they needed to sit down together to do so. Facing one another in the negotiating room enabled both sides to learn from what another what was possible. Specific revelations in that room allowed them to forge a compromise plan.

SECURING THE CAPACITY TO IMPLEMENT PLANS

As hard-fought as the project's visionary design phase was, its implementation phase was just as important to its long-term success. DiCicco delivered on his most basic promises. Though a few unexpected barriers threatened and delayed progress, the project maintained its course. Eventually, Jefferson Square's project leaders could celebrate having realized all of the main elements of their plans. How were DiCicco and his colleagues able to accomplish what they set out to do, when others so often failed?

DiCicco had only agreed to a plan that he thought was viable in the first place. The negotiations themselves were not just about what people deserved; they were about what anyone could realistically deliver. In addition, the careful arrangements made for relocations and financing left less to chance during implementation. Project planners fulfilled promises because they benefited from a combination of astute choices, luck, and access to resources.

Officials may have gotten lucky. As it turned out, government jumped into a real estate endeavor at the right place and time, although officials could not have counted on this. In the beginning, the situation seemed like it could be getting worse instead of better. The closing of the neighborhood's anchoring institution, Mount Sinai Hospital, in 1998 seemed like only another sign of how hard it would be to stop abandonment. But officials managed to turn the hospital's departure into an opportunity. Without a company interested in real development at the hospital site, DiCicco could imagine a plan for residential redevelopment without a new parking lot for the institution. And although much of the old hospital campus remained vacant, even after everything else was redeveloped, the very first construction was the publicly subsidized senior residential home on the corner of the old hospital campus.

In addition, the real estate market had started to boom by the time the newly constructed housing was ready. By the early 2000s, as the JSCDC put its brand new houses up for sale, conditions in the surrounding neighborhood had already changed. Though the rising real estate prices cost the project by making land acquisition in the second phase more expensive than anticipated, the impact on housing sales was dramatic. The financial success of the project relied heavily on being able to sell the houses at prices that would cover costs not paid for by public funds. Indeed, new houses that were expected to be priced starting at $85,000 in 1999[40] sold quickly for between $225,000 and $293,000 when they were offered in 2004. However, this real estate turn followed significant government spending in the area, beginning but not ending with the senior housing on the hospital site.

Public funding paid for about a third of the plans for Jefferson Square's redevelopment. DiCicco obtained over $7 million in government funding to pay construction and relocation costs,[41] which totaled $24 million. DiCicco and his allies secured over $6 million from the city (mostly funneling federal dollars),[42] $1.5 million from the state,[43] and $800,000 from foundations tied to banking.[44] The technically detailed revitalization plan may have helped DiCicco to access this money, but political power within the halls of government must have been asserted. (As noted, some contributions later came under scrutiny as part of Fumo's federal prosecution on corruption charges.[45]) To be sure, government money was not a pure blessing; it also led to political delays. Between the two stages of land acquisition, Mayor Street reportedly held the project up for a year out of concern that the financing was too generous and would create a dangerous precedent, encouraging people in other parts of the city to demand new houses worth $250,000 when threatened with displacement. Despite these concerns, Street eventually let the Jefferson Square project move forward as planned. DiCicco's political power, backed by Fumo, thus brought crucial financial resources with attendant political dangers to the project.

DiCicco and his aides also created remarkable administrative capacity that allowed them to attend to the details of construction, sales, and relocation. The JSCDC had been founded in 1997 exclusively for this single redevelopment project. Once the revitalization plan gained City Council approval, the JSCDC took on implementation. Newberg relied heavily on a small staff to complete land acquisition, construction, and even relocation. Though the RDA is the typical arbiter of relocation arrangements for eminent domain, the RDA's staff became little more than auditors after the JSCDC ironed out the details of individual compensation and relocation arrangements. Whether or not the JSCDC fulfilled particular displaced individuals' wishes (a topic discussed in the next chapter), it was an unusual departure for an independent organization to arrange compensation and relocation.

A ROARING SUCCESS

By most accounts, Jefferson Square's revitalization materialized as envisioned and was a political success. By 2004, many of the dramatic changes proposed in DiCicco's early plans had become reality. The project managers had acquired the originally targeted area, much of it by eminent domain. They had displaced the residents on Lawrence Street, Leithgow Street, and a few other streets, including most of the members of the King family. They had cleared and redeveloped the land, much of it as new twin houses with yards and garages that were sold at market prices, presumably to middle-class families. The fiercest critics of these changes as they had been planned years earlier praised what was actually implemented.

The King family and many other displaced homeowners gave the project their seal of approval. They were proud of a significant accomplishment—that twenty families who lost their old homes moved into new or rehabilitated ones very close by. Politicians and news media broadcast that the housing development was a market success and that the homeowners who fought against displacement were re-housed in the new development.

Ackelsberg later ran for City Council and said the following about the Jefferson Square relocations:

> It was a nice story. I actually told it occasionally on the campaign trail.... It was such a good deal. You move around the corner into a brand new house, right? That was the deal. And, it's not going to cost you anything more.... It's going to be kind of neutral on your budget.
>
> Irv Ackelsberg, Community Legal Services Managing Attorney[46]

Instead of the political embarrassment that it looked like at the peak of residents' discontent, Jefferson Square became a symbol of strength and pride for DiCicco. Not only had he used the government's power to transform a struggling neighborhood for the benefit of a variety of people, but he had responded to the demands of homeowners who wanted to stay in the neighborhood. DiCicco's project manager gave the following assessment:

> The highlight for me in my career is when twelve of the twenty existing homeowners got in a van with me and went to City Council and actually asked to get their houses condemned. Mrs. King sat right next to me and said, "This is a good deal."
>
> Jeremey Newberg, Capital Access President, Jefferson Square Project Manager[47]

Newberg and others celebrated the agreement between residents and DiCicco. If the orange signs in early 1998 signaled government's abuse of power, the joining of hands between residents and DiCicco in late 1999 symbolized the legitimate use of government power in service to serve its constituents.

In the interviews that I conducted with people familiar with the neighborhood prior to the redevelopment, reviews of the changes were generally positive. People said that the new and rehabilitated housing was better than the vacant lots and dilapidated housing that used to be on those blocks. They said the neighborhood was cleaner and quieter and that property was worth more. People also were generally pleased to see that many of the old residents had remained,[48] although the neighborhood, like any, had conflicts within it, and a few interviewees told me they were less than happy to see some of their neighbors stay.

The project planners saw it as a successful project of neighborhood revitalization that improved the place without destroying community networks. Neighbors benefited from a better environment, including newer

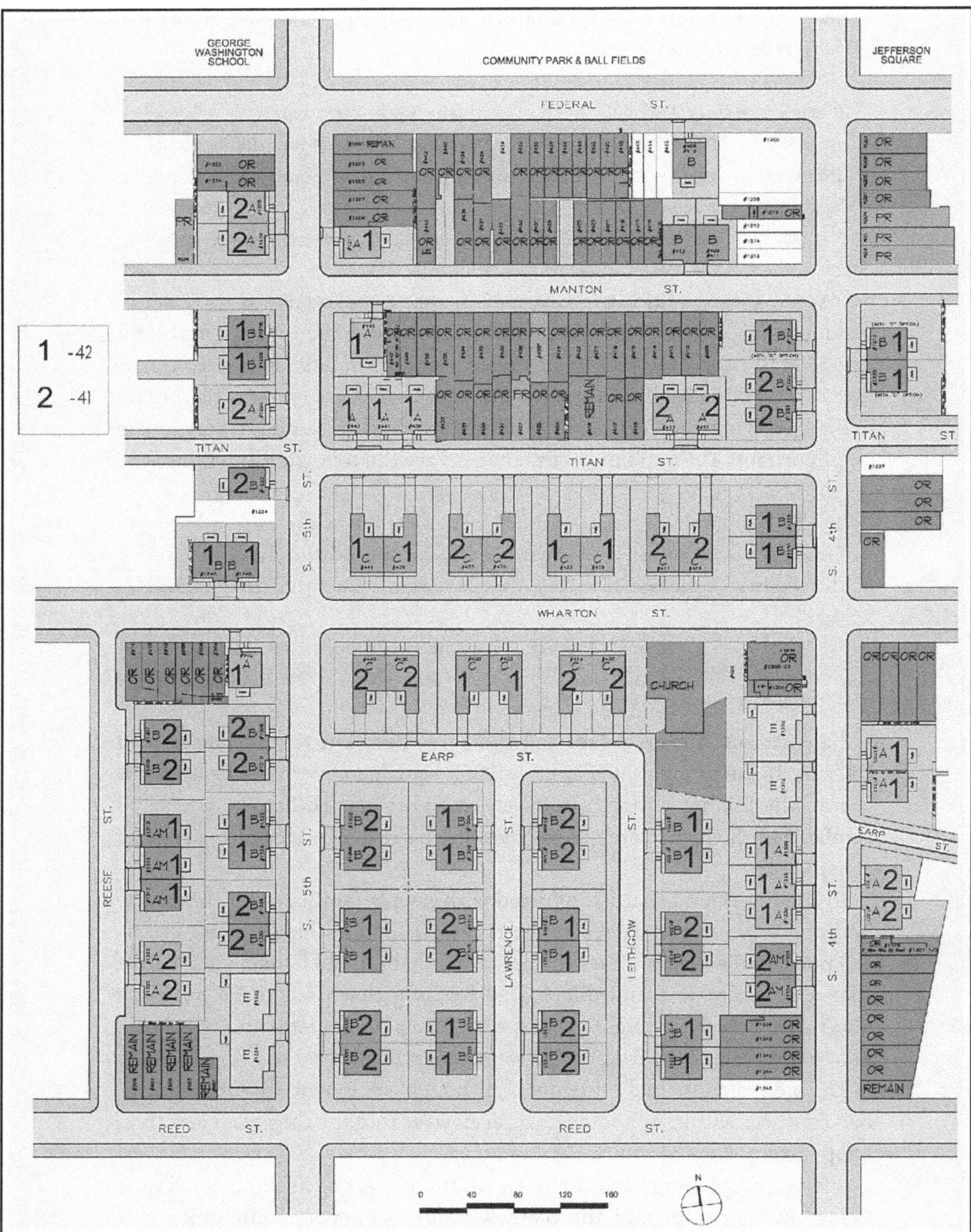
GEORGE WASHINGTON SCHOOL
COMMUNITY PARK & BALL FIELDS
JEFFERSON SQUARE
FEDERAL ST.
MANTON ST.
TITAN ST.
WHARTON ST.
EARP ST.
REED ST.
S. 5th ST.
S. 4th ST.
REESE ST.
LAWRENCE ST.
LEITHGOW ST.
CHURCH
1 -42
2 -41
0 40 80 120 160
N

houses, streets, and sidewalks and more people. The residents who were displaced and wanted to stay did so, and they reaped the benefits of redevelopment, too. Grant Johnson, a member of the JSCDC and project manager for Capital Access (Newberg's consulting company) as well as a new resident himself, emphasized that the "true mixed-income home ownership development where... existing owners benefit[ed] first" preserved the neighborhood's social fabric, so that residents knew "what neighbor to go to if there is a fire on the corner or who to talk to if somebody is sick and has not been seen outside of their house for a few weeks."[49]

In addition, people who wanted out could cash out, for more than they would have otherwise received. Speculators and slumlords were pushed out. An outsider might say, therefore, that everyone received a return on his or her investments.

Physical changes were plentiful, and new houses were quickly occupied. In October 2000, the JSCDC completed the rehabilitation of a thirty-seven-unit apartment complex for low-income seniors on the northwest corner of the old Mount Sinai Hospital's land. In March 2003, a public ceremony marked the groundbreaking for construction of the single-family homes,[50] and work began on the first of two planned phases. In this phase, JSCDC would build twenty-four new houses and renovate six row houses for low-income buyers; none of the homeowners to be relocated within the project would be moved until this first phase was complete, and they would then have the opportunity to move into these new houses.

In 2004, once some of the houses in the first phase were up, JSCDC put on sale everything that was planned for development (in the first and second stages), and the response was overwhelming. TV crews came out to report on the lines of interested buyers for the sixty-three houses to be sold at "market rate." The homes had buyers within one week of opening

PROPERTY LEGEND			
A	3 BR RELOCATION OR LOW INCOME HOUSE		20
AM	3 BR MARKET RATE HOUSE		5
B	3 BR MARKET RATE HOUSE		44
C	4 BR MARKET RATE HOUSE		14
D	3 OR 4 BR MARKET RATE H.C. ACCESSIBLE HOUSE (AT SPECIFIC LOTS SHOWN BY REQUEST - UP TO 5 UNITS)		0
E	3 BR H.C. ACCESSIBLE RELOCATION OR LOW INCOME HOUSE		4
OR	OWNER OCCUPIED REHAB		90
SR	SCATTERED SITE REHAB FOR RELOCATION		1
PR	PURCHASED REHAB FOR LOW INCOME OR RELOCATION		6
	TOTAL		184
	PHASE ONE PROPERTIES		

Figure 7.1:
Final Jefferson Square Plan, December 2003 (Version 33)
Source: Kramer+Marks Architects

Figure 7.2:
Virginia Nelson Holbrook and Sam Holbrook in House Taken for Jefferson Square, Picture of Virginia's Mother, Who Had Been a Nurse at Mount Sinai Hospital, on the Wall, circa 1990s
Source: Virginia Nelson Holbrook

their doors. Jeremey Newberg, hired by DiCicco to oversee the project, proclaimed, "On May 3, 2004, over one hundred people lined up in the rain—some camped out for two nights—so that they could buy a Jefferson Square home. By Friday, May 7, all ninety-three homes were sold."[51] (In addition to the sixty-three market-rate houses, twenty were reserved by those being relocated and ten were sold at subsidized rates to additional low- and moderate-income families.)[52] In the second phase of construction, market-rate houses for most of these buyers were built. By 2006, JSCDC had constructed eighty-seven housing units and had renovated six units on the project's main site (see Figures 7.1–7.8.) The finish date was later than expected, and the sales prices were significantly higher than originally projected. Sales on the market-rate houses closed in 2005, for between $225,000 and $293,000.[53]

Additional new developments and rehabilitations followed. Private owners renovated and constructed other buildings nearby, with and without government help.[54] Approximately fifty owner-occupied homes received

Figure 7.3:
New Dining Room of Virginia Nelson Holbrook and Sam Holbrook, Displaced in Jefferson Square Takings. Picture of Virginia's Mother, Who Had Been a Nurse at Mount Sinai Hospital, on the Wall, 2009
Source: Debbie Becher

Figure 7.4:
The King Family Assembled in Dorothy King's Living Room. Foreground from left to right, Peggy King Brookins, JoAnn King, Dorothy King, Richard King III, Shirley Corbin-Nelson with Other Family Members Reflected in the Background (2014)
Source: David Gehosky

Figure 7.5:
David Jones, Displaced by Jefferson Square, at His New Front Door (2009)
Source: David Gehosky

government assistance with rehabilitation projects, in amounts that varied by income.[55] The Mount Moriah Baptist Church, in the heart of the newly developed area, received JSCDC's help in securing city money for improvements. When the people at the church had spent that money, they raised another $150,000 independently for renovations.[56] A few of the men who had originally opposed the project, in part because they wanted to remake the neighborhood themselves, renovated buildings, too. Melvin Hanton managed to have one of his two condemned properties revested (given back) to him, a process that I discuss in more detail in Chapter 8. He completely restored a row house (not his own house), making a downstairs office and an upstairs apartment.[57] Another local man was constructing a set of new row homes as I conducted my interviews.[58]

Though it may have attracted buyers, the suburban design of low-density houses with side yards and garages also drew significant criticism. Early

Figure 7.6:
New Twin Houses in Foreground; Renovated Senior Housing on Part of Vacant Mount Sinai Hospital Campus in Background (2009)
Source: David Gehosky

Figure 7.7:
Full Blocks of New Twin Houses (2009)
Source: David Gehosky

Figure 7.8:
502 Wharton Street, Dorothy King's New House (2009)
Source: David Gehosky

on, at one of the Planning Commission meetings in 1999, at least one resident declared, "Everybody is for upgrading the neighborhood, but the plan should be like the rest of South Philadelphia, which is row houses."[59] The row houses so common in Philadelphia seemed to have been both an aesthetic and a functional preference for most of the people I interviewed, whether neighborhood residents, community organizers, or government officials. Some of them thought the character of row houses was more attractive than the twin houses with yards and garages that were built.[60] Others said open lawns in the middle of the city collected trash and invited intruders. Garages drew derision as well. Echoing her neighbors, JoAnn King noted, "Everyone is using a garage for storage. The vehicle is still parked in the street."[61] Apparently, the garages were too small for some cars, and residents often preferred the storage space because they had been accustomed to basements that they no longer had. Because the driveways were not used for cars, the redevelopment actually reduced space for street parking. For these reasons, even the planners themselves sometimes regretted these design features. An ironic result of the suburban-style houses, which had angered Dorothy King because of their intended appeal to more affluent whites, is that they were regularly mistaken for a newer public housing project—a point usually made with a note of derision, sadness, or humor.[62]

CONCLUSION

The Jefferson Square project moved to the positive side of the legitimacy boundary line. Officials made this possible by offering greater investment protection than had originally been planned. The project respected individual investments by guaranteeing displaced homeowners replacement houses in the new development and by phasing the construction to provide them extra security, by allowing them to stay in their old homes until the new ones were ready. The project continued to do away with residents' homes, but it respected collective investments by replacing the neighborhood's dilapidated houses with new houses, instead of a parking lot.

Although the conception of property as investment does not always determine the outcome of eminent domain cases, I have argued that political strength, constructive dialogue, and resources for implementation allowed Jefferson Square to embody an ideal of investment protection. Nevertheless, an alternative interpretation of what happened is that the politician's power prevailed and that the residents did not really get what they thought they deserved but only what they thought they could get. Residents might have lied to me, or even to themselves, when they said that they supported being displaced for the neighborhood's economic development. They may have offered their approval only because they acquiesced to power that they knew they could not fight. They might have sugarcoated their stories for me and the media, out of fear that DiCicco or his allies would retaliate if they uttered a critical word. Even if these interpretations are accurate, they do not detract from my own assessments of government legitimacy.

These concerns about residents' limited power emphasize that residents and planners alike treated the project as legitimate—but not necessarily as just. In fact, Newberg told me, "No one uses the word 'justice.'"[63] Many involved in the project seemed to think that many residents deserved better than what their neighborhood had handed them well before these plans were hatched. They did not deserve to struggle against the depopulation, job loss, crime, and vast drops in their properties' market value. Nor did they deserve the uncertainty and uprooting of redevelopment, no matter how physically comfortable the results.

Regardless of whether they achieved a just outcome, however, residents achieved a dramatic turnaround by securing a government action that appeared legitimate. Twenty families experienced an outcome—swift moves to new houses within the redevelopment footprint—that was significantly more favorable than their originally planned ejection from the neighborhood. The difference in the political fallout, from serious resistance to vocal support, was also spectacular.

By labeling this project a legitimacy success, I mean to suggest that most people involved evaluated it as a reasonable thing for government to do given existing circumstances, not that they thought it was the best thing that government could have done. Political support rests on legitimacy, not consensus. It was not necessary for everyone to adore the project or its particular details for it to earn legitimacy. Instead, the project needed to meet minimal standards—in this case, of investment protection. It needed to simply challenge the perception that provoked protest: that it was a land grab through which government would steal the value invested by residents. Critical evaluations of significant features of the project, such as the inclusion of suburban-style yards and garages, can and do coexist with votes of approval for the overall project.

Finally, just because this project earned significant political support that has lasted over a decade, there is no guarantee that it will continue. In other words, a boundary project's legitimacy is always precarious. By definition, a boundary project rests close to the legitimacy boundary line, even if it seems comfortably settled on one side or the other. The reconciled, compromise vision in Jefferson Square rested on a fragile compromise, not consensus. As noted earlier, Fumo, who funneled government funding to DiCicco for the project, eventually faced federal charges of fraud and theft; in March 2009, he was convicted on 137 counts. Fumo's use of nonprofit organizations in his financial shenanigans may have tarnished the JSCDC's reputation. This turn of events should remind us that the celebratory mood in Jefferson Square after the new residents first settled there was a snapshot in time and that the foundations of legitimacy for a boundary project always remain fragile. And these public determinations of legitimacy hide variation in individual judgments.

CHAPTER 8

Compensating for Property by Recognizing Investments

This chapter examines how government compensates individuals for taken properties and earns legitimacy by doing so. What do people who lose property claim they deserve? When do others agree that their claims are justified? When are their demands met, and when are they not? I answer these questions by looking closely at the compensation experiences of individuals enveloped by the American Street and Jefferson Square projects. The legitimacy of both projects was largely determined by compensation arrangements for condemnees and, in particular, homeowners. Protests were rooted in worries that people would lose their homes and would receive something less valuable in return. This chapter describes what individuals actually received and how officials, residents, and onlookers decided whether their compensation was reasonable.

When people judge government's compensation for property, they evaluate how well it accounts for the investments that people have made and lost. As noted earlier, investment is the sacrifice of any kind of value (including money, labor, time, and emotion) in the hope of future returns. My research on the American Street and Jefferson Square projects found that condemnees and officials approved of compensation efforts that recognized these characteristics of investments. When compensation efforts failed to recognize these characteristics, however, condemnees claimed that they were cheated—and officials sometimes agreed.

My investment-focused understanding of compensation stands in contrast to the conventional view, which focuses on market value.[1] Most authors who have written about compensation for eminent domain assume that government uses market prices as its standard and that eminent domain cases earn or lose legitimacy accordingly.[2] Many authors recognize, however, that identifying the market value of these properties is a challenging task that government often fails to fulfill, even if it is the standard.[3] By one argument, government earns legitimacy when it pays a property's actual market price, but it has legitimacy problems because its compensation sometimes inaccurately represents market value.[4] This inaccuracy can stem from benign errors in estimating value or from malevolent "lowballing" to save money, and condemnees who have the resources or wherewithal to litigate or organize politically can increase the offers more than those who do not.[5] By another set of arguments, government fails to earn legitimacy *because* it uses market price as a measure for compensation. Some claim that money will never compensate for the full sentimental and unique value of a property to an individual or the dignity of one's power to decide when to sell the property. Others believe that people are willing to accept payment for these different kinds of values but that government may have trouble figuring out how much money they are worth.[6]

Of course, accounting for someone's investment presents a huge challenge, for people's investments are hard for others to judge and vary widely. People invest different kinds and amounts of value and feel different levels of continued attachments to their properties. The protests that I have described involved long-time homeowners who had invested sweat, money, love, and time in their houses, but most taken properties involve very different kinds and amounts of investment. Indeed, most of those taken in Philadelphia during the period of my census were actually empty lots, and some people hold empty lots or buildings to simply speculate on the local real estate market.

In a legitimate compensation arrangement, compensation becomes an act of recognition—specifically, government's recognition of someone's investment. Government officials initiate the compensation process by evaluating what a condemnee has invested in the property being taken. They assess whether the condemnee is a property owner, whether and how they have cared for the property, how connected he or she is to the neighborhood, and whether he or she occupies the property. Officials also assess the property's physical, legal, and market condition. These basic assessments help them to determine the degree to which a condemnee has invested money, time, labor, and emotion in the property and in the area as a whole, as well as what kinds of compensation are likely to replace these investments.

For the second step of the compensation process, officials must identify the compensation, which can include money and/or a new property to match the lost investment.[7] If they have determined that only cash investments are being lost, they offer an amount of money deemed roughly equivalent. However, if they have determined that a combination of time, emotion, labor, and other values tied up in occupancy of housing (or a business) are being lost, they try to match the loss by providing roughly equivalent housing (or a business site). And if officials have determined that the condemnee has an important connection to the property's surrounding area, they attempt to find and offer the individual a new property in that area.

Throughout both steps of the compensation process, officials and condemnees maintain a healthy skepticism that the other may misrepresent the investment to his or her advantage. People who lose property make assertions to government both about what they have lost and what would count as an appropriate replacement, and they marshal evidence to support their claims. Whether genuine or disingenuous, they work to convince government officials and onlookers that they have made investments that warrant compensation. Similarly, officials demonstrate efforts to accurately assess what people have invested and provide compensation accordingly. When officials determine compensation, they evaluate constituents' claims by using observations about property conditions, documents, and other indicators of investment losses.

This two-part investment-recognition process is my observation of what officials actually do, both when adhering strictly to guidelines and when exercising discretion, and I have found that their success or failure determines the legitimacy of compensation. Legitimacy problems arise when constituents disagree with officials about what investments were lost, what counts as an appropriate replacement, or both.

Public reactions to the various compensation arrangements for the American Street and Jefferson Square takings shed light on how the compensation process can achieve or fail to achieve legitimacy. The two projects' overall reputations—negative in the case of American Street and positive in the case of Jefferson Square—did not always predict how people would perceive the projects' individual compensation arrangements. For example, the son of an elderly woman relocated to a new house in Jefferson Square told me that what happened to his family was "a blessing," but he also asked me to tell the stories of those whom he saw "lose everything."[8] Nor did the government's provision of vastly different compensation amounts for similar buildings always predict public disapproval. For houses that were worth about the same amount on the real estate market, one tenant and owner received a combined $35,000 and a homeowner received $52,000, and neighbors judged these arrangements to be fair. Conversely, neighbors sometimes disapproved when people got the same amount and type of compensation for houses of about equal market value. After two people received $22,000 in cash for houses on the same block in the American Street takings, some neighbors judged the compensation amount to be fair in one case but seriously unfair in the other. These judgments of legitimacy all involved people's opinions about whether compensation adequately recognized investments.

In all of the aforementioned cases, officials and citizens appealed to a similar logic of investment in judging compensation arrangements, although they did not always agree about what that logic prescribed in specific cases. Much of this chapter shows how government earned legitimacy for its compensation arrangements in a wide range of cases by recognizing various types and degrees of investment. Later, the chapter turns to cases in which the same processes led officials to seemingly disregard investments and thus fail to earn government legitimacy for its compensation arrangements.

MARKET VALUE FOR THE SPECULATOR

Officials and citizens expected speculators to cash out at market value and no more. Speculators (and slumlords) do even less for their properties than "flippers," who buy properties at low prices, quickly perform repairs and renovations, and attempt to sell for higher prices. Officials compensated people whom they deemed to be speculators and slumlords, or simply absentee owners who took little more than the minimum care for their properties, by paying cash for the estimated market value of the title lost. Onlookers often deemed this compensation appropriate, even if the owners disagreed.

In the Jefferson Square project, neighbors agreed that government acted reasonably by paying Curtis Dash (pseudonym)[9] the estimated market value of the property he lost, even though he said he deserved more. Dash had bought the property from a city agency for $29,000 at a sheriff's auction. When the RDA condemned the property a few months later, Dash demanded an additional $20,000 that he said he had spent in repairs. RDA officials refused to pay him any more than his purchase price because they did not believe he had invested more; they thought Dash knew the property was slated to be condemned and was trying to take advantage of the system.

In the American Street area, the government compensated a landlord named Mr. Herrero (pseudonym) $22,000 for the house he owned and rented out. As an absentee owner, he received only the property's estimated market price. Neighbors who knew of Mr. Herrero's arrangement did not complain that he was cheated or had received an overly generous amount, though many other American Street condemnees received much more, and neighbors and others familiar with the project decried what happened to other individuals. The practice of basing compensation on an estimated market price can earn legitimacy when it is applied to at least some absentee owners.

In the ideal, the absentee owner—someone who owns a property but either leases it or lets it remain vacant—represents the quintessential financial investor. Any labor or money an absentee owner commits probably has one purpose: the return of financial value, whether through rents paid, a sales price, or both. Accordingly, government officials offer what they call "real estate compensation," amounting to a check for the estimated full market value. In many cases, officials and observers agreed that compensation in cash, for the estimated sales price of a property, legitimately returns the absentee owner a rough equivalent of what was lost when government took his or her property.

RECOGNIZING VALUE PLURALISM

When officials and observers agreed that the market value of a property failed to represent the entirety of the lost investment, they considered it as part of, but not full compensation deserved. Officials and citizens acted as if government must also account for different and greater investments—and, surprisingly, it often managed to do so.

By replacing an old home with a new one, government sometimes overcame one of the biggest concerns about compensation: that governments cannot account for the many kinds of value people hold in residential properties. Indeed, officials did not parse out exact figures for labor, emotion, time, or even money lost. But by using broad categories that recognized that a home was at stake and needed to be replaced, they allowed for rough calculation and matching of these many types of value. Government seemed to adequately compensate some renters and homeowners by securing new, comparable, and secure places for them to call home. Thus, while officials compensated for the loss of ownership by assessing real estate values and providing them in cash, they usually compensated for the disruption of occupancy by assessing relocation costs and providing in-kind goods of an equivalent value.

Residential tenants and homeowners secured new housing through official rules that accounted for the loss of occupancy with "relocation

Table 8.1. COMPENSATION BY OFFICIAL CLASSIFICATIONS (COMPENSATION IN ITALICS)

		Ownership	
		No	Yes
Occupancy	Yes	**Tenant** *Relocation*	**Owner-occupant** *Real estate and relocation*
	No	**No warrant for compensation** *None*	**Absentee owner** *Real estate*

benefits." If the occupants owned the property as well, they also received real estate compensation. (Note that the American Street letters mentioning $20,000 as "real estate compensation" that so incensed residents and owners also noted that people "may be eligible for" an unnamed amount of "additional relocation benefits.")[10] In fact, official rules required qualifying people for compensation by verifying ownership and occupancy. These two dimensions actually created three official categories used to determine compensation: absentee ownership, tenancy, and owner-occupancy (see Table. 8.1). Relocation benefits were for tenants and owner-occupants, but not for absentee owners, and they included the market price of the physical move. More significantly, they ensured the occupant's relocation to a new housing unit that had qualities similar to those of the taken unit. Government almost always paid relocation benefits directly to the landlord or seller of a new housing unit, rather than to the condemnee directly as cash, to ensure that housing was replaced with housing. The vast amount of compensation for occupancy, therefore, was released only in-kind, through payments for "replacement housing."[11]

The Tenant

A tenant invests in a property in a very different way from an absentee owner, and compensation for tenancy accounts only for the loss of housing. A tenant pays rent every month but also puts in time—and, possibly, some labor and emotional value—while present in the building and neighborhood. In return, he or she expects to enjoy a secure, comfortable place to live. A tenant's relocation benefits include rent for a transition period (or a down payment for a purchase), as well as the costs of moving services and utility start-ups.[12]

Market prices of rent matter, as officials use a tenant's current rent to begin their calculations of how much they will pay toward a new home. But because they are providing a replacement for occupancy, officials make adjustments for income and housing availability so that the tenant can relocate somewhere suitable. Most important, relocation benefits can only rarely be accessed in cash; government pays the landlord or previous owner for the housing unit directly, on behalf of the tenant.

The experience of Julia Gomez (pseudonym), a tenant displaced by the American Street takings, illustrates how people approve of government when it compensates tenants in this way. Officials compensated Gomez's landlord with money that they earmarked as real estate compensation, but they compensated Gomez with relocation benefits. She used this compensation for a purchase instead of rent, and she received a $13,000 check as a down payment on a new house about a mile away from her old one. Gomez would not have been able to buy this house on her income and savings alone (and even with the benefits, she took out a loan for $37,000 to cover the remaining cost of the house). A neighbor of hers, relocated as a homeowner, looked at what happened to Gomez this way:

> They gave her a check, and she got a down payment... for a house. Now she owns her own house. And I said, "Well, good." At least that was good of them, because everybody thought they were going to just buy the houses from the people that owned them, and they were going to leave her hanging because that was not her house. But she got a house; she got a nice house. I mean, she got a better house than I do.
>
> Patricia Muñoz (pseudonym), condemnee[13]

Valerie Moore, another tenant displaced by Jefferson Square's redevelopment, approved of the compensation she received even more enthusiastically. She used her compensation to move to another rental, a row house about two miles away. Help from relocation workers catapulted her forward on a waiting list to get a Section 8 (subsidized) lease, and the workers also secured money for three years of rent. Moore told me that everything was paid for, that she was delighted to receive government's help to leave the neighborhood, and that she was happy in her new place. Being forced out of Jefferson Square literally opened doors to a different house that she much preferred and could not have accessed without relocation workers' assistance.[14]

The satisfaction expressed by these tenants became possible because government took responsibility for replacing what they had lost: housing. In both cases, government charged residents with the task of finding a home that would suit their needs and that they could afford, and government then provided resources to help secure the home. Once Gomez and Moore were categorized as tenants, government's efforts to compensate them focused entirely on finding and securing substitute housing. By managing to do just that, the compensation efforts earned legitimacy.

The Owner-Occupant

Ownership of a home generally indicates, albeit roughly, that someone has invested more than a tenant. As noted, a tenant invests money, time, and possibly labor and emotion while expecting to receive security and comfort. A typical homeowner, at least in the American imagination, invests more, and expects more in return. Government acknowledged this difference in providing compensation for homeowners. Like tenants' compensation, homeowners' compensation was directed toward the replacement of homes, not just market value, but also toward matching more substantial investments.

Homeowners received compensation for ownership and occupancy, but the compensation amounts often worked out to more than the amounts that would have resulted from an absentee owner and a tenant pooling their compensation. This happened through the provision of a "replacement housing payment," for homeowners, meant to cover the price difference between a new home and the old home, which was often greater than a similar payment for tenants based on rent differences. This payment required that the full amount of compensation for homeowners, the relocation benefits and the real estate compensation, tended to be distributed as a payment toward a new home, not as cash.

Miguelina de Jesus asserted her rights to secure exactly this kind of compensation from the American Street project, and she decided that she got what she deserved. She had raised her family in her house on American Street, but after a divorce she was living alone and had lost not only her family but many of her neighbors. De Jesus wanted to leave the neighborhood, but she would not be able to afford it from the small amount of money she would get from selling her house. She knew that the city's compensation would far exceed what speculators had recently offered her, so she waited. De Jesus told officials that she was not going to move unless she got enough money to "pick [her] own house."

De Jesus eventually received $30,000 in real estate compensation and $27,000 as replacement housing compensation. She knew that on the real estate market, the house she lost was not worth what government gave her, but she thought that government should pay her enough to move to a decent house in a different neighborhood. And this is exactly what she did: she used the compensation and her own $5,000 contribution to buy and move into a $60,000 house (plus settlement costs) several miles to the north, in a neighborhood near her daughter's family.[15] Notably, her total compensation of $57,000 was over one-and-a-half times as much as the $35,000 sum of a landlord's compensation and a tenant's compensation—Mr. Herrero's $22,000 and Gomez's $13,000, respectively, for a house with an only slightly lower estimated market value. Yet the recipients and onlookers judged all of these arrangements to be basically fair.

Like de Jesus, other homeowners sometimes happily used their compensation packages to secure housing outside the neighborhood that they could not have afforded otherwise. Many talked about the happy man who moved from the Jefferson Square site to Montana.[16] In general, government satisfied these homeowners by giving them not only the market value of their properties but also a lump sum to cover the cost of securing another, comparable place elsewhere.

In all of these cases, government recognized that homeowners make great investments of many types of value—generally greater than the investments of absentee owners and tenants combined—in their properties. As a result of this recognition, it was able to achieve legitimacy for its compensation arrangements, at least for those tenants and homeowners who wanted to leave the neighborhood.

RECOGNIZING FUTURE COMMITMENTS

To achieve legitimacy, government's compensation efforts needed to recognize that investments often involve future commitments, as when people intend to stay with and continue investing in their particular properties and neighborhoods. Notwithstanding the aforementioned legitimacy success stories, the categories of tenant, absentee owner, and owner-occupant did not always recognize these commitments among American Street and Jefferson Square condemnees. Thus, government sometimes needed to make finer distinctions than the official ones just described.

Officials and citizens tried to ensure that people who were significantly attached to a place and wanted to stay invested there received special recognition. Although officials did not speak about what they were doing in this way, they tried to distinguish absentee owners and homeowners who would maintain a future commitment (by sacrificing value) to their properties from those who would not. To recognize an absentee owner's or a homeowner's long-term attachment to a neighborhood, officials tried to secure a replacement property in the same or nearby location despite extra costs involved.

Differentiating Absentee Owners: The Investor and the Speculator

Government distinguished between two kinds of absentee owners: speculators, who had little intention of investing more in their properties, and investors, who planned to do so in the future. Its compensation for speculators stuck to the standard of cash for the property's market value, as discussed earlier. In contrast, its compensation for investors with long-term commitments and attachments to their properties included attempts to help them find substitute properties in the same neighborhood.

Officials' efforts to satisfy Melvin Hanton, an owner affected by the Jefferson Square project, demonstrated their willingness to honor absentee owners' future commitments. The RDA originally saw Hanton as a speculator. The two properties that he owned (one with his sibling) had sat vacant, with no indications—other than the payment of property taxes—that anyone tended to them. After the properties were taken, however, Hanton protested and claimed that he had a long history in the neighborhood and had planned to renovate his buildings. He had grown up in there in the 1940s and 1950s, moved away in the 1960s, returned with his wife in the 1980s, and moved away again after his mother died in the 1990s. He and his wife never sold the house they lived in as adults, and they had bought the building adjacent to it. Hanton also owned an interest in the house in which he had grown up and where his mother had lived until her death (see Figure 8.1).

Once Hanton convinced the RDA that he was a caring investor, it returned one of his properties through revestment—on the condition that he would renovate it and ensure its occupancy. One RDA staff member told me that he came to see Hanton as an investor, rather than a speculator, upon learning why Hanton had let his properties get in such poor condition despite his plans to repair them. "Evidently, he was sick for a while or he was out of the area and let them kind of fall into disrepair,"[17] the official said. During my 2009 interview with Hanton, he proudly demonstrated the high quality of the renovations to the building that was revested to him (see Figure 8.2). Moreover, he had no complaints about the RDA's stipulation that he restore the property, because, he said, he had planned to do so anyway.[18]

While government tried to accommodate people like Hanton by revesting property or offering property trades, they fought others' attempts to

Figure 8.1:
Childhood Home of Melvin Hanton (right), 1215 S. 4th Street, Taken
Source: JSCDC (circa 2000)

get anything beyond the minimum requirements for absentee owners, as demonstrated by the aforementioned case of Curtis Dash. While officials called people like Hanton "investors" to indicate a commitment to their properties, they labeled others "speculators" and "slumlords" to suggest a lesser attachment.

Owner-Occupants

Officials sometimes identified which homeowners were strongly committed to a neighborhood and found them homes very nearby, even if it required more money and effort than providing for relocation elsewhere. To recognize someone's long-term attachment to a neighborhood, officials tried to ensure that compensation came in the form of a property in that neighborhood.

Indeed, compensation arrangements made it possible for one homeowner displaced by the American Street condemnations to find a suitable relocation house in the neighborhood. Raymond Sosa's house (pseudonym), beautifully adorned on the inside, became the icon of the tragic loss

Figure 8.2:
Melvin Hanton's Property Revested and Renovation Completed (white door, left), 1207 S. 5th Street. New Jefferson Square House on Far Right (2009)
Source: Debbie Becher

of attachment to place. However, officials were able to replace this house with a brand new one just a few blocks away. Although Sosa would probably never consider it acceptable to have been forced from his home, "his whole vision changed" about the compensation when officials showed him the new house just a few blocks from his old one and explained that he would have no new mortgage, according to an RDA relocation worker.[19] By securing a house in the neighborhood, officials provided Sosa with compensation of greater financial value than he otherwise would have received. The total cost of building Sosa's new house was $125,000—much more than the $57,000 de Jesus received for moving out of the neighborhood from a similarly priced home. The RDA paid $20,000 in real estate compensation and $34,000 as a replacement housing payment for Sosa, so technically the compensation amount, $54,000, was quite similar to de Jesus's. However, the RDA also secured Sosa access to a project by the local community development corporation, which sold the house to Sosa for $52,000 (plus settlement costs); the community development corporation that built the house covered the rest of the costs of the $125,000 house, approximately $73,000, with federal subsidies for low-income homebuyers. By combining the real estate compensation, relocation benefits, and a connection to subsidized housing for low-income families, the RDA offered Sosa a sensible substitute in his old neighborhood—despite his continued objections to the condemnations.[20]

The Jefferson Square project compensated for homeowners' durable attachments to the neighborhood by allowing homeowners who wished to stay there—as over twenty of them did—to do so. The public's ultimate support for the project was partly based on DiCicco's eventual realization that many homeowners wanted to stay and the project's provisions for them. The project allocated much more money to relocation arrangements for homeowners who wanted to stay than to relocation arrangements for those who opted to leave, in order to preserve the former group's attachment to the neighborhood, even as they lost their houses.

Residents needed to stay in their new houses for a significant amount of time after the taking in order to access this larger compensation amount, however. Those who demonstrated a durable attachment by committing to stay received a subsidy covering the difference between the assessed value of their old house and the new one; for sales prices between $145,000 and $230,000, subsidies ranged from $90,000 to $115,000. The subsidy was turned into a mortgage that would pay itself off (self-amortize) over fifteen years, but only as long as the original owner or someone who inherited it from that owner actually lived in the house. According to an attorney who advocated for the residents, the idea was to prevent the recipient from "cashing in on the subsidy, pocketing the cash, and walking away."[21]

The new owners' indifference to the mortgage restrictions demonstrated that the strength of their desire to remain in the neighborhood outweighed their interest in financial gain. David T. Jones, Sr., who stayed in the neighborhood after being displaced from a house he had lived in since the 1960s, said of the restrictions, "I had no intentions of going anywhere, so that did not bother me at all." When I asked him whether he would have preferred to receive the compensation money allocated to his new house in the form of a cash payment, he replied, "I prefer the house. If I took the money, then I would have to go somewhere else. And I really did not want to go anywhere else."[22] Other homeowners concurred, saying, at the least, that they did not mind having their financial value tied up in a house in the neighborhood and, at the most, that they preferred it that way.[23]

Those who received so much more than the market value of their houses in the Jefferson Square redevelopment thought that they had not received a gift but only what they had deserved—adequate replacements for their investments. Resident Shirley Corbin-Nelson recounted a time she had vehemently corrected Jeremey Newberg when he implied the opposite, when he told her he was "giving her a new house." She responded, "You are not giving me shit! . . . Let me tell you one thing—I got a house. I lived in a house before you came, and you want what I have." And she recounted to me that "he looked at me and said, 'Shirley, I think you are right.' "[24]

FAILING TO RECOGNIZE INVESTMENT

In contrast to the success stories described above, there are cases in which government does not succeed in earning legitimacy. Condemnees believe that they have been cheated—and disinterested onlookers share their assessment. In these cases, which I call legitimacy failures, the two-part compensation process—identifying owners' investments and matching them with appropriate replacements—fails to earn government legitimacy. Government either misidentifies residents' investments or matches them with inappropriate replacements.

Identification Failures

Some compensation failures resulted from disagreements over what kind of investments were lost and, thus, needed to be replaced. In some of these cases, condemnees asserted that they deserved compensation as owners because they had maintained properties or held de facto titles. Other cases involved condemnees' claims that they planned to commit value to their properties in the future or that, because they had lived in their properties, they deserved relocation benefits as tenants or owner-occupants. Because government denied these claims, it offered the condemnees less compensation than they thought were warranted.[25] And when observers generally agreed that government had incorrectly identified a kind of investment, government failed to earn legitimacy.

Residents in the American Street neighborhood clashed with government over the evidence needed to identify them as owners. Two people claimed that they should have received compensation for lots they had been using for yards or storage, though they had no title or contract giving them the formal right to do so, and their neighbors agreed. Miguelina de Jesus said she should have been considered the owner of the lot next door to her house that she used as a yard, despite her lack of a title to the property. She knew that the use of vacant property was typical in a neighborhood overflowing with vacancies and that using adjacent lots had become a de facto form of ownership there. Furthermore, she believed that getting the title was a simple formality that, before the condemnation, probably would have cost her only a dollar and a trip downtown. Her failure to have done this cost her $2,000, however.[26]

Officials also refused to compensate Manuel Velez, whose story is described in the first pages of the book, for lots where he had a garage and kept his trucks. Velez considered the lots his own, despite his lack of a title to them, while government's official perspective was that he was "squatting" on them.[27] The properties were not worth much financially, but they led to a compensation dispute because Velez was determined to move to a new property with the same amount of land he had been using. His relocation worker, Maria Reyes, told me:

> He doesn't want any house. He wants a house with a yard to be able to park his trucks and other cars that he has that don't work. But he wants them because they're his. . . . You know, it's hard. But I was telling him, "No," [when he said,] "That's my truck and that's my lot." And I said, "Manuel, you know that is not yours. And I'm really, really sorry that you're going through this."
>
> Maria Reyes, RDA Relocation Technician[28]

Velez was sure that being forced to move to less land was a serious step down from what he had and would not meet the compensation goal of providing a house of equal or better condition. Like de Jesus, Velez also knew that using abandoned property was a socially respected form of investment.

Most of de Jesus's and Velez's neighbors probably would have agreed that government had cheated them by refusing to compensate for the lots. In response to the widespread abandonment of property in the American Street neighborhood, residents had developed their own rules for property use. By cleaning, using, and fencing land they did not own for yards, gardens, and storage, as well as to prevent dumping, residents protected everyone's property.[29] Government had even recognized this local standard by giving out titles to abandoned houses and lots for a dollar and back taxes—and locals knew it.[30] Thus, many neighbors agreed that use, not title, warranted compensation for ownership. To some officials, however, it seemed that the residents had been getting away with squatting until the condemnations. They treated the losses suffered by these "squatters" as unfortunate but perfectly justified consequences of government's involvement.

Another disagreement about what counted as ownership demonstrates how unique situations can cause misidentification of investments that lead to legitimacy failures. The government treated Velez as a tenant, rather than an owner-occupant, when it took what he (and everyone who knew him) believed to be his own house. This categorization cost him several thousand dollars in relocation payments and led to an extremely important symbolic loss. Velez's brother held the official title to the house; Velez told me that he had put the house in his brother's name as a formality because he was convinced that owning an asset would threaten his own Social Security benefits. Velez's brother received real estate compensation and passed it along to Velez. However, the sum of this compensation and Velez's tenancy relocation benefits amounted to less than the compensation that Velez would have received as an owner-occupant. Velez fought with officials about this for years, not understanding why they insisted on identifying him as a tenant rather than as an owner-occupant. After he finally moved, his daughter Milagros lamented:

> They treated my father as a tenant, so he lost a lot of money. He would have got... a couple thousand more, but they treated him as a tenant only because... my uncle's name was the one that was on the deed. They didn't want to hear it because they have a budget, and they want to give you the least possible. And so before, he never owed a mortgage. Now he owes a mortgage. So that wasn't fair.... Why would my uncle, if it was really his house... say it's my brother's house? But they didn't want to hear it.
>
> Milagros Velez, adult daughter of condemnee Manuel Velez[31]

In other cases, officials would not classify people who claimed they deserved compensation for occupancy as either as owners or tenants, so they received nothing at all. In Jefferson Square, Rosilyn Purvis thought she deserved something. She had lived with her grandmother in a house that her grandmother and uncle (the grandmother's son) owned together. For long stretches of time during a period lasting over twenty years, she stayed in the house in return for the care she gave her grandmother and some contributions toward the bills. When the redevelopment plans came along, Purvis's grandmother needed $5,000 to fix her heating system, and her health was deteriorating. For the sake of expedience, she sold her house to the JSCDC for $28,000 and received a spot in its newly rehabilitated senior apartment complex, before any single-family homes were built or renovated. Purvis moved into the new apartment with her grandmother, but when her grandmother died a year later, Purvis was left with nothing.[32] As a family member who had lived in the house, Purvis had a difficult time fitting into the RDA's compensation scheme. She told me that she "felt cheated," adding:

> I said, "Why wasn't I included?" I said, "Why did you make the homeowner— What about people that didn't have a deed? Would you just leave them out in the cold?"... [The compensation effort] seems like it worked out, but it didn't

Figure 8.3:
Former Home of Rosilyn Purvis and Her Grandmother at 1308 S. Lawrence Street (left), Taken. Vacant House Acquired for Jefferson Square from Mount Sinai Hospital (right), 1306 S. Lawrence Street
Source: JSCDC (circa 2000)

> work. I mean, it did help some people, but what about those in between the cracks?... It's like they said... "Oh well, too bad."
>
> Rosilyn Purvis, condemnee and co-resident with grandmother[33]

She explained that while she was neither a renter nor a homeowner, she still thought that she deserved something. When I told some officials how Purvis felt, they expressed concern but did not know how they would have helped, even if they had been aware of the problem.[34] Purvis admitted that she did very little to advocate for herself with authorities, in part because she could not produce any documents that they would treat as warrants for compensation. Though she had no title or lease, Purvis thought that she deserved help from government for being displaced and found it unjust that she could not even secure the benefits that a tenant would (see Figure 8.3).

In a similar situation, Joe Getka of Jefferson Square voiced his anger about officials' refusal to recognize that his son was living in a house he lost. Officials seemed to think of Getka as one of many owners of vacant properties who attempt to get unwarranted compensation for occupancy. They believed that he rehabilitated his property quickly and claimed his son had moved in at least in time (180 days before the official taking) to capture relocation benefits, but they refused to recognize this as genuine occupancy.[35]

In addition, Getka also alleged a government failure to acknowledge his long-standing attachment to his properties. He complained that by taking two of the three adjacent properties he owned (which the RDA said were vacant), officials had robbed him of his future plans. However, they would not acknowledge this loss. Despite his attempts to do so, Getka could not reclaim the properties or get other properties in the neighborhood that he considered suitable substitutes; his litigation resulted only in a slight increase in his real estate assessments. He protested that he was a proud investor and that he had planned to survive in retirement off the rental income from his little cluster of properties. Getka presented himself as both committed to the place and hoping to reap a profit. He had moved away from the neighborhood to the suburbs in 1969, but he prided himself on having invested in the area and said he had put a lot of work into the properties, in fact "killing [him]self working day and night" to ensure security for himself and his family. The takings, he said, were "devastating to us."[36] They would leave him with just one of a set of properties that he had hoped to use in combination, as a larger parcel where he "could build anything" he wanted in the future.[37] By giving him only a check for the properties' market price, government officials failed to recognize his hopes for that future.

Getka failed officials' tests of his future commitment. They initially tried to offer him extra consideration related to his attachment, but they eventually decided he was disingenuous and stopped. Once, officials offered a property swap so that he could build something himself on another site, but the properties would come with a requirement that Getka redevelop the new properties in short order and get them occupied. Getka balked because, he said, he was giving up properties with no such restrictions. At another point, Getka refused an offer to trade his properties for a new house in the development; he found it unacceptable because he was losing several parcels and the new house was only on one (see Figure 8.4).

When I met Getka in 2009, it was apparent that his years of fighting with government and his family about issues related to the taking had caused him deep pain. He said to me, repeatedly, with an earnest look in his eyes and his open hands stretched forward, "Why are they trying to hurt me?"[38] While officials may not have tried to hurt Getka, they had determined that he was not committed to owning and improving properties in the neighborhood, and they refused to provide him with extra compensation.

Figure 8.4:
Tenant-Occupied House Owned by Joseph and Helen Getka, (middle), 1234 S. 5th Street, Taken
Source: JSCDC (circa 2000)

Matching Failures

Even when government and condemnees agreed about the kind of investment lost, compensation failures sometimes arose during the second part of the compensation process, during which government attempted to match that loss with the appropriate replacement. At times, government's seemingly innocuous guidelines about replacement housing prevented condemnees from choosing new houses that they found suitable. In other cases, the rushed nature of the relocation process prevented condemnees from finding such housing.

Manuel Velez, whose problems persuading government of his ownership were discussed earlier, also sparred with officials over health and safety inspections. He found a few houses that he thought could substitute for his old one, but they failed RDA inspections. Velez was proud of his ability to convert a run-down place, bought for a relatively small amount of money, into something livable. He had used his "sweat equity" to build value in this way before, and he intended to do so again. But the RDA would not release relocation money for this kind of purchase. After proposing several different houses that failed RDA health and safety inspections, Velez gave up looking. Only when eviction was imminent, because new development was supposedly set to begin, did he settle on a replacement property that passed inspection. As described in Chapter 1, Velez told me all the reasons why he hated the new house during my interview with him there, complaining that he felt cramped by the much denser neighborhood and that the house's construction was shoddy.

Another requirement, that the new house be purchased from a non-relative, so stymied another displaced homeowner that she forfeited a large portion of the compensation available to her. American Street resident Aurora Caligna (pseudonym) eventually signed a paper waiving her right to most of a relocation payment that could have doubled the $22,000 she received as the market value of her taken house. She had asked the RDA to give her the payment for a house that her husband had bought already, but officials told her that she could not use the payment to purchase a house from a relative. Caligna tried to find a different house, but after choosing more than one place that failed health and safety inspections, she gave up, chose her husband's house, and surrendered the payment.

Sometimes, government's requirement that a new house be located before the funds could be released made the dislocated residents feel so rushed that they settled on something less than desirable. Limited by time—as well as by a lack of money, information, and assistance with finding a new house—they settled on houses they found unsatisfactory in order to access their payments.[39] These residents viewed their new houses as too costly, small, in bad repair, lacking in yard space, or in the wrong neighborhood.

Another American Street resident, Sonia Ortiz, for example, felt rushed when she began looking for a new house. (She had not wanted to leave her old house, and though she had over a year to look for a new one, she had maintained hope that residents would win their fight and stay in the neighborhood—thus, she may not have looked vigorously early on.) Ortiz felt a sense of urgency when a terrifying fire—which, she strongly suspected, was set by the people who wanted her out—broke out in the factory next door to her. In the time she had, she could not find a house for sale that she liked, that she could afford, and that was in the neighborhood. Eventually, she settled on a new house a few miles farther away from the center of the city. Ortiz told me that she liked this house but missed her old neighborhood and felt stressed by the additional mortgage.[40]

In the cases I have just described and others, government failed to earn legitimacy when citizens concluded that it categorized investment incorrectly or designed flawed matches. I demonstrated earlier that a system for recognizing investments allowed officials to regularly recognize many kinds of value, as well as long-term attachments to a place. However, individual situations did not all fit comfortably within these practices. Failures

Table 8.2. LEGITIMACY OF OWNER COMPENSATION BY PRACTICAL CLASSIFICATION

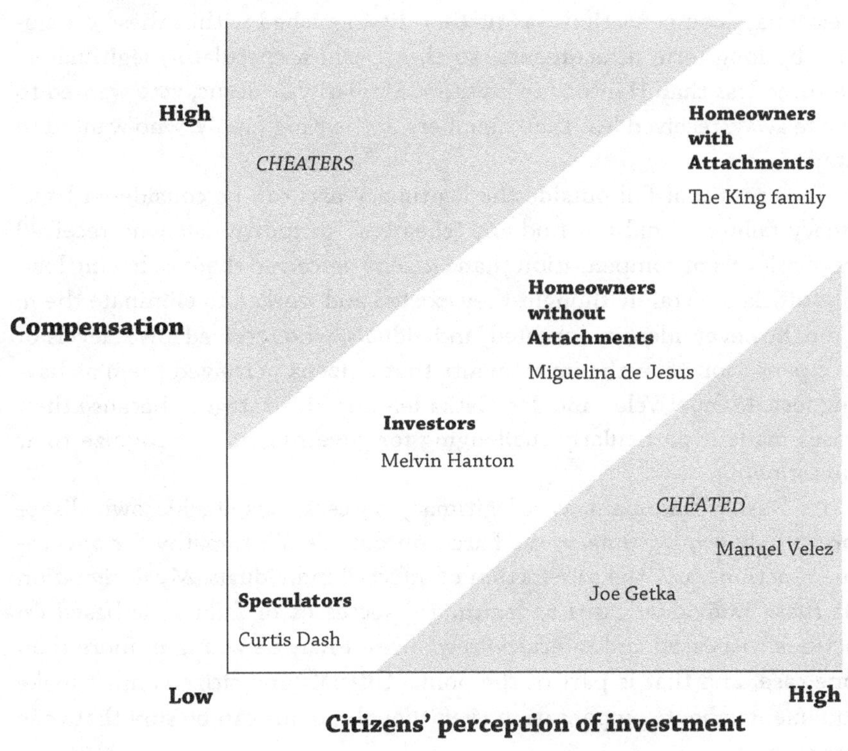

resulted not from discord over what government could or should compensate in general, but from disagreements over how individual cases fit into a classification system of kinds of investments lost and suitable matches. Therefore, conflicts over the appropriateness of government action do not result from differences along the familiar lines of exchange value versus use value and market value versus sentimental value. Instead, they result from differences in the more pragmatic classification and communication processes of the specific policy at hand.

A two-dimensional diagram simplifying a more complex process in Table 8.2 summarizes how the legitimacy of compensation arrangements depended on categorical representations of investment. (For parsimony's sake, only owners are included in the table.)

In the lighter area close to the x = y legitimacy diagonal are those cases in which the provided compensation roughly matched citizens' perceptions of the investments lost. Drawn as if market values of all properties referred to here were equal, the figure shows that absentee owners Curtis Dash and Melvin Hanton received less compensation than homeowners did. Legitimate compensation was further distinguished within these categories by long-term attachments, so that Dash, a speculator, legitimately received less than Hanton, an investor. Similarly, de Jesus, who wanted to move away, received less than members of the King family, who wanted to stay.

The cases that fell outside the legitimacy axis can be considered legitimacy failures. I did not find any "cheaters," or individuals who received higher levels of compensation than citizens perceived them as having lost, but officials certainly thought they existed and worked to eliminate them. I did, however, identify "cheated" individuals, who received lower levels of compensation than the investments that citizens perceived them as having lost. Manuel Velez and Joe Getka fell into this category because their cases made it particularly challenging for government to recognize their investments.

As Dash's placement as a legitimacy success (despite his own disapproval) shows, legitimacy was based on outsiders' sympathy for government actions, not the satisfaction of affected individuals. My designation of these individual cases as legitimacy successes or failures is based on actions witnessed and interview responses. I may be wrong in more than one case, and that is part of the point. Officials and citizens must make judgments about compensation even though no one can be sure that they are correct.

COMMUNICATING ABOUT WHAT PEOPLE DESERVE

Government depends heavily on communication as it strives to ensure the accuracy of its compensation judgments. Officials determine what condemnees deserve largely by asking them what they are losing and what could replace their losses and then verifying the condemnees' answers. When condemnees effectively express their understanding of the loss and what could replace it, a legitimate outcome is much more likely to result. However, this communication process is ripe with the potential for misunderstandings.

Tone and assertiveness mattered in the compensation cases I reviewed. The virulent anger expressed by Joe Getka, who was ultimately categorized as a mere speculator, appears to have damaged his case. Although officials tried to accommodate Getka at first, they eventually seemed to justify their dismissal of his claims by describing him as bitter and angry.[41] By contrast, although Melvin Hanton originally showed RDA officials his anger, he also approached them with a more conciliatory tone, at least sometimes, and convinced them to revest one of his properties. Other condemnees who felt cheated had avoided contact with officials altogether, refusing to advocate for themselves, to answer officials' requests for information, or even to make required decisions.[42] Quiescence did not get them what they thought they deserved, however; officials responded only to articulated requests.

Whether people voiced their demands often depended on their a priori assessments about their claims' legitimacy. Rosilyn Purvis, for example, remained mostly quiet about her sense of injustice, in part because of her view that she lacked any documents that authorities would treat as warrants for compensation.[43] In contrast, she noted, the King family had "something to work with . . . a deed."[44] Purvis attributed some of the Kings' ability to fight, which resulted in their successful self-advocacy and a transformation of the entire Jefferson Square project, to their possession of such documentation. Indeed, the Kings and others may have been willing to assert their arguments through loud and empathic speeches because they were confident of winning public approval. They knew they could make a compelling case not only by producing their titles, but also by sharing a few simple details about the decades they lived in the neighborhood and the number of family members who resided within a few blocks.

A priori judgments about legitimacy also may have led to quiescence on the part of condemnees who were categorized as speculators. Some of these individuals might have viewed themselves as deserving businessmen or businesswomen who took risks on a property's future. Nevertheless, they most likely assumed that their arguments for deserving more than minimal compensation would fall on deaf ears, and they certainly never threatened to call reporters to expose how officials were cheating them.

The cases above suggest that legitimacy is not just a consequence of how condemnees voiced their claims but also a motivator of that expression. Legitimacy is not really about what someone wants, or even what someone believes is fair; it is about being treated in a way that other people will think is fair. Purvis and others kept quiet because they believed that they were unlikely to draw sympathy. Other condemnees spoke more often and more loudly because they believed that their claims would be heard sympathetically, and this assertiveness may have resulted in greater compensation.

CONCLUSION

This book began with the question: When does government action become legitimate? We have seen that citizens and officials constantly constructed the boundaries of legitimacy as they considered government policies in real-life situations. They deployed various rules, categories, and narratives to make sense of what government was doing and what it should have been doing. Often, they decided that government action was legitimate when they characterized it as supporting people's investments, and they considered it illegitimate when it damaged investments.

Compensation arrangements reflect a more complicated attempt to replace investments lost than the legal standard of market value suggests. In some cases, government limited compensation to market value. Some people, on first glance, seemed to have invested nothing beyond the purchase price of their properties. Individuals who owned vacant lots or properties with vacant and neglected buildings warranted nothing more than market value, in a check.

In other cases, people demanded more and different compensation and garnered sympathy. For instance, even some people who lacked property titles or leases, and thus were neither legal owners nor renters, claimed to deserve compensation. They basically asserted that, given the local context, squatting was an investment that the community should recognize. Others who had legal titles or leases and who had stayed in neighborhoods that others abandoned were deemed more worthy of compensation than neighborhood newcomers. Even absentee owners who kept titles to vacant properties because they planned to fix them up in the future were judged to warrant greater compensation than speculators.

Thus, like the rest of the book, this chapter has shown how people claimed to be investors and how government earned legitimacy when it supported them as such. In contrast, those who were unlikely to be perceived as investors made few, if any, claims at all.

CHAPTER 9
The Politics of Property

My observations of Philadelphia's experiences with eminent domain only make sense once we understand that officials and citizens view property as investments of value that government is responsible for securing. The city's government routinely took private properties en masse that were vacant, dangerous, unsafe, and practically unsellable on the market, and these takings prompted little to no protest. In contrast, Philadelphia officials rarely even considered taking properties that were clearly cared for, inhabited, safe, and stably priced. This pattern cannot be explained by the assumption, implicit in our national discourse about eminent domain, that takings of private property for private reuse are the most likely to be controversial. But once we realize that officials and citizens viewed property as investment, we can understand how eminent domain decisions were made, why some of them were accepted, and why others led to conflicts.

As I described in the preceding chapters, citizens and officials alike appealed to a notion of investment as they made claims about what government could and should do throughout the American Street and Jefferson Square projects. These were borderline cases—with conditions falling between the two extremes mentioned above—in which eminent domain's protection of investment was less clear than usual. Therefore, government decisions were much more complex, considered, and prone to controversy than in most cases. Although the American Street project was greeted with skeptical optimism initially, its long history of implementation errors kept it from protecting investments and led to the widespread perception that it was a deeply misguided and disappointing initiative. The Jefferson Square project stirred initial controversy because it originally reflected officials' naïve understanding of community investments, but once this understanding was corrected, officials were able to implement a widely admired project.

In this chapter, I ponder the implications of my findings about legitimacy with respect to property beyond Philadelphia. First, I consider how reforms of eminent domain policy could reflect my conception of investment and, thus, earn legitimacy for government in a contemporary context. Second, I consider how the general meaning of private property could reflect my conception and earn this legitimacy.

EMINENT DOMAIN POLICY

Reform Recommendations Reflecting Property as Investment

I have devised several recommendations for eminent domain reform that, by reflecting a conception of property as investment, would enable government initiatives to earn legitimacy in today's urban environments. They would account for people's past investments in and future plans involving parcels of land, buildings, and geographic communities. By giving more power to individuals and businesses with established roots in areas targeted for redevelopment, such reforms would ensure the slowing, redesign, or even abandonment of the kinds of highly contested projects that have made national news.

However, the reforms would not doom a project simply because it involved a private redeveloper. If there is any way to limit government overreach in an era of ubiquitous public-private cooperation in land development, a first and admittedly controversial step is to acknowledge the inevitability of such cooperation. Rather than wish, will, or try to write public-private deal-making away, practical eminent domain reform would create protections that work within this form of governance. Policies that focus on protecting investment would give less import to distinctions between public and private entities and even between owners and non-owners. My recommendations reflect stakeholders' close-up evaluations of the real-life cases with which they were intimately involved, rather than sound bites offered by activists or news reporters. The reforms that I suggest would base government decisions on whether property has current value to an owner, renter, and nearby neighbors.

Easing Takings of Abandoned Properties, Restricting Takings of Valued Properties

My first suggestion for a reform may seem a bit counterintuitive, as it involves giving government more, rather than less, leeway in taking properties. Currently, many local authorities follow very cumbersome procedures for taking abandoned properties that are similar to their procedures for taking occupied and well-cared-for homes. The former procedures limit government's ability to revitalize neighborhoods and can inure officials to the procedures' ultimate intent—the protection of property that is valued by its current owners or occupants. A comprehensive set of reforms focusing on property as investment would make it easier for governments to take properties that have little to no discernable investment by the current owner.

Quick and simple processes for acquiring abandoned properties and the properties of neglectful absentee owners are necessary. Signals of abandonment and lack of care include tax delinquency, vacancy, and building-code violations. The substandard condition of a property with an absentee owner is a signal that the owner is a speculator or a slumlord. States, cities, and counties already have a vast array of guidelines for the acquisition of such properties and the punishment of irresponsible property stewardship. But these guidelines—partly because they are so respectful of property titles—can be extremely complex or inflexible and hamper governments' ability to encourage responsible stewardship.

Citizens are likely to endorse the easing of transfers of abandoned and speculative property because it will make government treat property as investment. In doing so, government will protect nothing more than the market value of property when its owners have invested nothing more than this market value and have shown no clear intention of investing more in the future. My study of Philadelphia showed that citizens and officials treated the takings of thousands of such properties as desirable. In addition, a primary official goal of the Philadelphia redevelopment projects studied here was to rid poor neighborhoods of speculators and slumlords, and this goal was supported by most local residents, business owners, and community leaders.

Some states already have what they call "quick take" procedures and "land banks" to facilitate the acquisition and management of abandoned properties. In late 2013, Philadelphia City Council Member Maria Quiñones-Sanchez—a representative of District Seven, where American Street is located, since 2008—sponsored a bill to create an autonomous Philadelphia land bank for managing the city's approximately 40,000 vacant properties. She was struggling against other members who wanted the council to retain control of these properties.[1]

No matter what kind of agency retains powers over vacant property, in practice, the treatment of absentee owners who claim not to have abandoned their properties may need to be delicate. If government is to respect owners' future plans as a type of investment, it must provide more protection for owners who have shown that they intend to steward a property. Owners who protest that they are land-banking with plans for eventual improvement, such as Joseph Getka of Jefferson Square, would merit greater consideration than many absentee owners. Perhaps government can provide more protection when the former type of owners treat their property with the minimal standard of care needed to avoid creating a nuisance.

Another possible reform would be to provide citizens who have previously demonstrated property stewardship with the opportunity to acquire titles taken from other, non-caring owners. Such a priority undergirds Philadelphia's current policy of offering vacant properties to adjacent homeowners.[2] In addition, the city of Richmond, California has a new policy allowing it to expropriate foreclosed properties from banks and return them to families who lost their mortgages. The policy is drawing nationwide attention, and other cities are considering following suit.[3] Indeed, the logic of investment dictates the importance of allowing governments, when possible, to quickly transfer properties to private parties who have shown a willingness to invest in them.

Compensation Standards for Valued Properties

In addition to expediting the process for taking abandoned properties, government should enhance its protections for properties that owners or inhabitants perceive and treat as valuable. Government needs to tread much more carefully when taking these properties than it does at present and when taking abandoned or speculative properties. By doing so, it can ensure that property investments—including high real-estate values, years of residence, labor, and emotional attachments—are more secure, even if property titles are not. Based on my research in Philadelphia, I recommend a series of broadly applicable reforms for the taking of valued properties that involve compensation guidelines, planning and negotiation processes, and accountability standards.

One of the most visible ways that government can demonstrate respect for property investment is by reforming its compensation guidelines. Indeed, I expect that the most politically feasible eminent domain reforms would be those related to compensation. Perhaps because compensation reform is so viable, it is a popular topic in law reviews, and my suggestions for such reform synthesize recommendations that have been laid out in much more detail in various journal articles.[4] I describe a few of these that could especially crystallize the conception of property as investment by adequately accounting for several distinct elements of investment.

Although governments may provide relocation benefits to compensate for physical displacement, these benefits are often so abysmally low that government appears insensitive to actual relocation costs. Compensation for the material cost of business relocations is even more limited than compensation for residential relocations, considering that the former may be consistently higher than the latter. Increasing maximum amounts for certain aspects of relocation compensation and bringing the compensation for business relocations more into line with actual costs would be good places to start adapting compensation rules.

Some of these reforms would involve changes to the Uniform Relocation Assistance and Real Property Acquisition Policies for Federally and Federally Assisted Programs Act of 1970 (URA),[5] the federal law regulating compensation. This act already treats the displacement of residents and businesses as particularly troublesome and deserving of compensation beyond the full market value of real estate lost. It provides for compensation directly related to occupancy, over and above any compensation provided for title. However, the URA also places appallingly low financial limits on the amounts available to recognize displacement costs. At present, it sets maximum relocation benefits covering the gap between market prices of condemned housing and replacement housing at $31,000 and $7,200 for owner-occupied and renter-occupied condemnations, respectively. In addition, it sets the maximum compensation for the costs of business of reestablishment beyond moving costs at $25,000 to $40,000.[6] Although the act and state laws allow agencies to ignore these limits if necessary as a "last resort,"[7] a better set of compensation standards would not create such a hurdle.

The current limitations on relocation benefits undermine the principle of full compensation for lost investments. If allowing displaced residents to stay in their immediate neighborhood was considered a potential requirement for suitable replacement housing, as many displaced residents would want, the current maximums would not suffice. Most of the residents displaced by the American Street takings received $22,500, the maximum replacement payment under the law at the time, before reforms raised it to $31,000. But this only allowed them to buy houses passing government health inspections a full two miles away from their old homes and farther from downtown. None of the Jefferson Square area residents would have been able to stay if $22,500 or $31,000 had been the maximum allowed payment above the market price of their former homes. For them, and for a few of the American Street residents, subsidies for affordable housing made the relocation to a nearby dwelling possible. Such a subsidy will not always be available, however, and not all displaced residents will choose such housing.

Therefore, the URA should be amended to increase the current maximum relocation benefits dramatically. Adding a lump sum figure to cover the non-market costs of displacement for any resident and any business would further increase the sense that government has fully recognized the lost investments.[8] In addition, URA protections should be repeated in state laws so that they apply to all projects, not just federally funded projects, that use eminent domain.

Although government at least already acknowledges displacement costs, even if it does not adequately account for them, it fails to provide any compensation whatsoever for the time that owners or inhabitants have invested in their properties. Currently, compensation rules mimic the instantaneous nature of market transactions, with appraisers, lawyers, and other officials striving to ensure that the calculation of market value for compensation purposes occurs on the exact date of the taking. This practice ignores the fact, well known to everyone involved with eminent domain, that the actual taking process always takes at least a few months and often stretches on for years. More important, the practice treats a person who bought a property six months before condemnation and another who bought a property twenty years earlier exactly alike—even though almost no one seems to think this is fair or reasonable.

Compensation practices need to recognize the years that owners and residents have spent with their property. One way of doing so would be to create "longevity allowances" and factor them into compensation rules. The allowances could account for investments of time in a very formulaic way, by allocating some cash amount or percentage of real estate value for each year that an individual has inhabited or owned a property.[9]

Even if this recommendation is anathema to many in legal and academic circles, it will probably seem like common sense to most Americans. The lengthy periods of time families had lived in their homes were often among the first pieces of evidence that protestors marshaled against government during the contentious stages of the American Street and Jefferson Square takings. Neighbors on N. Bodine Street, having lived there an average of twenty years, nevertheless spoke of the residents who had been there the longest, forty years, as the ones most pained by the displacement. The Kings and others asserted their rights to stay in their South Philadelphia neighborhood by talking about how they had stayed over the decades when others had fled. Indeed, news stories of highly contentious cases beyond Philadelphia often mention how long a family has lived in a threatened house, implying that the more years that were spent there, the more damage a removal would cause.

Because hopes for the future are central to investments, compensation calculations also should be changed to account for losses to future benefits, which present compensation rules typically ignore.[10] Critics of eminent domain often point to the current unwillingness of government to acknowledge these losses as evidence of its abuse of power. There is something wrong, they say, when the future profits from land flow to brand-new owners of condemned properties and the city coffers, rather than to those who stuck with the properties through hard times. This criticism is often vehement when government takes properties in areas where investments are finally beginning to pay off after years of waiting. Another strong point of contention is that the post-taking consolidation of several smaller parcels often creates an increase in real-estate value that flows to government or to a private redeveloper, rather than to the previous owners.

Compensation should recognize how expectations of future benefits from properties have been stymied by the takings.[11] Governments need to develop mechanisms for sharing the profits from land assembly that happens through eminent domain. For example, they might pay condemnees a portion of the market value of the larger consolidated parcel, rather than the market value of the singular taken parcel. Profit-sharing arrangements should also be constructed, so that if the redeveloped property continues to become more financially valuable to the city or new private owner, the particular owners and inhabitants who had banked on that area receive a significant portion of the benefits. Though costly, these compensation enhancements will be necessary if government is to appear respectful of the fact that it takes investments when it takes property.

Empowering Citizen Voices in Planning

Although the aforementioned reform recommendations might lessen the criticisms of compensation, this part of the eminent domain process occurs only after a valuable property has already been condemned. To earn approval for eminent domain, reforms also need to change the planning that determines whether properties will be taken at all.

Perhaps the biggest challenge to government legitimacy in redevelopment planning is the apparent disregard for owners' and occupants' wishes, and one way to help these people develop a powerful voice in planning is to ensure transparency throughout the process. Transparency requirements can support their ability to develop informed opinions and to speak with influence. Currently, a lack of transparency feeds on the precarious interplay among individuals' decisions about whether to support or fight a redevelopment plan and the larger community planning process. Residents commonly charge that government officials kept their plans hidden from public view until after the most important decisions about where and what to redevelop were made. At public meetings that EZ officials hosted for American Street's redevelopment and at the PCPC's meetings regarding Jefferson Square, residents asked repeatedly for information about which properties were being taken. Even though officials had such lists in their hands, they did not turn them over to the inquiring residents, and they either implied by omission or by direct statements that they did not exist.

In addition, after the broad designs for redevelopment are well known, privacy in individual deal-making often detrimentally affects others who have not yet signed agreements. Individuals faced with condemnation are constantly wondering what deals others were offered and what they accepted or rejected. Rumors are rampant and strongly influence decisions about what is possible and what is fair. Many of the residents displaced by the American Street takings seemed to have thought that their neighbors took lower compensation than the records indicated. This misinformation made them willing to accept compensation that did not feel right but that they assumed could not be pushed any higher. Among some of those who lost their properties in American Street and Jefferson Square, feelings of shame linger as they evaluate what happened to them in light of what they believe others received, and these beliefs are often incorrect. Officials generally treat individual compensation arrangements as confidential. The transparency requirements that I envision would continue to protect the privacy of arrangements about more personal issues such as liens incurred and family income. But they would put the amount and kind of assistance that government offers in return for some kind of concession, usually the property title, on the public record.

Officials often err on the side of hiding important, specific information—especially about compensation potential—because they are wary of violating confidentiality or making promises that they cannot or will not keep. A more troubling development is that in extremely contentious cases, confidentiality in deal-making has been expanded beyond officials' general practice. In the Atlantic Yards redevelopment planning, for example, residents who sold their properties signed gag orders prohibiting them from voicing opposition to the project or sharing any experience of maltreatment.[12]

If citizens are to gain power in the deal-making process, such practices must be stopped. Individuals must always be allowed to speak publicly about their opinions of the larger project and about their individual deals. Solid transparency requirements need to make information about any offers and agreements with individual condemnees public, so that everyone involved has the benefit of accurate information. Transparency must be required, and acts of concealment like gag orders and official retreats to generalizations must be soundly prohibited.

Transparency will not be enough to guarantee that citizen voices are heard. For instance, even if information is available on official documents, such as the addresses listed on the redevelopment proposal considered by the PCPC in relation to Jefferson Square, someone with condemnees' interests at heart needs intimate knowledge of the process to know when and where such documents exist. In order to help individual citizens targeted by eminent domain gain power in planning, the state should employ professionals to serve in a new kind of position, as individual advocates for condemnees.

Advocates would be contracted by government but would operate completely independently of officials handling the condemnations. I make this recommendation because of the problems that arise from the complexity and rarity of the eminent domain process. The professionals who have seen eminent domain planning happen many times have an extreme advantage over citizens who encounter it no more than once in their lives. Currently, the "repeat players" almost all work on the side of government officials pursuing the condemnations.[13] To reduce this power differential, professionals need to develop repeated experience in the local process on the side of the condemnees. A new professional position of independent advocates could allow people who do not work for government or private developers to develop such expertise and to use it to guide citizen-targets. The professional citizen advocates should be assigned to citizens from the earliest moment that a government's intentions to consider property for taking become evident.

The provision for such professional advocates needs to be separate from and in addition to compensation for attorneys that some eminent domain laws already cover. Attorneys' fees do not accomplish what I suggest here. The amount funded is often inadequate for an enduring contest.[14] The attorneys employed provide little to their clients in the way of professional expertise in this specialized field because very few attorneys have experience fighting eminent domain cases—especially for the poor, who do not tend to employ them at all. And perhaps most important, attorneys are employed primarily for their usefulness in appeals to the written rules, not for their acuity in political negotiations. Several of the condemnees I spoke with employed attorneys but did not see that their assistance made any difference.

The professional eminent domain advocates that I imagine, however, would advise clients about the larger political climate and bureaucratic process, with which they would be familiar from their repeated experiences. Historical precedents for independent advocates in other areas of citizen-government interaction, such as guardians ad litem for children involved in legal action and executors and trustees for wills, suggest that this recommendation is indeed plausible.[15]

My final recommendation for transforming the planning process is to create contracts for state-funded community organizers to work with and to form citizen-groups of those faced with eminent domain. Although support for individuals is important, the fact that planning involves entire areas means that citizens targeted by eminent domain must also be able to develop a powerful collective voice in order to have an impact. Furthermore, citizens often lament that scrambling to make individual deals divides them. Without help organizing, citizens surprised by redevelopment plans often lose the opportunity to capitalize on their collective power.

State-funded community organizers would help to boost the negotiating power of collectivities, rather than just individuals—and, in so doing, they would amplify the power of individuals allied with those collectives. While the individual advocates just described may help particular families or corporations get the best deal they can, within the context of the larger planning process, community organizers have much more potential to help change the direction of the planning itself. The importance of professionally trained and experienced community organizers was demonstrated with great clarity by the transformation of the Jefferson Square development. The Kings and other residents attested that this transformation would not have happened without Johanna Bauman, Reverend David Funkhouser, and attorney Irv Ackelsberg, all of whom advocated for St. John's Leadership Team rather than for individual residents. This organizing in reaction to eminent domain is likely to be temporary; organizations might dissolve after the redevelopment planning and implementation are complete.[16] More permanent community organizing can potentially lead to even greater grassroots control of eminent domain powers. For example, the Dudley Street Neighborhood Initiative in Boston, a neighborhood-based group, gained its own authority to take properties and used it laudably. This group demonstrated the crucial role of community organizing in determining whether the power of eminent domain is used to support or denigrate poor neighborhoods.[17]

This recommendation also stems from the understanding that decision-making about redevelopment is a long, drawn-out political process in which those invested in properties at stake deserve a voice. And yet, without help, they are extremely unlikely to wield political power that can rival that of the government officials or private redevelopers they encounter. Providing organizers to help give voice to community interests would reflect the existing practice of writing community benefits agreements that supposedly are negotiated by community spokespeople.[18] However, it would have the added advantage of creating a new organizational power outside existing community institutions with already entrenched interests. The government-funded community organizers that I imagine would be outsiders employed to work exclusively on redevelopment planning that may involve eminent domain.[19]

Unfortunately, while I believe it is one of the most worthwhile reforms that can be made, the provision of government-funded community organizers is also likely to be one of the most politically difficult to institute and protect. Politicians will be reluctant to provide such a resource and will be very tempted to cut the lifeline to any professionals explicitly organizing against official plans. There are precedents for government support for community organizing in President Johnson's Community Action program and, when requested through local grant planning, through other federal programming. And yet, these programs certainly have their limits, as the story of the lead organizer against eminent domain in Philadelphia so profoundly illustrates. Rosemary Cubas had begun building an organizing campaign for neighborhood improvement with EZ funds, but officials cut her off once her organizing turned to opposition of their eminent domain plans, and they explained quite bluntly that they could not fund resistance to their plans.[20] This experience serves as a warning that support for organizing will be difficult to secure, but perhaps even more difficult to protect over the long haul of project planning if citizens decide to oppose government plans. But of course, the possibility that opposition will emerge but lack a strong voice is what makes such a resource so important.

Accountability for Future Changes during Implementation

Even if governments manage to earn support for their respect of property during the planning and compensation process, their use of eminent domain is still denigrated when their optimistic redevelopment plans fail to come to fruition, as happens far too often. Consider how embarrassing it has been for New London, for instance, that Pfizer Corporation eventually decided to pull out of the city less than ten years after all of the necessary properties had been condemned and cleared so that it could locate there.[21] Similarly, the City of Philadelphia's reputation suffered when the original company that promised development on the first American Street site (the 2100 block) pulled out, while Chaes Foods vacated another large area two blocks north in order to build on the site. Another stain on the city's reputation resulted from the fact that American Street's other two sites, the

1700 block and the 2501 block, hosted only grass and wee ds several years after residents had been evicted.

The uncertainty of implementation creates a serious problem for eminent domain's legitimacy, when governments justify the power with their future plans for redevelopment. The fulfillment of plans is always uncertain, but this is particularly true of those that involve public-private redevelopment. These projects are subject to the same unpredictability that any long-term development project faces because of changes in the economic environment, but the public-private partnership adds another layer of uncertainty. Government counts on a private developer's commitment, and the developer bets on government's ability to deliver on its promises of land and other incentives and permissions. As countless project derailments around the country have demonstrated, no matter what agreements are negotiated, designs are drawn, and outcomes are predicted, no one can be sure what the future will hold for the publicly supported private redevelopment plans that emerge. If plans go awry before anyone's property is taken, there is no problem as far as eminent domain policy is concerned.

When people lose their properties for plans that are eventually abandoned, however, serious accountability to those condemnees is required if governments are to sustain any of the support they earned throughout earlier stages of a project. Accountability would include continued commitments to the original property owners and occupants—such as requiring their approval for dramatic changes to plans—even after their property is taken. During planning, officials and citizens can attempt to foresee problems and lay out penalties for withdrawals from earlier plans, with benefits going to condemnees.[22] In addition, checks should be in place to ensure that if no redevelopment occurs after a period of time or plans divert far away from original agreements, the previous owners have the option of getting their properties back at low or no cost.[23] With assurances of a voice in plan changes, as well as penalty payments and promises of returned properties for lack of development and changes of plans, redevelopment deals can provide citizens with increased security about the uncertain future.[24]

Finally, I recommend applying the above proposals for compensation, planning, and accountability to all eminent domain—for private as well as public reuse.[25] Whether property will be transferred to public or to private owners is irrelevant to the basic protections necessary for citizens' investments. My suggestions could force officials to respect property as an investment rather than as a title, and as I have argued, this largely requires putting less weight on the distinction between public and private property. The recent national debate about eminent domain abuse and my research specifically have narrowed our vision to a kind of eminent domain that seemed particularly egregious because property was being transferred to private rather than public owners. Nevertheless, I suspect that the reforms suggested here are needed just as much for citizens facing condemnation for public rather than private owners. In fact, it is very likely that many more property owners face eminent domain for publicly owned highways than for private redevelopment.[26] Moreover, because the former kind of eminent domain is so readily accepted as legitimate, condemnees currently have little reason to expect that political resistance would mobilize any support for their predicaments at all. Americans would probably just shrug and think that such condemnations are unfortunate sacrifices.

However, it could be the case that in takings for public entities, government ramrods the poor instead of the wealthy because properties are cheap and the poor are even more politically powerless than they are in takings for private reuse. Protections are necessary here because, in many cases, the redesigns of highways and increased compensation could save homes, farms, businesses, and hearts. But without any political pressure, state and federal departments of transportation are unlikely to make such concessions. My discussions with professional appraisers and attorneys acquainted with public takings suggest that the politics of these takings are, in fact, this lopsided. In addition, I have been repeatedly surprised by acquaintances who tell me of a dear relative who lost a home or a farm to a rural highway project or public conservation plan and felt powerless to do anything about it. One mild-mannered professor startled me with his story about how he remembered holding up protest signs to save the family farm at the age of five—and how it did no good. A state department of transportation "ruined my father," he said, when it refused to shift its highway design just a bit. Thus, carefully thought-out protections should be instituted for any use of eminent domain, regardless of whether a property's future lies in the hands of a public or private entity.

Problems with Common Reform Positions

The reform suggestions that I just described are not the only proposals for stemming eminent domain abuse. In fact, there are two other types of changes that were adopted by a majority of state legislatures in the *Kelo* aftermath. One type prohibits property takings for transfers to new private entities; after *Kelo*, thirty-one states passed a law either prohibiting takings for private reuse or for economic development.[27] The second kind of reform continued to allow takings for private reuse for the purpose of eliminating blight, but much more carefully defined blight or made the procedure to identify its existence more cumbersome. Thirty states enacted reforms of this kind between 2005 and 2008. Many of these were the same states that prohibited takings for private reuses, but they carved out exceptions for the elimination of blight.[28] We know very little about these reforms' impacts, but we can surmise their effects by imagining how different pre-*Kelo* eminent domain, about which we now know much more, would have been if they had been in place.

Although the first type of reform will certainly stop the kinds of high-profile cases that have made the national news, my research in Philadelphia indicates that its costs will also be quite high.[29] Had such laws eliminating takings for private reuse or for economic development been in place in Philadelphia in the 1990s and early 2000s, they would have prohibited a significant amount of the redevelopment activity that ultimately drew widespread support. Government would not have been able to take abandoned side yards for adjacent owner-occupants or to take lots on behalf of nonprofits interested in constructing affordable housing. Nor would it have been able to use eminent domain powers to address the severe problems caused by a lack of stewardship for properties in poor neighborhoods. Miguelina de Jesus, who was grateful for the above–market value compensation that allowed her to move away from her American Street home, would have remained trapped in her old neighborhood.

The ways in which eminent domain has been used and has earned support outside Philadelphia further demonstrate that restrictions on eminent domain for private transfers will hinder government's ability to achieve redevelopment. For example, if such restrictions had been in place in Massachusetts before the Dudley Street neighborhood organizing began, they would have prevented the highly esteemed transformation of the Roxbury area of Boston. There, local residents needed and used eminent-domain powers to save their neighborhood from absentee owners who were neglecting and even burning down their properties.[30] Limitations on private transfers will be detrimental to governments' abilities to acquire land for affordable housing built by private entities and more generally to transfer land from profiteers to stewards in extremely poor neighborhoods. Such reforms will stop governments from using resources to stem *private* abuses of land and buildings in poor neighborhoods. It is likely that with such reforms in place, public criticism will focus not on a lack of eminent domain power but on government's inability to provide affordable housing or to force private owners to steward their properties. Nevertheless, these changes to eminent domain laws will be a proximate cause for citizen dissatisfaction.

The second kind of common policy reform—toughening up the blight identification process[31]—will only help middle-class and wealthy Americans and will leave the poor without additional protection. If a neighborhood must qualify as blighted under a strict definition to allow a taking, most middle-class and wealthy properties and neighborhoods will be protected from eminent domain. But such a reform does nothing to protect the owners and inhabitants in blighted neighborhoods—poor people—from eminent domain. It does nothing to protect the individuals trapped there from having their interests in property summarily ignored. Indeed, although it seems intuitively attractive to create more stringent requirements that dictate where government can threaten property rights while preserving its ability to intervene in the neediest neighborhoods, this solution creates a dilemma. By protecting middle-class and wealthy neighborhoods, this type of reform simply sacrifices the poorest Americans to potential government abuse. Law professor David Dana wrote that "it is hard to understand any of the contours of *Kelo*-inspired reform as shaped by concern for the needs of the poor and poor neighborhoods," and that these reforms send a message, "repugnant in our constitutional tradition," that middle-class homeowners deserve more protection than poor renters.[32] Law professors Gerald Frug and David Barron commented in an op-ed about Massachusetts legislative proposals that "the legislation seems to suggest a simple, unjust rule: If you want to treat people unfairly, make sure it's poor people."[33]

The drawbacks of these most common eminent domain reforms might suggest the need to surrender the effort to curb abuse, and some government spokespeople have of course advocated such a path. They push for permission to continue to give governments broad discretion in using their eminent domain powers for redevelopment. Government officials and allies ask for continued latitude, while, perhaps, restating principles about the importance of planning and community involvement in planning.[34] It should be no surprise that they have often fought against limits on their eminent domain powers and have selected the most glowing accounts of eminent domain projects to convince the public of their benevolence. This position is understandable, given that they were put on the defensive by a sudden and powerful onslaught against their authority. However, it is hardly a solution for concerns about eminent domain abuse. It does nothing at all to protect citizens against the abuses of power experienced in cities across the country, and the seemingly broad discretion of government to deploy eminent domain is what inspired the national campaign against it.

The Libertarian Misdiagnosis of Abuse

When states reformed eminent domain policies, they were responding to a post-*Kelo* national debate that framed the problem with takings around whether government transferred property to public or private owners.[35] And yet, before the controversy that erupted in the early 2000s, that distinction had been of little import to eminent domain policy. For decades, if not centuries, governments' authority to take property and hand it over to new private users had been repeatedly invoked by legislatures and reaffirmed by the courts.[36] Still, the more recent cry that takings for private reuse constituted eminent domain abuse rallied support for a reigning-in of government power from all corners of the country. This national discussion did not emerge from an organic outpouring of local sentiment but from an effort by the libertarian Institute for Justice and (its spin-off) the Castle Coalition to organize a campaign around eminent domain, as discussed in Chapter 2. These organizations deliberately framed the issue around government's unacceptable involvement in the private affairs of property, a framing that served broader libertarian goals.

When eminent domain suddenly gained attention at the turn of the millennium, libertarian activists directed the national discussion. The Institute for Justice and Castle Coalition diagnosed the problem, selected illustrative cases to usher through court, and designed legislative reforms to tout as solutions. It published multiple reports on abuse,[37] wrote model laws[38] and lobbied for them, represented condemnees in court, trained citizens from all over the country to become activists, and consulted on local organizing efforts.[39] Titles of libertarian reports such as "The Supreme Assault on Private Property,"[40] "Public Power, Private Gain,"[41] and "Government Theft"[42] made the point that eminent domain abuse exposed the need to restrain government involvement in what they deemed to be the private affairs of property. National newspapers often simply broadcast the same message, with headlines such as "Across the Country, Americans Fight to Protect Their Property."[43]

Stories of eminent-domain abuse, framed as an illegitimate transfer from one private owner to another, seem to be about government invading what should be areas of private control. Thus, libertarian activists successfully incorporated their cause—the defense of private property as the right to control what is owned—into a debate over eminent domain. The now familiar objection to eminent domain reflects exactly the points that libertarian activists presented. The common response to a mention of eminent domain now, a few years after the *Kelo* debate, is to see government transfer of property to new private owners as blatantly violating the Fifth

Amendment's "public use" requirement and many state laws. From this perspective, a government can legitimately acquire property to give to a public school, park, or highway administration, but any handover to a private business, real-estate developer, or homeowner breaks down the sacred distinction between serving a public and a private interest and is thus an abuse of power.

Despite the broad resonance of this libertarian framing of the problem, my research in Philadelphia demonstrated that when citizens and officials raised cries of eminent domain abuse, they did so for different reasons. In fact, while several thousand properties that Philadelphia took over a decade and a half were intended for new private owners, only a minority of those takings sparked opposition. To be sure, when Philadelphians did protest, they often raised objections to the fact that private entities would get the properties. But this complaint was not their only one, and it certainly does not fully explain why government moved forward in some cases but not in others. Indeed, in the most controversial cases, officials could secure only the most fleeting interest by private developers, if any at all, before they acquired properties. Even when private developers were not directing the plans, government managed to cause citizen outrage. Philadelphia residents, business owners, and community leaders were infuriated not because private property was going to new private owners specifically, but because government officials treated their investments with disrespect.

Of course, the popular revulsion for public-private deal-making that hit the news, with the suspicion that private developers were calling the shots, is understandable, given the kinds of cases that gained national attention. Recently publicized cases all had very powerful private backers: Pfizer Corporation was relocating to New London, Columbia University is developing Manhattanville and Forest City Ratner Companies Atlantic Yards in New York, and the Trump Plaza Hotel and Casino wanted land in Atlantic City.

And yet, when we look closely at the details of these cases that at first glance seem so easily understood, we see that citizen objections emerged from government's failure to recognize investments, not from insistence on existing private owners' control. It was not the transfer to private entities that made these cases—commonly known as *Kelo*, Manhattanville, Atlantic Yards, and Atlantic City—seem wrong. In each of them, something happened during or as a result of the deal-making that convinced citizens that their investments were not secure. In the cases of eminent domain that became widely judged as instances of abuse, people close to the planning and negotiations decided that government never bothered to try, failed to secure, or violated the need to protect local investments.

In each of these cases, there was a moment at which citizens realized that government was not using the deals to support their investments. Accounts of what happened in New London, Connecticut suggest that the quasi-government New London Development Corporation (NLDC), which possessed eminent domain powers, never treated the reluctant homeowners with the respect they deserved. The NLDC failed to welcome them as parties deserving extensive consideration in planning and, if plans were to move ahead, in compensation. Apparently, the NLDC never even began to negotiate a deal that would have protected the interests of Fort Trumbull's recalcitrant owners. The Atlantic City Casino Redevelopment Authority also treated property owners as collateral damage, rather than as sources of ideas for planning or recipients of redevelopment's benefits. In New London and Atlantic City, government authorities acted as if they were willing to simply assert their power and bowl over residents, showing almost no desire to appease them. In these cases, once the local property owners understood that their interests were being so nonchalantly swept aside, they got mad and decided to fight.

In New York City's recent controversies, resistance developed because of government's lack of protection for a more diffuse group of constituents who were invested in the area but whose voices were not heard. These constituents included but were not limited to the direct property owners at risk. In both Manhattan (Manhattanville) and Brooklyn (Atlantic Yards), officials seemed to easily accept the private redevelopers' redesign ideas but were reluctant to consider alternatives presented by community organizations as more attentive to local wishes. The City Council (in approving rezoning) and the Empire State Development Corporation (New York's eminent domain authority) accepted Columbia University's plan for the redesign of a large area in upper Manhattan. They made relatively few concessions to the official community board's proposal, which arguably better reflected the wishes of local residents and businesses for the area's future.[44] A bit later in the projects' planning, government showed a greater reverence for community members' demands, probably because of their political organizing. The parties signed "Community Benefits Agreements" detailing exact amounts of money to flow to local organizations, numbers of affordable housing units to be built, conditions for relocations, and other benefits to flow from the redevelopment to the local community.[45] These agreements sparked some hope that local investments would be protected, but that hope was later dashed.

Even though government officials cleared early hurdles in New York by showing respect for investments through concessions in community benefits agreements, a lack of accountability for these agreements—and, thus, a sense that the project was not delivering benefits to those who had sacrificed to the area for so long—later fomented enduring resistance. In Manhattan, the outcome of Columbia University's financial commitment to share some of the development's benefits with the local community has continued to raise suspicion; the organization accepting the funds has failed to account for them.[46] Similarly, concerns about whether the Atlantic Yards' promises of affordable housing and funding to community organizations will reach the intended beneficiaries are voiced regularly. In both projects, New Yorkers have become extremely suspicious that the organizations that were at the table did not secure benefits for local residents, and for poor constituents in particular. In sum, resistance developed to Manhattanville and Atlantic Yards because city and state agencies overlooked alternative community-based visions for redevelopment early in the planning process and later failed to ensure accountability for benefits promised to local residents. Although the private redevelopers' power to direct government power draws vehement criticism in both of these projects with absolute giants set to receive the land (Columbia University and Forest City Ratner Companies), it is the continued and repeated lack of respect for local investment in place that has cemented the opposition. Thus, public-private cooperation fails to fully explain citizen objections in the most controversial cases, not only in Philadelphia but also in the nation at large.

Indeed, when we step back from the issue of eminent domain for private redevelopment, we can see how short a distance the objections to public-private cooperation really travel. These objections make little sense in light of countless other present-day policies that blend public and private resources. Since the 1980s, urban researchers have documented the prevalence of local government activity that takes the form of "deal-making."[47] These researchers have shown that, far from proving their legitimacy by demonstrating distance between public decisions and private interests, public officials spend much of their time hammering out the details of public plans with private developers. Typically, these developers have been promised contracts, land, tax incentives, zoning permissions, or other public resources. Notwithstanding trenchant critiques of these activities,[48] deal-making, private contracting, public-private partnerships, and public-private ventures have come to be expected forms of local governance.

Although they have joined the libertarian campaign against eminent domain abuse, left-leaning critics and activists have very good reasons to abandon the diagnosis of the problem as stemming from property transfers to private parties. Although many on the left are quite critical of private influence in planning for urban redevelopment, the history of eminent domain presents a stronger case against urban development through publicly controlled and owned projects. Early urban renewal programs were severely hampered by the lack of public resources for the planned redevelopment, including public housing. Even when they reduced the scale of their visions, progressive officials admitted their significant mistakes in underestimating the cost of reconstruction and political backlash and, thus, conceded the inability of governments to remake neighborhoods alone. In today's political climate, it is much less likely than in the mid-twentieth century that a plan for a publicly controlled, publicly owned development can secure the resources necessary for completion without private funding. And even if a purely public model for redevelopment can succeed in rare cases, it is unlikely to serve as a blueprint that cities across the country can use to address neighborhood problems successfully.

PRACTICAL MEANINGS OF PRIVATE PROPERTY

There is much more at stake in the debate over takings than the issue at hand. Within battles over eminent domain policy are politics about what private property means, about the acceptability of policies ranging from zoning to environmental regulations and from infrastructure to services spending. Indeed, the larger stakes of the eminent domain debate become clearer when compared to academic discussions about private property. When Americans voice opinions about what policies they support and why, they reveal their own practical theories of private property. These theories can contribute to long-standing academic debates among political theorists, legal scholars, and social scientists concerning how government can and should protect private property. In this section, I discuss how the practical theory of property as investment that I observed reflects adaptations of centuries of thinking about private property's meanings and impacts.

I clarify some basic ideas in classical and contemporary property theory to elucidate how they are revised by an investment-based theory of property that is practical in today's environment. All major classical theorists of private property, critical as well as celebratory, shared a basic understanding of property as control. Late twentieth-century political economists, however, observed a shift in demands on government with respect to private property. By noticing the importance of citizen demands for economic growth, these theorists redefined private property as an entitlement to value. They also preserved the classical critical distinction between use values and exchange values, which may now be less salient. Finally, as I have argued, today's citizens understand property as investment, expect individuals and government to share responsibility for property's value, and eschew the use value/exchange value distinction in their demands for government protection.

Although theories of property can seem timeless, they are always a product of politics at a certain time and place.[49] As American colonists and their successors established control over land in what is now the United States, they battled with indigenous tribes to establish notions of sovereignty and ownership. Today, advocates of liberal conceptions of property continue to struggle with those who support communal notions of land stewardship over the governance of reservations, public lands, and such common resources as water, air, fish, and wildlife. Less than two centuries ago, it was widely accepted in much of the United States that people could be owned as property, as slaves or as wives. Now, such a notion is practically unimaginable. Historians recount how nineteenth-century American governments granted formal property titles to people whom American governments would punish as squatters today.[50] They note that twentieth-century governments have increasingly been able to restrict the use of land inherent in property rights through zoning, health, and environmental regulations that would have been unthinkable a hundred years earlier. Recently, dramatic fights over changes in intellectual property rules have erupted. National and international regulations are being rewritten as music, video, and pharmaceutical producers attempt to protect against technologies and hackers taking control over dissemination out of their hands. Even though many of these changes—in who can own property, what can be owned, and how ownership and other rights are established—are beyond the scope of my concerns, they demonstrate just how unsettled seemingly fixed notions of property can be.[51] Property is a dynamic, contingent, and contested institution, and theories of government's relationship to property should reflect this dynamism.[52]

My concern is with the kind of security expected for real property (land and buildings) in the advanced capitalist United States. In this context, governments are larger and more intricately involved in activities that affect property's values than ever before. In addition, ownership of property is the majority experience, and neighborhood decline has become a familiar story. All of these factors help to explain the emergence of the expectation that government will protect property's value.

A new understanding of property, in fact, is needed for today's so-called neoliberal era of privatization, which differs dramatically from previous liberal periods. In today's neoliberal era of privatization, private property and private contracting are touted as solutions to any number of social issues.

But instead of withdrawing from the stage, governments are arguably more involved than ever before in how private activities are managed. It is perhaps just this involvement that so incenses libertarian activists who have attempted to revive a somewhat outdated notion of private property that requires government constraint.

Libertarian activists and intellectuals who treat property as control apply liberal ideas developed for a very different political and economic context to today's issues. Activists who have led the recent campaign against eminent domain abuse and contemporary libertarian-leaning legal theorists[53] base their ideas on classical liberal philosophers' arguments. Those philosophers argued that in protecting private property, government is responsible for enforcing private agreements, preventing privately induced harms, and otherwise restraining from intervention. They articulated and defended this notion of property as the best path to productivity and efficiency in the context of seventeenth-century English agricultural production and market exchange. John Locke used the example of agricultural land to argue that property security encourages people to labor, for people will only make the effort to plow, plant, fertilize, and weed if they know they can keep the harvest.[54] Adam Smith and Jeremy Bentham also defended the idea that property should confer private control, but for its promise of productivity and efficiency in market exchange. Following this tradition, law students learn that property is a set of rights through which owners are entitled to control an object's use, to exclude others from using it, and to transfer control to others.[55] However, the ideal of private control that inspired contemporary libertarians to attack eminent domain for private reuse hides more varied and complicated expectations about property that reflect contemporary American experience. The idea of private control cannot account for two crucial elements of protection inherent in a conception of property as investment: that government protects value, and that value comes in many forms.

Security of Value Rather Than Control

Expecting government to primarily enforce private control over property makes little sense when, despite symbolic prostrations to "free" markets, public actors are extremely involved in private economic endeavors. Indeed, the current neoliberal era is perhaps unique for its unprecedented combination of large, active governments with material support and cultural reverence for private activity. Classical theorists may have been unable to imagine this combination, and modern libertarians seem to want to dismantle it, but it accurately describes contemporary public policy. Today, governments respect the private, to be sure, but they also accept an established government involvement in the everyday life of property and property's value.[56] Despite a rhetoric praising "free" markets, markets are no more free from regulation than before the institution of neoliberal policies. Governments face what one sociologist has called a "neoliberal dilemma," for they control and support economic activity while appearing to cede power to markets.[57] Indeed, the seeds of the dissolution of earlier boundaries between public and private had been planted by the 1960s, when at least one property scholar declared that as governments began enlisting private entities to help fulfill responsibilities that they used to bear, the United States was "breaking down... distinctions between public and private" and "blurring or fusing" the two.[58] Classical ideas that property confers control cannot account for the active government involvement in property that is common today.

Many common contemporary policies demonstrate that Americans hold government responsible for actively protecting private property as value, just as a theory of private property as investment suggests. The legitimacy of a strong government hand in property value is evident in the wide acceptance of zoning and building codes, infrastructure such as parks and sidewalks, and services of law enforcement and schools. All of these policies are well understood to affect the value of living in, working with, owning, or leasing property in a neighborhood. Similarly, when the federal government funds housing developments, locates military operations, builds transportation infrastructure, and provides credit for ownership, it makes cities and neighborhoods more and less valuable, and citizens are well aware of this. To be sure, citizens regularly raise objections about how particular places should be zoned, about the best location for a park, or where to lay a sidewalk, but they much more rarely contest government's authority to regulate and spend in these ways. Thus, Americans today often take it for granted that governments can and should influence the value of property through many of their policies.

Not only do Americans readily accept government intervention in property to support its value, they even permit the expropriation of property under various laws other than eminent domain. Indeed, governments' authority to force property ownership from one private party to another in several other policies indicates that a conception of property as control has less salience than is commonly thought. With authority from foreclosure laws, governments take the property of an owner who fails to pay property taxes to local governments or mortgage payments to lenders. Asset forfeiture laws allow governments to seize properties used in the commission of crimes—most notably, since the 1980s, in response to drug crimes. There are even legal provisions for the transfer of property that was left to lie fallow by one owner and used by another for a period of time. These adverse possession laws enable the transfer of title to a long-term occupant—a squatter—after abandonment by a legal owner. In addition, government powers to abate public nuisances, by cleaning up land and repairing or demolishing buildings, have long existed. Municipalities seem to be reinvigorating these powers recently,[59] and property owners are challenging them in court for doing so.[60] Often, governments stick the owner with the costs of maintenance or demolition, and sometimes they take over the property title as well.[61] As evidenced by these various laws that allow for expropriation, the legitimacy of governments' general authority to usurp private control has become relatively well accepted.[62]

Value has become the emphasis for private property in a time of uncertainty. Americans recognize that control will not get them what they want from property if their property loses all value, and in today's uncertain environment, the possibility of a loss of value is all too familiar. Recently, millions of Americans living in middle-class neighborhoods watched their properties' real estate values drop as the national housing crisis exploded. Most Americans expected government, not just the private sector, to do something. Even before the national housing crisis, by the late 1990s and early 2000s, a generation of Americans had watched many neighborhoods and cities grow while others declined dramatically. Cities like St. Louis, Detroit, and Flint, as well as many neighborhoods within other cities, have experienced continued depopulation and disinvestment despite decades of attempts to spark growth. The sources of unprecedented uncertainty stretch beyond knowledge about real estate to disasters involving the application of scientific inventions—including nuclear accidents, oil spills, and massive chicken-farm waste—and financial inventions such as credit-default swaps and packages of subprime mortgages.[63] In today's uncertain environment, citizens expect government to secure the values that they enjoy with their properties, not simply protect their control over them.

Scholars first noticed the expectation that government would protect value in property during an earlier time of uncertainty—the local, national, and international economic crises of the 1970s and 1980s. Writing in that era, political economists observed how Western European and American politics of growth responded to inflation, oil crises, and manufacturing decline.[64] They noticed that in seemingly precarious circumstances of postwar retraction, postindustrialism, and municipal fiscal crises, citizens looked to national and local governments for guarantees of economic growth. Although economic vitality had always been a raison d'être for governments, these observers saw a qualitative shift in the kind of intervention that was expected. Jurgen Habermas, in particular, noted that the expectation of such a strong hand in economic activity clashed with the classical notion of nonintervention in private affairs.[65] These critical political economists saw that citizens voted for politicians who promised to keep jobs available, wages high, and real estate prices rising. Studying local American governments, John Logan and Harvey Molotch declared that the idea of growth as a public good had become so hegemonic that politicians who delivered high real estate values could practically be assured of winning votes.[66] Even though they did not identify a crucial component of the investment conception—that owners would be treated as if they deserve government's delivery of value to their properties only if they had made their own sacrifices to those same properties—these scholars made a major innovation by rejecting the idea of property as control in favor of an understanding of property as value.[67]

This changing conception of property highlighted the fact that political economists of the 1970s and 1980s were writing in a far different context from that of earlier critical scholars. Classical critics of capitalism, like the liberal political theorists they so vehemently critiqued, expected private property to secure control over the owned object. They analyzed policies that granted control over owned objects to private parties; for example, Karl Marx, Friedrich Engels, Max Weber, and Karl Polanyi all critiqued how the violent enclosures of the English commons created privately controlled parcels.[68] Of course, Marx and Engels also examined how private property protected private control over industry (the means of production). Emile Durkheim, Alexis de Tocqueville, and Thorstein Veblen also wrote about private property as control. They observed rampant land speculation in early rural America, the early development of urban rental housing, and private inheritance laws—all evidence that property amounted to control of land and buildings.[69] However, these realities shifted after the mid-twentieth century in the United States and Western Europe, as monetary stimulation, zoning regulations, manufacturing supports, and redevelopment initiatives proliferated. Those policies, which were designed to protect private value, became central to the analyses of late twentieth-century political economists.

Thus, although classical critics of capitalism and private property are not usually talked about for what they had in common with the liberal political theorists they so vehemently critiqued, they actually shared a very similar understanding of the kind of protection that private property conferred. Marx and Engels and other late nineteenth- and early twentieth-century critics of private property, like classical liberal theorists, expected private property to secure control over the object owned. Libertarians today continue the same tradition, and in so doing harken back to a context that has lost some relevance.

In response to changes in context, some scholarship in the critical tradition has shifted from condemning property as private control to condemning government for how it supports private property as value. But their conception of commodification also appeals more to the past than the present context.

Value Pluralism Rather Than Commodification

Although the critical scholars of the 1970s and 1980s took a novel approach when they identified value as the core of property, the urban political economists in particular relied what is now an outdated way of distinguishing value (use versus exchange) in their explanation of property politics. Recall that one of the basic tenets of property as investment, as I have defined it, is ambivalence or pluralism about the kind of value secured. The value of an investment can be made or returned in money or labor, but also in time, emotion, friendship, social networks, local schools and parks, or any other currency. Any of these may bring future income but also benefits such as wisdom, creativity, status, and self-assurance. This value pluralism differs starkly from the clean exchange value/use value distinction that is central to most critical theories of property.

As appealing as the division between monetary and non-monetary value is in the abstract, it has less practical meaning in daily life than it did when homeownership was less common and less important to family wealth. In the late twentieth century, a majority of Americans owned their own homes for the first time, and these homes offered sentimental comfort, physical shelter, *and* financial security. Until the national crisis beginning in 2008, real estate prices increased consistently, and the family home became the most significant financial asset of many Americans.[70] As Americans (on average) have become wealthier, not only through their homes but also through stock-market investments, it makes less sense for them to separate monetary value from household or personal security.[71] It is also possible that as inequalities increased in urban neighborhoods, Americans began to see a connection between financial and other kinds of value in real property. The vast differences between rich and poor neighborhoods are evident in both real estate prices and physical conditions, making use and exchange values in real property appear practically interchangeable.

In addition, Americans may find it more difficult to parse values into use and exchange components as governments' privatization sets prices on public goods. One may perceive public services that are characteristic of a social-welfare state—such as government-provided housing, schools, parks, and highways—as uses that come without a price tag. Neoliberal policies, however, have made this less likely by privatizing these goods, and thus putting price tags on them. They have put privately owned housing in the hands of more Americans (as discussed in Chapter 1) and shifted the provision of utilities, highways, housing, and school services from public to private entities. When government privately contracts for services, so that they are only available to citizens through private purchase, rental, or other kinds of fees, it creates a perception that use and exchange values are inextricable.[72]

Despite the inescapable overlap between use and exchange values in family wealth, neighborhood life, and government policy, critical political economists predicted that class differences in demands for use or exchange values in property would determine urban politics. As noted earlier, sociologists John Logan and Harvey Molotch argued that city politics in particular have required that politicians promise to protect the exchange value but not use value of property.[73] They said that by commodifying place, advocates of growth encourage public policies that pay attention to property prices but not to the more tangible and sentimental characteristics that make property valuable. When governments pursue properties' "highest and best use," for instance, they make only a financial calculation about what matters. Because poor neighborhoods' properties offer mostly use values, rather than exchange values, they receive little government support. Thus, conditions in poor neighborhoods worsen and neighborhoods become more and more divided between rich and poor.[74] Logan and Molotch contended that, instead of higher real-estate prices, the poor need, want, and will demand protection for the use-values of their homes and neighborhoods. These values include shelter, memories, relationships, community, and basic services. By analyzing political struggles to be defined by class-based attachments to these different kinds of value, contemporary political economists have adapted a distinction made by Marx and Engels to the treatment of property as value rather than control. Although they expected the politics to play out differently than their predecessors, growth theorists actually deployed an old division between use and exchange value derived from classical critiques of commodification under early capitalism.

Growth theorists borrowed the use value/exchange value distinction from classical critics who equated property in capitalism with "commodification." These critics said that commodification leads to the misrepresentation of the value of important goods like land because monetary price hides inherent use value. Marx and Engels argued that in the context of monetized markets, private property pushed owners to pursue their property's exchange (monetary) value, at the expense of such values as physical security, sustenance, and personal identity (use value). Much later, political economist Karl Polanyi famously equated private property with the "commodification" of goods, such as land and labor, with inherent values that cannot be represented in monetary terms. Indeed, he called land a "fictitious commodity," for capitalist private property drives owners to pursue its exchange-value and ignore its inherent use-value. Others who did not use this exact language also based their critiques of private property on the incumbent search for monetary profit, especially through land.[75] For instance, Alexis de Tocqueville and Thorstein Veblen condemned how nineteenth- and early twentieth-century Americans used land for monetary profit, without any tangible or personal interest in the particular place.[76] More recently, legal theorist Margaret Jane Radin distinguished between property, such as the home, that is significant to one's personal identity and property that is not, and thus is fungible.[77] Only the latter, she says, can be justly compensated with money. Of course, many of the sensibilities about property in these existing theories about property are still quite relevant. And yet, this does not diminish my contention that a conception of property as investment—in part because it eschews this distinction—is particularly well adapted to current circumstances. As I discuss next, old sensibilities about property live on, for we understand and reason with multiple conceptions of property, old and new alike.

The Simultaneous Life of New and Old Meanings of Property

I have just described how investment differs significantly from previously articulated bases of property theories, but my claim about what has changed is modest in important ways. First, I do not mean to suggest that the conception of property as investment has replaced more familiar notions. It is an alternative available to citizens and officials to invoke as they consider government activity and justify their positions to others. With a notion of investment protection, citizens and officials have one more choice when they evaluate and justify government action toward property. I hope to bring attention to the constant politics among multiple, competing notions of property, for notions of property are always somewhat unsettled,[78] and, to the extent that they are understood, are available for people to perform.[79]

The fact that Americans continue to invoke older ideas about property, as control and commodification, indicates that these traditional notions continue to have practical value. As I discussed earlier, it is possible that notions of property with a longer history will continue to be summoned in the heat of conflict to mobilize broad support, for they are well-entrenched and easily understood. While newer notions of property need more explanation, older notions may more quickly and easily motivate sympathy for one side of a conflict. Thus, even when creative notions of property surface, more traditional notions will endure.

Second, my argument about investment is modest because I understand emerging notions of property to have emerged at least partially from older understandings. Original notions of property appear as novel adaptations from historical antecedents, rather than as wholly fresh creations. The idea of investment newly synthesizes different theorists' presentations of how property engages the individual versus the collective. Investment implies interdependence between individual and collective action, an adaptation from previous theories that have emphasized one or the other.

The idea of property as investment preserves classical liberalism's emphasis on protection for the individual and the hopes for resulting productivity that serves all. When property is treated as investment, government creates an incentive for individuals to improve property, just as early proponents of private property expected. Property as investment reflects John Locke's liberal defense of private property as a way to preserve the value of an individual's labor for himself or herself. In today's urban America, owners want to know that they will benefit from completing bathroom or kitchen renovations, landscape improvements, equipment upgrades, paint jobs, or simple decorations. Either they enjoy the physical improvements when they stay or the increased price when they sell. Indeed, the idea of investment suggests that they deserve benefits today and tomorrow because of their own sacrifice of resources in the past. And yet, because they also understand that government activity keeps the area and, thus, their properties valuable, contemporary urban dwellers are not like Locke's imaginary farmer who took sole responsibility for the success or failure of the harvest.

While investment reflects the liberal notion that property protects benefits deriving from individual effort (in the ideal), it also reflects critical theories of property that have drawn attention to how collective action creates properties' value. Americans invoking a logic of investment expect neighbors and local government to significantly impact how their properties retain or lose their value. In this way, the idea of property as investment draws on critical writing about property. De Tocqueville, Marx and

Engels, and Polanyi all commented on how individual owners reap profit from government action (even if they proclaim individual responsibility). Of course, in the late twentieth-century, writers discussed how government became explicitly responsible for securing value—the financial value of property.[80]

By giving attention to government's responsibility for and to communities, the idea of investment actually draws on another important historical theory of property that I have not yet discussed: civic republicanism. Civic republicanism has been both an intellectual and practical counterpoint to liberalism, as activists and scholars alike have posited that a more communal conception of property as responsibility exists within the American tradition. In the context of postindustrial cities, civic republicans claimed that communal rights to continue operating factories against owners' wishes existed, and that they rested on the long history of a community's labor for and reliance on the factory.[81] A group of law professors who identify as "progressive property scholars" have been unearthing a progressive tradition of private property from American jurisprudence and draw heavily on this tradition that emphasizes the responsibilities to one another that private property incorporates.[82] By combining respect for long-term individual commitments with expectations of improvement in value, my investment conception of property synthesizes preexisting notions of property from self-identified liberal, critical, and progressive traditions. This practical amalgamation of preceding traditions, including liberal origins but heavily emphasizing critical and progressive elements, may be particularly useful for achieving emancipatory demands in today's urban environment.

HOW PROGRESSIVE IS A CONCEPTION OF PROPERTY AS INVESTMENT?

My research findings surprised me. At a moment when private property has reached new levels of grandeur, I begrudgingly expected that an uncritical reverence for the liberal understanding of property as individual control would have become hegemonic. Instead, I found that a reconstructed logic of property challenged that classical definition. I now wonder whether one consequence of today's overwhelming acceptance of private property is a change in what "private property" means. Perhaps the overwhelming of the private acceptance drove progressive-minded citizens to move from critique to reconstruction, in order to incorporate their ideals within the meaning of private property itself.

When citizens consider property as an investment that government is responsible for protecting, their demand for protection includes victims of eminent domain but also extends far beyond these victims. In contrast, when citizens consider property as control, their resulting objections to eminent domain for private transfers apply to a very small number of people—probably significantly less than 1 percent of the population faced with eminent domain. To be sure, as those people are disproportionately poor and African American, a strong case can be made that advocating for the liberal idea of property can serve social justice. Nevertheless, advocating the conception of property as investment leads to a damning critique of many more urban policies of contemporary governments.

To the extent that Americans expect governments to protect property as an investment, they declare the general oversight of poor neighborhoods—not only the use of eminent domain—to be abhorrent. This expectation holds government responsible for protecting citizens against the pervasive harms caused by neighborhoods that deteriorate around them.[83] While the standard of control holds government responsible for keeping its hands off urban property, the standard of investment holds it accountable for putting its hands in. The latter standard calls for government to secure property as privately and collectively enjoyed value, rather than as private control over an object. This difference can explain the non-libertarian sentiments expressed by an NAACP spokesperson testifying about eminent domain abuse at a Congressional hearing in 2011. He expressed concern that eminent domain powers outlined in *Kelo* " sanction easier transfers of property, wealth, and community stability from those with less resources to those with more,"[84] and he asserted that while hoping to "end eminent domain abuse," the NAACP also wanted to work with government to "focus[] on real community development concerns like building safe, clean and affordable housing in communities with good public schools, an effective accessible high quality health care system, small business development and growth, and a significant available living wage job pool."[85] To be sure, with its copious services and infrastructure and vehement regulatory enforcement, government already secures property, and thus people, in these ways in middle- and upper-class neighborhoods. By bringing government back into providing value security for all urban neighborhoods, a conception of property as investment allows the poor to demand the same kind of government respect and protection for property that wealthy and middle-class Americans have come to enjoy. The poor, like all others in America, have invested value of all kinds into the properties where they live and work.

When citizens understand property as investment, they expect government to do more than it would even if it adhered to critical theories about property as the protection of use values. To be sure, if government is to support use values, then it should provide schools, sidewalks, and sanitation services to make a neighborhood livable. The problem, however, with an overemphasis on use values is that it requires the poor to keep their value in non-monetary assets. The conception of investment makes some extremely important additions by suggesting that poor people deserve more than just tangible goods and services and sentimentality. It insists that, as much as any other Americans, the poor should be able to recoup the labor, time, effort, and money they have put into their properties by receiving money and/or the opportunity move into new communities of their choosing.

Although the word "investment" has financial connotations that may raise skepticism about its progressive potential among critics of capitalism, the fact that it has this and other connotations may be practically useful for challenging market ideals. Investment shares with property a recent obsession with financial value but a real ambiguity and long but forgotten history as a referent for primarily other forms of goods. Although recently the word "investment" has come to suggest a financial interest, in stock or real estate for instance, the word's root meaning is "to clothe"—an act that involves taking on a tangible object as part of one's person, thus incorporating a sense that objects contribute to personhood. Today, the word "investment" continues to signify forms of worth, such as knowledge and emotion, that make a person. Thus, "investment" is ambiguous with respect to kinds of value, so the conception of property as investment entitles people to government protection for many different kinds of value that they have invested, including but not limited to financial value.

Nevertheless, while the recent conception of property as investment carries some emancipatory power, its timing may be sadly ironic. The use of eminent domain in 1950s and 1960s urban renewal campaigns combined vast government authority with a pervasive disregard for the poor and people of color. It caused massive displacements of hundreds or thousands of residents and business owners. In contrast, this book has rendered a contemporary picture in which eminent domain targets abandoned land and speculators while minimally displacing occupants. Today's officials appear more sensitive to poor residents, at least formally colorblind, and even motivated to protect property as investment.

These improvements come at a time when municipal governments are extraordinarily weak. Thus, if America's urban poor have wrested some control of municipal governments through demands related to investment, they are exerting this control over entities that currently have less to give. Perhaps this timing is less of an unfortunate irony than an example of an opening being seized, as instances of weakened government authority might provide the best opportunities for redirecting that authority. Regardless, the current moment may offer progressives a chance to redirect eminent domain and other land-oriented policies from the nefarious goals of growth machines toward more progressive ends like support for individual and community investment of all kinds of worth.

Finally, perhaps the greatest progressive possibilities for property today lie in forms of tenure that defy the public-private distinction. It is possible that legal structures for ownership and leasing can powerfully enforce simultaneous individual and community responsibilities for the future of land and buildings. Indeed, ways of owning and leasing property that resist classification as either fully private or public may emerge anew or become newly popular. Cooperatives and community land trusts are the more familiar alternative forms of tenure that have flourished, but there are countless ways that estates have been constructed to give control and responsibility to commons, utilities, corporations, and even ecological regions.[86] These creative property arrangements deserve attention, for they challenge us to see the overlapping communal, individual, and government interests in property.

APPENDIX 1

Research Methods

QUESTIONS

As I researched the RDA's proposed and completed takings of private property for new private owners from 1992 to 2007, I had three main research objectives in mind. These objectives concerned only the acquisition process (as opposed to the disposition process, through which the RDA transfers titles it owns to new private owners). They were:

- To learn when government exercises its eminent domain power for urban redevelopment.
- To explain the discrete outcomes of attempts to invoke eminent domain (acquiescence, agreement, contestation, or government abandonment of project).
- To understand the compensation (including relocation) decision-making process and how it contributes to the outcomes described above.

After doing some preliminary research on the topic, I organized my empirical questions around a very condensed outline of the formal eminent domain process followed in Philadelphia. The questions that operationalize the above research objectives were as follows:

- From Idea to Project
  How does an urban redevelopment project that plans to use eminent domain emerge? What causes an idea to progress swiftly or to be delayed or detoured on its way to becoming a project?
- From Project to Discrete Outcomes

Once such a project emerges, what happens to a property in the near future, and what happens between government and the property owner?

- The Compensation Process and Its Impacts

How do negotiations and decisions about compensation occur, and how do they impact the outcomes in each of the stages above?

DATA COLLECTION AND ANALYSIS

I collected and analyzed data between the fall of 2005 and spring of 2009. My data collection began with research of general policy issues; I reviewed the news articles and policy documents listed in Table A.1 and summarized topics and resulting questions. In 2006, I observed several training sessions and meetings about eminent domain that were attended mostly by government officials, attorneys, appraisers, and/or anti-eminent-domain activists. My main purpose at these gatherings was to note which topics evoked discussion, conflict, and questioning and which ones seemed novel to me but were hardly remarked upon by the other attendees. During the spring of 2006, I also conducted approximately twenty interviews with general informants who represented different constituencies of "repeat players"[1] in the use (and, in most cases, Philadelphia's use) of eminent domain. I discuss my sampling methods for interviews later in this Appendix.

With guidance from The Reinvestment Fund, I researched the planning and development of Mayor Street's Neighborhood Transformation Initiative (NTI) in the summer of 2006. In the office where most of that planning happened, I learned how Street's campaign promise for an anti-blight program changed to a market investment program with strong City Council oversight. This change happened over two years in an attempt to sell the program to the public and negotiate with council members for the bill that would raise its funding.

In the fall of 2006, I observed several public meetings related to Philadelphia's eminent domain practice. In addition, I began working from within the offices most central to the functioning of eminent domain in the city, the RDA, and the Office of the Mayor's NTI and the Philadelphia EZ, where I was given temporary desks. I collected most of my archival material and a great amount of observational data over one year at the NTI office and over two years at the RDA office. (See Table A.2.)

At the RDA, I reviewed the archives of RDA Board of Directors meetings from 1992 to 2007. I collected information on the projects and properties pursued for acquisition, noted any discussions or actions that offered particular insights into my main empirical questions, and prepared these data

Item	Data Collected
Newspaper coverage	Text of articles returned in a keyword search for "eminent domain" in the *Philadelphia Inquirer* or the *Philadelphia Daily News* from January 1982 to January 2006 (from NewsBank database).
Policy analysis	Articles analyzing and making recommendations for city policy related to eminent domain, vacant properties, or other government attention to devastated Philadelphia real estate markets and neighborhoods, 1990–2007; evaluations and audits of the American Street EZ, the RDA, and the NTI.
Public meeting/ hearing testimony and minutes	Transcripts of all City Council hearings considering issues related to case studies; minutes from all PCPC meetings considering issues related to case studies; minutes from all meetings of the RDA Board, 1992–2007; minutes from all meetings of the American Street EZ Community Trust Board.
RDA Board action on takings	Related items from agendas for all meetings of the RDA Board, 1992–2007. Agendas contain memos from project managers to the board, usually stating the purpose and scope of the intended acquisitions.
Litigation related to "Preliminary Objections" to the taking	A motion to file "Preliminary Objections" to a Declaration of Taking that has been filed is the only way to litigate the actual taking (as opposed to the compensation). Court Dockets for all Declarations of Taking filed by the RDA with the Office of the Prothonotary of Philadelphia, First Judicial District of Pennsylvania, 1992–2007, were reviewed for this kind of litigation. All of the office's files on litigation related to case studies and other select cases were reviewed and summarized.
Litigation related to "Board of View" hearings	A motion to request a hearing in front of a "Board of View" after a Declaration of Taking has been filed is the first formal step in contesting the amount of real estate compensation. Basic information on all hearings requested and held from 1992 to 2007 was collected from the Bureau of Revision of Taxes of the City of Philadelphia.
Internal communications and project management	Staff member files related to case studies at the offices of the RDA, the PCPC, the Commerce Department. Internal files about consultation for the NTI at The Reinvestment Fund.
RDA management of property acquisitions	Files on property acquisition and relocation for each address pursued in case studies. Files included documentation of communications with condemnees, appraisals, settlement documents, internal communications, and more.

for entry into my own Microsoft Access database. Once the information was entered there, mostly by assistants, I was able to analyze it.

To research my two case studies, I collected documents, organized them chronologically, and used them to write a preliminary timeline about each

Table A.2. MAIN OBSERVATION SITES	
Observation Site	Time Period, Number, or Names of Sessions
Professional training sessions related to eminent domain	Lorman Education Services. Eminent Domain. Philadelphia, PA, January 24, 2005. Appraisal Institute. Condemnation Appraising: Basic Principles and Applications. Atlanta, GA, November 2–3, 2007. Pennsylvania Bar Institute. Preparing the Real Estate Valuation Case. Philadelphia, PA, November 18, 2008.
Professional meetings, presentations, and conferences related to eminent domain	Federal Reserve Bank of Philadelphia. The *Kelo* Decision—Balancing Community Revitalization with Property Rights. Reinventing Older Communities: People, Places, Markets. Philadelphia, PA, April 6, 2006. National Constitution Center. Eminent Domain Post *Kelo,* Templeton Lecture on Economic Liberties. Philadelphia, PA, April 10, 2006. Pennsylvania Association of Housing and Redevelopment Authorities. Coping with Changes in Eminent Domain. Champion, PA, June 6, 2006. Pennsylvania Bar Association. Eminent Domain after *Kelo*. Hershey, PA, June 8, 2006. Institute for Justice. Eminent Domain Conference. Arlington, VA, June 9–11, 2006. Building Industry Association of Philadelphia. Government Affairs Committee Meeting. Philadelphia, PA, January 9, 2007. New Jersey League of Municipalities. 92nd Annual Conference: Perceptions, Realities, Opportunities. Atlantic City, NJ, November 14, 2007. Smart Growth America National Vacant Properties Campaign and Brookings Institution Metropolitan Policy Program. Redesigning the Policy Framework for Shrinking Cities: Policy Conversations and Problem Solving on Right Sizing Strategies. Washington, DC, February 13, 2009.
Daily office activities	Redevelopment Authority of the City of Philadelphia, Development Department, October 2006–September 2008. Office of the Mayor's Neighborhood Transformation Initiative and the Philadelphia Empowerment Zone, January 2007–November 2007. The Reinvestment Fund, June–August 2006.
Public meetings	
RDA Board	Four meetings in 2006.
City Council Rules Committee	Two meetings, in 2006 and 2007.
Board of View Hearings	Four hearings, between 2007 and 2009.

study project. I used this timeline to develop questions for my interviews, and I used interviewees' responses to refine the timeline. Furthermore, I used the documents to verify interviewees' responses whenever possible. I also created spreadsheets to organize the documents' information regarding targeted properties and the RDA's interactions with owners and tenants.

The documents I used came primarily from government offices. For the American Street case study, I collected and reviewed all of the archival material I could locate at the RDA and NTI/EZ offices. For the Jefferson Square case study, I collected documents from the RDA and received important data from the JSCDC and at least one of its consultants. The JSCDC gave me spreadsheets of its own information on property acquisitions, relocations, and sales, along with conceptual plans for the project drawn by Kramer+Marks Architects.

Interviews

I planned interviews to gain different perspectives on the use of eminent domain from four groups with different interests: government, condemnees and neighbors, community organizations, and independent professionals (attorneys, appraisers, researchers, and planners). My interviewees were chosen because their significant general experience qualified them to serve as general informants or because they had been involved in one of the two case studies. I used recommendations from my acquaintances to identify the first few interviewees in the main government agencies of interest, and these interviewees referred me to others. More often, however, I used my archival research to identify potential subjects. For the case studies, I tried to interview anyone who seemed to have played an important role in the projects' unfolding, and I attempted to contact all owners of properties targeted in both cases. Once I made contact with people, they often wanted to know what research I had already done and to whom I had spoken, and this information usually prompted them to respond positively to my interview requests.

I conducted interviews with 104 subjects, all of whom represented government, condemnees, community organizations, or independent professions (see Table A.3). The primary topics of the interviews mirrored those of this book, and they were about equally divided among the interviews: general eminent domain practice ($n = 33$), the American Street case ($n = 40$), and the Jefferson Square case ($n = 31$). Interviews averaged just over an hour (72 minutes) and were loosely structured by interview guides.

Most interviewees had a significant amount of experience and knowledge about just a few of the many topics in the guides. After posing initial background questions, I attempted to allow the interviews to follow whatever thread the questions from my guide stirred, returning to the guide when I felt I had exhausted a line of questioning sparked by a particular statement. In addition, I followed up on interviewees' statements with requests for examples and evidence. Finally, when I could anticipate a counterargument or skeptical response to an interviewee's statement, I would probe by asking, "Other people would say such-and-such, which would conflict with what you are telling me. How would you respond?"

I informed all subjects of the purpose of my interviews and told them that their participation was voluntary. Furthermore, I informed them that any information they provided and its source might become public unless they asked me to keep it confidential or anonymous. Audio for most of the interviews (95 of 104) was recorded digitally and was subsequently transcribed so that I could refer back to interviewees' exact words. When I interviewed people without recording them, I took notes during and immediately after the interviews.

Table A.3. PERSONAL INTERVIEWS

Interviewee Type	Number[1]
Primary topic of interview	
General informant	33
American Street case	40
Jefferson Square case	31
Total	104
Primarily representative of	
Government	31
Condemnee or neighbor of condemnee	37
Community organization (including nonprofit development organizations)	24
Independent professional (attorney, appraiser, researcher, or planner)	12
Total	104
Form of recording	
Sound recording and transcript	95
Written notes only	9
Total	104

[1] Average interview length was 72 minutes. A few subjects were interviewed more than once, and a few interviewees were interviewed in groups of two or three. All interviews were conducted between 2005 and 2009.

Most of my interviewees had been significantly involved with and/or affected by either the case-study projects or eminent domain generally. This was partially due to my recruitment methods, which were affected by the contact information I had. If subjects recommended other interviewees to me, they usually provided a contact phone number, which I called to request an interview. I reached most professionals and community organization leaders by telephone, and they usually agreed to be interviewed. Moreover, I personally visited the initial relocation addresses of all residents dislocated from privately owned property in the case-study projects, and these visits also yielded a high response rate. When I was unable to reach condemnees (occupants and/or owners) in person, I mailed interview requests to the contact addresses I had for them. The post office returned many of these requests undelivered, but a few people who received the letters called me to set up interviews.

Many of the condemnees and neighbors who declined to be interviewed were those whom interviewees described as undesirable or problematic. A few of these people were neighborhood leaders—or people trying to be neighborhood leaders—who had been accused of misleading residents, often because of personal interests, during the project conflicts. Others had been accused of failing to take care of their property or themselves and/or of being involved in criminal activity involving drugs or prostitution. These condemnees and community leaders may have been reluctant to share their stories because they were wary of being judged negatively. In addition to their reluctance to speak with me, some of these condemnees were more difficult to locate than others, as they were less likely to keep in contact with my main informants and more likely to move frequently. It is also likely that many condemnees who declined to be interviewed lacked strong feelings about their experience with eminent domain; perhaps those who viewed their experiences as having less significance in their lives were less willing to make the effort to sit for an interview. Finally, there were a few people heavily involved in the American Street case who declined to be interviewed although they had fairly significant negative experiences. They told me that they had already told their stories enough times, when the newspapers and activists were interested, and that they did not feel like doing so again.

Because I relied mainly on archives and interviews for retrospective accounts, I could not capture the perspectives of the aforementioned groups. I believe that ethnography would be necessary to capture and retell their stories, and use them to deepen our understanding of government legitimacy.

CENSUS (OF EMINENT DOMAIN): DATA COLLECTION AND CODING

Data Sources

To track RDA activity for my census of eminent domain, I primarily consulted paper and/or electronic copies of several types of documents related to resolutions passed by the RDA Board to enter information into my own database. These documents included the resolutions themselves, staff memos explaining acquisition plans in board meeting agendas, and official minutes of the meetings where the resolutions were considered. I supplemented these documents when information on property acquisitions and dispositions was missing by consulting the City of Philadelphia's "Baseline" database, an incomplete electronic database used by the RDA. When necessary and possible, I verified conflicting information from these sources by accessing the Declarations of Taking filed in court and available from the Philadelphia Department of Records.

My secondary source of data for information on property at large in the city was from the City of Philadelphia Bureau of Revision and Taxes (BRT). I secured and merged annual databases of all parcels tracked by the BRT for tax purposes from 1994 to 2007.

Property Identification

In creating my census of properties targeted by the RDA, I used a number of techniques to compensate for the difficulties inherent in accurately tracking properties and projects over time. These difficulties can include official changes in property addresses, different recordings of addresses by different city agencies, and incorrect recordings of addresses.

I geocoded all addresses in the census to allow population of fields from other spatially organized data. This geocoding also corrected errors in addresses caused by misspellings of street names or missing or incorrect compass points. Addresses were geocoded first with PhillyCenterLine, an address locator based on the City of Philadelphia Streets Department's centerline shapefile. PhillyCenterLine matches addresses and address ranges to spatial coordinates and is set to a "match score" of 86 or above. This threshold matches on streets with same numeric and directional information, thus requiring users to enter them correctly, but allows for misspellings. I matched any addresses that were not located automatically or manually with PhillyCenterLine against Yahoo Geocoding.

I considered a street address existing in the city's Uniform Land Record (ULR) system to represent a single property. A simple street addresses, such as 10 N. 15th Street, therefore, was considered a single property, as were addresses with hyphens and suffixes, such as 10-18 N. 15th Street, 10R N. 15th Street, and 10½ N. 15th Street. In its own documents, the RDA often combines several addresses by using hyphens as shorthand. All hyphenated addresses received from RDA documentation that did not match addresses in the ULR were temporarily enumerated (e.g., 10–14 N. 15th Street became 10 N. 15th Street, 12 N. 15th Street, 14 N. 15th Street). If these enumerated addresses were in the ULR, I kept the records in the analysis and counted the addresses as separate properties.

If addresses (either in their enumerated or original forms) could not be matched to records in the ULR, however, they were not included in the analysis. After I enumerated all hyphenated addresses and corrected errors in street names, I found that some property addresses entered into my census of properties targeted for eminent domain fell into this category. One explanation for their lack of ULR matches is that less experienced project managers sometimes submit redevelopment proposals to the RDA Board with addresses that do not exist. As these project managers attempt to ensure that they cover every address on a block, they may list all of the possible addresses there, rather than verifying that each address has a title with the Department of Records. Such mistakes are generally caught, and the addresses are usually removed from the list by the time the Declaration of Taking resolution is prepared. Because these mistakes were not substantively meaningful to my analyses, I excluded all addresses (including when hyphenated or corrected for spelling or directional errors) that did not match records in the ULR.[2]

Property Characteristics

Establishing Private Ownership

I considered property involved in eminent domain to be privately owned if a public owner was not identified in three data sets, given priority in the following order: (1) the RDA's paper documentation, (2) the city's Baseline database, and (3) the BRT's 1994 database (the earliest database covering all city properties available).

Occupancy and Development

I created an "occupancy" variable to capture whether a building was vacant or inhabited, whether as a residence, business, or institution. The only occupancy data I considered reliable enough to use came from the RDA; although these data contain occasional errors, such errors represents the RDA's intent in pursuing properties better than corrected information. My primary source regarding occupancy was RDA paper documents, including staff memos to the RDA Board, and my secondary source was the Baseline database.

If properties were marked as occupied on one RDA source but not on another, I treated them as occupied in my analysis. Such contradictions usually occur either because the property was vacated somewhere in the process, or the RDA mistakenly identified the property as vacant or occupied during the planning stages. It is well known that the latter often happens because dwellings where people reside without utilities appear uninhabited based on views from the street and checks of utility bills. It was with this common occurrence in mind that I chose to code the buildings with conflicting information as occupied. (Although the RDA sometimes codes parcels used exclusively as storage spaces and garages as occupied lots, I considered these to be vacant lots in my analysis.)

I created a "development" variable to capture whether a property is undeveloped (either nothing or a storage building) or has a building that, though possibly in need of repair, could host a residence, business, or institutional use. As with my process for establishing private ownership, I populated the development variable first with data in RDA documents. If the variable was still null, I looked for the information in the Baseline database, and if still null, then in the BRT's 1994 database. My coding from the Baseline database used the variable called URAStatus, which included the categories "lot," "occupied commercial," and "occupied residential"; I coded properties in the latter two categories as buildings. In analyzing the BRT data, I used a building typology from The Reinvestment Fund to simplify codes for the building type field, and I coded properties as lots when the database indicated they were "vacant" or "parking."

Eminent Domain Outcomes

I coded all properties involved in eminent domain as having certain outcomes at the point that they were included in particular RDA Board resolutions (and mentioned in the memos and minutes related to such resolutions) or in specific kinds of legal motions. The possible outcomes were *pursued, taken, dropped, revested*, and *litigated*. If properties were revested or litigated, they were coded as having been formally contested. The board resolutions and legal motions were as follows:

1. Redevelopment Proposal resolutions: These resolutions approve the pursuit of plans to acquire particular properties. They allow RDA staff to send the plans to the PCPC for its recommendations and to the City Council for its approval.[3] Properties included in these resolutions were considered *pursued*.
2. Declarations of Taking resolutions: These resolutions allow RDA staff to file Declarations of Taking in court, thereby transferring property titles from previous owners to the RDA. Properties included in these resolutions were considered *taken*. Properties that were not included in these resolutions, despite having been included in Redevelopment Proposal resolutions, were considered *dropped*.
3. Revestment resolutions: These resolutions approve the return of property titles to previous owners after Declarations of Taking have been filed. Properties included in these resolutions were considered *revested*.
4. Petitions for Board of View hearings on compensation and Preliminary Objections to Declarations of Taking: These are motions that condemnees may file in the Court of Common Pleas to contest government actions. Properties for which a condemnee filed either of these motions were considered *litigated*.

PROJECT CHARACTERISTICS

The RDA Development Department manages acquisitions as "projects," which usually group multiple property addresses into a single plan for redevelopment. Because projects are not technically defined by legal code, they are not as easily tracked by official actions such as board resolutions. But because projects motivate RDA actions related to properties, their details are usually discussed when the RDA makes decisions. Development plans were gleaned from the memos that RDA project managers write to the board for consideration of the resolutions discussed above, and from meeting minutes recording board members' comments. I noted which property addresses were associated with which projects, and I coded projects by the characteristics of intended recipient, type of planned future use, and expected funding sources.

APPENDIX 2

The Reinvestment Fund's Residential Real Estate Market Analysis Methodology

The Policy Solutions Group at The Reinvestment Fund (TRF) categorized most of the city's census block groups for work under contract with the City of Philadelphia from 2000 to 2002. (TRF is a Philadelphia-based community development finance institution.) TRF created a typology that identified residential neighborhoods as "Reclamation," "Distressed," "Transitional," "Steady," "High Value/Appreciating," and "Regional Choice." It then applied this typology to most of the city's 1,816 block groups identified by the 2000 US Census. In my map and analysis, I used the label "Devastated" for TRF's "Reclamation" areas and the label "Stable or Improving" to combine TRF's "Steady," "High Value/Appreciating," and "Regional Choice" areas.

The Policy Solutions Group used a cluster analysis to create these six categories, which it called types of "markets." That analysis relied on the indicators shown in Table A.4 to reflect "those characteristics of the people and housing most representative of 'the market' . . . [and of] public and private housing programs." TRF's direct descriptions of its categories of "clusters," which it called market types, and variables used in the analysis are provided in the following text and in Table A.4.[1]

Reclamation: These markets have the oldest housing and the lowest average values. While the decade of the 1990s showed substantial percentage gain in sale prices (e.g., from $15,900 in 1990 to $20,700 in 1999), those prices remained well below the citywide average. Vacancy rates are very high and signs of physical deterioration are among the worst in the city. There is very little commercial presence. Although owner occupancy

Table A.4. INDICATORS OF NEIGHBORHOOD TYPE IN THE REINVESTMENT FUND'S ANALYSIS

Variable	Indicators	Data Source[1]
Owner occupancy rates	Percentage owner vs. renter occupied	US Bureau of the Census
Age of housing stock	Percentage of homes built after 1950	US Bureau of the Census
Housing sales price	Most recent sale year, value, type, and price	BRT[2]
Demolition activity	Percentage of units demolished	L & I[3]
Vacancy rates	Percentage of properties vacant	L & I
Presence of dangerous properties	Percentage of properties deemed dangerous and imminently dangerous	L & I
Housing assistance programs	Presence of non–market rate rental housing	US HUD[4]
Mix of commercial and residential uses	Percentage of properties categorized as commercial	BRT
Consumer credit profile	Percentage of households surveyed with high and very high risk credit scores	Experian

[1] Obtained 2000–2001.

[2] Bureau of Revision of Taxes of the City of Philadelphia.

[3] City of Philadelphia Department of Licenses and Inspections.

[4] US Department of Housing and Urban Development.

rates are high, so too are the rates of Section 8 tenancy. Resident credit scores reflected the highest average risk levels in the city.

Distressed: Some markets have home values well below the other markets. There was price appreciation in these markets, but the appreciation was based on a substantially lower base amount (e.g., from $39,800 in 1990 to $46,200 in 1999). The housing stock is old and in deteriorating condition. Demolitions, vacancies and dangerous property counts are elevated. Resident credit scores are, on average, low—meaning that mainstream financial credit is not likely to be readily available.

Transitional: These markets have housing values that exceeded the citywide average; change was minimal over the 1990s. Although in many of these markets the housing stock is relatively younger, some show signs of elevated levels of vacancies, dangerous properties, demolitions, and other indicators of physical deterioration. Transitional markets have about the lowest average level of commercial uses. These markets have the highest average level of owner occupancy. Resident credit scores reflect greater risk than Steady, High Value/Appreciating, and Regional Choice areas, meaning that access to traditional sources of credit will be reduced.

Steady: These markets have high housing values, but not as high as the Regional Choice and High Value/Appreciating markets. Price appreciation over the 1990s was not strong. Steady markets have very little commercial presence, and owner occupancy rates are high. The age of housing reflects a substantial portion of the homes built post-1950. Resident credit scores are generally high, but showing signs of erosion.

High Value/Appreciating: These areas, like the Regional Choice markets, have very high average housing values that fluctuate with the general economic cycle. Appreciation in this market was stronger than in the Regional Choice markets. Older housing in good condition is the norm. There are fewer rentals and less commercial presence than the Regional Choice markets. Resident credit scores are generally quite good.

Regional Choice: These areas have the highest average housing values; values tended to fluctuate along with the general economic cycle experienced in this and other cities. The housing stock is generally older and in good condition. Regional choice markets have a mix of both residential and commercial uses as well as owner- and renter-occupied stock. Resident credit scores tend on average to be the highest in the city.

APPENDIX 3
Case Study Area Characteristics

Table A.5 provides data on some general characteristics of the neighborhoods in which the book's case-study subjects—the American Street and Jefferson Square redevelopment projects—were set.

Table A.5. CASE STUDY AREA DEMOGRAPHIC AND REAL ESTATE MARKET CHARACTERISTICS, 1990 AND 2000

	American Street[1] (1990)	American Street (2000)	Jefferson Square[2] (1990)	Jefferson Square (2000)
Area size (acres)	207	207	54	54
Demographics				
Population size	3,431	3,301	2,530	2,774
Race/ethnicity				
White (%)	20	27	66	54
Black (%)	27	16	25	36
Hispanic (black or white) (%)	58	69	4	8
Foreign born (%)	11	17	19	6
Income and education				
Median household income				
Nominal dollars	\$21,403	\$23,782	\$21,204	\$21,912
2000 dollars[3]	\$28,198	\$23,782	\$27,937	\$21,912
Families below poverty level (%)	47	44	12	31
Percent graduated from college (%)	6	5	1	10

(Continued)

Table A.5. CONTINUED

	American Street[1] (1990)	American Street (2000)	Jefferson Square[2] (1990)	Jefferson Square (2000)
Residential real estate				
Total number occupied housing units	972	1,015	1,063	1,117
Housing cost				
Median value of owner-occupied homes				
Nominal dollars	$17,337	$29,863	$45,533	$48,000
2000 dollars	$22,842	$29,863	$59,991	$48,000
Median gross rent				
Nominal dollars	$370	$470	$315	$516
2000 dollars	$487	$470	$415	$516
Housing unit structure (percentage of total housing units)				
Housing units built before 1960 (%)	88	91	95	85
Single-family detached (%)	14	10	3	1
Single-family attached (%)	71	70	71	71
Multi-family (%)	13	19	25	27
Housing unit occupancy (percentage of total housing units)				
Owner-occupied (%)	43	46	60	52
Renter-occupied (%)	57	54	40	48
Vacant (%)	12	9	17	14

[1] The smallest collection of census block groups that encompassed all addresses targeted for takings was considered to represent the case study area. Data are from the US Bureau of the Census, Census 1990 and 2000. The American Street neighborhood statistics are combined from Census Tract (CT) 144, Block Group (BG) 7; CT 156, BG 1; CT 156, BG 2; CT 157, BG 3; CT 157, BG 4; CT 162, BG 3; CT 162, BG 4; CT 163, BG 4; and CT 163, BG 5.

[2] The Jefferson Square neighborhood statistics are combined from CT 25, BG 3; CT 27, BG 6; and CT 27, BG 7.

[3] Calculated with the CPI inflation calculator from the Bureau of Labor Statistics, which uses the average CPI for a given calendar year.

NOTES

CHAPTER 1

1. Reverend David Funkhouser, Pastor of St. John's Episcopal Church, testified that "[t]he community became aware of this [plan] in January 1998, when code violation notices were posted on the doors of the residents in the area." Philadelphia City Planning Commission, Meeting Minutes, April 15, 1999, p. 6.
2. Peggy King Brookins, interview, February 2, 2009. Since the family had moved to Philadelphia from South Carolina, they had lived in three different places, first an apartment at Randolph and Christian Street, then houses at Fifth and Christian Street and Third and Bainbridge Street.
3. Peggy King Brookins (family member of condemnees), personal communication with author, November 1, 2013. Dorothy King and Shirley Corbin-Nelson (condemnees) nodded their heads in agreement.
4. According to their "Claim for Replacement Housing Payment for 180-Day Homeowner" documents, Dorothy King moved into her house at 1313 S. Leithgow Street in 1965, JoAnn King at 1308 S. Leithgow Street in 1976, Mary and Joseph Black at 1303 S. Leithgow Street in 1977, Shirley Corbin-Nelson at 1306 S. Leithgow Street and Richard King, III at 1312 S. Leithgow Street in 1984.
5. Shirley Corbin-Nelson, interview, January 29, 2009.
6. Corbin-Nelson and JoAnn King, interview, January 29, 2009; Brookins, interview; Dorothy King, personal communication with author, November 1, 2013.
7. JoAnn King and Corbin-Nelson, interview.
8. Dorothy King, personal communication with author.
9. Santiago Burgos, *Status Report of First Year of the A.S.E.Z.—N.T.I. Pilot Early Action Planning Project* (Philadelphia, Philadelphia Empowerment Zone, December 2001); Cathy Califano (Economic Development director, Philadelphia Empowerment Zone) to Schmidt, Memorandum (Re: NTI Funding Request for the American Street Empowerment Zone), April 3, 2002.
10. Ana Rivera (condemnee), interview, April 13, 2008; Sonia Ortiz (condemnee), interview, April 16, 2008; Claudina Pantoja (condemnee), interview, April 22, 2008; Wanda Ocasio (condemnee), interview, July 13, 2008; Aida Cartegena (condemnee), interview, April 15, 2008.
11. Ibid.
12. Maria Reyes (relocation technician, RDA), interview, February 16, 2007.
13. Scott Bullock (senior attorney, Institute for Justice), interview, May 12, 2006.
14. Manuel Velez (condemnee), interview, July 16, 2008.

15. Velez, interview.
16. Community Leadership Institute, Philadelphia Folklore Project and Barry Dornfeld, *I Choose to Stay Here*. Philadelphia Folklore Project, 2004, 21 min.; Community Leadership Institute, *The Taking of Bodine: Never Forget*. Scribe Video Center, 2008, 10 min.
17. Velez, interview.
18. My use of "investment" as a kind of economic action in the sense developed by Max Weber and Talcott Parsons (2003 [1958]) differs from that of a few other sociologists. In their analysis of political philosophy texts, *On Justification*, Luc Boltanski and Laurent Thevenot (2006 [1991]) describe an investment concept that "links the benefits of a higher state to a cost or a sacrifice that is required for access to that state." Also, Anthony Giddens (1998) promoted a "social investment state," in which government takes responsibility for investing its resources.
19. Max Weber (1946 [1919]), pp. 78–79; Max Weber, Guenther Roth, and Claus Wittich (1978). Weber wrote that claims about the use of power attain legitimacy when people treat them as "valid" and act as if they are justified or appropriate, whether or not those people personally believe that the claims are proper. Sanford M. Dornbusch and W. Richard Scott (1975); Henry A. Walker, George M. Thomas and Morris Jr. Zelditch (1986); Henry A. Walker and Morris Jr. Zelditch (1993). Contemporary social research on legitimacy follows suit. Peter L. Berger and Thomas Luckmann (1967); Frank Dobbin and John R. Sutton (1998); Mary Douglas (1986); Lauren B. Edelman, Sally Riggs Fuller and Iona Mara-Drita (2001); William G. Roy (1997). Validation occurs through acts of compliance and the framings or cultural schema used in justifications.
20. In discovering a political culture of property, I hope to join sociologists of the economy who have shown alternative conceptions of other foundational capitalist institutions, as in research on the corporation by William Roy (1997), which showed different ideas and institutions of ownership; Neil Fligstein's (1990) discovery of shifts in "conceptions of control"; Frank Dobbin's (1994) comparative analysis of industrial policy; and Jens Beckert's (2007) comparative analysis of inheritance policy. I also join anthropologists, geographers, and sociologists who conducted field research to find such alternative conceptions, as seen in Wendy Espeland's (1998) and Nicholas Blomley's (2003) studies of indigenous encounters with liberal law; Deborah Davis's (2004), Katherine Verdery's (2003) and David Stark's (1996) studies of socialist transformations; and Isaac Martin's (2008) research on conservative activism.
21. The full text of what is commonly called the Takings Clause of the Fifth Amendment reads, "nor shall private property be taken for public use, without just compensation."
22. Richard Allen Epstein (1985).
23. Frank I. Michelman (1967).
24. Margaret Jane Radin (1982, 1993); Radin draws on philosopher Georg Hegel as well as sociologist Erving Goffman.
25. *Kelo v. City of New London*, 545 U.S. 469 (2005).
26. Obtained from a search of American newspapers in the LexisNexis database in 2013.
27. Lynne B. Sagalyn (2008).
28. Sean Flynn, "Across the Country, Americans Fight to Protect Their Property. Will the Government Take Your Home?," *Parade*, August 6, 2006.

29. Editorial, "United States: Hands Off Our Homes; Property Rights and Eminent Domain," *The Economist*, August 20, 2005, 34–35. Incidentally, "Hands Off My Home" is the name of the Institute for Justice's state-level campaign against eminent domain, launched immediately following the *Kelo* decision. Steven M. Teles (2008), p. 242.
30. Adam Liptak, "Case Won on Appeal (to Public)," *New York Times*, July 30, 2006.
31. *Casino Reinvestment Development Authority v. Banin*, 727 A.2d 102 (Superior Court of New Jersey, Law Division, Atlantic County 1998); Jayson Blair, "There Stays the Hotel and the Neighborhood," *New York Times*, December 31, 2000.
32. Antoinette Martin, "A Rising Tide in Waterfront Values," *New York Times*, June 4, 2010.
33. Janice Nadler, Shari Seidman Diamond, and Matthew M. Patton (2008), p. 295.
34. Ibid., p. 296.
35. Ibid., pp. 298, 304.
36. Ibid., p. 289.
37. Sagalyn (2008).
38. Monmouth University/Gannett NJ Poll, *The Power of Eminent Domain: Acceptable Uses Are Few Say Garden State Residents* (October 5, 2005). Nadler (2008, p. 301) also discusses this poll.
39. National Association for the Advancement of Colored People, AARP, Hispanic Alliance of Atlantic County, Citizens in Action, Cramer Hill Resident Association Inc. and Southern Christian Leadership Conference. Brief of the National Association of Colored People ("NAACP") et al as Amici Curiae in Support of Petitioners. *Kelo v. City of New London*, No. 04-108 (U.S. January 21, 2005); Hilary O. Shelton, "Statement of Mr. Hilary O. Shelton, Director, NAACP Washington Bureau & Senior Vice President for Advocacy and Policy before the U.S. Commission on Civil Rights," August 12, 2011.
40. Mindy Fullilove, *Eminent Domain and African Americans* (Washington, DC, The Institute for Justice, 2007), gives a commentary on the effect of recent takings on African Americans.
41. Nicholas Blomley (2007) exemplifies a direct attack on *Kelo* as allowing governments to pursue the "highest and best use" in economic terms. Susan Fainstein (2005b) critiques recent plans to bow to economic goals as the "new urban renewal" and (2005a) argues that taking for private reuse hurts the poor and benefits developers. John Logan and Harvey Molotch (1987) applied Karl Marx's distinction between use and exchange values to contemporary urban politics of real estate. Karl Polanyi (1994) theorized land as a fictitious commodity, driving governments to pursue the exchange value at the expense of the use value. Dave Harvey has often repeated this argument, as in his (2009) lambasting of a World Development Report that advocated the use of eminent domain for "higher value land uses."
42. Social theorists and researchers have elaborated on how property nurtures, guards, and signals various kinds of value. Karl Marx (1887), of course, expounded upon how private property can represent the financial value in a commodity for exchange. Erving Goffman (1961) and Margaret Jane Radin (1982) argued that clothing or personal jewelry can be a resource in the expression of personal identity. John Logan and Harvey Molotch (1987) described how property in the home, both through the house itself and the neighborhood in which it sits, is a medium for goods essential to daily life. Viviana Zelizer (2005) emphasized how property

such as food and clothing are the means through which mothers provide their children with physical security and show their love.

43. See Laura Underkuffler (2003) for a discussion of time as a crucial part of the meaning of property.
44. Nicole P. Marwell (2007); Mario Luis Small (2009); Carol B. Stack (1974).
45. United States Government Accountability Office, *Eminent Domain: Information About Its Uses and Effect on Property Owners and Communities Is Limited*, Report to Congressional Committees GAO-07-28 (Washington, DC, November 2006).
46. Vicki Lynn Been, "Eminent Domain and Economic Development" (Paper, Association of American Law Schools 2006 Annual Meeting. Joint Program of Sections on Property Law and Sate and Local Government Law, Washington, DC, 2006). Been spoke about the problematic lack of empirical information on eminent domain for economic development. Existing empirical studies of eminent domain for any purpose include one of New York City, Yun-chien Chang (2010), and one of five counties in the state of Massachusetts, Michael Malamut, *The Power to Take: The Use of Eminent Domain in Massachusetts*, Policy Paper (Boston, Pioneer Institute for Public Policy Research, December 2000). There are studies of compensation in litigated or publicly controversial cases of takings (for new private and public owners), including Nicole Garnett (2006); Thomas W. Mitchell, Stephen Malpezzi, and Richard K. Green (2009–2010); Ray Rivera, "Udot: Fair Deals or Land Grabs?" *Salt Lake Tribune*, October 24, 1999; Todd A. Schaffer and Clark Kelso, *Jury Verdicts in California Eminent Domain Cases: Some Descriptive Statistics* (Institute for Legislative Practice, November 11, 1999). For recent studies of compensation that do not select for controversy, see Yun-chien Chang, "Self-Assessment of Takings Compensation: An Empirical Study" (Paper 13, American Law and Economics Association Annual Meetings, 2008) Berkeley Electronic Press; Chang (2010); Curtis J. Berger and Patrick Rohan (1967); Patricia Munch (1976); Terrence M. Clauretie, William Kuhn, and R. Keith Schwer (2004); and Krisandra Guidry and A. Quang Do (1998). There is also a historical analysis of the legal innovation of "blight" designations to legitimize eminent domain: Wendell E. Pritchett (2003).

    The literature on 1950s and 1960s urban renewal is more vast. See, for example, Mindy Thompson Fullilove (2004); Herbert J. Gans (1962); Chester W. Hartman (1974); and James Q. Wilson (1966). For a longer list of sources on urban renewal, see Bernard J. Frieden and Lynne B. Sagalyn (1989), pp. 337–341. More recent well-known cases of redevelopment takings include the destruction of the Poletown neighborhood in Detroit for a General Motors plant, discussed by John J. Bukowczyk (1984), and the community-based initiative in Roxbury, Boston, discussed by Peter Medoff and Holly Sklar (1994).
47. Public interest groups and advocates for both sides of the post-*Kelo* debate about eminent domain reform have also produced empirically based reports in their attempts to effect policy change. See Dana Berliner, *Government Theft: The Top 10 Abuses of Eminent Domain* (Washington, DC, The Castle Coalition of the Institute for Justice, March 2002); Dana Berliner, *Public Power Private Gain: A Five-Year State by State Report Examining the Abuses of Eminent Domain* (Washington, DC, Institute for Justice, 2003); Dana Berliner, *Eminent Domain Abuse in a Post-Kelo World* (Washington, DC, Institute for Justice, 2006); Dana Berliner, *Redevelopment Wrecks: 20 Failed Projects Involving Eminent Domain Abuse* (Washington, DC, Institute for Justice, 2006); John D. Echeverria and Thekla Hansen-Young, *The Track Record on Takings Legislation: Lessons from Democracy's*

Laboratories (Washington, DC, Georgetown Environmental Law and Policy Institute, 2008); Department of the Public Advocate, *Reforming the Use of Eminent Domain for Private Redevelopment in New Jersey* (Trenton, NJ, Division of Public Interest Advocacy, The State of New Jersey, May 18, 2006); Department of the Public Advocate, *In Need of Redevelopment: Repairing New Jersey's Eminent Domain Laws: Abuses and Remedies, a Follow-up Report* (Trenton, NJ, Division of Public Interest Advocacy, The State of New Jersey, May 29, 2007); Department of the Public Advocate, *The Redevelopment of Mount Holly Gardens* (Trenton, NJ, Division of Public Interest Advocacy, The State of New Jersey, 2008); The Annie E. Casey Foundation, *Responsible Relocation: Redevelopment Roadmap* (Baltimore, MD, The Annie E. Casey Foundation, 2008); Jeff Benedict (2009); Matt Miller, *They Want to Erase Us Out: The Faces of Eminent Domain Abuse in Texas* (Austin, TX, The Institute for Justice Texas Chapter, January 2009); The Institute for Justice, *Building Empires, Destroying Homes: Eminent Domain Abuse in New York* (Washington, DC, 2009); Dick M. Carpenter II and John K. Ross, *Victimizing the Vulnerable* (Washington, DC, The Institute for Justice, June 2007); Dick M. Carpenter II and John K. Ross, *Empire State Eminent Domain: Robin Hood in Reverse* (Washington, DC, The Institute for Justice, January 2010).

48. During his first year in office, Mayor John Street (2000–2008) engaged The Reinvestment Fund (TRF), a local, nonprofit Community Development Finance Institution with a policy analysis arm, to help him plan and defend his anti-blight program, and together they came up with a "neighborhood market analysis" to guide decisions about government programming across the city. In its effort to compare and contrast neighborhood conditions, TRF developed several categories of neighborhoods (census block groups) based on indicators in 2000 of physical conditions (housing tenure, age, vacancy, and dangerous buildings) and financial conditions (resident credit scores and housing prices). Although TRF called its work a "market analysis," I believe its data indicate that its categories tell us as much about physical conditions as about financial conditions. The analysis was limited to the 1,684 of the city's 1,816 census block groups that had evidence of real estate markets and had Census 2000 data on housing cost and housing occupancy. Technically, the researchers performed a cluster analysis to create six market categories. That analysis relied on several indicators in 2000–2001 meant to reflect "those characteristics of the people and housing most representative of "the market'... [and of] public and private housing programs." The Reinvestment Fund, *Real Estate Market Analysis of Philadelphia for Mayor Street's Blight Elimination Plan* (Philadelphia, PA, 2001). I used the word "devastated" instead of TRF's label of "reclamation," which referred to policy recommendations for the worst conditions. See Appendix 2 for more detail on the TRF study methodology.

CHAPTER 2

1. See Kevin Fox Gotham (2001) for an alternative history of urban redevelopment policy.
2. *Berman v. Parker*, 26 U.S. 348, (1954).
3. Pa. Const. art. I, §10.
4. 1945 Pa. Laws 991. The "Urban Redevelopment Law" stated that the "acquisition and sound replanning and redevelopment of [blighted] areas... will promote the public health, safety, convenience and welfare;" therefore, the creation of Redevelopment Authorities and their pursuit of "economically and socially sound redevelopment... are declared to be public uses for which public money may be

spent, and private property may be acquired by the exercise of the power of eminent domain."

5. Ibid. §8(a), §10.
6. Ibid. §10.
7. 1964 Pa. Laws 84.
8. Carolyn Teich Adams (1991).
9. William Rafsky, *Community Renewal Program, City of Philadelphia: The Redevelopment Authority Program 1945–1962, Dollars, Acres, and Dwelling Units* (Philadelphia, PA, The Redevelopment Authority, September 1963).
10. Scott A. Greer (1966), p. 56.
11. United States National Advisory Commission on Civil Disorders, *Report of the National Advisory Commission on Civil Disorders* (Washington, DC, US Government Printing Office, March 1, 1968), p. 80.
12. Marc Fried (1963); Fullilove (2004); Gans (1962); Chester Hartman and Rob Kessler (1978).
13. Dennis R. Judd and Todd Swanstrom (1998), pp. 182–185.
14. Jordan Mechner, *Chavez Ravine: A Los Angeles Story.* Bullfrog Films, 2005, 24 min.; PBS, "Chavez Ravine: A Los Angeles Story," accessed June 5, 2013, http://www.pbs.org/independentlens/chavezravine/cr.html.
15. William Rafsky, "What Was Attempted" (Lecture, The Politics of Utopia: Towards America's 3rd Century, A series of community oriented lectures and discussions on Philadelphia's future as an urban center, Philadelphia, PA, 1975) The Political Science Department, Temple University, Section III.
16. Fullilove (2004); Herbert J. Gans (1962, 1966); Robert Halpern (1995); Hartman and Kessler (1978).
17. Sidney Wilhelm and Edwin Powell (1975), p. 119.
18. Rafsky, "What Was Attempted"; Adams (1991), p. 108.
19. Douglas S. Massey and Nancy A. Denton (1993); Kenneth T. Jackson (1985).
20. Raymond A. Mohl (1993a) described how, as plans were developed for Interstate 95 to cut through black areas of Miami from 1955 and 1957, only a few activists mobilized against it, pp. 122–124, for "Miami blacks were still more passive than active," but by the 1960s, they had successfully organized for other issues and forced the integration of several different public spaces, pp. 118–119.
21. Jane Jacobs (1961).
22. Henry Morgenthau III, *James Baldwin.* WGBH public television, 1963; Frieden and Sagalyn (1989), p. 273; Arnold R. Hirsch (1998), p. 273. For a discussion of highway construction and urban renewal as "black removal," see Mohl (1993b).
23. United States National Advisory Commission on Civil Disorders. *Report on Civil Disorders,* pp. 81–82.
24. In *Tumbling*, Diane McKinney-Whetstone (1996) gives a clever fictional representation of a local struggle with eminent domain, inspired by the fight over South Street.
25. Adams (1991), pp. 121–123.
26. Chester Hartman (2010 [1984]), p. 539.
27. Adams (1991), pp. 121–123.
28. Edmund Bacon, "What Was Attempted" (Lecture, The Politics of Utopia: Towards America's 3rd Century, A series of community oriented lectures and discussions on Philadelphia's future as an urban center, Philadelphia, PA, 1975) The Political Science Department, Temple University, Section IV. Bacon said that, as executive director of the Planning Commission, he had advocated the treatment of scattered

abandoned sites rather than large-scale clearances. A lack of political support had prevented him from implementing the former approach, he said.

29. Adams (1991); Rafsky, "What Was Attempted"; Rafsky, *Community Renewal Program*.
30. Rafsky, *Community Renewal Program*.
31. Neil Smith (1979), p. 164.
32. Loretta Lees, Tom Slater, and Elvin Wyly (2010).
33. Halpern (1995).
34. Judd and Swanstrom (1998), p. 200.
35. Ibid, pp. 227–231.
36. In 1960, Richardson Dilworth offered the Plan for Center City, which included a design for a wealthy, residential Society Hill, Adams (1991), p. 105.
37. Ibid., p. 109.
38. Halpern (1995).
39. Judd and Swanstrom (1998) p. 236 fn 111.
40. Ibid., p. 236 fn 115.
41. Frieden and Sagalyn (1989).
42. Judd and Swanstrom (1998), pp. 356–357.
43. Ibid., pp. 370–375.
44. Ibid., p. 382.
45. Bukowczyk (1984); Jeanie Wylie (1989).
46. Judd and Swanstrom (1998), p. 368.
47. Rowland Atkinson (2000); Peter Marcuse (1985).
48. Judd and Swanstrom (1998), p. 151.
49. William Julius Wilson (1987)
50. Douglas S. Massey, Jonathan Rothwell, and Thurston Domina (2009).
51. Judd and Swanstrom (1998).
52. Adams (1991).
53. Roman A. Cybriwsky, David Ley, and John Western (1986).
54. Margaret Pugh O'Mara (2005).
55. Robert P. Fairbanks (2009), p. 5. Conditions were also reflected in news reporter Steve Lopez's (1994) novel, *Third and Indiana*.
56. ABC News, *Badlands Part 1 and 2: The Death of an American Neighborhood*. ABC News Nightline, August 22, 1995.
57. Adams (1991), p. 23.
58. Christopher Howard, Michael Lipsky, and Dale Rogers Marshall (1998 [1994]); Michael McQuarrie (2013); Randy Stoecker (1997); Jordan Yin (1998).
59. Adams (1991), pp. 110, 113.
60. Barbara Ferman (1998 [1991]), p. 231.
61. Frieden and Sagalyn (1989).
62. McQuarrie (2005).
63. Bennett Harrison (1982).
64. Ibid.
65. Judd and Swanstrom (1998), p. 247.
66. Lees, Slater, and Wyly (2010), pp. xv, xvi, 448.
67. Margaret Dewar and June Manning Thomas (2012).
68. Thomas A. Jr. Finnerty, William D'Avignon, Anthony Kobak, and Jay Williams, *The Youngstown 2010 Citywide Plan*, (Youngstown, Ohio, The City of Youngstown, 2005).

69. Kaid Benfield, "Detroit: The 'Shrinking City' That Isn't Actually Shrinking," *The Atlantic* June 10, 2011; Jennifer Bradley, Richard Florida, Toni L. Griffin, Sam Staley, Michael A. Pagano, Terry Schwarz, Brad Whitehead, Ellen Dunham-Jones, and June Williamson, "The Incredible Shrinking City," *New York Times*, March 28, 2011.
70. Judd and Swanstrom (1998), p. 385.
71. Mark Alan Hughes (2000); Ann O'M Bowman and Michael A. Pagano (2004), pp. 79–81; Stephen Seplow, "Too Many Houses, Too Few Residents: Phila. Is Plagued by Abandoned Properties," *Philadelphia Inquirer*, May 10, 1999.
72. New Kensington Community Development Corporation, "Land Use," accessed June 10, 2013, http://www.nkcdc.org/land-use; New Kensington Community Development Corporation, "Greening," accessed June 10, 2013, http://nkcdc.org/media/images/nkcdc/greening.pdf; Pennsylvania Horticultural Society, "Launching the Green Strategy," accessed June 10, 2013, http://pennsylvaniahorticulturalsociety.org/phlgreen/ui_launchinggreencity.htm.
73. I offer a more in-depth analysis of the significance of racial differences in Becher, "Race as a Set of Symbolic Resources" (2015).
74. Martin Anderson (1964).
75. Teles (2008), pp. 237, 239.
76. Ibid., p. 241.
77. Castle Coalition, "About Us," The Institute for Justice, accessed June 5, 2013, http://castlecoalition.org/about.
78. Teles (2008), p. 242. See Michael W. McCann (1994) for an in-depth study of how activists can use a loss in court to mobilize public support for their cause.
79. John Kramer, "Media Advisory: Kelo Attorney to Testify before Michigan House on Eminent Domain Reform," Castle Coalition, A Project of the Institute for Justice, November 2005; Institute for Justice, "Financial Report," accessed August 2, 2013, http://ij.org/about/financialreport.
80. Debbie Becher (2015); Jennifer Bradley and Timothy J. Dowling (2008).
81. Teles (2008), pp. 238–239, 244.
82. Fullilove, *Eminent Domain and African Americans*, (Washington, DC, The Institute for Justice, 2007).
83. Gerald E. Frug and David Barron, "Make Eminent Domain Fair for All," *Boston Globe*, August 12, 2005; David Dana (2006); Robert G. Dreher and John D. Echeverria, *Kelo's Unanswered Questions: The Policy Debate over the Use of Eminent Domain for Economic Development*, (Washington, DC, Georgetown Environmental Law and Policy Institute, 2006).
84. Jerome I. Hodos (2011).
85. Philadelphia's population was 1,948,609 in 1970; 1,688,210 in 1980; 1,585,577 in 1990; 1,517,550 in 2000; and 1,526,006 in 2010. The United States Census Bureau, United States Census 1970, 1980, 1990, 2000, and 2010 accessed through Social Explorer, T1, at http://www.socialexplorer.com on January 29, 2014.
86. The median values of owner-occupied housing units for Philadelphia and the nation respectively were: $11,964/419,579 in 1970; $48,400/$78,500 in 1990; $59,700/$119,600 in 2000; and $142,800/$179,900 in 2010. The United States Census Bureau, United States Census 1970, 1990, and 2000, and ACS-1 year estimates for 2010 accessed through Social Explorer, T122 (1970), T80 (1990), T164 (2000), T101 (2010), at http://www.socialexplorer.com on January 29, 2014.
87. Median gross rents for units in Philadelphia and the nation respectively were: $452/$447 in 1990; $569/$602 in 2000; and $836/$855 in 2010. The United States Census Bureau, United States Census 1990 and 2000, and ACS-1 year

estimates for 2010 accessed through Social Explorer, T82 (1990), T167 (2000), T104 (2010), at http://www.socialexplorer.com on January 29, 2014.

88. Philadelphia and national poverty rates respectively were: 20.3%/13.1% in 1990; 22.9%/12.4% in 2000; and 26.7%/15.3% in 2010. The United States Census Bureau, United States Census 1990 and 2000, and ACS-1 year estimates for 2010 accessed through Social Explorer, T93 (1990), T183 (2000), T114-116 (2010), at http://www.socialexplorer.com on January 29, 2014.
89. The median household income in Philadelphia and the nation respectively were: $24,603/$30,056 in 1990; $30,746/$41,994 in 2000; and $34,400/$50,046 in 2010. The United States Census Bureau, United States Census 1990 and 2000, and ACS-1 year estimates for 2010 accessed through Social Explorer, T43 (1990), T93 (2000), T57 (2010), at http://www.socialexplorer.com on January 29, 2014.
90. Adams (1991).
91. Ibid. Although it might be hard to find many cities whose government entities are more fragmented than Philadelphia's, the city is probably not unique in this way. Mariana Valverde (2012).
92. Dick Simpson, James Nowlan, Thomas J. Gradel, Melissa Mouritsen Zmuda, Douglas Cantor, and David Sterrett, *Chicago and Illinois Leading the Pack in Corruption*, (University of Illinois at Chicago Department of Political Science, Illinois Integrity Initiative of the University of Illinois' Institute for Government and Public Affairs, April 18, 2012).
93. Karen Araiza, "Former L&I Commissioner: Stop the Corruption," *NBC10 Philadelphia*, August 4, 2013.
94. Tony Hanson, "'Sad Day,' Says Ramsey, as More Corruption Charges Filed Against Philly Cops," *CBS Philly*, June 4, 2013.
95. David Chang, MaryClaire Dale, and Dan Stamm, "Fumo Gets Home Confinement at His Mansion," *Associated Press/NBC 10* Philadelphia, August 7, 2013.
96. E. Digby Baltzell (1958).

CHAPTER 3

1. Because tax foreclosure is less available in Pennsylvania than in other states, eminent domain cases may be more common in Pennsylvania cities than in other states' cities. Pennsylvania requires a comparatively high accumulated amount of tax delinquency to justify foreclosure on a property due to unpaid taxes. Thus, Philadelphia government uses eminent domain for properties that other city governments might acquire through tax foreclosure, and its overall eminent domain numbers are probably higher than those of similar cities. This point does not detract, however, from the theoretical usefulness of studying eminent domain to understand conceptions of property. Eminent domain makes government's condemnation of property transparent, and thus engages citizens and scholars in considering this authority. In fact, the numbers of forcibly transferred property titles would be much greater if we included all of the property that government forcibly acquires through its police powers, such as tax foreclosures and drug forfeitures.
2. Five properties were both litigated and revested and, thus, were included in both of these figures. Four were vacant lots, and one was a vacant building.
3. Scott Bullock (senior attorney, Institute for Justice), interview, May 12, 2006.
4. 26 Pa. Cons. Stat. §203(b), §205 et seq. (Lexis, LexisNexis Academic through 2013 reg. session Act 86); 1945 Pa. Laws 991. Pritchett (2003) and Gold and Sagalyn (2011) provide histories of "blight" as a justification for eminent domain in pre-*Kelo* and post-*Kelo* statutes and judicial opinions, respectively.

5. John Linden [Pseudonym. Throughout the book, I use pseudonyms for all informants who did not take on public leadership roles and did not specifically give me permission to use their real names. All other names are accurate.] (planner, City of Philadelphia Planning Commission), interview, August 2, 2007.
6. Cathy Califano (deputy secretary, Philadelphia Office of Housing and Community Development and former Economic Development director, Philadelphia Empowerment Zone), interview, June 19, 2006.
7. Lorraine Warren [pseud.] (executive director, anonymous community development corporation), interview, February 8, 2007.
8. Susan Wachter, *The Determinants of Neighborhood Transformations in Philadelphia, Identification and Analysis: The New Kensington Pilot Study* (Philadelphia: The Wharton School, University of Pennsylvania, Spring 2005).
9. Philadelphia had an official program to help residents acquire "side yards." On the commercial side, there was no similarly named program that explicitly targeted adjacent owners, but officials considered and looked favorably upon businesses requesting property adjacent to their current operations. And my analysis presented earlier in the chapter shows that over half of the commercial projects approved for eminent domain were for expansions into adjacent properties. Similarly, almost three-quarters of takings for institutional developments were for expansions into properties next door to existing operations. The city's attempt to get vacant land into homeowners' hands as side yards was most recently formalized in a policy document that outlined the conditions under which the city would sell publicly owned land to an adjacent homeowner as a side yard, including a condition that the property be valued at less than $15,000 and be less than 3,000 square feet. City of Philadelphia, *Policies for the Sale and Reuse of City Owned Property* (April 20, 2012), http://www.phila.gov/pra/pdfs/CityPolicies for Sale Reuse Property_5.2012.pdf, accessed November 16, 2013.

CHAPTER 4

1. Community Leadership Institute, *The Taking of Bodine: Never Forget*. Scribe Video Center, 2008, 10 min.; Community Leadership Institute, Philadelphia Folklore Project and Barry Dornfeld, *I Choose to Stay Here*. Philadelphia Folklore Project, 2004, 21 min.; Amy L. Webb, "Neighborhood Transformation Investigated: Exclusive Report, Shoddy Record-Keeping and Missing Expense Reports Could Cost the City Millions," *Philadelphia City Paper*, December 9, 2003.
2. Scott Bullock (senior attorney, Institute for Justice), interview, May 12, 2006; Elizabeth Segarra (staff organizer, Community Leadership Institute [CLI]), interview, February 26, 2007.
3. *ABC News*, "Badlands Part 1 and 2: The Death of an American Neighborhood"; Steve Lopez (1994).
4. The United States Bureau of the Census, United States Census 1990 and 2000. See Appendix 3 for more census data on the area.
5. Barbara Kaplan and Elizabeth Kozart (Philadelphia City Planning Commission), memorandum: American Street Corridor Land Use Report, October 6, 1997.
6. Dougherty, interview, January 29, 2007.
7. Miguelina de Jesus (condemnee), interview, March 17, 2008.
8. Urban Partners, American Street Empowerment Zone: Economic Development Strategy (Philadelphia, PA, Prepared for City of Philadelphia, Philadelphia Empowerment Zone, October 2001). The businesses were primarily warehouse operations, light construction-related businesses, and automotive repair shops.

About a third of the businesses within the boundaries of the American Street Industrial Corridor of the Philadelphia Empowerment Zone were services (31 percent); a third were retail (28 percent); and the final third was split between manufacturing (14 percent), wholesale trade (12 percent), and construction (8 percent).

9. Tomasita Romero (informal community leader), interview, March 12, 2008.
10. Frederick F. Wherry and Tony Rocco (2011).
11. Community Leadership Institute et al., *I Choose to Stay*.
12. Claudina Pantoja (condemnee), interview, April 22, 2008; Aida Cartegena (condemnee), interview, April 15, 2008.
13. Sonia Ortiz (condemnee), interview, April 16, 2008.
14. Manuel Velez (condemnee), interview, July 16, 2008. Others also spoke of having done major, costly renovations to their houses. Pantoja, interview; de Jesus, interview.
15. Segarra, interview, February 26, 2007.
16. Romero, interview.
17. Ibid.
18. Velez, interview.
19. Cartegena, interview. Ortiz (2008) and others spoke similarly about cleaning up and using the lots next to their houses.
20. Ibid.; Ortiz, interview; C. Pantoja, interview.
21. Jasmin Pantoja (adult daughter of condemnee Claudina Pantoja), interview, April 22, 2008; Cartegena, interview; Wanda Ocasio (condemnee), interview, July 13, 2008; Ana Rivera (condemnee), interview, April 13, 2008.
22. Ortiz, interview; C. Pantoja, interview.
23. C. Pantoja, interview.
24. Velez, interview.
25. J. Pantoja, interview.
26. Rivera, interview.
27. Ortiz, interview.
28. Ocasio, interview.
29. Walt DeTreux (former chief of staff to City of Philadelphia Council Member Richard Mariano, District Seven), interview, March 22, 2007.
30. Eugenia Burgos (informal community leader and former ASCTB member), interview, March 12, 2008.
31. Asociación de Puertorriqueños en Marcha, "About Us: A Brief History of APM," accessed March 18, 2007, http://www.apmphila.org/about.html. The Asociación de Puertorriqueños en Marcha (APM) began its work by filing a lawsuit in 1970 against the state over local provision of care to Latinos with mental retardation. Women's Community Revitalization Project, "Affordable Housing for Low Income Women and Their Families," accessed March 29, 2007, http://www.wcrpphila.com/Frahousing.html. The Women's Community Revitalization Project (WCRP) was conceived by a neighborhood coalition when it won a $50 million settlement from a challenge to Fidelity Bank's lending practices in 1986.
32. National Council of La Raza, "Norris Square Civic Association," accessed March 18, 2007, http://www.nclr.org/content/affiliates/detail/1232/. The Norris Square Civic Association (NSCA) was founded in 1982 by a group of young mothers focusing on community development and resident empowerment. The Hispanic Association of Contractors and Enterprises was originally founded to accomplish development in the early 1980s and tends to focus more on commercial construction.

33. Romero, interview.
34. Urban Partners. ASEZ: Economic Development, pp. 14–15, 35.
35. James Hartling (partner, Urban Partners), interview, January 22, 2007.
36. DeTreux, interview. DeTreux added that Dougherty is "a great guy, a really good guy."
37. Dan Gunderson (director of Development, Philadelphia/Camden Empowerment Zone) to Duane Bumb (Commerce), Paul Deegan (PIDC), Vince Dougherty (Commerce), Fernando Gallard (MBAT), Kirk Goodrich (RDA), Bill Hankowsky (PIDC), Steve Mullin (PIDC), Tony Palimore (PIDC), Graig Schelter (PIDC), Andy Toy (Commerce), memorandum (Re: American Street Site Assembly), July 16, 1997.
38. Kaplan and Kozart, American Street Corridor Land Use Report.
39. Califano, interview.
40. Burgos, interview.
41. Linden, interview. Linden thought that the barriers preventing trucks from reaching American Street via I-95 would discourage businesses from locating there.
42. Dougherty continued: "We, all of the players (Commerce, PIDC, RDA, City Planning, PHA...) had this very nice meeting in October 1997 to get the American Street site assembly program back on track, prioritize sites and start to deal with the issues of occupied houses, PHA houses, etc. Almost six months later, we seem to be no further along than we were six months ago, which is no further along than six months before that, which is no... Most of the developable sites we have acquired were acquired thru Commerce's efforts, either directly... or indirectly... RDA (according to Tony P) is not responding to status requests on condemnations...." Dougherty to Bumb (deputy director, Philadelphia Department of Commerce), e-mail exchange, March 25–31, 1998.
43. Dougherty to Mullin, memorandum (Re: Coordination/Cooperation between OHCD & Commerce), January 15, 1998.
44. Dougherty to Bumb, memorandum, August 1997.
45. Dougherty, interview.
46. Guillermo Salas (president-cofounder, Hispanic Association of Contractors and Enterprises), interview, February 16, 2007.
47. Ibid.
48. The Philadelphia Empowerment Zone, "Ez Facts," accessed December 21, 2006, http://empowermentzone.org/ez_facts/index.html; The Philadelphia Empowerment Zone, Making Revitalization a Reality (2004). The $29 million reserved for the American Street (a designated 1.7-mile-long stretch bordering N. American Street) came from a total of $79 million awarded to the city. In 2000, the area had a population of 14,000, according to the Philadelphia Empowerment Zone, "2007 HUD Secretary's Opportunity and Empowerment Zone Award Submission."
49. Celestino Martinez [pseud.] (City of Philadelphia employee), interview, January 24, 2007.
50. Undated flyer provided by Elizabeth Segarra, staff organizer, Community Leadership Institute, February 26, 2007.
51. Scott Herbert, Avis Vidal, Greg Mills, Franklin James, and Debbie Gruenstein, Interim Assessment of the Empowerment Zones and Enterprise Communities (EZ/EC) Program: A Progress Report (Washington, DC, U.S. Department of Housing and Urban Development, November 2001). The Philadelphia/Camden Empowerment Zone (along with one of the other six Empowerment Zones and

four of the twelve Enterprise Communities studied) received the highest possible ranking in "overall resident influence."

52. Dougherty, interview. Dougherty's colleagues working on land assembly were from the Philadelphia Industrial Development Corporation (PIDC), the RDA and OHCD.
53. Cathy Califano (Economic Development Director, Philadelphia Empowerment Zone) to Jonathon Schmidt, memorandum (Re: NTI Funding Request for the American Street Empowerment Zone), April 3, 2002. A land-use study of the area found that the area had almost sixteen acres of developable land, but no "potential developable parcels" greater than one acre.
54. Dougherty to Bumb, memorandum. In 1997, a planner posed this question for the Planning Commission to consider: "Another 12 acres of land could potentially become available, but would require the taking of more houses and the demolition of buildings. How much land is needed and what size parcels should we consider? Do we want to consider taking blocks that are zoned residential, but whose few remaining houses are in really bad shape?" Kaplan and Kozart, American Street Corridor Land Use Report.
55. Dougherty to Bumb, memorandum.
56. In addition, the site assembly program had practically run out of money. In July 1998, Dougherty wrote, "With only $277,000 left in the pot and no new funds budgeted, we can't go much further on the ASSAP [American Street Site Assembly Program]." Dougherty to Mullin, memorandum (Re: Coordination/Cooperation between O.H.C.D. & Commerce).
57. Dougherty, e-mail, August 5, 1998.
58. Califano, interview; James Flaherty (former member and president ASCTB, former executive director, Kensington South Neighborhood Advisory Committee), interview, March 22, 2007.
59. Patricia Smith (former director, Neighborhood Transformation Initiative), interview, June 29, 2006.
60. Santiago Burgos, Status Report of First Year of the A.S.E.Z.—N.T.I. Pilot Early Action Planning Project (Philadelphia, Philadelphia Empowerment Zone, December 2001).
61. Jeremy Thomas (project manager II, Philadelphia Department of Commerce), interview, March 25, 2008.
62. Minutes of the American Street Empowerment Zone Community Trust Board Minutes (hereafter cited as Minutes, ASCTB), October 17, 1995.
63. Jannet Ramos (neighbor of condemnees), personal communication with author, March 15, 2008; Burgos, interview; Patricia DeCarlo (executive director, Norris Square Community Association), interview, February 2, 2007; Segarra, interview.
64. Burgos, interview.
65. Ramos, personal communication with Author.
66. Minutes, ASCTB, March 5, 1996.
67. "The Commerce Department is confident that once the parcel is assembled, an end user will be secured on a timely basis. Several companies have expressed interest in the parcel already." Burgos. Status Report of First Year.
68. Minutes, ASCTB, June 29, 1995, October 17, 1995, October 24, 2001, January 23, 2002, October 23, 2002.

CHAPTER 5

1. Maria Reyes (relocation technician, RDA), interview, February 16, 2007.

2. Matthew Walker (project manager, RDA) to Melvis Dunbar (relocation director, RDA), Memorandum (Re: Project Relocation Activities: Model Cities 28–Reline Centers 2100 N. American Street), November 23, 2001.
3. Segarra, interview.
4. As Herb Gans (1962) discovered, residents of Boston's West End did not believe news of impending slum clearance until they saw the bulldozers.
5. Ortiz interview.
6. Matthew Walker (former project manager, RDA), interview, February 29, 2008. The RDA board would not approve the taking, until decision-makers at the RDA felt certain that funding for the project was guaranteed. Walker said he felt that his hands were tied until the agreement was signed, something that finally happened in June 2002. Walker, Project Timeline (Philadelphia, Redevelopment Authority of the City of Philadelphia, January 30, 2002). Representatives of the RDA, the Commerce Department, and the EZ do not appear to have expected the agreement to delay the project for so many months, as its signing did not even appear on the project timeline. Santiago Burgos, Second Year Status Report of the A.S.E.Z.—N.T.I. Early Action Planning, (Philadelphia, Philadelphia Empowerment Zone, December 2002). Later, the EZ reflected back and reported on the reasons for the delays. One reason involved negotiations with the RDA over funding for the acquisitions, and another involved inclusion in the greater Model Cities URA, which made delays in takings in other parts of the city hold up the process for those along American Street.
7. For example, an appraiser visited Ortiz's house but performed an exterior inspection only and did not necessarily have any contact with her. Benchmark Appraisers appraised the property for $20,000 on January 17, 2002, based on this inspection.
8. Outline for the Town Meeting to Be Hosted on March 7, 2002, by the EZ and Several Community Organizations, acquired from files of the Philadelphia Empowerment Zone.
9. Ibid.
10. Redevelopment Authority of the City of Philadelphia. Condemnation Budget, First Entry, 2002. The offer letters were originally expected to go out on December 4, 2001. They were actually sent on July 1, 2002, and July 8, 2002, and Richard Harrell, a RDA relocation worker, visited some residents' homes on July 29, 2002, August 1, 2002, and August 7, 2002, according to multiple RDA case files.
11. The case notes in one RDA file read, "Worker met with [owner-occupant name] this afternoon to complete the preliminary data. Worker explained the relocation process. [Name] speaks very little English. Worker will mail out a GIN letter requesting certain items." These notes are fairly representative of the other files, except for the comment about the owner speaking little English.
12. Raúl Argullo [pseud.] (condemnee), personal communication with author, April 22, 2008.
13. Rivera, interview.
14. The RDA stamped this letter as received on May 3, 2002. Ortiz told me that she did not hire a lawyer, however. She, Rivera, and Cartegena all said that they could not afford lawyers; Cartegena added that hiring one would have been a waste of money because "nobody could have helped us." Oritz, interview; Rivera, interview; Cartegena, interview. De Jesus, who wanted to move and was generally satisfied with the way relocation was handled, said she did not need a lawyer because she was capable of handling the negotiations herself. De Jesus, interview. Pantoja

and Velez hired lawyers but told me they were no help in the end, although Velez also spoke of plans to hire another lawyer to help him sue. Pantoja, interview; Velez, interview.

15. Council of the City of Philadelphia, Public Hearing, Committee on Rules (hereafter cited as City Council), December 9, 2002. Department of Records, pp. 184.
16. Ibid., pp. 186.
17. Salas, interview.
18. Burgos, interview.
19. City Council, December 9, 2002, pp. 208–209.
20. Webb, "Neighborhood Transformation Investigated." Cubas died of cancer in 2006, before I could interview her for this research.
21. Segarra, interview.
22. Luis Mora (executive director, American Street Financial Services Corporation), interview, February 26, 2008; Ortiz, interview; Flaherty, interview. Ocasio (2008) remembered hearing that a Wal-Mart or a K-Mart was planned for the 2100-block site that was condemned.
23. Flaherty, interview; Califano, interview.
24. Califano, interview.
25. Segarra, interview; Martinez, interview.
26. DeTreux, interview; Califano, interview.
27. DeTreux, interview.
28. Mora, interview.
29. Burgos, interview.
30. She refers here to numbers of properties that Mayor Street's office proposed it would acquire with NTI funds.
31. Segarra, interview.
32. Domenic Vitiello (assistant professor of City and Regional Planning, University of Pennsylvania), interview, April 8, 2008.
33. Santiago Burgos (director, Program Operations, Philadelphia EZ) to staff, memorandum (Re: Misinformation Campaign in Asez), November 5, 2002. The EZ hosted its own community meetings that were attended by hundreds of people on October 16 and October 24, 2002. It mailed follow-up bilingual information packets on November 14, but its attempts to allay fears through education about the formal process continued to seem evasive. For example, the packets posed the question, "What happens if one lives within the Industrial Corridor Urban Renewal Area?" and answered it with, "NOTHING, unless a project is planned." Moreover, the EZ did not hand out detailed information about the exact projects that were planned.
34. Romero, interview.
35. DeTreux, interview.
36. Burgos, interview. Flaherty, interview. Flaherty also mentioned that he would receive calls because of flyers that activists distributed in his neighborhood saying that the government was taking homes on Second Street. He would try to allay resident fears with what he knew about acquisition plans.
37. Reyes, interview.
38. The RDA came very close to evicting two of the residents, which would have made them ineligible for relocation assistance. Each time, the RDA called off the eviction when residents resumed a cooperative stance and promised to move soon.
39. Before putting compensation money toward the new house, the settlement would pay off any balance attached to the title. If there was a credit—for example, in

taxes paid for the future—it would be returned to the condemnee in cash. If there was a debt, the creditors would be paid from the compensation money. The settlement would wipe off a median $12 of credit and $3,490 of debt attached to the condemned titles.

40. One condemnee took out an $8,000 loan to pay off an outstanding utility bill.
41. City Council, December 9, 2002, p. 184.
42. Council of the City of Philadelphia, Public Hearing, Committee on Rules, December 5, 2001. Department of Records, pp. 12–15.
43. Ibid., pp. 12–15.
44. Twenty-Eighth Amendment to the Model Cities Urban Renewal Plan, Philadelphia City Council, Bill 010648 (passed December 13, 2001). N. American Street, along with most of lower North Philadelphia, was included and certified as blighted under the Model Cities Urban Renewal Plan created in the 1960s. The plan has been amended over twenty times since, each time passing through the RDA Board, the City Planning Commission, and the City Council to reaffirm the blight designation and specify new property addresses targeted for acquisition.
45. Kaplan and Kozart, American Street Corridor Land Use Report; Califano, interview. Richard Singer, the president of Honor Foods, also described this as a problem that the American Street Business Association was fighting. Singer, interview, March 27, 2007.
46. Urban Partners. Asez: Economic Development; Burgos. Status Report of First Year.
47. Bob Grossman (associate director, Philadelphia Green, Pennsylvania Horticultural Society), interview, February 2, 2007. This approach to vacant land was so popular that it spread across the city, with the program managing a $3 million city contract by 2007.
48. RDA Board, Model Cities Urban Renewal Plan, Declaration of Taking 28c, Resolution 17002.
49. Singer, interview; Dougherty, interview; Dougherty to Steve Mullin (Commerce), memorandum (Re: Coordination/Cooperation between O.H.C.D. & Commerce), January 15, 1998; Dougherty to Darrell Clarke (City of Philadelphia Council Member, District Five), memorandum (Re: American Street Zoning Policy), February 6, 2004. In the latter memo, Dougherty wrote to Clarke to request his support for a policy allowing only industrial uses on the American Street Corridor.
50. Owner of Reline Centers of America, personal communication with author by telephone, January 26, 2007. Reline's facility relocated from just south of the American Street land assembly sites to 6801 State Road, in the far northeast section of the city.
51. Dougherty, personal communication with author by e-mail, April 3, 2009.
52. Reinaldo Pastrana (president, Lance Investments) to Dougherty, letter, October 29, 2003; Dougherty to Pastrana (Lance Investments), letter, July 29, 2005; ibid. A well-known developer of retail properties, Pastrana wrote to the Commerce Department in October 2003 about developing the 2100 block of N. American Street for three commercial clients. He asked again, in writing, for a chance in January 2005. A month later, the Department of Commerce granted him a 120-day "land reservation" to arrange financing, and it granted him a 30-day extension in June. Pastrana appears to have abandoned the idea without developing a formal plan.

53. In May 2005, as Pastrana's reservation on the land was nearing expiration, David Park Sang of C&C Poultry (a.k.a. Chaes Foods on the 1901 block of N. American) requested the land. In late July, once Pastrana had failed to provide proof of intent to develop the land, the Commerce Department gave a 90-day reservation to Sang so that he could pursue a "development proposal." Dougherty to Pastrana, letter. Anthony Diver Tamora Building Systems to Sang, letter, July 6, 2005. Sang enlisted a design firm to develop a proposal for construction of a $4.4 million combined office and warehouse facility.
54. Dougherty, personal communication with author by e-mail.
55. Ibid.
56. Walker, interview.
57. Segarra, interview.
58. Ramos, personal communication with author.
59. Dougherty, personal communication with author by e-mail.
60. DeCarlo, interview.
61. Mora, interview.
62. Minutes, ASCTB, March 5, 1996.
63. Aurora Urrea [pseud.] (neighbor of condemnees), personal communication with author, March 15, 2008.
64. Arturo Martin [pseud.] (neighbor of condemnees), personal communication with author, March 15, 2008.
65. Ramos, personal communication with author.
66. Ortiz, interview.
67. Eva Gladstein (NTI director, former Philadelphia EZ executive director), interview, April 21, 2006.
68. Michael Koonce (deputy executive director and former executive director, RDA), interview, February 10, 2009.

CHAPTER 6

1. Jefferson Square Community Development Corporation, *Summary of Jefferson Square Master Plan*, July 28, 1998.
2. Rita Giordano, "For Jefferson Square, 2 Approvals: Two City Agencies Gave Their Blessings to Plans for the Controversial Project in South Philadelphia," *Philadelphia Inquirer*, April 28, 1999, quoting Gina Caruso of the St. John's Leadership Team, a group representing residents.
3. Tom Kirsch, "Mt. Sinai Hospital," Opacity, accessed March 21, 2012, http://www.opacity.us/site109_mount_sinai_hospital.htm.
4. Gilbert Gaul, "Mt. Sinai Hospital Seeks Life Support from Specialization," *Philadelphia Inquirer*, November 29, 1989; Andrea Gerlin, "Hospital Closing Leaves a Scar. Idled Workers and Neighbors Hope Mt. Sinai Will Reopen. A Health-Care Upheaval Has Left It Darkened and Littered," *Philadelphia Inquirer*, June 25, 1998; Kirsch, "Mt. Sinai Hospital."
5. Virginia Nelson Holbrook (condemnee), interview, February 9, 2009.
6. Valerie Moore (condemnee), interview, March 14, 2009.
7. Brookins, interview.
8. Ibid.; Melvin Hanton (condemnee), interview, February 26, 2009; JoAnn King, interview; Moore, interview; Corbin-Nelson, interview.
9. Corbin-Nelson, interview.
10. Brookins, interview; Corbin-Nelson, interview. These personal observations are also reflected in the US Census 1990 and 2000 (CT25BG3, CT27BG6, and

CT27BG7). In the 1990s, the percentage of whites in the general area dropped from 66 to 54 percent.

11. Brookins, interview.
12. Hanton, interview. He said the streets "changed because of drugs," which were responsible for the area's "crash."
13. See Appendix 3 for sources and more detail.
14. Johanna Bauman (United Communities of Southeast Philadelphia Community Organizer), interview, July 1, 2007.
15. Sam Holbrook (condemnee), interview, February 9, 2009.
16. Clarence Smith, interview, February 16, 2009.
17. Brookins, interview.
18. Ibid.; Corbin-Nelson, interview.
19. David T. Jones, Sr. (condemnee), interview, February 7, 2009; Brookins, interview; Corbin-Nelson, interview.
20. Gina Caruso (neighbor of condemnees), interview, July 19, 2007.
21. Council of the City of Philadelphia, Public Hearing, Committee on Rules, June 15, 1999. Department of Records (hereafter cited as City Council, June 15, 1999), p. 40.
22. "Research Action," unknown author, notes from a March 5, 1998, meeting at Morning Glory Café of Jeremey Newberg representing Frank DiCicco's office, David Funkhouser, Darlene Scott (resident), and Peter Moor.
23. Bauman, interview; Kathy Furber (neighbor of condemnees), interview, August 1, 2007.
24. Corbin-Nelson, interview.
25. Brookins, interview.
26. Furber, interview; David Funkhouser (former Pastor, St. John's Episcopal Church), interview, July 30, 2007.
27. Bauman, interview; United Communities Southeast Philadelphia, "About Us," accessed November 5, 2013, http://ucsep.org/about-us/. Bauman's employer, United Communities Southeast Philadelphia, formed from the merging of former settlement houses and now has a mission of social and economic justice and community sustainability.
28. Bauman, interview.
29. For example, minutes of a Philadelphia City Planning Commission (PCPC) meeting on April 15, 1999 suggest that despite residents' requests, they did not offer any specific property lists or talk about the dates when those would be considered. Those lists must have already been in the works because the RDA Board would consider a Redevelopment Proposal listing the property addresses in less than two weeks, on April 27, and at the PCPC would consider it in three weeks, on May 6.
30. City Council, June 15, 1999, pp. 104–105.
31. Caruso, interview.
32. Ms. Vollbrecht, testimony, City Council, June 15, 1999, p. 110.
33. Jeff Brown (RDA) to Nick Scafidi (RDA), memorandum (Re: Jefferson Square Urban Renewal Area Condemnation Timeline), 2001. On May 5, 1999, DiCicco and Newberg held a community meeting where they shared a conceptual drawing that showed exact plans. The parking lot appeared on the plan drawn by Kramer+Marks Architects January 4, 1999 (Scheme # 7), but was not on the previous design (Scheme #6) from May 26, 1998. Mary Black's testimony (City Council, June 15, 1999, pp. 92–93) exemplified residents' angry reaction.

34. Rita Giordano, "City Council Delays Vote on Housing: The Jefferson Square Project Created Outrage among South Philadelphia Residents Who Fear Being Displaced," *Philadelphia Inquirer*, June 16, 1999. Black testified at an earlier PCPC meeting that "she could not understand how homes could be taken for a parking lot," PCPC Meeting Minutes, April 27, 1999, p. 7.
35. Jeremey Newberg, interview, June 12, 2006. Newberg told me via e-mail on January 12, 2014, that before JSCDC, Capital Access received a $20,000 contract from the Pennsylvania Senate Appropriations Committee, facilitated by Senator Fumo for planning. JSCDC later contracted with Capital Access annually to manage the project. Also see note 41.
36. Gerlin, "Hospital Closing"; Peter T. Kilborn, "Philadelphia Shaken by Collapse of a Health Care Giant," *New York Times*, August 22, 1998; Steve Massey, Pamela Gaynor, Christopher Snowbeck and Mackenzie Carpenter, "Anatomy of a Bankruptcy," *Pittsburgh Post-Gazette*, January 17–24, 1999.
37. City Council, June 15, 1999, pp. 89–90.
38. Ibid., pp. 103–104.
39. Jefferson Square Community Development Corporation (JSCDC), *Summary of Jefferson Square Master Plan* (Philadelphia, PA, March 1999, hereafter cited as *Summary*, 1999). They formed JSCDC in February 1998, EIN Number 23-2955963, and it began purchasing properties in late 1998. The JSCDC employed Jeremey Newberg's consulting company, Capital Access, to manage the project planning. In response to City Council members' questions at their June 15, 1999 meeting, Newberg said that Capital Access was being paid $3,000 per month for his and his two employees' services, pp. 86–87.
40. Graham Troy, "Councilman Frank Dicicco Leaves Office with Praise for His Stance on Development," philly.com, December 28, 2011, accessed December 1, 2013, http://articles.philly.com/2011-12-28/news/30565398_1_tax-abatement-private-development-new-zoning-code. "The Jefferson Square Master Plan was completed according to the vision of Councilman DiCicco and input from the Staff of Senator Fumo and the [Jefferson Square] Advisory Group," Jeremey Newberg, *Jefferson Square Master Plan: Status Report and Development Options*, (Philadelphia, PA, Capital Access Advisors, June 4, 1997, hereafter cited as *JS Master Plan: Status Report*), p.1.
41. Craig R. McCoy, "100 Camp Out to Buy New Townhouses in South Philadelphia," *Philadelphia Inquirer*, May 4, 2004. McCoy reported that Fumo arranged for $1.5 million in state grants and $600,000 in nonprofit donations. Editorial, *Philadelphia Daily News*, March 18, 2009. The editorial, "The Lessons of Fumo's Disgrace," raised questions about funding from Fumo-linked nonprofits. Craig R. McCoy and Mario F. Cattabiani, "Fumo Probe Turns to Nonprofits, Ikea; Federal Officials Seek Records from the 5 Groups, and from the Furniture Retailer," *Philadelphia Inquirer*, May 7, 2004. Craig R. McCoy, "Fumo: A Valued Connection," *Philadelphia Inquirer*, January 18, 2004. McCoy reported, "Newberg said his company, Capital Access Inc., receives $45,000 a year from Jefferson Square as project manager. Fumo has also arranged for the company to make $65,000 from the state as a consultant, while he works on the nonprofit project, Newberg said. Arnao, the Fumo staff member and director of Citizens Alliance, is Jefferson Square's board chairman."
42. City Council, June 15, 1999, p. 58.
43. Linda Dottor, planner for the PCPC, had notes in her files indicating that in 1994, before DiCicco was elected to City Council, Mt. Sinai hospital had requested city government's help with its efforts to "improve the community immediately

surrounding" the hospital. Mt. Sinai began strategic planning for a "priority area" directly to its north, from Reed to Wharton Streets, between Fourth and Fifth Streets. The hospital's committee on the subject set the following goals: increased hospital parking, patient recreation space, improved surrounding community appearance, and increased stability of nearby residential areas. From 1994 through 1996, the hospital worked to develop a "Mt. Sinai Community Enhancement Plan." Fred Druding, Sr., interview, August 2, 2007. Druding said he was brought on as a consultant by the hospital in the mid-1990s, when it hosted a series of meetings for long-range planning for neighborhood rehabilitation called the Fifth Street Renaissance.

44. Minutes to a PCPC meeting give this account of a statement by DiCicco: "... He has been concerned about the situation since 1997 when Mt. Sinai closed down, and he is concerned about delaying a decision any further. The majority of the blighted conditions was [*sic*] created by Graduate Health Systems, and the community has suffered as a result of that closing. This is a serious situation and a tenant is very close to signing with the new owners of the Mt. Sinai building for a sub-acute care facility to be operated by Kessler Rehabilitation. A senior citizens home of 35–37 units will also be developed on the Mt. Sinai site. Any community resident that is forced to relocate would have first preference for admittance. Kessler Rehabilitation needs additional parking and if they do not get that parking, they will not sign the lease. The building will continue to be vacant. If Kessler becomes a tenant, it will create 250–350 jobs for the community. This is about economic and job development for people who live in the community. The councilman said that when he met with representatives of Kessler, they had looked at the condition of the surrounding community and were concerned for the employees, patients, and visitors. If there is a delay, 300 jobs could be lost." PCPC Minutes, April 15, 1999. "Mr. Newberg said that one of the reasons Mt. Sinai had closed was because they could not attract day patients, nurses, and doctors to work there because of parking and safety issues. The new hospital has said that they need 250 parking spaces which relates to 250–300 jobs. If Mt. Sinai does not reopen, the neighborhood will be disadvantaged." PCPC Minutes, April 27, 1999. At the June 15, 1999 City Council hearing, DiCicco reported that New Tower Investments bought two of the hospital properties and that he had been party to negotiations with a New Jersey company, Kessler Rehabilitation Services, as a potential tenant. He said the company had been thinking about opening a facility there, though "they needed additional parking... and they were also concerned about the blight and deterioration and the vacant lots and other poor conditions of that community," pp. 44–46.
45. Druding, Sr., interview. Druding was a former resident of the 1300 block of South Fifth Street.
46. Ibid.
47. Jeremey Newberg, *Jefferson Square Master Plan Phase I (Draft)* (Philadelphia, PA, Capital Access Advisors, under the supervision of Honorable Frank DiCicco, February 20, 1997, hereafter cited as *JS Master Plan Phase I*), p. 4.
48. Ibid., p. 2.
49. Ibid., p. 4. Of the 324 properties included in the "Phase I Target Area," the draft report identified 128 as vacant lots, 43 as vacant structures, and 153 as occupied structures. (The report distinguishes 153 structures as 39 that were "blighted, yet occupied" and 114 that were "habitable."), p. 2.
50. Sharon Wallis (neighbor of condemnees), interview, February 5, 2009.

51. Newberg, *JS Master Plan: Status Report*, p. 2.
52. Frank DiCicco, "Tending the Rose of Jefferson Square," *Philadelphia Inquirer*, February 27, 2003; DiCicco, testimony, City Council, June 15, 1999, pp. 42, 54–55.
53. Brookins, personal communication.
54. By the end of 1998, the *Philadelphia Inquirer* reported, "At DiCicco's request, inspectors from the city Department of Licenses and Inspections went through the neighborhood early this year, and they declared a number of homes, some of them occupied, imminently dangerous. Seven homes in the 1300 blocks of Leithgow and Lawrence fell into that category. That means the homes have to be fixed up or torn down. "At this point, we're trying to work with the residents," L & I Commissioner Frances Egan said. "We're trying to give them a little time." Julie Stoiber, "Neighbors Protest Planned New Look: A Councilman Wants to Revitalize Part of South Philadelphia. Residents Want a Say," *Philadelphia Inquirer*, December 3, 1998. At the June 15, 1999 City Council hearing, Councilman DiCicco took full responsibility for sending out the inspectors: He said, "About a year and a half ago, when L & I at my direction were going through the neighborhood from Federal Street to Reed Street, from Fourth Street to Fifth, I directed [L & I] to do a survey of the neighborhood to identify any properties that may be in need of repair or to be demolished. As a result of their survey, several properties that are owner-occupied were slated to be demolished. At that moment, a great awareness by the community became known," pp. 46–47.
55. The February 1997 *JS Master Plan Phase I* (pp. 10–13) details an "acquisition strategy" according to three categories of owners: institutions (72 properties, including 24 publicly owned properties), "small investors with three or more properties" (103 properties) and "individuals and/or estates" (170 properties). About "Investors and Institutions (other than Mt. Sinai hospital, churches, and public authorities), it says, "The prospects of Mt. Sinai expansion, gentrification and recently, riverboat gambling, motivated some speculative investment in the area over the past ten years. The Advisory Group will explore use of straw parties to negotiate acquisition of investor-owned properties. The goal is to work with the City to develop a package of tax incentives *and expanded building code enforcement to persuade investors before cash offers or Eminent Domain are pursued as secondary options*" (emphasis added.) By contrast, individual owners, it said, "will be approached with offers to sell homes, rental properties and/or vacant lots. The package of incentive for sellers may include: relief from back real estate taxes, waiver of liens . . . , first opportunity to purchase new houses constructed at a favorable price, assistance with re-location, cash, acquisition through eminent domain. *For reluctant owners of rental properties and vacant lots, requests will be made for L & I for new building code inspections and diligent enforcement of violations as well as pressure for payment of any back taxes.* For existing homeowners who choose to remain in their homes, a package of services for minor to substantial rehabilitation of their homes will be provided. In the past six months, six owners have approached Mt. Sinai Hospital with solicitations to sell their properties" (emphasis added). Notice that code enforcement and pressure to pay back taxes is reserved for investors and individual owners of rental properties and vacant lots, but is not mentioned as an approach for homeowners who chose to remain.
56. Newberg, *JS Master Plan Phase I*, p. 15; in later plans from 1999, the statement about existing residents reads a bit differently: "JSCDC seeks to serve families

earning low- and moderate- incomes. This includes existing residents who may be new buyers or existing homeowners. In addition, the [plan] seeks to attract new families to purchase and become part of this revitalized community." JSCDC, *Summary,* 1999, p. 3. The November 1999 version has a very similarly worded paragraph. JSCDC, *Jefferson Square Revitalization Plan: Urban Renewal Plan Submission,* November 1999 (hereafter cited as *JS Urban Renewal Plan Submission*).

57. Ibid., p. 4.
58. Bauman, interview.
59. Newberg, *JS Master Plan Phase I,* p. 10. DiCicco thus made an error that, if he had read Herb Gans's (1962) close study of the clearance of the West End of Boston a half century earlier, he might have avoided.
60. Jeremey Newberg, representing DiCicco in a March 5, 1998 small meeting, "implied that the Kings are land speculators by reading us a list of properties that they own," "Research Action."
61. Druding, Sr., interview.
62. Bauman, interview.
63. JSCDC, *JS Urban Renewal Plan Submission,* p. 3.
64. Frank DiCicco (First District City Councilperson), personal communication with author by telephone, June 1, 2009.
65. A one-page list of "work to be done and issues to resolved in January" showed how little they knew as they embarked on this project about relocation benefits and eminent domain generally. The to-do list included "Research relocation laws and how the City enforces them," and "Research Eminent Domain: Who has done it before? City staff who manage it?" Newberg, *JS Master Plan Phase I,* p. 18.
66. Ibid., p. 7. The financing section of the February 1997 *JS Master Plan Phase I* mentions relocation costs for occupied residences, but it simply says that they will be estimated later in the year. In the June 4, 1997 *JS Master Plan: Status Report,* the line item for "Relocation" in the "Project Development Costs" spreadsheet is set to zero. The acquisition costs are based on sale/compensation prices of $4,000 per vacant lot, $10,000 per vacant structure, $15,000 per "blighted, yet occupied structure," and $35,000 per "habitable structure." (p. 2). In addition, early plans referred to targeted properties in ways that would have made it hard to see clearly how many were occupied. The *JS Master Plan: Status Report* began the description of the 203 private, individually owned properties to be acquired as "vacant lots and structures" (p. 2), failing to indicate that the majority were occupied. Similarly, the Financing section in the February 1997 *JS Master Plan Phase I* began by describing targeted properties as "vacant lots and buildings."(p. 7). Where the types of properties are differentiated further in the same report (p. 2), the word "habitable" is used to label over a hundred occupied structures. Although the word "habitable" does not make clear that these structures were indeed occupied, I verified in a phone conversation (on April 29, 2009) with Grant Johnson (Project Manager, JSCDC and Capital Access) that all "habitable" properties were occupied. Much later, in November 1999, the *JS Urban Renewal Plan Submission* presented to City Council still used this confusing labeling on early pages (pp. 3, 14), but later in the document (p. 17) made clear which properties targeted for condemnation were occupied (48) or vacant (135) by changing the label to "habitable and occupied."
67. Newberg, Jeremey to Frank DiCiccio, David Cohen (Office of the Mayor), (John Kromer (OHCD), Charles Hoffman (Office of State Senator Fumo), George Marks

(Kramer/Marks Architects), memorandum re: Jefferson Square Master Plan: City Participation, February 26, 1997, noted on p. 3 of a copy in RDA files.

68. Kirk Brown, testimony, City Council, June 15, 1999, pp. 120–121.
69. DiCicco, testimony, City Council, June 15, 1999, pp. 38–39.
70. Newberg, *JS Master Plan Phase I*, p. 4.
71. DiCicco, "Tending the Rose"; DiCicco, testimony, City Council, June 15, 1999, p. 53.
72. DiCicco, testimony, City Council, June 15, 1999, pp. 53–54.
73. Druding, Sr., interview. He said that after several community meetings held at the hospital before 1997, he had drawn up a plan for both rehabilitation and new construction of row homes, following some demolition and relocation.
74. Ibid.
75. Newberg, *JS Master Plan Phase I*, p. 1.
76. Newberg, *JS Master Plan: Status Report*, p. 2. Although the 1997 plans stated that the houses would be sold to low- and moderate- income buyers, the 1999 plans said that the new construction houses would also be sold to "market rate buyers." *Summary*, 1999, p. 3
77. Newberg, testimony, City Council, June 15, 1999, p. 63.
78. Ibid., p. 121.
79. Stoiber, "Neighbors Protest Planned New Look."
80. Newberg, *JS Master Plan Phase I*, p. 4.
81. Ibid., p. 15; DiCicco, testimony, City Council, June 15, 1999, p. 40.
82. The article includes a photo of Fred Druding, Sr., and two others whom it describes as "key players in the planned South Fifth Street Renaissance Project." It quotes Mount Sinai's president as saying that Graduate Health System's purchase of Mount Sinai included 40 to 50 properties in the Greenwich Square area, but that it had no plans for them except for a parking lot expansion. Frank Lewis, "Working for a Community's Health," *South Philadelphia Review*, February 8, 1996.
83. Bauman, interview.
84. DiCicco, testimony, City Council, June 15, 1999, pp. 94–95.

CHAPTER 7

1. Brookins, interview.
2. June Cairns (former United Communities Southeast Philadelphia executive director), interview, July 21, 2007. Bauman's employment as a community organizer was part of an effort to rejuvenate the organization's attachment to local residents.
3. Kathy Furber (member of St. John's Episcopal Church), testimony, City Council, June 15, 1999, p. 101. Furber said the church hired Funkhouser in October 1996 and started to work with a community organization to address the neighborhood's housing, crime, and education problems in February 1997. The church held several months of leadership programs and workshops and became interested in community organizing, although the church did not know the exact path this effort would take, she said. In January 1998, neighbors asked for the church's help in response to the appearance of condemnation posters on Leithgow and Lawrence Street, and the church responded by getting involved in the Jefferson Square controversy and holding community meetings, according to Furber.
4. Funkhouser, interview.
5. Corbin-Nelson, interview.
6. Ibid.

7. Bauman, interview.
8. Cairns, interview.
9. Bauman, interview.
10. Ackelsberg, interview.
11. Caruso, interview.
12. Funkhouser, interview; Furber, interview. Furber devoted herself to the group as the record keeper and as a persistent, empathetic presence.
13. Dorothy King, testimony, City Council, June 15, 1999, pp. 102–103.
14. Sam Holbrook and Virginia Nelson Holbrook, interview.
15. Wallis, interview.
16. Funkhouser, testimony, City Council, June 15, 1999, p. 114.
17. Corbin-Nelson, interview.
18. DiCicco, testimony, City Council, June 15, 1999, p. 53.
19. Ibid., p. 66.
20. Most recently, DiCicco and Newberg had worked to sell their vision at a meeting with community members on May 5, 1999 and at the Philadelphia City Planning Commission meeting where the proposal would be approved on May 6, 1999.
21. DiCicco said, "In the last three or four weeks we have ceased negotiating to buy any occupied properties because we don't want to be accused of making a deal that may be less of a deal than you can get should you decide to sell by way of the [RDA]. So [JSCDC] is only looking to purchase vacant land and vacant buildings going forward." DiCicco, testimony, City Council, June 15, 1999, p. 52.
22. Bauman, interview.
23. Bauman, interview; Caruso, interview; Brookins, interview.
24. DiCicco, personal communication.
25. Ibid.
26. Brookins, testimony, Council of the City of Philadelphia, Public Hearing, Committee on Rules, December 8, 1999. Department of Records (hereafter cited as City Council, December 8, 1999), p. 177.
27. Ibid., p. 182.
28. DiCicco, personal communication.
29. City Council, December 8, 1999, p. 178.
30. Brookins, testimony, City Council, December 8, 1999, pp. 187–189.
31. Cohen, testimony, City Council, December 8, 1999, p. 176.
32. Ackelsberg, testimony, City Council, December 8, 1999, pp. 183–197.
33. DiCicco, testimony, City Council, December 8, 1999, p. 167.
34. Brookins, testimony, City Council, December 8, 1999, p. 179.
35. The JSCDC had provided a twenty-seven-page *Jefferson Square Revitalization Plan: Urban Renewal Plan Submission*, dated November 1999, which presumably captured the content of the agreement that had been reached. Section 1 of the bill, passed by City Council a week after the public hearing, read, "The redevelopment proposal dated April 1999 including the detailed redevelopment area plan, the maps, and all other documents and supporting data which form part of the proposal submitted by the [RDA] for the Jefferson Square Redevelopment Area, Jefferson Square Urban Renewal Area (hereinafter called "Project"), and *including the Jefferson Square Revitalization Plan dated November, 1999* (which Plan contains the relocation provisions applicable to current residents), having been duly reviewed and considered, is approved. The [RDA] is authorized to take such action as may be necessary to carry it out, except *that involuntary relocation of current residents of the Redevelopment Area is conditioned on compliance with the commitments*

contained in the Jefferson Square Revitalization Plan dated November, 1999 and will occur only if sufficient funding exists to comply with such commitments" (emphasis added). Council of the City of Philadelphia, Bill 990331 (December 16, 1999).

36. Hon. Frank DiCicco (member, City Council of Philadelphia First District), Jeremey Newberg (secretary and treasurer, JSCDC), Ruth Arnau (chairperson, Board of Directors, JSCDC), Peggy Brookins and Gina Caruso (co-chairs, St. John's Leadership Team), and Irv Ackelsberg (Community Legal Services, Inc., and counsel, St. John's Leadership Team), "Memorandum of Understanding Regarding Relocation Provisions Applicable to Bill No. 990331, December 1999.
37. Linden, interview.
38. Honeyman, interview, August 2, 2007. Honeyman coordinated the citywide program of community organizing under which Johanna Bauman was employed with United Communities. He did some of the organizing work himself both before and after Bauman resigned.
39. Brookins, interview.
40. JSCDC, *JS Urban Renewal Plan Submission*.
41. Early in planning, Newberg stated that the project would need $4.5 million in subsidies. Newberg, *JS Master Plan Phase I,* pp. 7–9. Early plans also requested city contributions through waivers of tax liens and transfer taxes, demolitions of buildings, and waivers of liens for demolitions. The project eventually secured and spent over $7 million in government funding and almost $1 million in private funding, detailed in notes 42 and 43.
42. The city gave the project at least $6,0122,000, mostly by funneling federal dollars to it. In 2001, DiCicco said the project had already received $6 million in city funds. Rita Giordano, "Jefferson Square Moves Forward in South Philadelphia. Funding Is in Flux, and More Properties Might Be Condemened. The Plan Is Bound for the Planning Commission and Council," *Philadelphia Inquirer*, February 21. In an internal letter, John Kromer (director, Office of Housing and Community Development, City of Philadelphia) wrote that the city had committed $6 million to the project, the first half in Economic Stimulus funds to support acquisition, the second half in CDBG or HOME funds to support acquisition and development of up to 38 units of housing, Letter to Bobincheck (associate director, Office of Strategic Planning and Policy, Pennsylvania Housing Finance Agency), June 14, 2001. The city subsidized the project in other ways as well, for instance, by waiving unpaid taxes and liens. In December 1999, the city solicitor wrote that the city that would waive about $122,000 in unpaid taxes and other liens on properties that JSCDC would acquire (JSCDC would have to pay $355,000 to clear liens totaling $477,000 for unpaid taxes, utilities, and other fees). Stephanie L. Franklin-Suber (city solicitor), letter (Re: Jefferson Square Letter Agreement, BRT Account Nos.—Schedule 'A') to Newberg, December 21, 1999.
43. In 2004, *The Philadelphia Inquirer* reported that "Newberg is on State Sen. Vincent J. Fumo's legislative payroll as a housing consultant. Over the years, Fumo has arranged for the development to get $1.5 million in state grants, as well $600,000 in loans and grants from Fumo-backed nonprofits." Craig R. McCoy, "100 Camp Out to Buy New Townhouses in South Philadelphia," May 4. I located records for just over a million of the state funding: Samuel A. McCullough (secretary, Department of Community and Economic Development, Commonwealth of Pennsylvania) informed Newberg that the JSCDC application received a $200,000 grant under the Employment and Community Conservation program in a letter dated June 24, 1998, and a $345,000 grant under the Community Revitalization

Assistance Program in a letter dated June 2000. In 2003, Brian Hudson (executive director, Pennsylvania Housing Finance Agency) wrote to Newberg that the Pennsylvania Housing Finance Agency was awarding an additional $500,000 in funding through the Homeownership Choice program. Letter Re: Homeownership Choice Program, July 14.

44. The Federal Home Loan Bank of Pittsburgh (a cooperative of community financial institutions) contributed $500,000 of this funding. Bendel (director, Community Investement), letter to Desiderio (vice president, PNC Financial Services), June 25, 2001. The First Union Regional Foundation contributed $300,000. Denise McGregor Armbrister (director) letter (Re: Grant #6348) to Newberg, May 15, 2001.
45. See note 41, Chapter 6.
46. Ackelsberg, interview, July 27, 2007.
47. Newberg, interview.
48. For example, Hanton, interview; Jeremy Morton [pseud.], personal communication with author, February 9, 2009.
49. Johnson, interview, February 10, 2009.
50. JSCDC, *Jefferson Square Neighborhood Revitalization Plan: Ground Breaking Ceremony Program*, (Philadelphia, PA, March 14, 2003).
51. Capital Access, *Jefferson Square: The Right Home. The Right Price* (Philadelphia, PA, May 2005).
52. JSCDC renovated an additional house just west of the new development for a homeowner with an unusually large family and a need to relocate quickly.
53. Raw data provided by Grant Johnson.
54. Johnson, interview. He said that Quaker Window and Mount Moriah church made significant repairs.
55. Maureen Mastroieni, "Collaborative and Market-Driven Approaches to Economic Development and Revitalization," *Entrepreneur*, Spring 2007.
56. Johnson, interview.
57. Hanton, interview.
58. Ibid.; Johnson, interview. Ed Nesmith built a set of row homes, and Melvin Hanton renovated his row house bordering the project.
59. Samuel Dorn (resident of 421 Wharton Street), PCPC Meeting Minutes, April 27, 1999, p.8.
60. Hanton, interview; Troy Adams (RDA project manager), interview, March 21, 2007.
61. JoAnn King, interview. In other interviews, Virginia Nelson Holbrook and David T. Jones, Sr. echoed this observation.
62. Adams, interview; Ryan Molle, interview, February 16, 2009.
63. Newberg, interview.

CHAPTER 8

1. This view follows a tradition of sociological research on valuation in market and legal settings where many facets of social relationships are seen to become part of the negotiation of value. See Charles W. Smith (1989); Olav Velthuis (2005); Viviana A. Rotman Zelizer (1994a, 2005).
2. For a discussion of fair market value of the property lost as the legal standard for just compensation, see David A. Dana and Thomas Merrill (2002); Thomas W. Merrill (2002–2003). "Eminent domain law has adopted fair market value as the compensation benchmark despite its tension with the goal of full compensation

for purely practical reasons—that is, '[b]ecause of serious practical difficulties in assessing the worth an individual places on a property at a given time,'" Abraham Bell and Gideon Parchomovsky (2006–2007) quoting *US v. Acres of Land*, 441 U.S. 506, 511 (1979). Pennsylvania's eminent domain law now defines just compensation as "the difference between the fair market value of the condemnee's entire property interest immediately before the condemnation and as unaffected by the condemnation and the fair market value of the property interest remaining immediately after the condemnation and as affected by the condemnation," 26 Pa.C.S. § 702 (2013).

3. The few published empirical studies on compensation amounts suggest that compensation may accurately affect market price on average, but there may be wide variation in the accuracy of compensation settlements. In studies of recent takings, average compensation settlements seem to fall, on average, at or just above full market value. In an analysis of all 1,430 (non-litigated) takings compensations settled in New York City between 1990 and 2002, Yun-chien Chang (2010) found that the average compensation settlement was 101 percent of a property's market sale price, estimated with a hedonic regression model on nearby sales in city records. In an analysis of compensation for 75 of the 132 single-family homes condemned for a state highway project in San Diego County in 1991, Krisandra Guidry and A. Quang Do (1998) found that owners, on average, received 5 percent more than the market price estimated with a hedonic regression model. In her study of compensation parcels assembled in St. Joseph County, Indiana in 2000 for a General Motors plant, Nicole Garnett (2006) found that on average, compensation for the real estate price of condemned properties almost matched appraised values, at 103 percent. There is also evidence that condemnations in recent years yield some premium over market price. In an analysis of compensation for 60 of the 115 residential properties taken for the expansion of the McCarran International Airport in Las Vegas between 1993 and 1996, Terrence Clauretie, William Kuhn, and Keith Schwer (2004) found condemnees to have received an average of 17 percent above their properties' market value estimated using hedonic regressions. In the Indiana project that Garnett studied, owners who negotiated pre-condemnation sales prices received an average of 41 percent more than their assessed property values; county officials apparently entered the negotiations after hearing from compensation "experts" that assembling land that is not on the market usually requires payments of approximately 20 to 25 percent above market value. In the same project, those who did not negotiate a pre-condemnation sale but had properties condemned (for an average of 103 percent of assessed value) received, on average, an additional 54 percent of assessed market price earmarked to cover relocation or replacement housing expenses, Garnett (2006). Under-compensation may be less universal than revealed by older studies by Berger and Rohan (1967) and Munch (1976). Still, inaccuracies remain common. In his study of New York City condemnations, Chang (2010) found that most properties were compensated inaccurately at extreme levels, either less than 50 percent or more than 150 percent of estimated market value. Compensation for properties condemned for the airport in Las Vegas systematically overestimated market prices for higher-valued properties and underestimated market prices for lower-valued properties (a similar finding to that of Munch [1976]).
4. Incomplete information prevents officials and condemnees from actually knowing, when faced with a forced transfer, the price at which a property would have exchanged between a willing buyer and seller taking into account all possible uses

to which a property might be dedicated, Dana and Merrill (2002), pp. 169–170. Because full market value is impossible to know, Thomas Merrill says that it is "a fiction" in takings cases and that valuation "necessarily entails an element of discretionary choice," Merrill (2002–2003). The fact that condemning authorities devote minimal resources to appraising properties en masse can exacerbate incomplete information problems, Berger and Rohan (1967).

5. Government has some incentives to keep costs down and at least sometimes lowballs offers by initiating negotiations with condemnees with prices below its own appraisals of market value, Berger and Rohan (1967); Mitchell, Malpezzi and Green (2009–2010). Although few may litigate offers (only 10 percent in Berger and Rohan's [1967] study), litigation raises awards, on average (Berger and Rohan [1967]; Ray Rivera, "UDOT: Fair Deals or Land Grabs?," *Salt Lake Tribune*, October 24, 1999; Schaffer and Kelso, *Jury Verdicts*) and can induce condemning authorities to get more detailed assessments from outside appraisers, Berger and Rohan (1967). Political organizing also achieves results, in terms of higher values in compensation, Garnett (2006); Mitchell, Malpezzi and Green (2009–2010).
6. Scholars worry that neither the fair market value standard nor, in some cases, any financial compensation, Lewinsohn-Zamir (2013), can account for the elements of property that one experiences as part of his or her person, Radin (1982), including the dignity or autonomy inherent in one's control over when to alienate one's property, Lee Anne Fennell (2004); Michelman (1967). For example, Fennell (2004) claims that government cannot compensate for lost autonomy with money because, "[t]he extra dollars, in a sense, are the wrong currency" (p. 959). Others complain that legal standards lead to under-compensation by omitting financial factors that they seem to think are possible to represent in dollars such as business goodwill lost; transaction costs involving legal, settlement, moving, and replacement fees; and benefits gained by the taker through land assembly. See, for example Laura H. Burney (1989); Malamut. *The Power to Take: The Use of Eminent Domain in Massachusetts*, (Boston, Pioneer Institute for Public Policy Research, 2000); Christopher Serkin (2004–2005); Fennell (2004); Dana and Merrill (2002); Merrill (2002–2003); Garnett (2006). Although Fennell (2004) claims that an ability to opt-in, not cash, is required to account for autonomy in takings for private reuse, she and Bell and Parchomovsky (2006–2007) have argued that self-assessment mechanisms can measure subjective valuation in dollars. However, Chang, *Self-Assessment* shows evidence that self-assessments relying on tax fillings lead to under-valuation because owners will ignore risks of condemnation and instead pay attention to the definite cost of tax payments. Robert C. Ellickson (1973, pp. 736–737) briefly defends for cash payments for longevity, and Rachel D. Godsil and David V. Simunovich (2008) propose a lump sum for the loss of homeowner status.
7. For discussions about how people use different forms of media to distinguish kinds of exchanges, especially how they distinguish cash from tangible goods, see Viviana A. Zelizer (1994b, 2005).
8. Jeremy Morton [pseud.], personal communication with author, February 9, 2009.
9. Unlike in other chapters, where the information about individuals that I conveyed is based largely on interviews with them, much of the financial information in this chapter comes from RDA files. Therefore, I have obscured the identities of some individuals in this chapter by giving them pseudonyms, even if I used their real names in previous chapters.

10. Anyone uneducated in RDA practice (most people) would not notice the important distinction between real estate compensation and relocation benefits, so most people latched on to the $20,000 figure as what government would pay to displace people. Though money earmarked for real estate never reached above $30,000 for most owners, most residents received tens of thousands of dollars more in money earmarked as relocation benefits. Most of the American Street families received fairly significant amounts for relocation costs, in addition to their real estate compensation.
11. Office of Community Planning and Development, "Form Hud-40057: Claim for Replacement Housing Payment for 180-Day Homeowner." Money is also released to cover other expenses such as the cost of moving one's belongings and settlement fees. Also see Office of Community Planning and Development, "Form Hud-40054: Claim for Moving and Related Expenses." The federal Uniform Relocation Assistance and Real Property Acquisition Policies for Federally and Federally Assisted Programs Act of 1970 and Pennsylvania's eminent domain laws define a "comparable replacement dwelling" identically, as a dwelling that is "(1) Decent, safe and sanitary; (2) Adequate in size to accommodate the occupants; (3) Within the financial means of the displaced person; (4) Functionally equivalent; (5) In an area not subject to unreasonable adverse environmental conditions; and (6) In a location generally not less desirable than the location of the displaced person's dwelling with respect to public utilities, facilities, services and the displaced person's place of employment," 42 U.S.C.S. § 4601 (2013); 26 Pa.C.S. § 103 (2013).
12. Office of Community Planning and Development, "Form Hud-40072." Tenants who need it are meant to receive help finding an apartment; payment for the difference between rent in the new location and what a household seems able to afford, based on its income for five years; and moving expenses. If a family qualifies for public housing assistance, it will get priority to enter a public housing-assistance program—usually Section 8, a rental voucher program.
13. Interview, 2008.
14. Valerie Moore, interview with author, March 14, 2009.
15. Romo took out a loan for $10,000 to pay her $5,000 contribution and a lien for water outstanding on the condemned property.
16. Ackelsberg, interview; Adams, interview; Furber, interview; Caruso, interview; Newberg, interview.
17. Adams, interview.
18. Hanton, interview.
19. Reyes, interview.
20. Segarra, interview; Milagros Velez (adult daughter of condemnee), interview, July 12, 2008; Muñoz, interview; Rivera, interview; Gomez, interview.
21. Ackelsberg, interview.
22. Jones, interview.
23. Corbin-Nelson, interview; Janet Dennis, interview, February 10, 2009; Nelson Holbrook and Virginia Nelson Holbrook, interview.
24. Interview; J. King, interview.
25. One would imagine that the most basic problem of this kind would occur if someone could not produce a clean title, to document ownership, and thus could not demonstrate that compensation is deserved. That people act as if they own properties though they do not really have clean titles is not so surprising. Titles often have a myriad of problems because of murky histories of transfers and liens,

quite common in poor neighborhoods. Those "clouds" on titles rarely matter until someone wants to transfer the title and record the transfer officially and clearly. If government had not come along with its eminent domain plans, and no one tried to transfer ownership legally (because of a sale or an inheritance), there is a good chance no one would even notice problems with a property title for a very long time, perhaps not even for several generations. These kinds of problems can usually be cleared up, though they take time and sometimes money.

26. Romo, interview.
27. In addition, one RDA project manager described him as "this guy who's basically living in this house, squatting in this house. You know, it's his brother's house" Raymond Boyle [pseud.], interview, February 7, 2007. As Grant Johnson surveyed the area being acquired for Jefferson Square, he found several people he tagged as squatters, interview.
28. Interview.
29. Vacant lots require maintenance and property-tax payment, yet legal owners had few incentives to care for properties worth just a couple of thousand dollars, if that much. Many owners simply ignored their legal rights and responsibilities. Lots that owners abandoned often appeared unkempt and invited dumping. Nearby residents and business owners coped with the nuisances, and they used large swaths of vacant land they did not own, for storage, yards, gardens, or just clean open space. Residents maintained some of the privately owned land that was not theirs, in part for their own enjoyment and in part to make clear that the area was cared for and therefore watched, something neither governments nor real estate markets were handling. Unless these residents could gain formal title, I believe that they were unlikely to build anything more permanent than a garden or garage.
30. Many of the people displaced from the first American Street site had even become owners of their houses by securing titles to abandoned properties from government for a dollar and back taxes. They had been tenants of a single landlord for several years until he died, and no one else bothered to contact them or collect the rent, so they stayed as squatters until government granted them official recognition. Even more commonly, government executed similar transfers for vacant lots adjacent to properties that people already owned.
31. Milagros Velez, interview.
32. The situation was different and better for Janet Dennis, who was in a similar situation. The older relative she was caring for lived through the relocation, and Dennis moved with her. When I interviewed Dennis, she was attempting to follow legal channels to secure her rights to the title for the house.
33. Interview, April 19, 2009.
34. When Purvis had asked Newberg about her problem early on, he suggested that she get her name on the deed and thus become a legal owner. But she thought that her grandmother was too ill to talk about the issue and that her uncle would be suspicious that she was after the "money," when she really just wanted the "benefits." Purvis understood how she "fell through the cracks," as she put it: "My name was not in any of her documents, even though I paid a lot of bills and took care of the house and everything, I didn't get the benefits of it. So that was that," ibid. Grant Johnson, the JSCDC staff member who spent most of his time for several years attending to the displacements and managing the construction, did not remember Purvis when I mentioned her, though he remembered almost everyone

else by name. The only sign that he attended to her concerns is a note about her as a "possible tenant" on one of his spreadsheets.

35. Johnson, personal communication. Getka accused RDA officials of harassing his son to back up their assertion that he was trying to cheat the system. He shows me pictures of a beaten-down front door, with scribbles telling the son to keep out of the house, Joe Getka (condemnee), interview, February 22, 2009.
36. Getka, interview.
37. Ibid.
38. Ibid. Even when officials believed that a long-term attachment to a property was the investment at stake for an absentee owner, they did not always find a way to compensate adequately. Dorothy King's daughters complained that their mother lost something valuable in the properties that she owned but rented out, which, unlike their houses, she had to give up for a small price, Brookins, interview; JoAnn King, interview; Corbin-Nelson, interview.
39. Ortiz, interview, Muñoz, interview; Pantoja, interview; Reyes, interview.
40. Ortiz, interview.
41. Even though Getka knew that he spoke angrily to people at the RDA, he told me, he did not seem to know what else to do when he was not getting a fair deal. RDA Project Manager Adams described a bit of bewilderment about how to read Getka.
42. Purvis said she avoided advocating for herself, in part, out of fear of launching an angry attack on officials that would not help her cause. Hanton, who got one property back when he convinced officials that he was invested in it, failed to get more consideration with another property that he owned with his siblings. He took partial responsibility for that loss, for not being assertive and clear. He was absent for long periods of time because of sickness and conflict among his co-owners (his siblings) about what they wanted done with that property, interview. Indeed, RDA officials expressed frustration at what seemed to them to be Hanton's avoidance when they were trying to accommodate him. Adams expressed frustration about Hanton's failure to communicate his wishes about the other property until it was too late, interview. Quiescence was widespread among American Street condemnees, even though a few managed to get the project into the news. Rivera's statements were exemplary. She was resigned to her disappointing fate and gave up on trying to get what she thought she deserved after problems with inspections and restrictions about buying from relatives. She told me, "Nobody could do anything," and said repeatedly, "The city tells you you have to go, you have to go," interview.
43. Interview.
44. She also said, "They have a lot more fight than I do," because they had a whole family of people who spoke up for one another, interview.

CHAPTER 9

1. Editorial, "Blight Costs City Too Much," *Philadelphia Inquirer*, December 2, 2013, accessed December 12, 2013, http://articles.philly.com/2013-12-02/news/44622783_1_land-bank-properties-north-philadelphia; Claudia Vargas, "Bill for Philly Land Bank Stuck in Tug-of-War," *Philadelphia Inquirer*, November 21, 2013, accessed December 12, 2013, http://articles.philly.com/2013-11-21/news/44288291_1_land-bank-city-council-council-members.
2. City of Philadelphia, *Policies for the Sale and Reuse of City Owned Property*, Philadelphia Redevelopment Authority, April 20, 2012, 10 pages, accessed

December 12, 2013, http://www.phila.gov/pra/pdfs/City%20Policies%20for%20 Sale%20Reuse%20Property_5.2012.pdf, pp. 6–7. City-owned vacant land worth less than $15,000 and smaller than 3,000 square feet may be transferred for a nominal cost to adjacent homeowners on blocks that are predominantly occupied.

3. Shaila Dewain, "More Cities Consider Using Eminent Domain to Halt Foreclosures," *New York Times*, November 15, 2013.
4. The Annie E. Casey Foundation. *Responsible Relocation*; Dreher and Echeverria, *Kelo's Unanswered Questions*. These reports contain some of the kinds of reforms that I propose, which depart from the two more common approaches.
5. 42 U.S.C.S. §§4601–4655 (2013).
6. Ibid. §4623, 4624, 4622. These numbers were actually even lower when I did my research. Before Congress passed a reform to the law on July 6, 2012 (effective July 6, 2014), the limits were $22,500 for owner-occupied residences, $5,250 for tenants, and from $10,000 to $20,000 for businesses. In Pennsylvania, similar provisions set the maximum residential replacement payments for homeowners at $27,000, for tenants at $6,300, 26 Pa.C.S. §§ 903–4 (2013).
7. Ibid, §4626; 26 Pa.C.S. § 905 (2013).
8. Godsil and Simunovich (2008).
9. See note 6, Chapter 8.
10. Pennsylvania's eminent domain law, enacted in 2006, is fairly typical in prohibiting any increase in value from the condemnation from affecting compensation, 26 Pa.C.S. § 704 (2013).
11. Fennell (2004) describes the increased value of property created by a taking, often through consolidation of parcels, as "surplus from transfer." She explains that this surplus is not usually recognized as compensable to the condemnee and, instead, goes in full to the condemnor. James A. Krier and Christopher Serkin (2004, pp. 868–873) argue that with a standard of "gain-based compensation," this surplus can and should be fully transferred to the condemnee, who ought not be "precluded from sharing in some or all of the economic gains created by the government action," p. 868.
12. Chris Smith, "Mr. Ratner's Neighborhood," *New York Magazine*, August 14, 2006; Patrick Gallahue, "Tout of Bounds: Ratner Forces Apt. Sellers to Hype Nets Arena," *New York Post*, June 16, 2004.
13. For a brilliant interpretation of how "repeat players" hold significant advantages over "one-shotters" in legal settings, see Marc Galanter (1974).
14. The Pennsylvania Eminent Domain law passed in 2006 provided, for example, "The owner of any right, title or interest in real property acquired or injured by an acquiring agency . . . shall be reimbursed in an amount not to exceed $4,000 as a payment toward reasonable expenses actually incurred for appraisal, attorney and engineering fees," 26 Pa.C.S. § 710 (2013).
15. My proposal for an advocate should not be confused with steps taken by a few states to establish offices of a public advocate (New Jersey) or ombudsman (Missouri and Utah) to assist with eminent domain or property-rights issues more generally. While these offices are described as advocating for citizens' rights, they are charged with acting independently of any party's interest. The advocates I propose would be expressly employed to treat citizens targeted with eminent domain as clients.
16. Debbie Becher (2012).
17. Medoff and Sklar (1994).

18. For analysis of the use of community benefits agreements, see Murtaza H. Baxamusa (2008); Vicki Been (2010), Julian Gross (2008); Patricia Salkin and Amy Lavine (2007/2008).
19. As Michael Heller and Rick Hills (2008) propose, preventing eminent domain from moving forward until a majority of owners in an area vote for a redevelopment proposal could magnify community control as well, but it would most likely give great influence to a few powerful voices. Professional assistance with organizing could create more equity in collective decision-making, even if such an institutional mechanism were adopted.
20. Debbie Becher (2010).
21. Patrick McGeehan, "Pfizer to Leave City That Won Land-Use Case" *New York Times*, November 13, 2009.
22. The neglect of uncertainty in urban planning is addressed in Guy Benveniste (1989); Karen S. Christensen (1985); Michael Gunder (2008); Peter Marris (1996); Charles Edward Lindblom (1959).
23. These recommendations provide greater protection than those that already exist in state laws, such as Pennsylvania's provisions for the "abandonment of project." These provisions require that the condemnor offer to sell the property back to the condemnee at the original compensation price, if the project for which it was taken is abandoned within ten years. 26 Pa.C.S. § 310 (2013).
24. Nevada and Texas have "buy-back" provisions, but they are so weak that they hardly provide any protection against the costs to the condemnee in the case of project failure. These laws allow original owners to buy properties back when governments that do not make progress toward promised redevelopment plans within ten (Texas) or fifteen (Nevada) years. The standards for demonstrating progress toward plans are very low, and the public authority is afforded great flexibility in changing the plans. In addition, after ten or fifteen years of limbo, it seems that the condemnee should have to pay only a small fraction of the condemnation price to get a property back.
25. The NAACP made a similar recommendation; see Shelton, "Statement before U.S. Commission."
26. Malamut, *The Power to Take: The Use of Eminent Domain in Massachusetts*.
27. Castle Coalition, "Enacted Legislation since Kelo," accessed July 15, 2013, http://castlecoalition.org/about/component/content/510?task=view. The thirty-one states were: Alabama, Alaska, Arizona, Colorado, Florida, Georgia, Idaho, Illinois, Indiana, Kansas, Kentucky, Louisiana, Maine, Michigan, Minnesota, Montana, Nevada, New Hampshire, New Mexico, North Carolina, North Dakota, Ohio, Oregon, Pennsylvania, South Carolina, South Dakota, Texas, Vermont, Virginia, Wisconsin, and Wyoming. They enacted a wide variety of limits on the purposes to which eminent domain could be put, often prohibiting private reuse but also preventing economic development and other previously accepted purposes from counting as "public use." These provisions often created exceptions, including those for takings to eliminate blight.
28. Martin E. Gold and Lynne B. Sagalyn (2011), pp. 1156–1157.
29. In 2006, Pennsylvania prohibited the taking of "private property in order to use it for private enterprise," with some exceptions, including if the condemnation served "for the development of low-income and mixed-income housing projects," 26 Pa.C.S. § 204 (2013). Note that the act approved on May 4, 2006, which vastly overhauled Pennsylvania's eminent domain law, exempted the areas already

certified as blighted in Pennsylvania's larger cities, including Philadelphia, from the new provisions until December 31, 2012, 26 Pa.C.S. § 203 (2013).

30. Frug and Barron, "Make Eminent Domain Fair," *The Boston Globe*, August 12, 2005; Medoff and Sklar (1994).
31. Pennsylvania's new blight definitions are in 26 Pa.C.S. § 205 (2013).
32. Dana (2006).
33. Frug and Barron, "Make Eminent Domain Fair."
34. For example, see Douglas R. Porter, *Eminent Domain: An Important Tool for Community Revitalization* (Washington, DC, Urban Land Institute, 2007).
35. Gold and Sagalyn (2011).
36. Pritchett (2003).
37. The Castle Coalition, a 2002 spinoff from the Institute for Justice (IJ), took control of much of the campaign, while the IJ continued to take responsibility for litigation. A few of the early publications include Berliner, *Government Theft*; Berliner, *Public Power*; Berliner, *Eminent Domain Abuse*; Berliner, *Redevelopment Wrecks*. Several additional publications of local and national scope can be found on the organization's website, Castle Coalition, "Castle Coalition & IJ Publications," accessed July 15, 2013, http://castlecoalition.org/about/38.
38. Castle Coalition, "Model Charter Provision or Ordinance for Local Governing Body," accessed July 15, 2013, http://castlecoalition.org/survivalguide/311?task=view. Here, the Castle Coalition recommended municipal reforms that either prevented takings for private business, for economic development, or for any private party. Its statement on model language for legal reforms to "prevent the use of eminent domain for private redevelopment" recommended the prohibition of takings for private reuse as the best possible constitutional reform and the elimination of enabling statutes as the best statutory reform. Castle Coalition, "Model Language for State Constitutional Amendments," accessed July 15, 2013, http://castlecoalition.org/legislativecenter/182?task=view; Castle Coalition, "Model Language for State Statutes Limiting Eminent Domain Abuse," accessed July 15, 2013, http://castlecoalition.org/survivalguide/310?task=view. Also see Castle Coalition, *50 State Report Card: Tracking Eminent Domain Reform Legislation since Kelo* (Washington, DC, Institute for Justice, August 2007); Institute for Justice, *Legislative Action since Kelo* (Washington, DC, Castle Coalition, 2006).
39. The Castle Coalition website solicited visitors to "report an abuse of eminent domain" and provided a form for that purpose. It also asked supporters to lobby local legislatures, write letters to the editor, and organize local events. The organization's "Survival Guide" gives advice about how to handle one's own eminent-domain case, organize a grassroots campaign, and reform eminent domain laws. Castle Coalition, "Get Involved Now," accessed July 15, 2013, http://castlecoalition.org/getinvolved. I attended the Castle Coalition's National Conference, June 9–11, 2006 in Arlington, Virginia, "Moving Forward: Winning the Battle Against Eminent Domain Abuse in a Post-Kelo World." It seemed to be primarily a training conference for local organizers. The Castle Coalition consulted with Rosemary Cubas, who led the anti-eminent-domain group that organized in Philadelphia, Bullock, interview; Segarra, interview.
40. Robert James Bidinotto, "The Supreme Assault on Private Property: An Interview with Scott Bullock (2005)," *The New Individualist*, accessed July 15, 2013, http://www.atlassociety.org/tni/supreme-assault-private-property-interview-scott-bullock.
41. Berliner. *Public Power*.

42. Berliner. *Government Theft*.
43. Flynn, "Across the Country."
44. Daniel Amzallag and Betsy Borias, "Council Signs Off on Manhattanville Expansion," *Columbia Daily Spectator*, December 19, 2007.
45. Maggie Astor, "Community Benefits Agreement for Manhattanville Approved," *Columbia Daily Spectator*, May 8, 2009. For reporting on the broader phenomenon of Community Benefits Agreements in large redevelopment projects, see Gross (2008); Salkin and Lavine (2007/2008); Baxamusa (2008); Been (2010).
46. Casey Tolan, "2012–13 in Review: As Manhattanville Benefits Are Dispensed, Questions Arise over Hiring Policies," *Columbia Daily Spectator*, May 13, 2013; Colin Kinniburgh, "Holding Columbia Accountable," *Columbia Daily Spectator*, April 5, 2012; Casey Tolan, "Cb9 Calls for Audit of Columbia's Manhattanville Commitments," *Columbia Daily Spectator*, March 22, 2013.
47. Lynne B. Sagalyn (2001); Frieden and Sagalyn (1989).
48. Mariana Valverde (2012); Susan Fainstein (1995); David Harvey (1989).
49. Crawford Brough Macpherson (1978).
50. James Willard Hurst (1956).
51. Blomley (2003); Bruce G. Carruthers and Laura Ariovich (2004).
52. Legal historians and a few historical sociologists have described more personal conceptions of American real property in the nineteenth century. Morton J. Horwitz (1992) provided a historical overview; Hurst (1956) exposed how property signified freedom for settlers; Orlando Patterson (1982) studied property as the absence of freedom for slaves; and Hendrik Hartog (2000) showed how property robbed wives of a sense of self.
53. Epstein (1985); Ilya Somin (2007); Robert C. Ellickson (1991). Mainstream economists share libertarians' disdain for government intervention in property's value. Economist Martin Anderson (1964, 1965) most famously made the connection to eminent domain in a treatise in the Harvard Business Review against urban renewal in the 1960s, decrying "the federal bulldozer." He argued that taking property for private redevelopment was wrongheaded because it distorted market price. Without eminent domain and the resulting distorted incentives, he argued, private developers would have produced more and better housing. Author field notes, Castle Coalition National Conference, "Moving Forward." Robert Ellickson trained Dana Berliner, litigation director for the Institute for Justice, in property law.
54. John Locke (1986 [1690]).
55. Singer (2000).
56. Valverde (2012).
57. Greta R. Krippner (2007).
58. Charles A. Reich (1964), pp, 746.
59. A-mila West, "Parker City Council Meets to Decide on City Clean-up Procedures," *News Channel 7*, *wjhg.com*, December 4, 2013, accessed December 13, 2013, http://www.wjhg.com/news/headlines/Parker-City-Council-Meets-to-Decide-on-City-Clean-up-Procedures-234344651.html; Valerie Garman, "PCB Takes Action on Dilapidated Buildings," *News Herald*, 2013, accessed December 13, 2013, http://www.newsherald.com/news/government/pcb-takes-action-on-dilapidated-buildings-1.235134?page=0; Erin Schattauer, "Bozeman Getting Proactive about Dilapidated Buildings," *Bozeman Daily Chronicle*, November 30, 2013, accessed December 13, 2013, http://www.bozemandailychronicle.com/news/city/article_cb862b10-5957-11e3-85e1-0019bb2963f4.html?mode=story. The city

councils of Parker City, Florida; Palm City Beach, Florida; and Bozeman, Montana are considering expanding their public nuisance codes. Editorial, "Flagstaff Eyesores Have Been Ignored for Far Too Long," *Arizona Daily Sun*, November 15, 2013, accessed December 13, 2013, http://azdailysun.com/news/opinion/editorial/flagstaff-eyesores-have-been-ignored-for-far-too-long/article_3ff12d62-4dbc-11e3-a51c-0019bb2963f4.html. The editorial praised Flagstaff, Arizona for taking new approaches to applying old ordinances to repair, clean up, and demolish nuisance properties. Chelsey Levingston, "200 Hamilton, Middletown Vacant Properties to Be Demolished," *Journal-News*, December 9, 2013, accessed December 13, 2013, http://www.journal-news.com/news/news/200-hamilton-middletown-vacant-properties-to-be-de/ncDX9/. Hamilton and Middletown, Ohio, made the news for using federal funds to demolish hundreds of properties left vacant by the housing crisis.

60. *City of Dallas v. Stewart*, 361 S.W.3d 562, (Supreme Court of Texas, 2012); *Bonner v. City of Brighton*, 828 N.W.2d 408 (Court of Appeals of Michigan, 2012).
61. For example, Hamilton, Ohio typically took property titles when it demolished buildings, but Middletown did not. Levingston, "200 Hamilton, Middletown Vacant Properties."
62. Joseph William Singer (2000) discusses in detail how scholars wrongly, but frequently, treat these situations as either exceptions to or minor consequences of the fundamental idea of property as control or ownership. Singer proposes to incorporate these and other seeming anomalies into the meaning of property by understanding property as instituting obligations, not just rights.
63. Ulrich Beck (1992) provides a compelling analysis of uncertainty as a unique contemporary condition.
64. Jürgen Habermas (1975 [1973]); Harvey Luskin Molotch (1976);Logan and Molotch (1987).
65. Habermas (1975 [1973]).
66. Logan and Molotch (1987).
67. Katherine Verdery (2003) also found that in the context of a late twentieth-century post-socialist transformation, the state becomes responsible for making property valuable, not simply for protecting owners' control.
68. Marx (1887); Max Weber (1981 [1923]); Polanyi (1944).
69. Emile Durkheim and George Simpson (1933 [1893]); Thorstein Veblen (1945 [1923]); Alexis de Tocqueville and Henry Reeve (1835).
70. Shawna Orzechowski and Peter Sepielli, "Net Worth and Asset Ownership of Households: 1998 and 2000," US Bureau of the Census, Department of Household Economic Studies, 2003, accessed August 22, 2013, http://www.census.gov/prod/2003pubs/p70-88.pdf. In 2000, home equity (the value of a home minus the mortgage) accounted for the largest share (32 percent) of household net worth. Just over two-thirds of households owned homes, with a median equity of $59,000.
71. Note that Logan and Molotch (1987) themselves began their book with this dilemma about the American home but took it in another direction.
72. Even before privatization of public services, cost-benefit analyses and other forms of commensuration and value quantification in public-policy analysis, as analyzed by Wendy Nelson Espeland (1998), may have blurred distinctions among kinds of value.
73. Logan and Molotch (1987).

74. Sharon Zukin (2010); Peter Marcuse (2008, 2010 [1986]); Kevin Fox Gotham, Jon Shefner and Krista Brumley (2001).
75. Polanyi (1944).
76. Tocqueville and Reeve (1835); Veblen (1945 [1923]).
77. Radin (1982).
78. Blomley (2003); Singer (2000); Laura Underkuffler (1996).
79. Nicholas Blomley (2013).
80. Molotch (1976); Logan and Molotch (1987).
81. Staughton Lynd (1988).
82. Eduardo M. Peñalver (2009); Gregory S. Alexander, Eduardo M. Peñalver, Joseph William Singer and Laura Underkuffler (2009); Gregory S. Alexander and Eduardo M. Peñalver (2012); Singer (2000).
83. Gans (1962) offered a similar critique in his iconic study of urban renewal.
84. Shelton, "Statement before U.S. Commission," p. 2.
85. Ibid., p. 6.
86. Charles C. Geisler (2000); Marcuse (2008); John Emmeus Davis (2008).

APPENDIX 1

1. Galanter (1974). The term "repeat players" is meant to contrast with "one-timers."
2. I began address correction with a superset of 13,560 of addresses from RDA documents and the Baseline databases. After removing 661 addresses from this larger set due to a lack of ULR matches, and eliminating properties that did not warrant inclusion a census of eminent domain cases between 1992 and 2007, I had identified 7,000 properties. These are analyzed in Chapter 3. Note that many of the 661 addresses eliminated for a lack of ULR match would not have ended up in the eminent-domain census anyway, due to reasons apart from their problematic address information.

3. The city condemned some properties through an alternative method (called "spot blight," "ACT 94," or "citywide condemnation"), in which properties were identified as blighted and did not require Redevelopment Proposals. For the purposes of analysis, I considered those properties both pursued and taken when the RDA Board authorized the Declaration of Taking.

APPENDIX 2

1. This methodology documentation (description of market types and variables used) obtained from The Reinvestment Fund, 2006.

BIBLIOGRAPHY

Adams, Carolyn Teich. *Philadelphia: Neighborhoods, Division, and Conflict in a Postindustrial City*. Philadelphia: Temple University Press, 1991.

Alexander, Gregory S., and Eduardo M. Peñalver. *An Introduction to Property Theory*. New York: Cambridge University Press, 2012.

Alexander, Gregory S., Eduardo M. Peñalver, Joseph William Singer, and Laura Underkuffler. "A Statement on Progressive Property." *Cornell Law Review* 94 (2009): 743–744.

Anderson, Martin. *The Federal Bulldozer: A Critical Analysis of Urban Renewal, 1949–1962*. Cambridge, MA: MIT. Press, 1964.

——. "The Federal Bulldozer." *Harvard Business Review* 43 (1965): 6–21.

Atkinson, Rowland. "The Hidden Costs of Gentrification: Displacement in Central London." *Journal of Housing and the Built Environment* 15, no. 4 (2000): 307–326.

Baltzell, E. Digby. *Philadelphia Gentlemen: The Making of a National Upper Class*. Glencoe, IL: Free Press, 1958.

Baxamusa, Murtaza H. "Empowering Communities Through Deliberation the Model of Community Benefits Agreements." *Journal of Planning Education and Research* 27 (2008): 261–273.

Becher, Debbie. "The Participant's Dilemma: Bringing Representation and Conflict Back In." *International Journal of Urban and Regional Research* 34, no. 3 (2010): 496–511.

——. "Political Moments with Long-Term Consequences." In *Remaking Urban Citizenship: Organizations, Institutions, and a Right to the City*, edited by Michael P. Smith and Michael McQuarrie, 203–220. New Brunswick, NJ: Transaction Publishers, 2012.

——. "Race as a Set of Symbolic Resources: Mobilization in the Politics of Eminent Domain." In *Race and Real Estate*, edited by Adrienne Brown, Kim Scheppele, and Valerie Smith. New York: Oxford University Press, 2015.

Beck, Ulrich. *Risk Society: Towards a New Modernity*. London: SAGE Publications, 1992.

Beckert, Jens. *Inherited Wealth*. Princeton, NJ: Princeton University Press, 2007.

Been, Vicki. "Community Benefits Agreements: A New Local Government Tool or Another Variation on the Exactions Theme?" *The University of Chicago Law Review* 77 (2010): 5–35.

Bell, Abraham, and Gideon Parchomovsky. "Taking Compensation Private." *Stanford Law Review* 59 (2006–2007): 871–906.

Benedict, Jeff. *Little Pink House: A True Story of Defiance and Courage*. New York: Grand Central Publishing, 2009.

Benveniste, Guy. *Mastering the Politics of Planning: Crafting Credible Plans and Policies That Make a Difference*, 1st ed. San Francisco: Jossey-Bass, 1989.

Berger, Curtis J., and Patrick Rohan. "The Nassau County Study: An Empirical Look into the Practices of Condemnation." *Columbia Law Review* 67 (1967): 430–458.

Berger, Peter L., and Thomas Luckmann. *The Social Construction of Reality*. New York: Anchor Books, 1967.

Blomley, Nicholas. "Legal Geographies—*Kelo,* Contradiction, and Capitalism." *Urban Geography* 28, no. 2 (2007): 198–205.

——. "Performing Property, Making the World." *Canadian Journal of Law and Jurisprudence*, no. 1 (2013): 23–48.

——. *Unsettling the City: Urban Property and the Politics of Land*. New York: Routledge, 2003.

Boltanski, Luc, and Laurent Thévenot. *On Justification: Economies of Worth*. Princeton, NJ: Princeton University Press, 2006 [1991].

Bowman, Ann O'M., and Michael A. Pagano. *Terra Incognita: Vacant Land and Urban Strategies,* Washington, DC: Georgetown University Press, 2004.

Bradley, Jennifer, and Timothy J. Dowling. "Eminent Domain as Trojan Horse: How the Property Rights Movement Is Misusing *Kelo* to Advance a Radical Agenda." In *Land and Power: The Impact of Eminent Domain in Urban Communities,* edited by Timothy N. Castano, 39–38. Princeton, NJ: The Policy Research Institute for the Region, Woodrow Wilson School of Public and International Affairs, Princeton University, 2008.

Bukowczyk, John J. "The Decline and Fall of a Detroit Neighborhood: Poletown vs. G.M. and the City of Detroit." *Washington and Lee Law Review* 41 (1984): 49–76.

Burney, Laura H. "Just Compensation and the Condemnation of Future Interests: Empirical Evidence of the Failure of Fair Market Value." *Brigham Young University Law Review* (1989): 789–821.

Carruthers, Bruce G., and Laura Ariovich. "The Sociology of Property Rights." *Annual Review of Sociology* 30 (2004): 23–46.

Chang, Yun-chien. "An Empirical Study of Compensation Paid in Eminent Domain Settlements: New York City, 1990–2002." *Journal of Legal Studies* 39 (2010): 201–244.

Christensen, Karen S. "Coping with Uncertainty in Planning." *Journal of the American Planning Association* 51 (1985): 63–73.

Clauretie, Terrence M., William Kuhn, and R. Keith Schwer. "Residential Properties Taken under Eminent Domain: Do Government Appraisers Track Market Values?" *Journal of Real Estate Research* 26, no. 3 (2004): 317–327.

Cybriwsky, Roman A., David Ley, and John Western. "The Political and Social Construction of Revitalized Neighborhoods: Society Hill, Philadelphia, and False Creek, Vancouver." In *Gentrification of the City*, edited by Neil Smith and Peter Williams, 92–120. Boston: Allen & Unwin, 1986.

Dana, David. "The Law and Expressive Meaning of Condemning the Poor after Kelo." *Northwestern University Law Review* 101, no. 2 (2006): 5–22.

Dana, David A., and Thomas Merrill. *Property: Takings,* New York: Foundation Press, 2002.

Davis, Deborah. "Talking about Property in the New Chinese Domestic Property Regime." In *The New Economic Sociology*, edited by Frank Dobbin, 288–307. Russell Sage Foundation, 2004.

Davis, John Emmeus. "Homes That Last." *Shelterforce* (Winter 2008). http://www.shelterforce.org/article/1237/homes_that_last/ (accessed December 20, 2013).

Dewar, Margaret, and June Manning Thomas, eds. *The City after Abandonment*. Philadelphia: University of Pennsylvania Press, 2012.

Dobbin, Frank. *Forging Industrial Policy: The United States, Britain, and France in the Railway Age*. Cambridge: Cambridge University Press, 1994.

Dobbin, Frank, and John R. Sutton. "The Strength of a Weak State: The Rights Revolution and the Rise of Human Resources Management Divisions." *American Journal of Sociology* 104, no. 2 (1998): 441–476.

Dornbusch, Sanford M., and W. Richard Scott. *Evaluation and the Exercise of Authority*, 1st ed. San Francisco: Jossey-Bass Publishers, 1975.

Douglas, Mary. *How Institutions Think*, 1st ed. Syracuse, NY: Syracuse University Press, 1986.

Durkheim, Emile, and George Simpson. *Émile Durkheim on the Division of Labor in Society*. New York: Macmillan, 1933 [1893].

Edelman, Lauren B., Sally Riggs Fuller, and Iona Mara-Drita. "Diversity Rhetoric and the Managerialization of Law." *American Journal of Sociology* 106, no. 6 (2001): 1589–1641.

Ellickson, Robert C. "Alternatives to Zoning: Covenants, Nuisance Rules, and Fines as Land Use Controls." *The University of Chicago Law Review* 40, no. 4 (1973): 681–781.

——. *Order without Law: How Neighbors Settle Disputes*. Cambridge, MA: Harvard University Press, 1991.

Epstein, Richard Allen. *Takings: Private Property and the Power of Eminent Domain*. Cambridge, MA: Harvard University Press, 1985.

Espeland, Wendy Nelson. *The Struggle for Water: Politics, Rationality, and Identity in the American Southwest*. Chicago: University of Chicago Press, 1998.

Fainstein, Susan. "Eminent Domain Benefits Developers, Not the Public." *Gotham Gazette*, December 12, 2005a. http://www.gothamgazette.com/index.php/development/3078-eminent-domain-benefits-developers-not-the-public (accessed December 20, 2013).

——. "The Return of Urban Renewal: Dan Doctoroff's Grand Plans for New York City." *Harvard Design Magazine* 22 (Spring/Summer 2005b): 1–5.

——. "Urban Redevelopment and Public Policy in London and New York." In *Managing Cities: The New Urban Context*, edited by Patsy Healey, Stuart Cameron, Simin Davoudi, Stephen Graham, and Ali Madani-Pour, 127–143. Chichester; New York: J. Wiley, 1995.

Fairbanks, Robert P. *How It Works: Recovering Citizens in Post-Welfare Philadelphia*. Chicago: University of Chicago Press, 2009.

Fennell, Lee Anne. "Taking Eminent Domain Apart." *Michigan State Law Review* (2004): 957–1004.

Ferman, Barbara. "Chicago: Power, Race, and Reform." In *City Politics: The Political Economy of Urban America*, 2nd ed., edited by Dennis R. Judd and Todd Swanstrom, 223–235. Boston: Longman, 1998 [1991].

Fligstein, Neil. *The Transformation of Corporate Control*. Cambridge, MA: Harvard University Press, 1990.

Fried, Marc. "Grieving for a Lost Home." In *The Urban Condition: People and Policy in the Metropolis*, edited by Leonard J. Duhl, 151–171. New York: Basic Books, 1963.

Frieden, Bernard J., and Lynne B. Sagalyn. *Downtown, Inc.: How America Builds Cities*, Cambridge, MA: MIT Press, 1989.

Fullilove, Mindy Thompson. *Root Shock: How Tearing Up City Neighborhoods Hurts America, and What We Can Do About It*, 1st ed. New York: One World/Ballantine Books, 2004.

Galanter, Marc. "Why the 'Haves' Come Out Ahead: Speculations on the Limits of Legal Change." *Law & Society Review* 9 (1974): 95–160.

Gans, Herbert J. *The Urban Villagers: Group and Class in the Life of Italian-Americans*, updated and expanded ed. New York: Free Press, 1962.

——. "The Failure of Urban Renewal." In *Urban Renewal: The Record and the Controversy*, edited by James Q. Wilson, 50–67. Cambridge, MA: MIT Press, 1966.

Garnett, Nicole. "The Neglected Political Economy of Eminent Domain." *Michigan Law Review* 105 (2006): 101–150.

Geisler, Charles C. "Property Pluralism." In *Property and Values: Alternatives to Public and Private Ownership*, edited by Charles C. Geisler and Gail Daneker, 65–88. Washington, DC: Island Press, 2000.

Giddens, Anthony. *The Third Way: The Renewal of Social Democracy*. Cambridge: Polity Press, 1998.

Godsil, Rachel D., and David V. Simunovich. "Protecting Status: The Mortgage Crisis, Eminent Domain, and the Ethic of Homeownership." *Fordham Law Review* 77 (2008): 949–998.

Goffman, Erving. *Asylums: Essays on the Social Situation of Mental Patients and Other Inmates*. Garden City, NY: Doubleday, 1961.

Gold, Martin E., and Lynne B. Sagalyn. "The Use and Abuse of Blight in Eminent Domain." *Fordham Urban Law Journal* 4 (2011): 1119–1173.

Gotham, Kevin Fox. "Urban Redevelopment, Past, and Present." In *Critical Perspectives on Urban Development*, edited by Kevin Fox Gotham, 1–32. Oxford: Elsevier Science, 2001.

Gotham, Kevin Fox, Jon Shefner, and Krista Brumley. "Abstract Space, Social Space, and the Redevelopment of Public Housing." In *Critical Perspectives on Urban Development*, edited by Kevin Fox Gotham, 277–312. Oxford: Elsevier Science, 2001.

Greer, Scott A. *Urban Renewal and American Cities: The Dilemma of Democratic Intervention*. Indianapolis: Bobbs-Merrill, 1966.

Gross, Julian. "Community Benefits Agreements: Definitions, Values, and Legal Enforceability." *Journal of Affordable Housing and Community Development* 17 (2008): 35–58.

Guidry, Krisandra, and A. Quang Do. "Eminent Domain and Just Compensation for Single-Family Homes." *The Appraisal Journal* 66, no. 3 (1998): 231–235.

Gunder, Michael. "Ideologies of Certainty in a Risky Reality: Beyond the Hauntology of Planning." *Planning Theory* 7, no. 2 (2008): 186–206.

Habermas, Jürgen. *Legitimation Crisis*. Boston: Beacon Press, 1975 [1973].

Halpern, Robert. *Rebuilding the Inner City: A History of Neighborhood Initiatives to Address Poverty in the United States*. New York: Columbia University Press, 1995.

Harrison, Bennett. "The Politics and Economics of the Urban Enterprise Zone Proposal: A Critique." *International Journal of Urban and Regional Research* 6, no. 3 (1982): 422–428.

Hartman, Chester. "The Right to Stay Put." In *The Gentrification Reader*, edited by Loretta Lees, Tom Slater, and Elvin Wyly, 531–541. Abingdon, UK: Routledge, 2010 [1984].

Hartman, Chester, and Rob Kessler. "The Illusion and Reality of Urban Renewal: San Francisco's Yerba Buena Center." In *Marxism and the Metropolis: New Perspectives* in *Urban Political Economy*, edited by William K. Tabb and Larry Sawers, 153–178. New York: Oxford University Press, 1978.

Hartman, Chester W. *Yerba Buena: Land Grab and Community Resistance in San Francisco*. San Francisco: Glide Publications, 1974.

Hartog, Hendrik. *Man and Wife in America: A History*. Cambridge, MA: Harvard University Press, 2000.

Harvey, David. "From Managerialism to Entrepreneurialism: The Transformation in Urban Governance in Late Capitalism." *Geografiska Annaler: Series B, Human Geography* 71, no. 1 (1989): 3–17.

——. "Reshaping Economic Geography: The World Development Report 2009." *Development and Change* 40, no. 6 (2009): 1269–1277.

Heller, Michael, and Rick Hills. "Land Assembly Districts." *Harvard Law Review* 121, no. 6 (2008): 1467–1527.

Hirsch, Arnold R. *Making the Second Ghetto: Race and Housing in Chicago, 1940–1960*, 2nd ed. Chicago: University of Chicago Press, 1998.

Hodos, Jerome I. *Second Cities: Globalization and Local Politics in Manchester and Philadelphia*. Philadelphia: Temple University Press, 2011.

Horwitz, Morton J. *The Transformation of American Law, 1870–1960: The Crisis of Legal Orthodoxy*. New York: Oxford University Press, 1992.

Howard, Christopher, Michael Lipsky, and Dale Rogers Marshall. "Citizen Participation in Urban Politics." In *City Politics: The Political Economy of Urban America*, 2nd ed., edited by Dennis R. Judd and Todd Swanstrom, 199–210. Boston: Longman, 1998 [1994].

Hughes, Mark Alan. "Dirt into Dollars: Converting Vacant Land into Valuable Development." *Brookings Review* 18 (Summer 2000): 36–39.

Hurst, James Willard. *Law and the Conditions of Freedom in the Nineteenth-Century United States*. Madison: University of Wisconsin Press, 1956.

Jacobs, Jane. *The Death and Life of Great American Cities*. New York: Random House, 1961.

Jackson, Kenneth T. *Crabgrass Frontier: The Suburbanization of the United States*. New York: Oxford University Press, 1985.

Judd, Dennis R., and Todd Swanstrom. *City Politics: The Political Economy of Urban America*, 2nd ed. Boston: Longman, 1998.

Krier, James E., and Christopher Serkin. "Public Ruses." *Michigan State Law Review*. no. 2 (2004): 859–875.

Krippner, Greta R. "The Making of US Monetary Policy: Central Bank Transparency and the Neoliberal Dilemma." *Theory and Society* 36, no. 6 (2007): 477–513.

Lees, Loretta, Tom Slater, and Elvin Wyly. "Introduction." In *The Gentrification Reader*, edited by Loretta Lees, Tom Slater, and Elvin Wyly, ix–xxvi. Abingdon, UK: Routledge, 2010.

Lewinsohn-Zamir, Daphna. "Can't Buy Me Love: Monetary versus In-Kind Remedies." *University of Illinois Law Review* 2013, no. 1 (2013): 151–194.

Lindblom, Charles Edward. "The Science of 'Muddling Through.'" *Public Administration Review* 19, no. 2 (1959): 79–88.

Locke, John. *The Second Treatise on Civil Government*. Amherst, NY: Prometheus Books, 1986 [1690].

Logan, John R., and Harvey Luskin Molotch. *Urban Fortunes: The Political Economy of Place*. Berkeley: University of California Press, 1987.

Lopez, Steve. *Third and Indiana: A Novel*. New York: Viking, 1994.

Lynd, Staughton. "The Genesis of the Idea of a Community Right to Industrial Property in Youngstown and Pittsburgh." In *The Constitution and American Life,* edited by David P. Thelen, 266–295. Ithaca, NY: Cornell University Press, 1988.

Macpherson, Crawford Brough. *Property: Mainstream and Critical Positions.* Oxford: Blackwell, 1978.

Marcuse, Peter. "Gentrification, Abandonment, and Displacement: Connections, Causes, and Policy Responses in New York City." *Urban Law Annual; Journal of Urban and Contemporary Law* 28 (1985): 195–240.

——. "The Housing Change We Need." *Shelterforce* (Winter 2008).

——. "Abandonment, Gentrification, and Displacement: The Linkages in New York City." In *The Gentrification Reader,* edited by Loretta Lees, Tom Slater, and Elvin Wyly, 333–347. Abingdon, UK: Routledge, 2010 [1986].

Marris, Peter. *The Politics of Uncertainty: Attachment in Private and Public Life.* New York: Routledge, 1996.

Martin, Isaac. W. *The Permanent Tax Revolt: How the Property Tax Transformed American Politics.* Stanford: Stanford University Press, 2008.

Marx, Karl. *Capital: A Critical Analysis of Capitalist Production.* London: Sonnenschein Lowrey, 1887.

Marwell, Nicole P. *Bargaining for Brooklyn: Community Organizations in the Entrepreneurial City.* Chicago: University of Chicago Press, 2007.

Massey, Douglas S., and Nancy A. Denton. *American Apartheid: Segregation and the Making of the Underclass.* Cambridge, MA: Harvard University Press, 1993.

——. Jonathan Rothwell and Thurston Domina. "The Changing Bases of Segregation in the United States." *The ANNALS of the American Academy of Political and Social Science* 626, no. 1 (November 2009): 74–90.

McCann, Michael W. *Rights at Work: Pay Equity Reform and the Politics of Legal Mobilization.* Chicago: University of Chicago Press, 1994.

McKinney-Whetstone, Diane. *Tumbling.* New York: William Morrow, 1996.

McQuarrie, Michael. "Privatization and Low-Income Housing in the United States since 1986." *Research in Political Sociology* 14 (2005): 15–51.

——. "No Contest: Participatory Technologies and the Transformation of Urban Authority." *Public Culture* 25, no. 1 (2013): 143–175.

Medoff, Peter, and Holly Sklar. *Streets of Hope: The Fall and Rise of an Urban Neighborhood.* Boston: South End Press, 1994.

Merrill, Thomas W. "Incomplete Compensation for Takings." *New York University Environmental Law Journal* 11 (2002–2003): 110–135.

Michelman, Frank I. "Property, Utility, and Fairness: Comments on the Ethical Foundations of 'Just Compensation' Law." *Harvard Law Review* 80 (1967): 1165–1214.

Mitchell, Thomas W., Stephen Malpezzi, and Richard K. Green. "Forced Sale Risk: Class, Race, and the 'Double Discount.'" *Florida State University Law Review* 37 (2009–2010): 589–658.

Mohl, Raymond A. "Race and Space in the Modern City: Interstate-95 and the Black Community in Miami." In *Urban Policy in Twentieth Century America,* edited by Arnold R. Hirsch and Raymond A. Mohl, 100–158. New Brunswick, NJ: Rutgers University Press, 1993a.

——. "Shifting Patterns of American Urban Policy Since 1900." In *Urban Policy in Twentieth Century America,* edited by Arnold R. Hirsch and Raymond A. Mohl, 1–45. New Brunswick, NJ: Rutgers University Press, 1993b.

Molotch, Harvey Luskin. "The City as a Growth Machine: Toward a Political Economy of Place." *American Journal of Sociology* 82, no. 2 (1976): 309–332.

Munch, Patricia. "An Economic Analysis of Eminent Domain." *Journal of Political Economy* 84 (1976): 473–497.

Nadler, Janice, Shari Seidman Diamond, and Matthew M. Patton. "Government Takings of Private Property: Kelo and the Perfect Storm." In *Public Opinion and Constitutional Controversy*, edited by N. Persily, J. Citrin, and P. Egan, 287–310. Oxford: Oxford University Press, 2008.

O'Mara, Margaret Pugh. *Cities of Knowledge: Cold War Science and the Search for the Next Silicon Valley*. Princeton, NJ: Princeton University Press, 2005.

Patterson, O. *Slavery and Social Death: A Comparative Study*. Cambridge, MA: Harvard University Press, 1982.

Peñalver, Eduardo M. "Land Virtues." *Cornell Law Review* 94 (2009): 821–888.

Polanyi, Karl. *The Great Transformation*. New York: Farrar & Rinehart, 1944.

Pritchett, Wendell E. "The 'Public Menace' of Blight: Urban Renewal and the Private Uses of Eminent Domain." *Yale Law and Policy Review* 21, no. 1 (2003): 1–52.

Radin, Margaret Jane. "Property and Personhood." *Stanford Law Review* 34 (1982): 957–1013.

——. *Reinterpreting Property*. Chicago: University of Chicago Press, 1993.

Reich, Charles A. "The New Property." *Yale Law Journal* 73 (1964): 733–787.

Roy, William G. *Socializing Capital: The Rise of the Large Industrial Corporation in America*. Princeton, NJ: Princeton University Press, 1997.

Sagalyn, Lynne B. *Times Square Roulette: Remaking the City Icon*. Cambridge, MA: MIT Press, 2001.

——. "Positioning Politics: *Kelo*, Eminent Domain, and the Press." In *Land and Power: The Impact of Eminent Domain in Urban Communities*, edited by Timothy N. Castano, 39–48. Princeton, NJ: The Policy Research Institute for the Region, Woodrow Wilson School of Public and International Affairs, Princeton University, 2008.

Salkin, Patricia, and Amy Lavine. "Negotiating for Social Justice and the Promise of Community Benefits Agreements: Case Studies of Current and Developing Agreements." *Journal of Affordable Housing* 17, no. 1–2 (2007/2008): 113–144.

Serkin, Christopher. "The Meaning of Value: Assessing Just Compensation for Regulatory Takings." *Northwestern University Law Review* 99, no. 2 (2004–2005): 677–742.

Singer, Joseph William. *Entitlement: The Paradoxes of Property*. New Haven, CT: Yale University Press, 2000.

Small, Mario L. *Unanticipated Gains: Origins of Network Inequality in Everyday Life*. Oxford: Oxford University Press, 2009.

Smith, Charles W. *Auctions: The Social Construction of Value*. New York: Free Press, 1989.

Smith, Neil. "Gentrification and Capital: Practice and Ideology in Society Hill." *Antipode* 11, no. 3 (1979): 24–35.

Somin, Ilya. "Is Post-Kelo Eminent Domain Reform Bad for the Poor?" *Northwestern University Law Review* 101, no. 4 (2007): 1931–1943.

Stack, Carol B. *All Our Kin: Strategies for Survival in a Black Community*. New York: Harper & Row, 1974.

Stark, David. "Recombinant Property in East European Capitalism." *American Journal of Sociology* 101, no. 4 (1996): 993–1027.

Stoecker, Randy. "The Community Development Corporation Model of Community Development: A Critique and an Alternative." *Journal of Urban Affairs* 19, no. 1 (1997): 1–23.

Teles, Steven M. *The Rise of the Conservative Legal Movement: The Battle for Control of the Law*. Princeton, NJ: Princeton University Press, 2008.

Tocqueville, Alexis de, and Henry Reeve. *Democracy in America*. London: Saunders and Otley, 1835.

Underkuffler, Laura. "Property: A Special Right." *Notre Dame Law Review* 71, no. 5 (1996): 1033–1058.

——. *The Idea of Property: Its Meaning and Power*. Oxford; New York: Oxford University Press, 2003.

Valverde, Mariana. *Everyday Law on the Street: City Governance in an Age of Diversity*. Chicago: University of Chicago Press, 2012.

Veblen, Thorstein. *Absentee Ownership and Business Enterprise in Recent Times: The Case of America*. New York: Viking Press, 1945 [1923].

Velthuis, Olav. *Talking Prices: Symbolic Meanings of Prices on the Market for Contemporary Art*. Princeton, NJ: Princeton University Press, 2005.

Verdery, Katherine. *The Vanishing Hectare: Property and Value in Postsocialist Transylvania*. Ithaca, NY: Cornell University Press, 2003.

Walker, Henry A., George M. Thomas, and Morris Jr. Zelditch. "Legitimation, Endorsement, and Stability." *Social Forces* 64, no. 3 (1986): 620–643.

Walker, Henry A., and Morris Jr. Zelditch. "Power, Legitimation, and the Stability of Authority: A Theoretical Research Program." In *Theoretical Research Programs: Studies in the Growth of Theory,* edited by J. Berger and Morris Zelditch, Jr., 364–381. Stanford, CA: Stanford University Press, 1993.

Weber, Max. "Politics as Vocation." In *From Max Weber: Essays in Sociology,* edited by H. H. Gerth and C. Wright Mills, 77–128. New York: Oxford University Press, 1946 [1919].

——. *General Economic History*. New Brunswick, NJ: Transaction Books, 1981 [1923].

Weber, Max, Guenther Roth, and Claus Wittich. *Economy and Society: An Outline of Interpretive Sociology*. Berkeley: University of California Press, 1978.

Wherry, Frederick F., and Tony Rocco. *The Philadelphia Barrio: The Arts, Branding, and Neighborhood Transformation*. Chicago: University of Chicago Press, 2011.

Wilhelm, Sidney, and Edwin Powell. "Who Needs the Negro?" In *Contemporary Social Issues: A Reader*, edited by Giallombardo, Rose, 118–199. Santa Barbara, CA: Hamilton Publishing, 1975.

Wilson, James Q. *Urban Renewal: The Record and the Controversy*. Cambridge, MA: MIT Press, 1966.

Wilson, William Julius. *The Truly Disadvantaged: The Inner City, the Underclass, and Public Policy*. Chicago and London: University of Chicago Press, 1987.

Wylie, Jeanie. *Poletown: Community Betrayed*. Urbana: University of Illinois Press, 1989.

Yin, Jordan. "The Community Development Industry System: A Case Study of Politics and Institutions in Cleveland, 1967–1997." *Journal of Urban Affairs* 20, no. 2 (1998): 137–157.

Zelizer, Viviana A. Rotman. *Pricing the Priceless Child: The Changing Social Value of Children*. Princeton, NJ: Princeton University Press, 1994a.

——. *The Social Meaning of Money*. New York: Basic Books, 1994b.

——. *The Purchase of Intimacy*. Princeton, NJ: Princeton University Press, 2005.

Zukin, Sharon. *Naked City: The Death and Life of Authentic Urban Places*. Oxford: Oxford University Press, 2010.

INDEX